SWIFT™ iOS 24-HOUR TRAINER

Continues

Swift™ iOS 24-Hour Trainer

Swift™ iOS 24-Hour Trainer

Abhishek Mishra

wrox™
A Wiley Brand

Swift™ iOS 24-Hour Trainer

Published by
John Wiley & Sons, Inc.
10475 Crosspoint Boulevard
Indianapolis, IN 46256
www.wiley.com

Copyright © 2016 by John Wiley & Sons, Inc., Indianapolis, Indiana

Published simultaneously in Canada

ISBN: 978-1-119-07355-0
ISBN: 978-1-119-07346-8 (ebk)
ISBN: 978-1-119-07342-0 (ebk)

Manufactured in the United States of America

10 9 8 7 6 5 4 3 2 1

ABOUT THE AUTHOR

ABHISHEK MISHRA has been developing software for over 18 years and has experience with a diverse set of programming languages and platforms. He is the author of *iPhone and iPad App 24-Hour Trainer* and the technical reviewer of *Professional iOS Programming*. He holds a Master's degree in Computer Science from the University of London and is a freelance consultant and trainer specializing in mobile application development. His clients include British Sky Broadcasting, Centrica PLC, Expedia Inc., Kantar Media, and Havas Media. He lives with his wife and daughter in London.

ABOUT THE TECHNICAL EDITOR

CHAIM KRAUSE is a Simulation Specialist for the U.S. Army. One of his responsibilities is to develop small games for use at the Army University. Chaim has been developing software for about 30 years, progressing through BASIC, Delphi/Pascal, C++, Java, Objective-C, and C# on platforms from the TRS-80 through Windows, OS X, Android, and iOS. He has also worked with Arduinos. Chaim has been the Technical Editor for a dozen books on topics as varied as iPhone/iPad, Android, iWatch, Arduino, and Unity. When not working in front of a computer at his day job, Chaim is often sitting in front of a computer at home playing wargames or developing his own game. Chaim can be reached at chaim@chaim.com.

CREDITS

ACQUISITIONS EDITOR
Aaron Black

PROJECT EDITOR
Christina Haviland

TECHNICAL EDITOR
Chaim Krause

PRODUCTION EDITOR
Joel Jones

COPY EDITOR
Nancy Rapoport

MANAGER OF CONTENT DEVELOPMENT & ASSEMBLY
Mary Beth Wakefield

PRODUCTION MANAGER
Kathleen Wisor

MARKETING DIRECTOR
David Mayhew

MARKETING MANAGER
Carrie Sherrill

PROFESSIONAL TECHNOLOGY & STRATEGY DIRECTOR
Barry Pruett

BUSINESS MANAGER
Amy Knies

ASSOCIATE PUBLISHER
Jim Minatel

PROJECT COORDINATOR, COVER
Brent Savage

PROOFREADER
Nancy Bell

INDEXER
Nancy Guenther

COVER DESIGNER
Wiley

COVER IMAGE
© nyul/iStockphoto

ACKNOWLEDGMENTS

This book would not have been possible without the support of the team at John Wiley and Sons—Aaron Black, Christina Haviland, Nancy Rapoport, and Mariann Barsolo. I would also like to thank Chaim Krause for taking the time to read the entire manuscript and his keen eye for detail. It has been my privilege to work with you. Thank you.

CONTENTS

INTRODUCTION

WHEN I FIRST BEGAN LEARNING IOS DEVELOPMENT, I started out like most developers, from the humble Hello World application. I was overwhelmed with new concepts, such as view controllers and table views. My background with C++ did not help much when it came to working with Objective-C, and I had to start from scratch. There was no book written on the subject and everything had to be learned from Apple's documentation and personal blogs.

Eventually I came to grips with Objective-C, and with practice, I grew more proficient. With the launch of iOS 7, Apple announced a new language called Swift, and it felt almost like going back to square one again, as I learned how to perform familiar tasks with a new language.

This book is written to help someone new to iOS development learn the basic concepts and (I hope) avoid making the mistakes I made when starting out myself. That being said, this book should also be useful for an experienced Objective-C developer who is looking to transition over to Swift. This book adopts a hands-on Try It approach, and you get to try out each new concept as you progress through the book.

iOS application development is a huge topic, and it is just not possible to include every single topic related to iOS application development in this book. When selecting topics to include in this book, I have tried to strike a balance between the absolute basics and more advanced topics such as Test Driven Development, CloudKit, and UI testing.

This book has been written for you, the reader. I hope that after reading this book, you can take your first steps into the wildly exciting world of iOS App development.

WHO THIS BOOK IS FOR

This book is for beginners with little programming experience who want to pursue a career in the exciting world of iOS development. It is also for experienced Objective-C developers who want to learn Swift programming.

Although you do not need to have any prior programming experience, a little knowledge will help you move faster through the initial lessons, particularly the basics of object-oriented software development. If you are a more experienced developer, then this book can help you get up-to-speed with new concepts relating specifically to iOS 9 development and Swift.

WHAT THIS BOOK COVERS

This book covers iOS 9 application development with Swift 2. That includes development for both the iPhone and the iPad. The lessons in this book use XCode 7.0 and make use of new Swift features such as the `guard let` clause. All of the lessons use storyboards to construct user interfaces.

The book starts off with an introduction to the Swift language followed by lessons that will teach you how to perform common tasks such as displaying alerts, pickers, and collection views. Toward the end of the book, you will find slightly more advanced topics such as iCloud document storage, CloudKit, Test Driven Development, and UI testing.

The appendixes cover ways to test and deploy your apps, ranging from deploying a build to your personal device to distributing your app to beta testers via TestFlight.

HOW THIS BOOK IS STRUCTURED

This book consists of 33 short lessons and 3 appendixes. Each lesson introduces a single topic and ends with a step-by-step Try It section where you get to apply the concepts you've learned in the lesson to create a simple iOS application. The source code for the Try It exercises is available for download at www.wrox.com/go/swiftios. Lessons toward the beginning of the book are simpler and progress in complexity as you work your way through the book.

If you are an absolute beginner to iOS development, you should progress through the lessons from cover to cover, sequentially. If you have prior experience with iOS development and want to read this book for a particular topic of interest, then you can jump right in with the relevant lessons.

iOS development is a vast topic and no single book can cover everything related to iOS development. However, several lessons contain sources for where to find additional information on the web.

When you're finished reading the book and watching the accompanying videos, you'll find lots of support in the P2P forums.

INSTRUCTIONAL VIDEOS

Learning is often enhanced by seeing in real time what's being taught, which is why most lessons in the book have a corresponding video tutorial available at www.wrox.com/go/swiftiosvid. And of course it's vital that you play along at home—fire up Xcode and try out what you read in the book and watch on the videos.

CONVENTIONS

To help you get the most from the text and keep track of what's happening, I've used a number of conventions throughout the book.

> **NOTE** *Boxes like this one hold important, not-to-be forgotten information that is directly relevant to the surrounding text.*

> **REFERENCE** *References like this one point you to other lessons in the book, the book's website, and the instructional videos that accompany a given lesson.*

As for styles in the text:

➤ I highlight new terms and important words when they are first introduced.

➤ I show URLs within the text like this: www.wrox.com.

➤ I present code in monofont type like this: persistence.properties.

ERRATA

We make every effort to ensure that there are no errors in the text or in the code. However, no one is perfect, and mistakes do occur. If you find an error in one of our books, such as a spelling mistake or faulty piece of code, we would be very grateful for your feedback. By sending in errata you may save another reader hours of frustration and at the same time you will be helping us provide even higher quality information.

To find the errata page for this book, go to www.wrox.com and locate the title using the Search box or one of the title lists. Then, on the Book Search Results page, click the Errata link. On this page you can view all errata that has been submitted for this book and posted by Wrox editors.

> **NOTE** *A complete book list including links to errata is also available at* www.wrox.com/misc-pages/booklist.shtml.

If you don't spot "your" error on the Errata page, click the Errata Form link and complete the form to send us the error you have found. We'll check the information and, if appropriate, post a message to the book's errata page and fix the problem in subsequent editions of the book.

P2P.WROX.COM

For author and peer discussion, join the P2P forums at http://p2p.wrox.com. The forums are a web-based system for you to post messages relating to Wrox books and related technologies and interact with other readers and technology users. The forums offer a subscription feature to e-mail you topics of interest of your choosing when new posts are made to the forums. Wrox authors, editors, other industry experts, and your fellow readers are present on these forums.

At `http://p2p.wrox.com`, you will find a number of different forums that will help you not only as you read this book, but also as you develop your own applications. To join the forums, just follow these steps:

1. Go to `http://p2p.wrox.com` and click the Register link.

2. Read the terms of use and click Agree.

3. Complete the required information to join as well as any optional information you wish to provide and click Submit.

4. You will receive an e-mail with information describing how to verify your account and complete the joining process.

> **NOTE** *You can read messages in the forums without joining P2P, but in order to post your own messages, you must join.*

Once you join, you can post new messages and respond to messages other users post. You can read messages at any time on the Web. If you would like to have new messages from a particular forum e-mailed to you, click the Subscribe to this Forum icon by the forum name in the forum listing.

For more information about how to use the Wrox P2P, be sure to read the P2P FAQs for answers to questions about how the forum software works as well as many common questions specific to P2P and Wrox books. To read the FAQs, click the FAQ link on any P2P page.

SECTION I
Hello iOS!

Hello iOS!

Hello and welcome to the exciting world of iOS application development. iOS is Apple's operating system for mobile devices; the current version at the time of this writing is 8.0. It was originally developed for the iPhone (simply known as iPhone OS back then), and was subsequently extended and renamed in June 2010 to iOS to support the iPad, iPhone, and iPod Touch.

At its core, iOS is Unix-based and has its foundations in MacOS X, which is Apple's desktop operating system. In fact, both iOS and MacOS X share a common code base. As new versions of mobile operating systems have appeared, Apple has brought over more functionality from MacOS X. This is part of Apple's strategy to bridge the difference between desktop and mobile computing.

With the launch of version 8.0, Apple has not only pushed the boundaries on what is achievable on smart phones and tablet computers, but has also given us a brand new programming language called Swift. This book covers iOS development with Swift only, but at the time of this writing, it is possible to create iOS applications with both the older language Objective-C as well as Swift.

This lesson introduces you to the arena of iOS development.

iOS DEVELOPER ESSENTIALS

Before you get started on your journey to becoming an iOS developer, you will need some essential resources. This section covers these basic requirements.

A Suitable Mac

To develop apps for the iPhone and the iPad using the official set of tools provided by Apple, you will first need an Intel-based Mac running Mac OS X Yosemite (10.10) with a minimum 4GB of RAM and at least 11GB of free space on your hard disk. You do not need a top-spec model to get started. In fact a Mac Mini or a low-end MacBook will work just fine.

Processor speed is not going to make much difference to you as a developer. You will be better off investing your money in more RAM and hard disk space instead. These are things you can never get enough of. A large screen does help, but it is not essential.

A Device for Testing

If you are reading this book, chances are that you have used an iPhone, iPad, or iPod Touch and probably even own one or more of these nifty devices.

As far as development is concerned, there aren't many differences between developing for any of these devices. The obvious differences are screen size and the fact that only iPhones can make phone calls. When you are starting out as an iOS developer, you will test your creations on the iOS Simulator. The iOS Simulator is an application that runs on your Mac and simulates several functions of a real iOS device (more on this later).

At some point, however, you will want to test your apps on a physical device. As good as the iOS Simulator may be, you must test on a physical device before submitting your app to the App Store.

Another good reason to test on a physical device is that the processor on your Mac is much faster than that on the iPhone/iPad. Your app may appear to execute much faster on your Mac (in the iOS Simulator) than it does on the real thing.

If the app you are going to make is targeted at iPhone users, you can also use an iPod Touch as the test device. These are significantly cheaper than iPhones and for the most part offer the same functionality as their phone counterparts.

Most of Apple's devices support iOS 8; however, iOS 8 is not supported for the following:

➤   iPhones prior to the iPhone 4S

➤   iPads prior to the iPad 2

➤   iPod Touch devices prior to the iPod Touch 5th generation

An iOS Developer Account

To develop your apps you will need to download the latest version of Xcode and the iOS SDK (Software Development Kit). To do this, you must sign up to the Apple Developer Program to become a registered developer.

The signup process is free and you can immediately begin to develop your first apps. Limitations exist as to what you can do for free. To submit your apps to the App Store, get access to beta versions of the iOS/SDK, or test your apps on a physical device, you need to become a paying member.

Most of the concepts and apps presented in this book will work just fine with the free membership. The only exceptions would be examples that require the camera, accelerometer, and GPS for which you would need to try the app on a physical device.

You can choose from two forms of paid membership as a registered Apple Developer: Individual and Enterprise.

Individual

The Individual iOS Developer Program costs $99 a year and is for individuals or companies that want to develop apps that will be distributed through the App Store. You can also test/distribute your apps on up to 100 devices without having to go through the App Store. This form of deployment (without having to submit them to the App Store) is called ad-hoc distribution and is a great way to submit a preview of the app to a client. This form of distribution is covered in detail in Appendix C.

Enterprise

The Enterprise iOS Developer Program costs $299 a year and is for large companies that want to develop apps for internal use and will not distribute these apps through the App Store. With the Enterprise iOS Developer Program there is no restriction to the number of devices on which your in-house application can be installed.

To start the registration process, visit the iOS Dev Center (see Figure 1-1) at `https://developer` `.apple.com/programs/enroll/`.

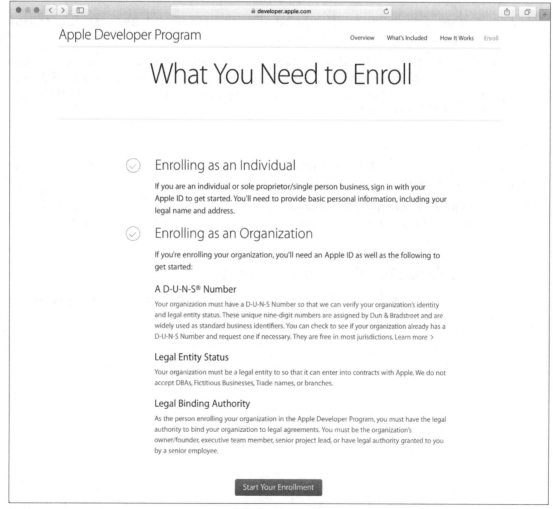

FIGURE 1-1

The Official iOS SDK

The Apple iOS SDK (Software Development Kit) is a collection of tools and documentation that you can use to develop iOS apps. The main tools that make up the SDK are:

➤ **Xcode:** Apple's integrated development environment (IDE) that enables you to manage your products, type your code, trace and fix bugs (debugging), and lots more.

➤ **Interface Builder:** A tool fully integrated into the Xcode IDE that enables you to build your application's user interface visually.

➤ **iOS Simulator:** A software simulator to simulate the functions of an iPhone or an iPad on your Mac.

➤ **Instruments:** A tool that will help you find memory leaks and optimize the performance of your apps. Instruments are not covered in this book.

In addition to these tools, the iOS SDK also includes extensive documentation, sample code, How-To's, and access to the Apple Developer Forums.

The iOS SDK is available as a free download to registered members (registration is free). However, there are benefits to paid membership, including the ability to debug your code on an iOS device, distribution of your applications, and two technical support incidents a year where Apple engineers will provide you code-level assistance.

Downloading and Installing

You can download and install Xcode 7 for Mac OS X El Capitan and the iOS SDK from the Mac App Store (see Figure 1-2).

If you have a paid membership, you can download the latest version of Xcode as well as prior versions by logging in to the iOS developer portal at `https://developer.apple.com/devcenter/ios/index.action`.

The Typical App Development Process

Whether you intend to develop iOS apps yourself or manage the development of one, you need to be familiar with the basic steps in the development process (see Figure 1-3). This section introduces these steps briefly.

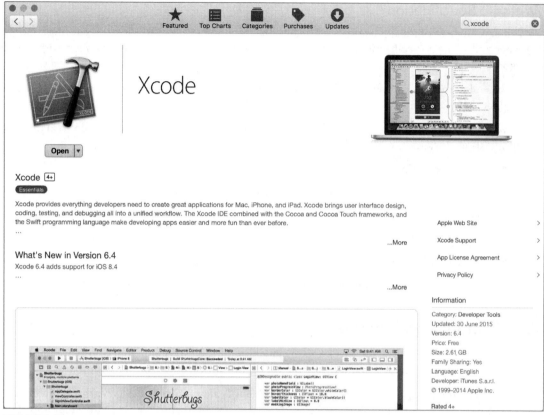

FIGURE 1-2

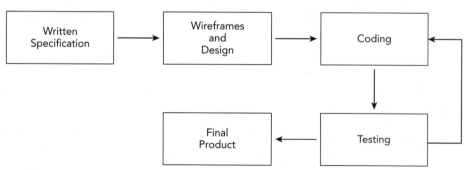

FIGURE 1-3

Writing a Specification

The development of an app begins with a concept. It is good practice to formally put this concept on paper and create a specification. You do not necessarily need to type this specification, although it's a good idea to do so.

At the end of the project you should come back to the specification document to see how the final product that was created compares with the original specification.

As you build your experience developing iOS applications, this difference will become smaller. The specification must address the following points:

- ➤ A short description in 200 words or less
- ➤ The target audience/demographic of the users
- ➤ How will it be distributed (App Store, or direct to a small number of devices)
- ➤ A list of similar competing apps
- ➤ A list of apps that best illustrate the look-and-feel your app is after
- ➤ The pricing model of competing apps and potential pricing for your app

Wireframes and Design

A wireframe is a large drawing that contains mockups of each screen of your app as well as lines connecting different screens that indicate the user's journey through your application.

Wireframes are important because they can help identify flaws in your design early on (before any coding has been done). They can also be used to show potential clients how a particular app is likely to look when it's completed.

There is no right or wrong way to make a wireframe. If it is for your personal use, you can just use a few sheets of paper and a pen. If it is for a client, you might want to consider using an illustration package.

Coding

The actual process of creating an iOS app involves using the Xcode IDE to type your code. iOS apps can be written in either Swift or Objective-C. This book covers iOS development with Swift only.

An iOS app typically consists of several files of Swift code along with resource files (such as images, audio, and video). These individual files are combined together by a process called *compilation* into a single file that is installed onto the target device. This single file is usually referred to as the application binary or a build.

Testing

It might sound obvious, but you must test your app after it has been developed. As a developer, you test your code frequently as you write it. You must also perform a comprehensive test of the entire application as often as possible to ensure things that were working in the past continue to do so.

This form of testing is called *regression testing.* It helps to make a test plan document. Such a document basically lists all the features that you want to test and the steps required to carry out each test. The document should also clearly list which tests failed. The ones that fail will then need to be fixed and the test plan document can provide the replication procedure for the defect in question.

When your app is ready, you will want to list it in the iTunes App Store. To do so involves submitting your app for review to Apple. Apple has several criteria against which it reviews applications and if your app fails one or more of these criteria it will be rejected—in which case you will need to fix the appropriate code and resubmit. It is best to test your apps thoroughly before submitting them in the first place. Distributing your apps via the App Store is covered in Appendix D.

You must always test on a real iOS device before submitting your app for the App Store review process, or giving it to a client to test. Testing on the iOS Simulator alone is not sufficient.

If you are developing for a client, you will probably need to send the client a testable version of your work periodically for review. The recommended way to do this is by using Apple's TestFlight service, which is covered in Appendix C.

Home Screen Icon

Unless you provide an icon for your application, iOS will use a standard gray icon to represent your application in the home screen (see Figure 1-4).

FIGURE 1-4

To replace this icon, you will need to provide one or more PNG files with appropriate dimensions. These dimensions are listed in Table 1-1 and are different for iPhone-based and iPad-based applications.

TABLE 1-1: Home Screen Icon Sizes

DEVICE	ICON SIZE (IN PIXELS)
iPhone 4s	120 x 120
iPhone 5 and iPhone 6	120 x 120
iPhone 6Plus	180 x 180
iPad Retina and iPad Mini Retina	152 x 152
iPad and iPad Mini (without Retina)	76 x 76

You learn to use these icons in this lesson's Try It section.

Application Launch Image

A *launch image* is a placeholder image that you must provide as part of your iOS application. When a user taps your application's icon on the home screen, iOS displays this image while the app starts up.

Once your application has finished loading, iOS gives it control and simultaneously hides the launch image. The overall effect of the launch image is to give your users the perception that your application has launched quickly.

> **NOTE** *The launch image provided as part of your application may not always be used. When an app is suspended into the background state (perhaps because the user tapped the home button on the device), iOS creates a snapshot of the current screen before suspending the app. If the app is resumed within a short period of time then this cached image is used in place of the launch image. However, if the user killed the app, uninstalled it, or hasn't used the app for an extended period of time then the launch image will be used.*

Prior to iOS8, as a developer you had to provide a static PNG version of the launch image for every screen size and orientation that was supported by your app.

While it is still possible to provide static launch images, with the launch of iOS 8 Apple has introduced the concept of a single *launch file*. A launch file is an XIB (or a storyboard file) that describes the user interface for the launch image. An empty document called `LaunchScreen.storyboard` is provided with every iOS project that you create.

The idea behind providing a single launch file over several individual launch images is that iOS will generate the launch images it needs from the launch file for the device on which the app is being used.

You learn to use a launch file in this lesson's Try It section.

TRY IT

In this Try It, you build a simple iPhone application using Xcode 7 that displays the text "Hello Swift" in the center of the screen. You will also provide application icons and a launch file.

Lesson Requirements

➤ Launch Xcode.

➤ Create a new project based on the Single View Application template.

➤ Edit a storyboard in Interface Builder.

➤ Display the Xcode Utilities area.

➤ Set up an application icon.

➤ Set up a launch file.

➤ Test an app in the iOS Simulator.

> **REFERENCE** *The code for this Try It is available at* www.wrox.com/go/ swiftios.

Hints

Download and install the latest version of Xcode and the iOS SDK on your Mac; then launch Xcode.

Step-by-Step

➤ Create a Single View Application in Xcode called HelloSwift.

1. Launch Xcode.

2. To create a new project, select the File ⇨ New ⇨ Project menu item.

3. Choose the Single View Application (see Figure 1-5) template for iOS and click Next.

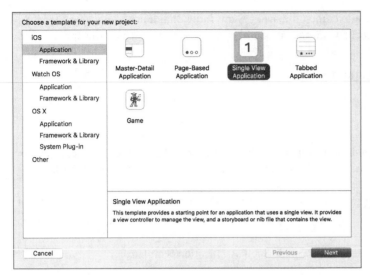

FIGURE 1-5

4. Use the following information in the project options dialog box (see Figure 1-6) and click Next.

> **Product Name:** HelloSwift

> **Organization Name:** Your company

> **Organization Identifier:** com.wileybook

> **Language:** Swift

> **Devices:** Universal

> **Use Core Data:** Unchecked

> **Include Unit Tests:** Unchecked

> **Include UI Tests:** Unchecked

5. Select a folder where this project should be created.

6. Ensure the Source Control checkbox is not selected.

7. Click Create.

> Edit the `Main.storyboard` file in Interface Builder (see Figure 1-7).

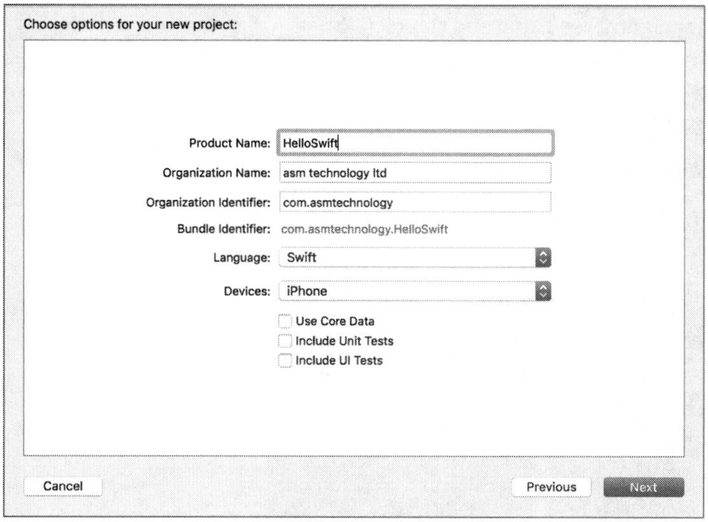

Choose options for your new project:
Product Name: HelloSwift
Organization Name: asm technology ltd
Organization Identifier: com.asmtechnology
Bundle Identifier: com.asmtechnology.HelloSwift
Language: Swift
Devices: iPhone
Use Core Data
Include Unit Tests
Include UI Tests
Cancel
Previous
Next

FIGURE 1-6

HelloSwift: Ready | Today at 06:14
HelloSwift
AppDelegate.swift
ViewController.swift
Main.storyboard
Assets.xcassets
LaunchScreen.storyboard
Info.plist
Products
View Controller Scene
View Controller
Top Layout Guide
Bottom Layout Guide
View
First Responder
Exit
Storyboard Entry Point
Simulated Metrics
View Controller
Is Initial View Controller
Key Commands
wAny hAny

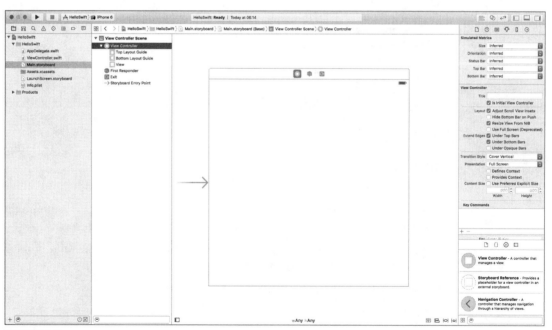

FIGURE 1-7

1. Ensure the project navigator is visible and the HelloSwift project is selected and expanded. To show the project navigator, use the View ⇨ Navigators ⇨ Show Project Navigator menu item. To expand a project, click the triangle next to the project name in the project navigator.

2. Click the `Main.storyboard` file to select it.

3. Ensure the Attribute inspector is visible by selecting the View ⇨ Utilities ⇨ Show Utilities menu item.

4. Click the white background area of the default scene in the storyboard.

5. Under the View section of the Attribute inspector, click once on the Background item to change the background color. This is shown in Figure 1-8. Pick any color you want.

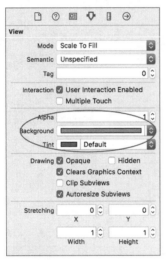

FIGURE 1-8

6. From the Object library in the bottom-right corner, select Label and drop it onto the View (see Figure 1-9). You can use the search box to narrow your choices.

7. Change the text displayed in the Label to "Hello Swift" by editing the value of the Text attribute in the Attribute inspector.

8. Position the label anywhere within the scene using the mouse.

➤   Create layout constraints.

1. Select the label in the storyboard scene by clicking on the label once. Change the size of the label so that the label is large enough to show the text "Hello Swift" fully. To do this use the Editor ⇨ Size To Fit Content menu item.

2. Select the label in the storyboard and bring up the Align constraints popup window by clicking the Align button at the bottom right corner of the storyboard (see Figure 1-10).

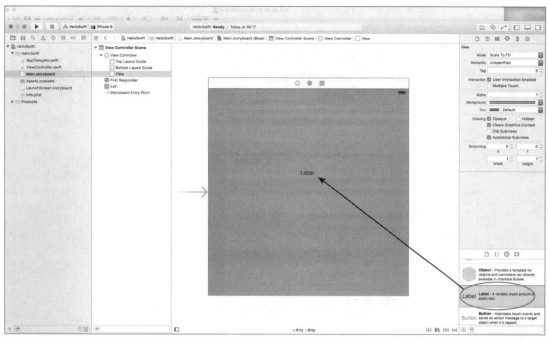

FIGURE 1-9

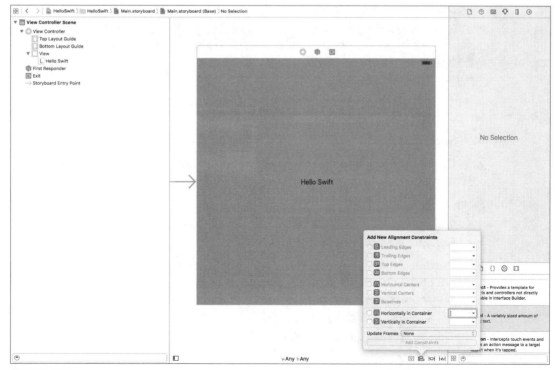

FIGURE 1-10

In this popup window, setup the following options (see Figure 1-11):

➤   Horizontally in Container: Checked

➤   Vertically in Container: Checked

➤   Update Frames: All Frames In Container

FIGURE 1-11

Click the Add 2 constraints button in the popup to apply these layout constraints to the label and dismiss the popup.

NOTE *Selecting All Frames in Container in the Update Frames combo box will force the scene to update the position of the label using the constraints you have just specified.*

➤   Set up a launch file.

  1.   Select the LaunchScreen.Storyboard file in the project navigator.

  2.   Use the Attribute Inspector to change the background color of the launch file to a different color than that of the scene in the main storyboard.

➤   Set up an application icon.

  1.   Select the Assets.xcassets item in the project navigator to open the asset bundle. Select the AppIcon asset within this bundle.

  2.   Use drag-and-drop to assign images to the iPhone App and iPad App placeholders. You can obtain the images from the resources available for this lesson on the book's website at www.wrox.com/go/swiftios.

      ➤   iPhone App 2x: Use the file iPhoneAppIcon2x.png.

➤   iPhone App 3x: Use the file
`iPhoneAppIcon3x.png`.

➤   iPad App 1x: Use the file
`iPadAppIcon1x.png`.

➤   iPad App 2x: Use the file
`iPadAppIcon2x.png`.

After these assignments are made, your scene should resemble Figure 1-12.

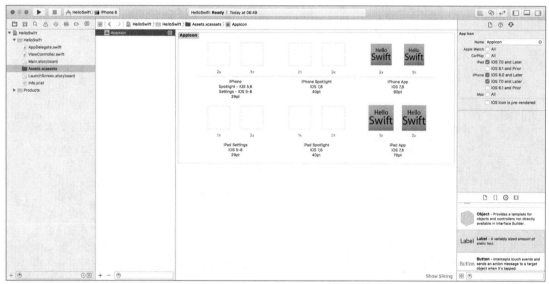

FIGURE 1-12

➤   Test your app in the iOS Simulator by clicking the Run button in the Xcode toolbar. Alternatively, you can use the Project ➪ Run menu item.

REFERENCE *To see some of the examples from this lesson, watch the Lesson 1 video online at* `www.wrox.com/go/swiftiosvid`.

A Tour of Xcode and the iOS Simulator

Xcode is Apple's IDE (integrated development environment), which you use to create iOS applications. The word "integrated" refers to the fact that Xcode brings together several different tools into a single application.

Xcode contains several tools, but the ones you'll use most of the time are the source code editor, debugger, and the Interface Builder. At the time of this writing, the current version of Xcode is 7.0.

The iOS Simulator is an application that runs on your Mac and allows you to test your apps without using an actual iOS device. The iOS Simulator is part of the standard iOS SDK installation. When you run your app in Xcode, you have the choice of launching it in the simulator or an actual device. If you choose to launch it in the simulator, Xcode will launch the iOS Simulator automatically.

In this lesson, you explore various commonly used features of Xcode and the iOS Simulator.

THE WELCOME SCREEN

When you launch Xcode, you are presented with the welcome dialog box (Figure 2-1). You can use the welcome dialog box to quickly create a new project, connect to a source code repository, open a recently used project, or create a Swift playground.

FIGURE 2-1

The first step in creating an iOS application is to create an appropriate project in Xcode. An Xcode project has the file extension `.xcodeproj` and tells the Xcode IDE (among other things) the name of your application, what kind of application it is (iPhone/iPad/Universal), and where to find the code files and resources required to create the application.

CREATING A NEW PROJECT

When you create a new project in Xcode, you first need to select a template on which to base the project. Xcode templates contain files that you need to start developing a new application. Xcode provides a list of project templates to select from (Figure 2-2).

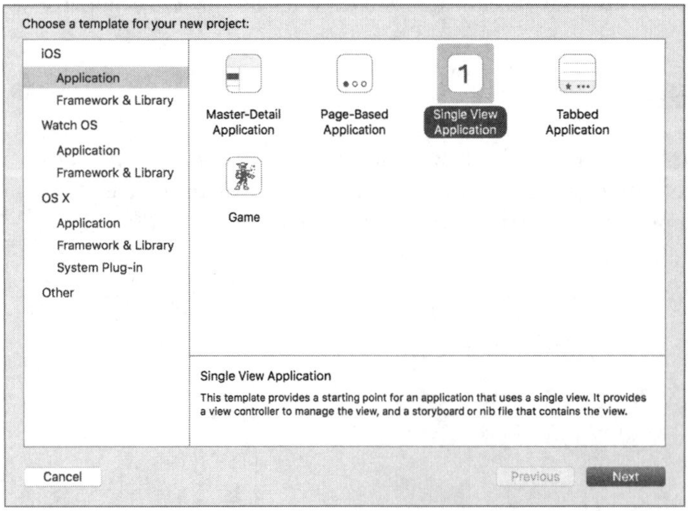

FIGURE 2-2

The Xcode template window has multiple template categories to choose from. In this book, you create iOS applications, and thus need to make sure the iOS template category is selected.

After you have selected a suitable template, Xcode presents the project options dialog box (Figure 2-3).

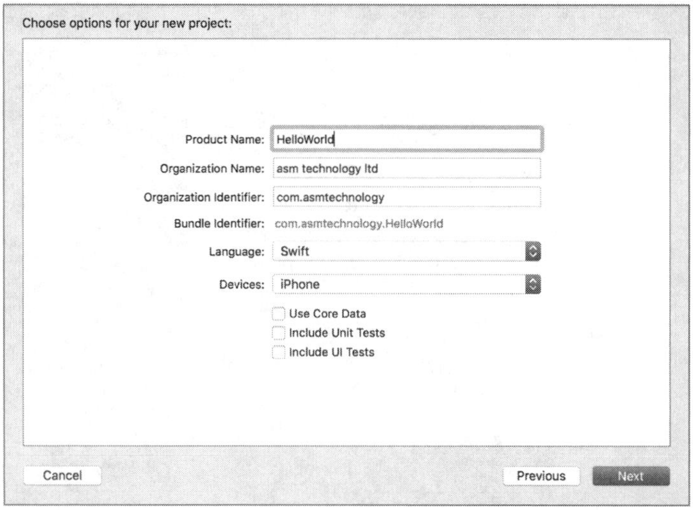

FIGURE 2-3

This is where you provide the name of the project and the name of your company, choose the language (Objective-C or Swift), and specify the target device (iPhone, iPad, or Universal).

To uniquely identify your application in the iTunes store (and on an iOS device), each project must have a unique identifier. This identifier is known as a *bundle identifier* and is created by combining the name of the project along with a company identifier that you provide in the project options dialog box. It is best to provide your website domain name in reversed format as the company identifier because domain names are guaranteed to be globally unique.

Checking the Use Core Data checkbox will add necessary boilerplate code to allow your application to persist objects into a database using Core Data. Core Data is covered in Lesson 26; for the moment you can leave this box unchecked.

Checking the Include Unit Tests and Include UI Tests checkboxes will create a project that includes unit interface tests and user tests, topics that are covered in Lessons 33 and 34, respectively. For the moment you should leave these boxes unchecked.

When you click Next, Xcode will ask you to provide a location on your Mac where you would like to save the new project. Toward the bottom of this dialog box, you have the option to create a new Git repository for version control. Version control is beyond the scope of this book, so just uncheck the Source Control option in the dialog box.

AN OVERVIEW OF THE XCODE IDE

The Xcode IDE features a single window, called the *workspace window* (Figure 2-4), where you get most of your work done.

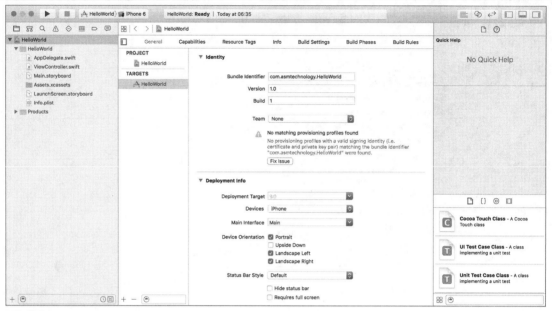

FIGURE 2-4

The Navigator Area

The left side of the workspace window is the navigator area (Figure 2-5).

FIGURE 2-5

The navigator area consists of eight tabs; each of these tabs (called navigators) shows different aspects of the same project. You can switch between navigators using the navigator selector bar at the top of the navigator area (Figure 2-6).

FIGURE 2-6

The Project Navigator

The project navigator (Figure 2-7) shows the contents of your project. Individual files are organized within groups that are represented as folders in a tree structure. The top-level node of this tree structure represents the project itself. These groups are purely logical and provide a convenient way to organize the contents of your project. A group may not necessarily correspond to actual folders on your hard drive.

When a new project is created, Xcode will create two groups (folders) under the project node. Figure 2-7 shows what the project navigator would look like if you were to create a new project using the Single View Application template called HelloWorld without unit tests or user interface tests.

As you can see, the top-level node is called HelloWorld, and the two groups below that node are:

FIGURE 2-7

➤ **HelloWorld:** Contains the source code for your application.

➤ **Products:** Contains the finished products, created after the source code compiles successfully.

In most cases, you will work with a single project at a time in the Xcode workspace window; however, it is possible to open multiple projects in the project navigator using a workspace file. A workspace file has the file extension .xcworkspace and contains references to one or more project files. You will not be creating workspaces in this book; however, if you were to open a workspace file, the workspace window would display information on multiple projects contained within the workspace (Figure 2-8).

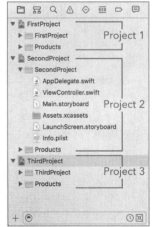

To create a new group, right-click an existing node in the project navigator and select New Group from the context menu. You can move files between groups by using simple drag-and-drop operations in the project navigator. If the groups in the project navigator correspond to actual folders on your Mac, then moving things around in the project navigator will not move the corresponding files into new locations on your Mac.

FIGURE 2-8

To delete a file, simply select the item and hit the backspace key on your keyboard. Xcode then asks you if you intended to delete the actual file from your Mac or just remove the reference from the project. The process of deleting a group is similar to that of a file; keep in mind that deleting a group deletes any files within that group.

At the bottom of the project navigator is a set of icons. You can use these icons to filter what is displayed in the project navigator based on certain criteria.

> **NOTE** *To learn more about the project navigator, read the Project Navigator Help document at* `http://developer.apple.com/library/ios/#recipes/ xcode_help-structure_navigator/_index.html`.

The Symbol Navigator

The symbol navigator (Figure 2-9) shows the classes in your project along with their methods and member variables. A top-level node in a tree-like structure represents each class. Expanding the class node reveals all its member variables and methods.

FIGURE 2-9

The Find Navigator

The find navigator (Figure 2-10) lets you find all occurrences of some text, across all files of the project.

A root-level node in a tree represents each file that has one or more occurrences of matching text. Expanding the node reveals the exact positions within that file where these matches were made.

The Issue Navigator

The issue navigator (Figure 2-11) lists all compile-time errors and warnings in your project. While compiling a file, Xcode raises an issue each time it finds a problem with the file. Severe showstopping issues are flagged as errors, whereas less severe issues are flagged as warnings.

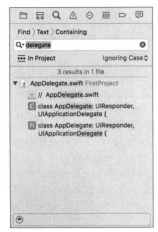

FIGURE 2-10

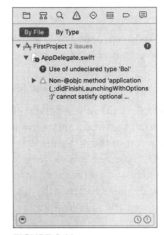

FIGURE 2-11

Each file with one or more errors/warnings is represented by a root-level node in a tree-like structure. Expanding the node reveals the exact positions within that file where these errors/warnings were encountered.

The Test Navigator

The test navigator (Figure 2-12) gives you a snapshot of all the unit tests created with the project. A root-level node in a tree-like structure represents each test suite. Expanding this node reveals the test fixtures within that test suite. Clicking a test fixture (method) will open the corresponding code in the editor area. To run a test, you could click the play icon to the right of the test fixture.

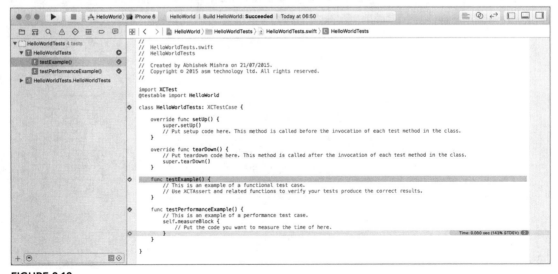

FIGURE 2-12

The Debug Navigator

The debug navigator is used during an active debugging session and lists the call stack for each running thread. Debugging is an advanced topic and is not covered in this book.

The Breakpoint Navigator

The breakpoint navigator lists all breakpoints in your code and allows you to manage them. A breakpoint is an intentional pause-point that you can set in your project. When the app is being executed, Xcode interrupts the execution of the application when it encounters one of these pause-points and transfers control to the debugger. This is extremely useful when trying to figure out why a particular piece of code does not work and you want to inspect the values of variables and content of memory. Breakpoints and the debugger work only when the application is being executed in debug mode. Breakpoints and debugging are advanced topics, and are not covered in this book.

The Report Navigator

The report navigator shows you a history of build logs and console debug sessions. Building is the complete process of creating an executable application from your source code files. Compilation is a part of the build process. Each time you build a new executable, Xcode creates a build log that contains, among other things, a list of files that were compiled.

The Editor Area

The right side of the workspace window is the editor area (Figure 2-13). Xcode includes editors for many file types, including source code, user interface files, XML files, and project settings, to name a few.

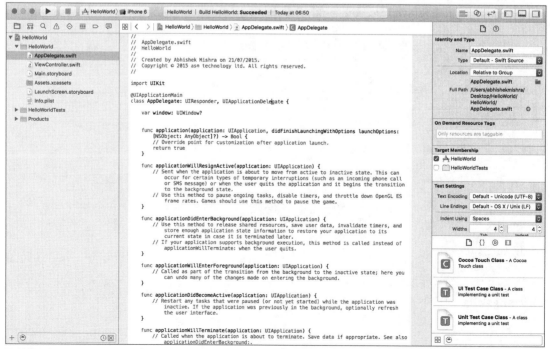

FIGURE 2-13

The content of the editor area depends on the current selection in the navigator area. When you select a file in the navigator area, Xcode tries to find an appropriate editor for that file type. If it can't find one, it opens the file using Quick Look (which is also used by the Finder).

Jump Bars

At the top of the editor area is the jump bar (Figure 2-14). The jump bar displays the path to the current file being edited and can be used to quickly select another file in the workspace. The jump bar also has back and forward buttons to move through a history of files edited. Each element in the path displayed in the jump bar is a pop-up menu (Figure 2-15) that you can use to navigate around your project.

FIGURE 2-14

FIGURE 2-15

The contents of the jump bar depend on the type of file you're viewing. When editing a user interface file, for example, the jump bar enables you to navigate to individual interface elements.

The Source Editor

When you select a source-code file in the navigator area, or a text/XML file, Xcode uses the source editor to open the file. This is the editor with which you will spend most of your time when you write your code. The source editor has several helpful features, such as syntax highlighting and code completion hints. You can configure individual features of the source editor using Xcode preferences.

The Assistant Editor

The assistant editor (Figure 2-16) was introduced in Xcode 4 and enables you to view multiple files side-by-side.

The assistant editor is not visible by default and can be accessed by using the editor selector buttons in the Xcode toolbar or by selecting View ➪ Assistant Editor ➪ Show Assistant Editor. Option-clicking a file in the project navigator or symbol navigator opens it in the assistant editor. You can create additional assistant editor panes by using the + button in the jump bar of the assistant editor.

The Version Editor

If your project is under version control, you can use the version editor to compare the current version of a file with a previous version. Like the assistant editor, the version editor is not visible by default and can be accessed by using the editor selector buttons in the Xcode toolbar. Version control is not covered in this book.

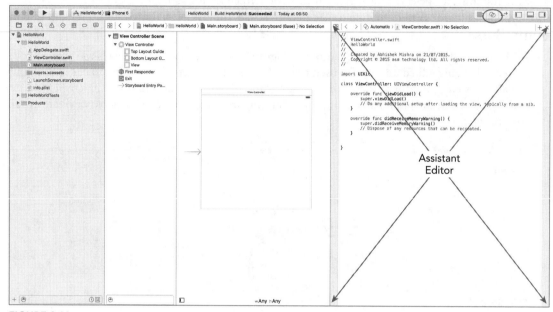

FIGURE 2-16

The Utilities Area

The utilities area (Figure 2-17) supplements the editor area. You can display it by selecting View ⇨ Utilities ⇨ Show Utilities or by clicking the utility button in the toolbar.

The Inspector Area

The top portion of the utilities area contains the inspector area (Figure 2-18). Like the navigator area, the inspector area also contains multiple tabs that can be switched using a selector bar at the top of the window.

The number of tabs available depends on the currently selected item in the project navigator. Regardless of what is selected in the project navigator, the first two tabs are always the file inspector and the quick help inspector. The file inspector provides access to the properties of the current file. The quick help inspector provides a short description of the current file.

The Library Area

The bottom portion of the utilities area contains the library area (Figure 2-19). This area contains a library of file templates, user interface objects, and code snippets that you can use in your applications.

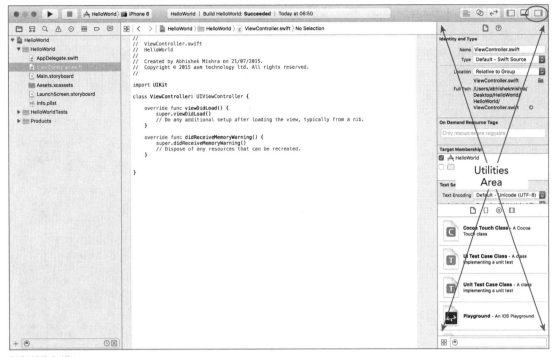

FIGURE 2-17

FIGURE 2-18

FIGURE 2-19

The library area also provides a convenient method to access all the media files in your project. A selector bar at the top of the library area provides access to four different library categories.

The Debugger Area

The debugger area (Figure 2-20) also supplements the editor area. You can access it by selecting View ⇨ Show Debug Area or by clicking the debugger button in the toolbar.

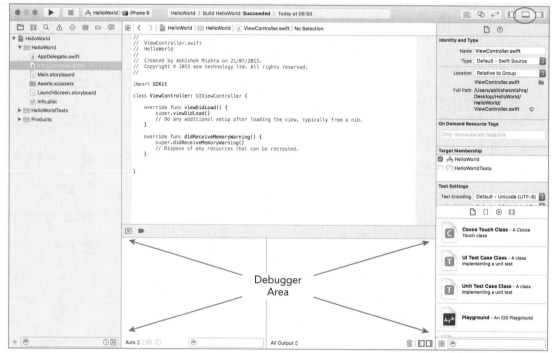

FIGURE 2-20

The debugger area is used while debugging an application and to access the debug console window. You can use this area to examine the values of variables in your programs.

The Toolbar

The Xcode toolbar (Figure 2-21) is located at the top of the workspace window. Use the first two buttons on the left side to run/stop the active build scheme. Immediately following the stop button is the Scheme/Target multi-selector. When you create an iOS project, Xcode creates a scheme with the same name as the project and several build targets.

FIGURE 2-21

The build targets that are typically generated for a project include:

➤   iOS Device

➤   iPad 2 (if it is an iPad or Universal project)

➤   iPad Air (if it is an iPad or Universal project)

➤ iPad Retina (if it is an iPad or Universal project)

➤ iPhone 4S (if it is an iPhone or Universal project)

➤ iPhone 5 (if it is an iPhone or Universal project)

➤ iPhone 5S (if it is an iPhone or Universal project)

➤ iPhone 6 Plus (if it is an iPhone or Universal project)

➤ iPhone 6 (if it is an iPhone or Universal project)

You can use the Scheme/Target multi-selector to switch build targets and create/edit schemes. Managing schemes is an advanced topic beyond the scope of this book.

To the right of the Scheme/Target multi-selector is a status window. Following the status window, the toolbar contains the editor selector and utility selector buttons, which have been covered in the previous sections.

FEATURES OF THE iOS SIMULATOR

When you run an application from the Xcode IDE, unless you have selected a device in the Scheme/Target multi-selector, your application will be launched in the iOS Simulator. Figure 2-22 shows the iPhone 5S simulator. You can use the iOS Simulator to simulate different device and SDK versions. To switch devices use the Hardware ⇨ Device menu.

FIGURE 2-22

You can rotate the simulator by using the Rotate Left or Rotate Right menu items from the Hardware menu. The iOS Simulator allows you to simulate a variety of one and two-finger multitouch gestures. Single-finger gestures such as taps and swipes can be performed by clicking and dragging with the mouse. The only two-finger gesture that you can simulate is the pinch. To do so, hold down the Option key on your keyboard while clicking and dragging with the mouse in the simulator window. Shake gestures can be performed by using the Hardware ⇨ Shake Gesture menu item.

If you are developing an app that requires location data, you can use the iOS Simulator to simulate a test location while you are running your application within the simulator. Select Debug ⇨ Location ⇨ Custom Location to specify a latitude and longitude pair (Figure 2-23). Creating location-based applications is covered in Lessons 29 and 30.

FIGURE 2-23

The simulator can also simulate changing locations. This is particularly useful if your app is designed to be used while on the move. From the Debug ⇨ Location menu, you can select from a list of prerecorded location sets. The simulator will then periodically cycle between the locations in the selected set. The sets are:

➤ Apple Stores

➤ City Bicycle Ride

➤ City Run

➤ Freeway Drive

Installing and Uninstalling Applications

To install an application to the iOS Simulator, you need to open its corresponding .xcodeproj file in Xcode and click the Run button in the Xcode toolbar.

You cannot delete the default iOS Simulator applications (such as Photos, Settings, Game Center, Safari, and so on). To uninstall (delete) one of your applications from the iOS Simulator, click and hold the mouse button down on the icon of the app until all the icons start to wiggle. Once they start to wiggle, you will notice an X button on the top-left corner of each icon.

Release the mouse button if you are still holding it down; the icons will still continue to wiggle. Click the X button on the icon of the app you want to delete. An alert window will appear asking you to confirm this action.

Limitations of the iOS Simulator

As good as the iOS Simulator may be, it has its limitations. For starters, you cannot make calls, send or receive text messages, or install apps from the App Store.

The performance of the iOS Simulator depends on the speed of your Mac, and in certain cases your application may appear to execute much faster on your Mac (in the iOS Simulator) than it does on the real device.

Accelerometer, camera, and microphone functions are not supported in the iOS Simulator. If you are developing OpenGL/ES-based applications, you should keep in mind that several OpenGL/ES functions are not supported on the iOS Simulator.

The iOS Simulator is a useful tool to test your apps but it is definitely not a replacement for testing on a real device.

TRY IT

In this Try It, you launch Xcode and open the project that you created in the Try It for Lesson 1. This project was built using the Single View Application template. Once the project is opened in Xcode, you will open a file in the editor area and display the assistant editor, debugger, and utilities areas.

Lesson Requirements

➤ Launch Xcode.

➤ Create a new project using a template.

➤ Open a file in the editor area.

➤ Show the assistant editor.

➤ Show the debug area.

➤ Show the utilities area.

Hints

This Try It builds on the HelloSwift project you created at the end of Lesson 1.

Step-by-Step

1. Open the HelloSwift project you created at the end of Lesson 1 by double-clicking the `HelloSwift.xcodeproj` file in the finder.

2. Open the `AppDelegate.swift` file in the Xcode editor. Ensure the project navigator is visible and the iOSTest project is open.

3. Show the assistant editor using the editor selector buttons on the Xcode toolbar.

4. Show the debug area using the view selector buttons on the Xcode toolbar.

5. Show the utilities area using the view selector buttons on the Xcode toolbar.

> **REFERENCE** *To see some of the examples from this lesson, watch the Lesson 2 video online at* `www.wrox.com/go/swiftiosvid`.

3

Introducing Swift

Prior to the launch of iOS8, Objective-C was the official language used to make native applications. With the launch of iOS 8, Apple provided an alternative language called Swift. Now it is possible to code iOS (and Mac OSX) applications in both Objective-C and Swift. This book targets Swift 2.0, which is supported on iOS 9 and later. This lesson introduces some of the basic concepts of Swift.

INTRODUCING XCODE PLAYGROUNDS

Playgrounds are a new feature of Xcode (available from versions 6 and above) that allow you to rapidly prototype Swift code. You cannot create a complete app in a playground, but if you want to quickly try out an algorithm or just want to get a feel for the Swift programming language, then playgrounds are for you.

To create a playground, you can either select the Get started with a playground option in the Xcode welcome screen (Figure 3-1), or select the File ➪ New ➪ Playground menu item.

FIGURE 3-1

Xcode will then ask you to provide a name for the playground as well as the platform. In this book, only iOS playgrounds are explored (Figure 3-2).

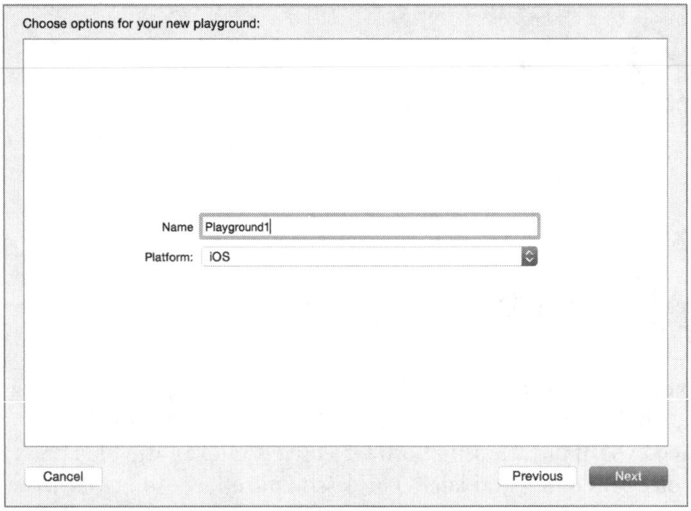

FIGURE 3-2

Xcode will then prompt you to provide a location where the playground should be saved on your hard disk. You can, of course, use any location of your choice.

The main playground screen is divided into two parts (Figure 3-3).

➤ **Editor area:** This forms the left-hand side of the playground screen and is where you type your Swift statements. Every time you press Enter on your keyboard to type a new line, the playground will try to execute the line you have just finished.

➤ **Results area:** This forms the right-hand side of the playground and is where results are displayed. When the playground executes a line of Swift code, it will try and put the result in the same vertical position as the line of code that was executed.

If the Swift code you have typed in the editor area contains `print` statements, then the output of these statements will be visible in the console. To display the console in a playground, use the View ⇨ Debug Area ⇨ Activate Console menu item.

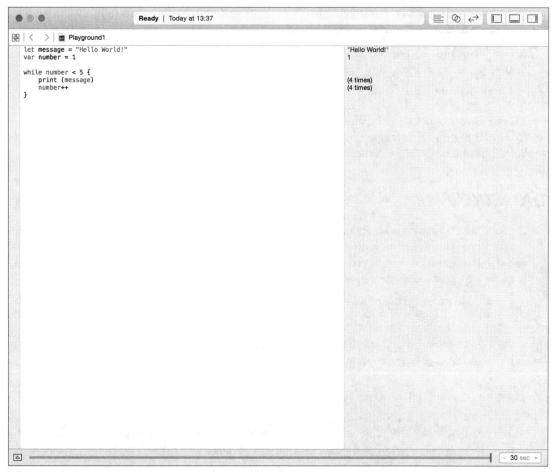

FIGURE 3-3

CONSTANTS AND VARIABLES

The `let` keyword is used to create a constant. A constant is a quantity whose value cannot change once it is assigned. The following statement creates a constant called `maximumScore` with a value of 200:

```
let maximumScore = 200
```

If you are familiar with programming in C or Objective-C, you will immediately notice that Swift statements do not need to end in a semicolon.

A variable quantity is one whose value can change over the life of the application. A variable is defined using the `var` keyword as follows:

```
var currentScore = 20
```

There are a few rules that you must stick to when it comes to naming constants and variables. Constants and variables cannot begin with a number, contain spaces, or contain mathematical symbols. You cannot change a constant into a variable or vice versa.

DATA TYPES

Unlike C or Objective-C, Swift does not require you to specify a data type when you are declaring a constant or variable. The Swift compiler uses type inference to work out the data type from the value you assign. If, however, you wish to be explicit, you can specify the data type of a constant or variable while declaring them as follows:

```
let maximumScore:Int = 200
var bookCategory:String = "fiction"
```

Once a constant or variable has been created with a certain type, its type cannot be changed. Table 3-1 lists some of the common data types in Swift.

TABLE 3-1: Common Swift Data Types

TYPE	DESCRIPTION
Int	Used to represent whole positive or negative numbers such as 1, 2, 300, 5000.
Float	Used to represent positive or negative fractional numbers such as 11.9482.
Double	Used to represent positive or negative fractional numbers (with a greater degree of precision than Float), such as –11.948281731.
Bool	Used to represent Boolean values; can be true or false.
String	Used to represent a sequence of characters enclosed in double quotes, such as "Hello World!"
Character	Used to represent a single character in a string.

Variables in Swift are classed as either value types or reference types depending on how they behave when they are passed as parameters to a method. (A method is a block of code that will be described later).

A value type is a variable whose value is copied when it is passed as a parameter to a method. Any changes made by the method to the variable only apply to its private copy of the original variable and do not affect the value of the original variable in any way.

A reference type, on the other hand, is passed by reference. If the receiving method changes the value of a reference type then the change will be visible outside the scope of the function.

COMMENTS

Comments are used to add some descriptive text to your code that you want the compiler to ignore. Typically, these are used to provide a human readable description about what is happening in the code for reference purposes. Comments in Swift are similar to C-style comments. A single line comment begins with two forward slashes (//). For example:

```
// this is a single line comment.
```

When the compiler encounters a line that starts with two forward slashes, it ignores everything on that line.

If you would like to create a comment that spans over multiple lines, you could use multiple single line comments. Alternatively you can use a multi-line comment. A multi-line comment begins with a forward slash asterisk (/*) and ends with an asterisk forward slash (*/) for example:

```
/* this is a very
long comment that spans
three lines */
```

STRINGS

A string is a sequence of characters represented by the `String` type, and each character in a string is of the `Character` type. For example:

```
var stringVariable = "the man in the moon"
```

You can initialize an empty string as follows:

```
var anEmptyString:String = ""
```

If you have programmed in Objective-C, you will be familiar with the concept of mutable and immutable strings. A mutable string is one whose contents can be changed, and Objective-C uses two different classes (`NSString` and `NSMutableString`) to indicate whether a string can be mutated. You will be pleased to know that there is only one `String` type in Swift; mutability is established by creating a string variable. If you wish to create an immutable string, create a string constant as follows:

```
let immutableString = "this string cannot be changed"
```

Strings can be concatenated (added together) to produce longer strings using the + operator as follows:

```
let firstString = "Happy"
let secondString = "Birthday"
var concatenatedString = firstString + secondString
```

The variable `concatenatedString` will now contain `"HappyBirthday"` (without a space, as there is no space in any of the original strings.

You can append a string to an existing string variable using the += operator as follows:

```
var myString = "two times two is "
myString += "four"
```

The variable `myString` will now contain `"two times two is four"`. The space between *is* and *four* is part of the original value of `myString`.

Swift uses string interpolation to create a new string from a mix of constants, variables, and expressions. If you are an Objective-C programmer, then string interpolation in Swift is similar to Objective-C's [`NSString stringWithFormat`] class method. This is best explained with an example:

```
var patientName = "Jason"
var patientHeight = 84
var message = "\(patientName) is \(patientHeight) cm tall."
```

The result of this snippet will be a string that contains `"Jason is 84 cm tall."` In this example the variables `patientName` and `patientHeight` are inserted as `\(patientName)` and `\(patientHeight)` placeholders. When the message variable is evaluated, these placeholders are replaced by actual values and any associated type conversions are performed automatically.

Placeholders aren't restricted to names of constants and variables; you can put a complete expression in a placeholder. For example, the statement

```
let result = "\(2 + 2) is equal to four"
```

will create a string constant called `result` with the value `"4 is equal to four"`.

TUPLES

A tuple is a compound value that groups multiple values. The individual values within a tuple can be of different data types. The following line of code declares a tuple called `applicantDetails` with two values—the first is an Int, the second a String.

```
let applicantDetails = (12, "Henry")
```

There are a few different ways to access individual values in a tuple. One way is to use index numbers starting at zero:

```
print("Applicant age is \(applicantDetails.0)")
print("Applicant name is \(applicantDetails.1)")
```

If you have named the elements in the tuple when it is defined, you can use these names to access individual values, as you can see in the following code snippet:

```
let applicantDetails = (applicantAge:12, applicantName:"Henry")
print("Applicant age is \(applicantDetails.applicantAge)")
print("Applicant name is \(applicantDetails.applicantName)")
```

You can also split a tuple into separate variables, which you can then access as follows:

```
let applicantDetails = (12, "Henry")
let (applicantAge, applicantName) = applicantDetails
print("Applicant age is \(applicantAge)")
print("Applicant name is \(applicantName)")
```

The output of any of these three methods would be the same:

```
Applicant age is 12
Applicant name is Henry
```

OPTIONALS

An optional is a new concept in Swift. An optional variable can either contain a value or have no value. The closest thing in Objective-C would be the use of nil to indicate the absence of an object, but in Objective-C, nil cannot be used with primitive data types, structures, or enumerations. Unlike Objective-C, Swift's optionals can be used to indicate the absence of a value for any data type.

While declaring a variable, you indicate that it is an optional by appending a (?) to the data type. Thus, an optional Double is a Double? For example:

```
var optionalDouble : Double? = 17.7681
```

If you define an optional without providing a value, it is automatically set to nil. Alternately, you can set an optional variable to contain no value by assigning nil to it as follows:

```
optionalDouble = nil
```

nil is interpreted as a valueless state to an optional. If an optional contains a value, you can access this value by unwrapping the optional. To unwrap an optional, simply add an exclamation mark to the end of the variable name.

If you attempt to unwrap an optional that has no value, your app will be terminated with a runtime error. You can test whether an optional has a value by comparing it with nil in a simple if statement, as in the following:

```
var score : Int? = 10
if (score != nil)
{
    print("Your score is \(score!)")
}
```

Another way to execute a bunch of statements if an optional contains a value is to use an optional binding. An optional binding allows you check if an optional has a value and, at the same time, extract this value into a constant or variable. Optional bindings can only be used in if and while statements, both of which are covered later in this lesson. Consider the following example:

```
var score : Int? = 10
if let unwrappedScore = score
{
    print("Your score is \(unwrappedScore)")
}
```

In this example, the optional `score` will automatically be unwrapped into the constant `unwrapped-Score` if it contains a value. `unwrappedScore` can now be used just like a normal constant and does not need any further unwrapping.

If an optional is guaranteed to always contain a value, then you can skip having to unwrap it every time by implicitly unwrapping it when you declare the optional. An implicitly unwrapped optional is declared with an exclamation mark after the data type, instead of a question mark. Attempting to assign `nil` to an implicitly unwrapped option will result in a compile time error.

Some scenarios where you may want to use an implicitly unwrapped optional are:

➤   As a return value from a function, this ensures the function will not return `nil`.

➤   As an argument to a function, this ensures the function cannot be called with a `nil` argument.

➤   When creating `IBOutlets` to elements in `xib` files. Interface builder and `xib` files will be covered in Lesson 9.

In the following example, `score` is an implicitly unwrapped optional:

```
var score : Int! = 10
print("Your score is \(score)")
```

CONTROL FLOW STATEMENTS

A *control flow statement* allows you to modify the order of statements executed, execute certain statements multiple times, or execute certain statements conditionally.

if-else

The `if` statement is one such control statement. In its basic form an `if` statement executes a block of statements only if a specific condition is met.

```
if condition evaluates to true
{
    statement to execute
}
```

The *test condition* is usually a Boolean variable, or an expression that evaluates to a Boolean variable. If the test condition evaluates to `true`, the following statement (or block of statements) is executed. The following is a simple example:

```
var numberOfRedMarbles = 20;
var numberOfBlueMarbles = 5;
if numberOfRedMarbles > numberOfBlueMarbles
{
    print("Game over, you won!");
}
```

In this hypothetical game example, a player is required to collect a certain number of red and blue marbles. A player wins the game if he collects more red marbles than blue ones. The test condition in this case is the expression

```
numberOfRedMarbles > numberOfBlueMarbles
```

which evaluates to `true` in this particular case. Note the complete `if` statement contains both the test condition and the block of statements that go with the test condition.

The else Clause

A modified version of the `if` statement allows you to specify an additional block of statements that are executed should the test condition fail. This additional alternate-scenario statement is completely optional and should you need to specify it, you can use the modified form of the `if` statement:

```
if condition evaluates to true
{
    statements to execute
}
else
{
    some other statements to execute
}
```

This modified form of the `if` statement is known as the if-`else` statement. The `else` portion is optional. The statement (or block of statements) following the `else` clause is executed only if the test condition evaluates to `false`. A simple example follows:

```
var numberOfRedMarbles = 20;
var numberOfBlueMarbles = 5;
if numberOfRedMarbles > numberOfBlueMarbles
{
    print("Game over, you won!");
}
else
{
    print("Better luck next time!");
}
```

In this example, if `numberofRedMarbles` is greater than `numberofBlueMarbles` then

```
print("Game over, you won!");
```

will be executed. Otherwise,

```
print("Better luck next time!");
```

will be executed. Now it just so happens to be the case that 20 is greater than 5 and hence the block associated with the `else` clause will not execute in this example.

In the examples so far, the conditional expressions are trivial (such as 20 is greater than 5) and strictly speaking, the `if` statement is not being used to its true potential. In a real-world application, the values of the operands in the conditional expression would be dynamic—for instance, the number of times a tap is detected, or the number of alien spaceships destroyed by the player as a game proceeds. In these cases, the `if` and `if-else` statements are extremely useful.

Just as with an `if` statement, statements that appear after the `if-else` statement would continue to execute regardless of what happened in the `if-else` statement.

switch-case

A switch-case statement is convenient when you want to examine a variable and take a different course of action for different values of the variable.

```
switch variable {

case value:
    statements

case value:
    statements

default:
    statements
}
```

The variable being examined in a switch-case statement can be an Integer, Boolean, Tuple, or Optional. You use the `case` clause to handle a specific value (or set of values). If the value of the variable is found to match one of the scenarios handled by a `case` statement, then the corresponding statement (or block of statements) will be executed. The following example shows a `switch-case` statement:

```
let numberOfMarbles = 1;

switch numberOfMarbles {

case 1:
    print("You have just one marble.")

case 2,3,4,5:
    print("You have a few marbles.")

default:
    print("You have way too many marbles!")
}
```

The last case in a switch-case statement is always labeled `default`. The default case is executed if none of the preceding cases have matched the value of the variable. Once a case is executed, control moves out of the entire `switch-case` block and the statement following the `switch-case` block will be executed.

Every `case` must have at least one statement; the following will NOT work in Swift:

```
let numberOfMarbles = 1;

switch numberOfMarbles {

case 0:
case 1:
    print("You have just one marble.")

case 2,3,4,5:
    print("You have a few marbles.")

default:
    print("You have way too many marbles!")
}
```

It is possible to achieve the overall effect of a `switch-case` statement with multiple `if-else` statements, but the resulting code would be cumbersome.

Loops

A loop is a programming construct used to execute a bunch of statements multiple times. Typically, a Boolean expression is evaluated either at the beginning or at the end of each pass of the loop. If the expression evaluates to `true` then the loop will continue for another pass.

for Loop

The `for` loop has its roots in the C programming language. The general form of this loop is

```
for initial expression; termination expression; increment expression
{
    loop statements
}
```

where:

➤ **Initial expression:** This expression usually involves an assignment (where a value is assigned to a variable).

➤ **Termination expression:** This expression usually involves a comparison operator and evaluates to either `true` or `false`. If this expression evaluates to `false` the body of the loop will not be executed.

➤ **Increment expression:** This expression usually adds an integer to the variable used in the initial expression.

The loop statements are a block of Swift statements that are executed at each pass of the loop. These statements are also known as the *body* of the loop.

When a `for` loop is encountered, the following happens:

1. The initial expression is evaluated.

2. The termination expression is evaluated.

3. If the termination expression evaluates to `false`, the `for` statement terminates, and execution continues at the first statement after the loop block.

4. If the termination expression evaluates to `true`, the loop statement/block is executed once.

5. The increment expression is evaluated, and execution continues from Step 2.

For an example of a `for` statement in action, consider the following snippet:

```
for var number = 10; number < 15; number++ {
    print("The value of number is \(number)")
}
```

This snippet would result in the following output:

```
The value of number is 10
The value of number is 11
The value of number is 12
The value of number is 13
The value of number is 14
```

In this example, the initial expression sets the value of the variable `number` to `10`:

```
number = 10
```

The termination expression is a conditional expression that evaluates to `true` or `false`. In this case, the expression tests if the value of `number` is less than 15:

```
number < 15
```

The increment expression adds `1` to the value of the variable `number`:

```
number++
```

Without this expression, the value of `number` would never change, and the termination expression would never evaluate to `false`. Consequently the loop would go on indefinitely.

for-in Loop

The `for-in` loop executes a block of statements for each item in a range or collection. Unlike the `for` loop, there is no termination expression to be evaluated. The general form of this loop is

```
for item in range
{
    loop statements
}
```

where:

➤ **Item:** This is a variable that is automatically assigned the next value in the collection of values being iterated across.

➤ **Range:** This is an ordered collection of values over which the loop iterates.

The following snippet provides an example of the `for-in` statement in action:

```
for number in 1...3
{
    print("The value of number is \(number)")
}
```

This snippet would result in the following output:

```
The value of number is 1
The value of number is 2
The value of number is 3
```

In this example, the range of values across which the loop iterates is expressed as a closed range of numbers from 1 to 3 using the range operator (...). The variable number does not have to be declared before it is used as Swift will implicitly declare it because it is included in the loop.

You can also use the `for-in` loop to iterate across an array or dictionary. An example of iterating over an array of strings follows:

```
let places = ["Geneva", "Rome", "Zurich"]
for place in places
{
    print("\(place) is a nice city to visit.")
}
```

This snippet would result in the following output:

```
Geneva is a nice city to visit.
Rome is a nice city to visit.
Zurich is a nice city to visit.
```

while Loop

The `while` loop executes a block of statements as long as a specified condition holds true. The general form of the `while` statement is:

```
while loop condition
{
    loop statements
}
```

The *loop condition* is typically a Swift expression that evaluates to `true` or `false`. The loop statements are a block of Swift statements that are executed at each pass of the loop. These statements are also known as the *body* of the loop.

When a `while` loop is encountered, the following happens:

1. The loop condition is evaluated.

2. If the loop condition evaluates to `false`, the `while` statement terminates, and execution continues at the first statement after the loop block.

3. If the loop condition evaluates to `false`, the loop statement/block is executed once, after which execution continues from Step 1.

The following code snippet provides an example of a `while` loop in action:

```
var number = 1
while number < 5
{
    print("The value of number is \(number)")
    number = number + 1;
}
```

This snippet would result in the following output:

```
The value of number is 1
The value of number is 2
The value of number is 3
The value of number is 4
```

In this example, the loop condition is a conditional expression that evaluates to `true` or `false`. In this case, the expression tests if the value of `number` is less than 5:

```
number < 5
```

It is worth noting that the value of `number` is incremented by 1 in the body of the `while` loop. If this were not done, then `number` would always equal 1, and this loop would never terminate.

repeat-while Loop

The `repeat-while` loop first executes a block of statements and then checks a specified condition to determine if the preceding block should be executed again. The general form of the `while` statement is:

```
repeat {
    loop statements
}
while loop condition
```

Once again, *loop condition* is typically a Swift expression that involves a conditional operator and evaluates to `true` or `false`. The loop statements are a block of Swift statements that are executed at each pass of the loop. These statements are also known as the *body* of the loop.

When a `repeat-while` loop is encountered, the following happens:

1. The loop body is executed.
2. The loop condition is evaluated.
3. If the loop condition evaluates to `false`, the `repeat-while` loop terminates, and execution continues at the first statement after the loop block.
4. If the loop condition evaluates to `true`, execution continues from Step 1.

Consider the following example of a `repeat-while` loop in action:

```
var number = 1
repeat
{
    print("The value of number is \(number)")
```

```
        number = number + 1
}
while number < 5
```

This snippet would result in the following output:

```
The value of number is 1
The value of number is 2
The value of number is 3
The value of number is 4
```

It's important to note that the body of the `repeat-while` loop is guaranteed to execute at least once because the loop condition is evaluated after the loop body is executed.

CONTROL TRANSFER STATEMENTS

Control transfer statements change the order in which your program's instructions are executed. They are commonly used to break out of a loop prematurely, or skip one or more iterations.

You can use the `break` statement as part of the statements that form the body of a `for`, `for-in`, `while`, or `repeat-while` loop, to end the loop prematurely. Programs that use loops generally rely on the loop to come to a natural end at some point.

However, sometimes you need to break out of a loop prematurely (perhaps in response to some external factor) and in such cases you can use the `break` statement. The `break` statement is written on its own, on a single line:

```
break
```

Any other statements in the block after the `break` statement will not be executed. The following example demonstrates the use of the `break` statement. In this example a `while` loop is used to iterate over integers between 1 and 200 and print the first number that is divisible by both 5 and 7

```
var number = 1
while number < 200
{
    if ((number % 5 == 0) && (number %% 7 == 0) {
        print("The first number divisible by both 5 and 7 is \(number)")
        break
    }
}
    number = number + 1;
}
```

The `continue` statement, when used in the body of a loop, causes execution to skip one iteration of the loop. The `continue` statement is also written on its own, on a single line:

```
continue
```

Any statements after a `continue` statement will be skipped for that iteration. The following example demonstrates the use of the `continue` statement. In this example a `while` loop is used to iterate over integers between 1 and 200 and print all numbers that are not divisible by 13.

```
var number = 1
while number < 200
{
    if ((number % 13 == 0){
        number = number + 1
        continue
    }

    print("\(number) is not divisible by 13.")
    number = number + 1;
}
```

TRY IT

In this Try It, you launch Xcode and create a new Swift playground. You will then perform a few basic operations with optionals.

Lesson Requirements

➤ Launch Xcode.

➤ Create a new Swift playground.

➤ Perform basic operations with optionals.

> **REFERENCE** *The code for this Try It is available at* www.wrox.com/go/ swiftios.

Hints

To view the console inside the playground window, use the View ➪ Assistant Editor ➪ Show Assistant Editor menu item.

Step-by-Step

➤ Create a new Swift playground.

1. Launch Xcode and create a new Swift playground by selecting the File ➪ New ➪ Playground menu item.

2. In the playground options screen, use the following values:

➤ **Name:** Playground1

➤ **Platform:** iOS

3. Save the playground onto your hard disk.

➤ Create a simple program in the playground.

1. Delete the default contents of the playground file.

2. Type the following lines:

```
import UIKit

var blueBallCount : Int! = 20
var redBallCount : Int? = 100

if redBallCount != nil
{
    print("number of red balls is \(redBallCount!)")
    print("total number of balls is \(redBallCount! + blueBallCount)")
}
else
{
    print("redBallCount has no value")
}
```

3. Observe the results of this program in the Assistant Editor. You should see two lines:

```
"number of red balls is 100"
"total number of balls is 120
```

➤ Modify the program slightly.

1. Change the third line of code to

```
var redBallCount : Int?;
```

2. Once again, observe the results of this program. You should now see only one line:

```
" redBallCount has no value"
```

REFERENCE *To see some of the examples from this lesson, watch the Lesson 3 video online at* www.wrox.com/go/swiftiosvid.

4

Functions

A function is a collection of instructions that perform a specific task; the task is usually something that needs to be performed multiple times over the life of the application. A function has a name, which is used to call it from other parts of your application. A function may return a value (perhaps the result of a computation) and could also have one or more input parameters.

DECLARING FUNCTIONS

Every function has a name; the name given to a function typically describes what it does. Functions are declared in Swift using the `func` keyword. The following example declares a simple function called `greetUser` that prints a line to the console using `print`:

```
func greetUser ()
{
    print("Hello there!")
}
```

To call this function from other parts of your code, you will simply need to mention the name of the function:

```
greetUser()
```

PARAMETERS AND RETURN VALUES

As mentioned earlier, functions can return values and accept input parameters; both of these are optional but at the very least, most functions accept one or more input parameters. The following example declares the function `cubeNumber`, which accepts a single integer as input and returns its cube as output.

```
func cubeNumber (inputValue:Int) -> Int
{
    return inputValue * inputValue * inputValue
}
```

Any input parameters are declared in the parentheses, and the return type of the function is specified using the return arrow (->). Functions aren't restricted to a single input parameter. The following example declares the function greetUserBetter, which accepts an Int and String as input parameters and writes a line to the console.

```
func greetUserBetter(age:Int, userName:String)
{
    print("Hello \(userName). You are \(age) year(s) old.")
}
```

To call this function from other parts of your code, you will simply need to mention the name of the function and supply the values for the two arguments in the order in which they were declared:

```
greetUserBetter(12, userName:"John")
```

Functions can only return a single value (or none at all), but you can still use tuples to return multiple values from a function. Essentially the multiple values that the function would like to return will be grouped into a single tuple and returned. This is demonstrated in the following example:

```
func retrievePersonnelDetails(personnelID:String) -> (String?, Int?)
{
    if personnelID == "100-182"
    {
        return ("John Woods", 37)
    }
    else if personnelID == "100-876"
    {
        return ("Jason Lee", 45)
    }

    return (nil, nil)
}
```

It is worth mentioning that the return value for this function is a tuple of optionals. This implies that for some cases of personnelID this function will return the tuple (nil, nil), indicating that no data was available. You could instead have used an optional tuple (as opposed to a tuple of optionals) for the return value. Using an optional tuple means that the function will return (String, Int), or nil.

Swift allows you to specify an optional external name (known as an argument label) for each parameter to a function. The idea is to provide descriptive names for each parameter that indicate the purpose of the parameter. The retrievePersonnelDetails function could be declared using external and internal parameter names as follows:

```
func retrievePersonnelDetails(acmeEmployeeNumber personnelID:String) ->
(String?, Int?)
```

When this method is now called, you will use the external parameter name:

```
retrievePersonnelDetails(acmeEmployeeNumber:"100-876")
```

If you want a function parameter to accept zero or more items of the same type, you will need to declare the parameter as a variadic parameter. A variadic parameter is declared by adding three period characters (...) to the end of the data type in the functions parameter list. The values of a variadic parameter are presented to the function as an array. Variadic parameters will be explored in this lesson's Try It.

TRY IT

In this Try It, you create a new Swift playground and build a function that uses several concepts covered in this lesson, including returning tuples, variadic parameters, and external parameter names.

Lesson Requirements

➤ Launch Xcode.

➤ Create a new Swift playground.

➤ Create a function that finds the minimum and maximum height from a variable number of heights.

➤ Display the results in the console.

> **REFERENCE** *The code for this Try It is available at* www.wrox.com/go/ swiftios.

Hints

To view the console inside the playground window, use the View ➪ Debug Area ➪ Activate Console menu item.

Step-by-Step

➤ Create a new Swift playground.

1. Launch Xcode and create a new Swift playground by selecting File ➪ New ➪ Playground.

2. In the playground options screen, use the following values:

    ➤ **Name:** FunctionPlayground

    ➤ **Platform:** iOS

3. Save the playground onto your hard disk.

➤ Create the minmax function.

1. Delete the default contents of the playground file.

2. Type the following lines:

```
func minmax(heights inputValues:Int...) -> (Int, Int)
{
    var minHeight = 100000
    var maxHeight = -10000
    for height in inputValues
    {
        if height > maxHeight
        {
            maxHeight = height
        }

        if height < minHeight
        {
            minHeight = height
        }
    }

    return (minHeight, maxHeight)
}
```

➤ Call the `minmax` function.

1. Type the following lines after the end of the `minmax` function definition:

```
let result = minmax(heights:10, 12, 8, 5, -2, 13)
print("Shortest height = \(result.0). Tallest height = \(result.1)")
```

2. Observe the results of this program in the console. You should see the following line in the console:

```
Shortest height = -2. Tallest height = 13
```

> **REFERENCE** *To see some of the examples from this lesson, watch the Lesson 4 video online at* `www.wrox.com/go/swiftiosvid`.

Closures

A *closure* is a block of code that can be passed around and used in your code. Functions are special cases of closures. Closures in Swift are similar to blocks in Objective-C and can capture any constants and variables in their enclosing scope.

FUNCTION TYPES

In the last lesson you learned about functions—which are a special case of closures. Just like primitive data types Int, String, Double, and so on, functions have their own data types in Swift. The data type of a function is called a *function type* and is simply a collection of the parameters and return values of the function. For example, if given the function cubeNumber:

```
func cubeNumber (inputValue:Int) -> Int
{
    return inputValue * inputValue * inputValue
}
```

its function type is simply (Int) -> Int.

It is possible for different functions to have the same function type. In the following example, you can see that the function type for another function called squareNumber is exactly the same as for cubeNumber:

```
func squareNumber (inputValue:Int) -> Int
{
    return inputValue * inputValue
}
```

Function types are first class data types. You can declare a variable to be of a function type and assign an appropriate function to that variable as follows:

```
var mathFunction: (Int) -> Int = squareNumber
```

Function types can be used as parameters to functions as well as return values.

CLOSURE TYPES

There are three types of closures in Swift: global closures, nested closures, and closure expressions. Each of these will be explored in this section.

Global Closures

Global closures are the functions you have learned about so far, declared with the `func` keyword. Unless explicitly specified, these global closures are part of the public interface of the class in which they are declared. You can restrict the visibility of the global closure to the containing class by using the private keyword.

Nested Closures

A nested closure is a function defined within the body of another function. The nested closure would not be visible to code outside the enclosing function but could still be used within the enclosing function. The enclosing function can, however, return one of the nested functions to the caller. For this to happen, the return type of the enclosing function would have to be a function type. In the following example, the function `mathFunctionFactory` returns one of two nested closures depending on the input parameter:

```swift
func mathFunctionFactory(operationId : String) -> (Int) -> Int
{
    func squareNumber(inputValue : Int) -> Int
    {
        return inputValue * inputValue
    }

    func cubeNumber(inputValue : Int) -> Int
    {
        return inputValue * inputValue * inputValue
    }

    return (operationId == "square") ? squareNumber : cubeNumber
}
```

You could use `mathFunctionFactory` to square a number as follows:

```swift
var mathFunction : (Int) -> Int = mathFunctionFactory("square")
println("The square of 2 is \(mathFunction(2))")
```

Closure Expressions

Closure expressions are a way to write inline closures. They are the equivalent of blocks in Objective-C, or lambdas in other languages. Usually when one mentions the word *closure* in Swift, they are referring to closure expressions. The syntax of the closure expression is as follows:

```
{ (parameters) -> return type in
statements
}
```

The cubeNumber function discussed earlier in this lesson could be written using a closure expression as follows:

```
var cubeNumber : (Int) -> Int =
{
    (inputValue : Int) -> Int in
     return inputValue * inputValue * inputValue
}
```

Note that cubeNumber is now a variable of function type (Int) -> Int and is assigned a closure expression of the same function type. The closure expression is everything between the pair of curly braces.

```
{
    (inputValue : Int) -> Int in
    return inputValue * inputValue * inputValue
}
```

The body of the closure expression starts after the in keyword. The definition of the closure's parameters and return types always precedes the in keyword.

If you have looked at the closure version of cubeNumber, you may have noticed that mentioning the function type twice seems redundant. Swift can infer the function type of the closure expression automatically. Thus, the closure version of cubeNumber can be reduced to this:

```
var cubeNumber : (Int) -> Int =
{
    inputValue in
    return inputValue * inputValue * inputValue
}
```

When you program with closures, it is unlikely you will store them in a variable as in the preceding example. Most of the time, a closure is used as a parameter to a function. This is illustrated in this lesson's Try It.

TRY IT

In this Try It, you create a new Swift playground and build a function that performs a simple arithmetic operation on two numbers. The operation to be performed on the numbers is passed to the function as a closure.

Lesson Requirements

➤ Launch Xcode.

➤ Create a new Swift playground.

➤ Create a function that performs a mathematical operation on two numbers using a closure.

➤ Display the results in the console.

> **REFERENCE** *The code for this Try It is available at* www.wrox.com/go/ swiftios.

Hints

To view the console inside the playground window, select View ➪ Debug Area ➪ Activate Console menu item.

Step-by-Step

➤ Create a new Swift playground.

1. Launch Xcode and create a new Swift playground by selecting File ➪ New ➪ Playground.

2. In the playground options screen, use the following values:

   ➤ **Name:** ClosurePlayground

   ➤ **Platform:** iOS

3. Save the playground onto your hard disk.

➤ Create the minmax function.

1. Delete the default contents of the playground file.

2. Type the following lines:

```
func calculator(firstOperand : Double,
                secondOperand : Double,
                calculatorFunction:(Double, Double) -> Double)
```

```
{
    let result : Double = calculatorFunction(firstOperand, secondOperand)
    print("operand 1 = \(firstOperand), operand 2 = \(secondOperand),
 result = \(result)")
}
```

➤ Call the `calculator` function.

1. Type the following lines after the end of the `calculator` function definition:

```
calculator(12.4,
            secondOperand:17.5,
            calculatorFunction:{
                (v1:Double, v2:Double) -> Double in
                 return v1 - v2}
)
```

2. Observe the results of this program in the console. You should see the following line in the console:

```
operand 1 = 12.4, operand 2 = 17.5, result = -5.1
```

REFERENCE *To see some of the examples from this lesson, watch the Lesson 5 video online at* www.wrox.com/go/swiftiosvid.

Error Handling

Error handling refers to the process of handling error conditions in your app. Swift 2.0 adds new statements that give you the ability to throw, catch, and manipulate runtime errors. Prior to Swift 2.0, if your function wanted to indicate failure, it would do so by returning an *Optional variable* with a `nil` value. Errors provide a streamlined solution to the problem of indicating failure within a function and handling the failure.

THE ERRORTYPE PROTOCOL

An error can be represented by a class, struct, or enumeration that implements the `ErrorType` protocol. In most cases, you will use enumerations to represent errors. The following code snippet lists an enumeration called `NetworkError` that could be used to represent error conditions encountered while making a network request.

```
enum NetworkError: ErrorType {
    case ResourceNotFound
    case ServerError(httpErrorCode:Int)
    case NetworkTimeout
}
```

`NetworkError` could be used to represent three potential scenarios:

➤ `ResoureNotFound`: The URL you were trying to reach couldn't be located.

➤ `NetworkTimeout`: The network request timed out.

➤ `ServerError`: Any other error generated by the server, the HTTP error code will be included as an associated value—`httpErrorCode`.

THROWING AND CATCHING ERRORS

To indicate that a function can throw a runtime error, you must add the `throws` keyword to the end of the function declaration:

```
func doSomething() throws {
...
}
```

If your function returns a value, then you must add the `throws` keyword before the return arrow (`->`):

```
func downloadResource(resourceName:String) throws -> NSData?
{

}
```

If a function is not declared with the `throws` keyword, it cannot throw a runtime error. To throw an error from a throwing function, you can use the `throw` keyword:

```
func downloadResource(resourceName:String) throws -> NSData?
{
    if resourceName.isEmpty
    {
        throw NetworkError.ResourceNotFound
    }

    return nil;
}
```

When calling a function that can throw, you must write `try` in front of the function call. This keyword is used to indicate the fact that the function being called may throw an error and the lines of code after the function call may not be executed as a result. The following snippet shows how you would call the `downloadResource` function.

```
let homeScreenBanner:NSData? = try downloadResource("homeScreenBanner.png")
```

Adding a `try` statement before a function call does not catch or handle any of the errors that can be generated by the function. It simply serves to highlight the fact that the function you are calling can throw one or more errors. To catch and handle errors, you wrap the call to the function in a do . . . catch statement: The general form of the do . . . catch statement is presented next:

```
do{
    try  A function that throws an error
}
    catch An Error Matching Pattern {
}
```

If a function throws an error, that error propagates up the call stack until a suitable `catch` clause is found that can handle the error. If no `catch` clause is found, then the application is terminated with a runtime error. A `catch` clause is followed by an optional pattern used to match errors and a bunch of statements that will be executed if the match is a success.

You can have multiple `catch` clauses in a `do . . . catch` statement. You can also create a catch-all clause by omitting the pattern. Multiple `catch` clauses, and a `catch-all` clause are demonstrated in the following code snippet:

```
func loadHomeScreenImages() {

    do {
        let homeScreenBanner:NSData? = try downloadResource("homeScreenBanner.png")
    } catch (NetworkError.NetworkTimeout) {
  print("Network error occurred!")
    } catch {
        print("Some other error occurred!")
    }
}
```

`catch` clauses must be exhaustive; you need to either provide a `catch` clause for every exception that can be generated by the throwing function or include a `catch-all` clause.

You can, however, decide to handle some of the errors and pass the rest higher up the call stack. To do so, simply append the `throws` keyword to the method that is handling the partial list of errors. For example, the following code snippet will compile fine even though it does not handle every possible error that the `downloadResource` method can throw:

```
func loadHomeScreenImages() throws {

    do{
        let homeScreenBanner:NSData? = try downloadResource("homeScreenBanner.png")
    }
    catch (NetworkError.NetworkTimeout)
    {
        print("Network error occured!")
    }
}
```

This code will compile because `loadHomeScreenImages` itself is declared as a method that can throw errors (in this case, propagate errors from the `downloadResource` function).

Suppressing Error Handling

If you are sure that a throwing function will, in fact, not throw an error at runtime, you can opt to suppress error handling by using the forced try expression (`try!`). The following snippet uses the forced try expression in the call to `downloadResource` to suppress error handling.

```
func loadHomeScreenImages() {
    let homeScreenBanner:NSData? = try! downloadResource("homeScreenBanner.png")
    print("\(homeScreenBanner)")
}
```

If a method that is called with the forced try expression generates a runtime error, then your application will be terminated.

The defer Statement

When a runtime error occurs, code execution usually leaves the current block of code and propagates up the call stack until an appropriate `catch` expression is found. Often you may want to execute some cleanup code when an error occurs, before code execution leaves the current scope. The `defer` statement allows you to do just that.

A `defer` statement delays execution until the current scope is exited:

```
func downloadResource(resourceName:String) throws -> NSData?
{
    if resourceName.isEmpty
    {
        throw NetworkError.ResourceNotFound

        defer {
            // insert cleanup code here.
        }
    }
    else
    {
        return NSData(contentsOfURL: NSURL(string: resourceName)!)
    }

    return nil;
}
```

You cannot execute any code in a `defer` block that would cause execution control to jump out of the block. Therefore, you cannot use the `break` statement or the `return` statement, or throw an error.

TRY IT

In this Try It, you create a new Swift playground and build a function that divides two numbers and throws an exception if the denominator is zero.

Lesson Requirements

➤ Launch Xcode.

➤ Create a new Swift playground.

➤ Create a function called `divideNumbers` that divides two numbers and throws an exception.

➤ Create a function that calls `divideNumbers` and handles any exceptions that are thrown by `divideNumbers`.

➤ Display the results in the console.

> **REFERENCE** *The code for this Try It is available at* www.wrox.com/go/
> swiftios.

Hints

To view the console inside the playground window, select View ⇨ Debug Area ⇨ Activate Console.

Step by Step

➤ Create a new Swift playground.

1. Launch Xcode and create a new Swift playground by selecting File ⇨ New ⇨ Playground.

2. In the playground options screen, use the following values:

    ➤ **Name:** ExceptionsPlayground

    ➤ **Platform:** iOS

3. Save the playground onto your hard disk.

➤ Create an enumeration to represent errors.

1. Delete the default contents of the playground file.

2. Type the following lines:

```
enum ArithmeticError: ErrorType {
    case DivisionByZero
}
```

➤ Create the `divideNumbers` function.

Type the following lines after the definition of the `ArithmeticError` enumeration:

```
func divideNumebrs(numerator n:Double, denominator d:Double) throws -> Double
{
    if d == 0
    {
        throw ArithmeticError.DivisionByZero
    }

    return n / d
}
```

➤ Create a function that calls the `divideNumbers` function and handles any errors that may be generated.

Type the following lines after the definition of the divideNumbers enumeration:

```
func performDivision(number1:Double, _ number2:Double)
{
    do{
        let result = try divideNumbers(numerator: number1,
                                       denominator: number2)

        print("\(number1) divided by \(number2) equals \(result)")

    }
    catch
    {
        print ("number2 is zero!")
    }
}
```

➤   Call the performDivision function.

1.   Type the following line after the end of the performDivision function definition:

```
performDivision(10, 2)
```

2.   Observe the results of this program in the console. You should see the following line in the console:

```
"10.0 divided by 2.0 equals 5.0\n"
```

REFERENCE *To see some of the examples from this lesson, watch the Lesson 6 video online at* www.wrox.com/go/swiftiosvid.

Object-Oriented Programming with Swift

Over the years, computer application developers have developed various strategies to create applications that can solve complex problems. One of the earliest approaches to problem solving was the concept of structured programming.

Structured programming (which predates object-oriented programming) centered on a divide-and-conquer philosophy. A complex program was broken down into a set of tasks, and then each task into a set of simpler sub-tasks. A key feature of structured programming is that there is a clear separation between data and the code that operates on that data.

Structured programming is still in use in some types of applications today, but it has a few drawbacks:

➤ People generally think of data (account numbers) and what they can do with it (compute balance, interest, and so on) as related concepts. It is not natural to think of them in isolation.

➤ Programmers were constantly reinventing the wheel, creating solutions for things that had been solved over and over again by others. Structured programming did not address the need to reuse existing functions (either written by you or someone else) conveniently.

➤ A new approach to programming, *object-oriented programming (OOP)*, was created. Essentially, OOP tries to address the deficiencies in the structured programming model by:

  ➤ Providing techniques to achieve re-use of software components.

  ➤ Coupling data with the functions that act on them.

Core to object-oriented programming is the idea of treating data and functions that act upon them as an independent entity known as an *object*.

CREATING CLASSES WITH SWIFT

A *class* can be thought of as a template or blueprint of an object. This is best understood by an example. If you were to go down to your local car dealer, you would likely find several cars there. Each of these cars share some common characteristics with each other; for instance, each has seats, wipers, four wheels, and so on. Looking at this situation from an object-oriented perspective, you can say that each of these cars is an instance of a class of objects called automobiles. The `Automobile` class (see Figure 7-1) could then be thought to define some characteristics that are common to each instance (such as the fact that each car has four wheels).

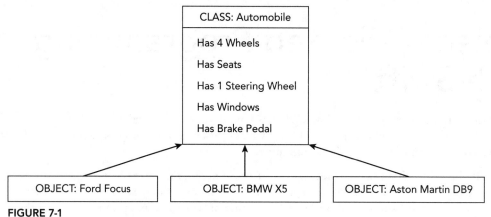

FIGURE 7-1

Classes are created in swift using the `class` keyword followed by the name of the class. Unlike Objective-C, the external interface and implementation of a class is contained in a single file. A bare-bones `Automobile` class would resemble the following:

```
class Automobile : NSObject
{

}
```

The statements that will make up the body of the class are contained within the pair of curly braces. Just like Objective-C, Swift classes generally inherit from NSObject either directly or indirectly.

PROPERTIES

Common characteristics between the various instances of the `Automobile` class can be easily represented using variables; for example, the number of wheels could be represented by an integer variable named `wheelCount` and so on. Table 7-1 lists the characteristics of the `Automobile` class and the equivalent variables that could be used to represent them.

TABLE 7-1: Characteristics of the Automobile Class

CHARACTERISTIC	VARIABLE
Has 4 wheels	`Int wheelCount`
Has seats	`Bool hasSeats`
Has 1 steering wheel	`Int numberOfSteeringWheels`
Has windows	`Bool hasWindows`
Has brake pedal	`Bool hasBrakePedal`

Unlike Objective-C, Swift does not have an explicit @property syntax. Properties in Swift are simply public member variables of the class. With this in mind, the `Automobile` class now becomes:

```
class Automobile : NSObject
{
    var wheelCount:Int?
    var hasSeats:Bool?
    var numberOfSteeringWheels:Int?
    var hasWindows:Bool?
    var hasBreakPedal:Bool?
}
```

Notice how every variable is declared as an optional type. The class does not have an `init()` method at this point so the default values of all these variables will automatically be `nil`, and you need optionals to handle `nil` values in Swift.

METHODS

To be compliant with the principles of object-oriented design, this `Automobile` class must also define some operations that do something with these variables (see Figure 7-2). Whatever these operations may be, each concrete instance of the `Automobile` class will be able to perform them.

These operations are best thought of as commands you could give to a car (instance of `Automobile` class). This is perhaps where object-oriented solutions differ from real-world situations. In the real world, you can't command a car to drive itself (except in the movies); you need to drive the car. In an object-oriented world, however, the car would drive itself and all you would have to do is tell the car to start driving. Table 7-2 lists a few possible operations that the `Automobile` class could define.

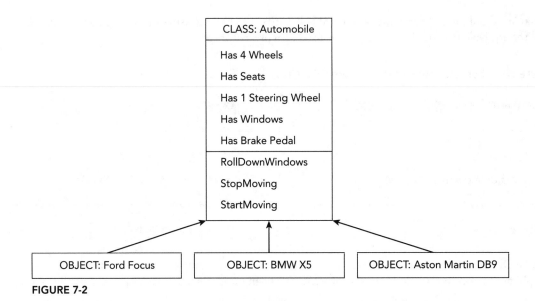

FIGURE 7-2

TABLE 7-2: Operations in the Automobile Class

OPERATION	DESCRIPTION
rollDownWindows	The car rolls down all its windows.
stopMoving	The car stops moving.
startMoving	The car starts moving.

Just as you use variables to represent the common characteristics, each of these operations would be represented using blocks of code (methods). These blocks of code would operate on the data (variables) within the class to achieve the desired outcome. The following is the modified definition of the `Automobile` class:

```
class Automobile : NSObject
{
    var wheelCount:Int?
    var hasSeats:Bool?
    var numberOfSteeringWheels:Int?
    var hasWindows:Bool?
    var hasBreakPedal:Bool?
    var speed:Int?

    func rollDownWindows () {
        println("windows are now open");
    }

    func stopMoving() {
        speed = 0
```

```
            println("car has stopped moving")
        }

        func startMoving() {
            speed = 10
            println("car is moving")
        }
    }
```

An *initializer* is a special method in a class that is used to create an instance of the class. This is similar to the concept of a constructor in other languages. The process of initialization typically involves setting up default values for member variables and any other setup tasks that may be necessary. Unlike Objective-C, initializers in Swift do not return a value.

When it comes to specifying default values for member variables, you can either specify them at the time of declaration or set them up in an initializer. The initializer for the Automobile class would be:

```
init (numWheels:Int, seats:Bool,
      steeringWheelCount:Int, windows:Bool,
      breakPedal:Bool) {
    wheelCount = numWheels
    hasSeats = seats
    numberOfSteeringWheels = steeringWheelCount
    hasWindows = windows
    hasBreakPedal = breakPedal
}
```

You can also create an initializer without any parameters; however, because the Automobile class inherits from NSObject, you will end up overriding the default no-parameter initializer provided by NSObject. A default initializer for the Automobile class would resemble the following:

```
override init() {
    wheelCount = 4
    hasSeats = true
    numberOfSteeringWheels = 1
    hasWindows = true
    hasBreakPedal = true
}
```

A *deinitializer* is a method that is called immediately before a class is deallocated. Deinitializers are written with the deinit keyword, and are called automatically for you.

```
deinit {
}
```

Swift uses ARC (Automatic Reference Counting) to manage your memory for you so you do not usually need to use deinitializers. However, if you are managing your own resources outside of ARC, you will need to use a deinit method to free these resources.

To find out more about ARC, refer to the Automatic Reference Counting guide available at:

```
https://developer.apple.com/library/ios/documentation/Swift/Conceptual/Swift_
Programming_Language/AutomaticReferenceCounting.html
```

INSTANTIATING OBJECTS

When it comes to using a class, in most cases you need to instantiate it into a concrete object first. All subsequent interaction will be with the object and not the class. The `Automobile` class in this example is not an actual car; it is just the definition of what a car should be.

The following example shows how an instance of the `Automobile` class may be instantiated and used:

```
var bmwThreeSeries: Automobile = Automobile(numWheels:4,
                     seats:true, steeringWheelCount:1,
                     windows:true, breakPedal:true)

bmwThreeSeries.rollDownWindows()
bmwThreeSeries.startMoving()
bmwThreeSeries.stopMoving()
```

INHERITANCE

When developing an application, you are likely to create more than one class. The classes you define are likely to have some relationships with each other. Object-oriented programming allows you to specify different types of relationships between classes.

The concept of *inheritance* implies that a new class can be created that inherits the functionality of an existing class. This new class will provide the functionality of the parent class and provide some additional functionality of its own. Inheriting from a base class is known as *subclassing*. By subclassing an existing class, the designer of an object-oriented solution is reusing the functionality present in an existing class and not duplicating it. The parent class is commonly referred to as the base class, and the child as the subclass.

As an example, consider a hypothetical class `Dog` (see Figure 7-3). Such a class could either be created in isolation, or more likely inherit from a more general class `Mammal`. The attributes and methods present in the `Mammal` class would be a part of the `Dog` class. In addition, the `Dog` class would add a few attributes and methods of its own.

When you use inheritance to create a relationship between two classes, you are essentially creating an *is-a* relationship between them. In the preceding example, a `Dog` is a `Mammal`. When one class inherits from another, the parent class is known as the superclass and the derived class is known as the subclass.

To indicate a class inherits from a superclass, you indicate the name of the superclass after the subclass, separating the two names with a colon. For example, if `Mammal` is the superclass, and `Dog` a subclass, then this relationship can be defined in Swift as follows:

```
class Mammal : NSObject{

    var isMale:Bool = false

    func play() {
        println("Mammal's play() called")
    }
```

```
    func rest() {
        println("Mammal's rest() called")
    }

    func eat() {
        println("Mammal's eat() called")
    }
}

class Dog : Mammal{

    var hasFourLegs:Bool = true

    func bark(){
        println("Dog's bar() called")
    }
}
```

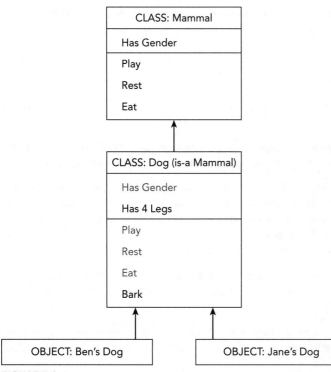

FIGURE 7-3

A subclass can provide its own implementation of a method that is defined in a superclass. This behavior is called *method overriding*, and the subclass's version of the method will be used instead of the superclass. When overriding a superclass method, Swift requires that you prefix your overriding version in the subclass with the override keyword. Within your overriding version, you can access the variables and methods of the superclass using the super keyword. In the following code snippet, the Dog class overrides the eat method, which it would have otherwise inherited from Mammal:

```
class Dog : Mammal{

    var hasFourLegs:Bool = true

    override func eat() {
        super.eat()
        println("Dog's eat() called")
    }

    func bark(){
        println("Dog's bar() called")
    }
}
```

The overriding version of eat in the Dog class first calls the superclass's version of eat. This is not strictly required but is a good idea. If you want to prevent a method from being overridden in a subclass, you need to append the final keyword before the method declaration.

COMPUTED PROPERTIES

Swift provides the concept of computed properties. These are similar to custom getters and setters in Objective-C.

A getter is a method that provides read-only access to a private member variable of an object. A setter is a method that allows another object to change the value of a private member variable.

In object-oriented design it is common practice to create private member variables in a class and selectively provide getters/setters to define the operations that can be performed on these variables. This practice is known as encapsulation and allows one to use a class without knowing the details about how specific functionality is implemented in the class. Encapsulation also provides the class designer with a degree of control over how the class will be used.

It is not necessary to have both getter and setter methods for a member variable. Providing just a getter method (without a setter method) would in effect make the underlying member variable read-only.

Computed properties do not actually store a value; instead, you provide a getter and (an optional) setter method that compute the value of the property based on other properties of the class. This is illustrated in the following example:

```
class Rectangle : NSObject {

    var length:Double
    var breadth:Double
```

```
    init(length:Double, breadth:Double) {
        self.length = length
        self.breadth = breadth
    }

    var area : Double {
        get{
            return length * breadth
        }
    }
}
```

ENUMERATIONS

An enumeration is a data type that groups a set of named values. The named values are referred to as elements of the enumeration. Unlike C, Swift enumerations can contain computed properties, initializers, and member methods.

Enumerations in Swift are defined using the enum keyword, and the member values within that enumeration are prefixed with the case keyword, as shown here:

```
enum EmployeeType {
    case CEO
    case CTO
    case Manager
    case Receptionist
    case Developer
    case ProductOwner
}
```

To use this enumeration, you will need to declare an appropriate variable and assign it one of the values in the enumeration as follows:

```
var acmeEmployee : EmployeeType = EmployeeType.Developer
```

PROTOCOLS

A *protocol* can be thought of as a contract that a class agrees to abide by. Technically speaking, the class is said to implement the protocol in question. But what form does this contract take?

This contract (protocol) is basically a list of methods. These methods can be grouped as either required or optional. Any class that wishes to conform to a protocol must provide implementations of all required methods in the protocol. A class can implement multiple protocols (see Figure 7-4), and multiple classes may implement a given protocol.

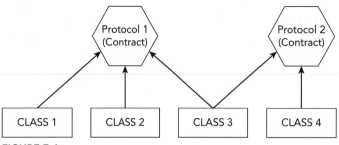

FIGURE 7-4

Just because a class implements a protocol does not mean that the class cannot have additional methods of its own (in addition to the ones defined in the protocol). The manner in which protocols are used depends on the designer of the object-oriented system. In other object-oriented languages like C++, protocols are known as interfaces.

Protocols are defined in Swift using the `protocol` keyword:

```
protocol MessageListener {

}
```

A class conforms to a protocol by including the names of the protocol in its declaration after a colon. A class can conform to multiple protocols by listing the names of the protocols separated by commas. If a class has a superclass, the name of the superclass must be listed before any protocols. The following code snippet lists a class called `NetworkManager` that is a subclass of `NSObject` (inheritance) and implements the `MessageListener` protocol:

```
class NetworkManager: NSObject, MessageListener {

}
```

If a protocol contains member variables (property definitions), then conforming classes will need to provide appropriate properties with the same name in their declarations. The protocol does not specify the manner in which a conforming class may implement properties. A conforming class could provide a stored property or a computed property implementation. A protocol, however, does specify whether each property must be gettable, settable, or both. The following snippet shows the `MessageListener` protocol with a few property definitions as well as the corresponding implementation in the `NetworkManager` class:

```
import Foundation

protocol MessageListener {
    var hasNewMessage:Bool {get}
    var messagePollInterval:Int {get set}
}

class NetworkManager: NSObject, MessageListener {

    private var isDirty : Bool = false
```

```
private var pollInterval : Int = 10

var hasNewMessage : Bool {
    get {
        return isDirty
    }
}

var messagePollInterval: Int {
    get {
        return pollInterval
    }

    set {
        self.pollInterval = newValue
    }
}
}
```

A protocol can also contain method names that conforming classes must implement. The following code snippet builds on the MessageListener protocol and NetworkManager class by adding methods:

```
protocol MessageListener {
    var hasNewMessage:Bool {get}
    var messagePollInterval:Int {get set}

    func beginListening()
    func endListening()
}

class NetworkManager: NSObject, MessageListener {

    private var isDirty : Bool = false
    private var pollInterval : Int = 10

    var hasNewMessage : Bool {
        get {
            return isDirty
        }
    }

    var messagePollInterval: Int {
        get {
            return pollInterval
        }

        set {
            self.pollInterval = newValue
        }
    }

    func beginListening() {
        println("NetworkManager beginListening() is called")
```

```
        }

        func endListening() {
            println("NetworkManager endListening() is called")
        }
    }
```

If a method or property is prefixed with the `optional` attribute in the protocol, then conforming classes need not provide implementations for these. If a protocol contains an optional property or method in its definition, then the entire protocol must be marked with the `@objc` attribute, as you can see in the following code snippet:

```
@objc protocol ConnectionDelegate {
    optional func setupConnectionAttributes(ipaddress:String, port:Int) -> Bool
}

class NetworkManager: NSObject, MessageListener, ConnectionDelegate {

    private var isDirty : Bool = false
    private var pollInterval : Int = 10

    var hasNewMessage : Bool {
        get {
            return isDirty
        }
    }

    var messagePollInterval: Int {
        get {
            return pollInterval
        }

        set {
            self.pollInterval = newValue
        }
    }

    func beginListening() {
        println("NetworkManager beginListening() is called")
    }

    func endListening() {
        println("NetworkManager endListening() is called")
    }

    // NOTE: this class does not need to provide an implementation for
    // the optional method in the ConnectionDelegate protocol, but it does
    // in this case
    func setupConnectionAttributes(ipaddress:String, port:Int) -> Bool{
        return false
    }
}
```

TRY IT

In this Try It, you create a new Swift playground and build a class called Calculator that performs arithmetic calculations.

Lesson Requirements

➤ Launch Xcode.

➤ Create a new Swift playground.

➤ Create a class called `Calculator` that performs arithmetic calculations.

➤ Display the results in the console.

> **REFERENCE** *The code for this Try It is available at* www.wrox.com/go/ swiftios.

Hints

To view the console inside the playground window, use the View ➪ Debug Area ➪ Activate Console menu item.

Step-by-Step

➤ Create a new Swift playground.

1. Launch Xcode and create a new Swift playground by selecting the File ➪ New ➪ Playground menu item.

2. In the playground options screen, use the following values:

   ➤ **Name:** ClassPlayground

   ➤ **Platform:** iOS

3. Save the playground onto your hard disk.

   ➤ Create the `Calculator` class.

4. Delete the default contents of the playground file.

5. Type the following lines:

   ```
   import UIKit

   class Calculator : NSObject
   ```

```
{
    func AddTwoNumbers(firstNumber:Double, secondNumber:Double) -> Double {
        return firstNumber + secondNumber
    }

    func SubtractTwoNumbers(firstNumber:Double,
                            secondNumber:Double) -> Double {
        return firstNumber - secondNumber
    }

    func MultiplyTwoNumbers(firstNumber:Double,
                            secondNumber:Double) -> Double {
        return firstNumber * secondNumber
    }

    func DivideTwoNumbers(firstNumber:Double,
                          secondNumber:Double) -> Double? {
        if (secondNumber == 0) {
            return nil
        }

        return firstNumber / secondNumber
    }
}
```

➤ Create an instance of the `Calculator` class and call some of its methods.

1. Type the following lines after the end of the `Calculator` class definition:

```
var arithmeticCalculator:Calculator = Calculator()

let num1 = 17.5
let num2 = 19.76

let sum  = arithmeticCalculator.AddTwoNumbers(num1, secondNumber: num2)
let difference  = arithmeticCalculator.SubtractTwoNumbers(num1,
secondNumber: num2)
let product  = arithmeticCalculator.MultiplyTwoNumbers(num1,
secondNumber: num2)
let division  = arithmeticCalculator.DivideTwoNumbers(num1, secondNumber:
num2)

print("\(num1) + \(num2) is \(sum)")
print("\(num1) - \(num2) is \(difference)")
print("\(num1) * \(num2) is \(product)")
print("\(num1) / \(num2) is \(division!)")
```

2. Observe the results of this program in the console. You should see the following output in the console:

```
17.5 + 19.76 is 37.26
17.5 - 19.76 is -2.26
```

```
17.5 * 19.76 is 345.8
17.5 / 19.76 is 0.885627530364372
```

> **REFERENCE** *To see some of the examples from this lesson, watch the Lesson 7 video online at* www.wrox.com/go/swiftiosvid.

Supporting Multiple Device Types

If you have been developing iOS applications for a few years, you will have noticed the steady increase in the number of iOS-enabled devices in the market today. In this lesson, you learn about some of the differences between the different iOS devices and how to support them from a single code base.

When it comes to supporting the different devices, broadly speaking there are two main device families, iPhones and iPads. The obvious difference is the screen size, but there are some more subtle differences. For example, iPads cannot make phone calls or send text messages.

You could create separate binaries of your application for the iPhone and iPad, although the commonly accepted method is to create a single binary that works on both device families. Such a binary is called a universal application.

To create a universal application project in Xcode, set the device type to be Universal in the project options dialog box (see Figure 8-1). Although you can use any Xcode template to create a universal application, this lesson is based on the Single View Application template.

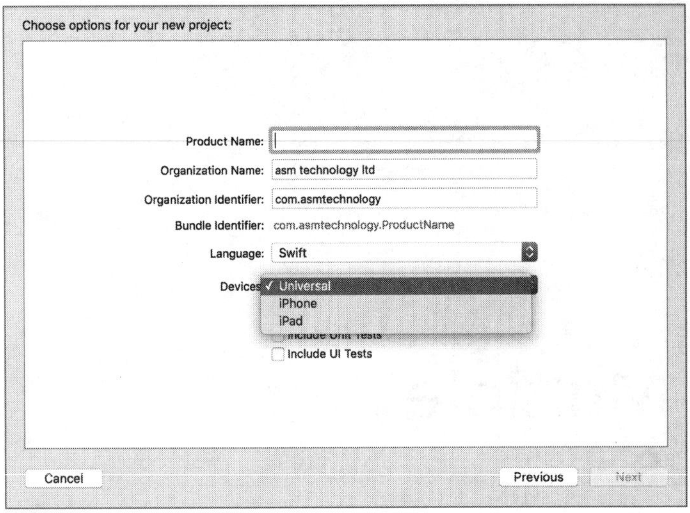

FIGURE 8-1

DEVICE DIFFERENCES

While there are two main iOS device families (iPhones and iPads), within each family there are several devices. This section introduces the differences between these devices.

Screen Size

By far, the most visible aspect of a device is its screen size. There is a subtle difference in units when it comes to expressing screen dimensions from a hardware versus a software point of view.

From a hardware point of view, screen size is expressed in terms of physical pixels, whereas iOS applications refer to the same screen size in device-independent units and not pixels. Starting with iOS4 and the introduction of the Retina display on the iPhone 4, Apple has introduced a new device-independent coordinate system. Application developers express sizes and positions in this new system.

Depending on the physical device on which the app is executed, these device-independent coordinates are converted to device-dependent coordinates by multiplying them with a scale factor. In the case of a device that does not have a Retina display (such as the iPhone 3GS), this scale factor happens to be 1. Table 8-1 provides a summary of screen sizes both in hardware pixels and device-independent units.

TABLE 8-1: Summary of Screen Sizes

DEVICE TYPE	SCALE FACTOR	PHYSICAL SIZE (PIXELS)	LOGICAL SIZE (UNITS)
iPhone 4S	2	640 x 960	320 x 480
iPhone 5/5S	2	640 x 1136	320 x 568
iPhone 6	2	750 x 1334	375 x 667
iPhone 6Plus	3	1242 x 2208	414 x 736
iPad 2, iPad mini	1	768 x 1024	768 x 1024
iPad mini Retina, iPad Air, iPad Air 2	2	1536 x 2048	768 x 1024

Icon Size

Every application has an icon that is used to represent it on the springboard, settings app, and spotlight search results. The sizes of these icons have changed over the years as iOS has evolved. Table 8-2 presents the sizes of these icons for iOS 7.0 and 8.0.

TABLE 8-2: Icon Sizes

DEVICE	IOS VERSION	ICON TYPE	ICON SIZE (PIXELS)
iPhone 4S/5/5S	7.0	Springboard	120 x 120
iPhone 6	8.0	Springboard	120 x 120
iPhone 6 Plus	8.0	Springboard	180 x 180
iPad 2, iPad mini	7.0	Springboard	76 x 76
iPad mini Retina, iPad Air, iPad Air 2	8.0	Springboard	152 x 152
iPhone 4S/5/5S	7.0	Spotlight results	80 x 80
iPhone 6	8.0	Spotlight results	80 x 80
iPhone 6 Plus	8.0	Spotlight results	120 x 120
iPad 2, iPad mini	7.0	Spotlight results	40 x 40

continues

TABLE 8-2 *(continued)*

DEVICE	IOS VERSION	ICON TYPE	ICON SIZE (PIXELS)
iPad mini Retina, iPad Air, iPad Air 2	8.0	Spotlight results	58 x 58
iPhone 4S/5/5S	7.0	Settings app	58 x 58
iPhone 6	8.0	Settings app	58 x 58
iPhone 6 Plus	8.0	Settings app	87 x 87
iPad 2, iPad mini	7.0	Settings app	29 x 29
iPad mini Retina, iPad Air, iPad Air 2	8.0	Settings app	58 x 58

As an iOS developer, you will need to include your application icon in different sizes as part of your project. This is typically done using an asset bundle. Every Xcode project has an asset bundle called `Assets.xcassets` and within this bundle is an entry called `AppIcon` that represents the application icons (see Figure 8-2).

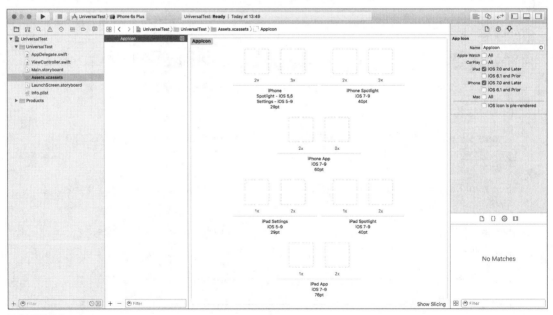

FIGURE 8-2

Device Orientation

There are four device orientations for iOS devices:

➤ Portrait

➤ Portrait upside-down

➤ Landscape left (the Home button is on the left)

➤ Landscape right (the Home button is on the right)

It is common for iPhone applications to support a single orientation (portrait), but for iPad applications, Apple recommends that you support every orientation. You can configure the layouts supported by your application in the Xcode project settings page (see Figure 8-3). You will notice that the default orientation options for iPhone applications are set up so as to exclude support for the portrait upside-down mode. This makes sense because people generally do not use their iPhones upside-down.

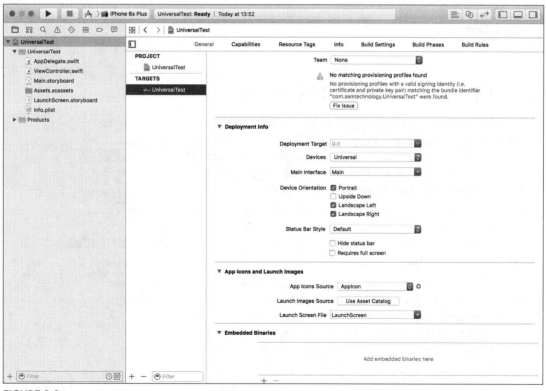

FIGURE 8-3

When you use the Xcode project settings page to set up the list of orientations supported by your app, behind the scenes Xcode adds entries to the "Supported interface orientations and Supported interface orientations (iPad)" keys in your project's Info.plist file (see Figure 8-4). The Info .plist file can be found in the Supporting Files group in the project explorer.

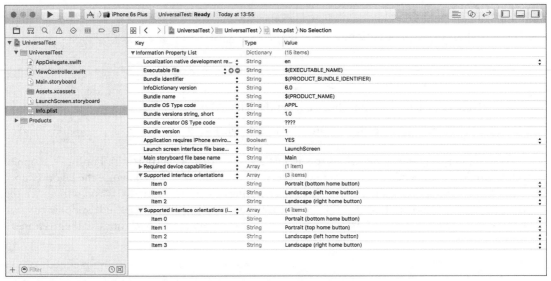

FIGURE 8-4

THE UNIVERSAL XCODE TEMPLATE

If you create a new universal Xcode project using the Single view Application template, the project navigator will resemble Figure 8-5. Notice the project contains a single view controller file and a single storyboard. This may be a surprise to you if you have been developing applications prior to iOS8.

Prior to iOS 8, a universal application template consisted of two different storyboards, one for the iPhone and one for the iPad. This has now been done away with but introduces a slight complication into the mix.

FIGURE 8-5

The iPad user interface for an app is usually different from the iPhone version. In general, because the iPad screen is larger, developers tend to use different on-screen layouts and in some cases even provide the user with additional options on the iPad version of the same app.

With just a single storyboard file, how can this be accomplished? The answer to this is the new Adaptive layout feature of iOS8 with support for size classes. Adaptive layout will be discussed in the next lesson.

TRY IT

In this Try It, you launch Xcode and create a new universal project using the Single View Application template. You then add a label to the main scene of the storyboard and examine the application on both the iPhone and iPad simulators.

Lesson Requirements

➤ Launch Xcode.

➤ Create a new project using a template.

➤ Use the interface editor to update a storyboard scene.

➤ Launch the app in the iPhone simulator.

➤ Launch the app in the iPad simulator.

> **REFERENCE** *The code for this Try It is available at* www.wrox.com/go/ swiftios.

Hints

To run an application in the iOS Simulator first select the appropriate device in the scheme selector drop-down; then select Product ⇨ Run.

Step-by-Step

➤ Create a new universal project in Xcode.

1. Launch Xcode and create a new application by selecting File ⇨ New ⇨ Project.

2. Select the Single View Application template from the list of iOS project templates.

3. In the project options screen use the following values:

➤ **Product Name:** UniversalTest

➤ **Organization Name:** your company

➤ **Organization Identifier:** com.yourcompany

➤ **Language:** Swift

➤ **Devices:** Universal

➤ **Use Core Data:** Unchecked

> ➤ **Include Unit Tests:** Unchecked

> ➤ **Include UI Tests:** Unchecked

4. Save the project onto your hard disk

➤ Open the `Main.storyboard` file in the Xcode editor.

1. Ensure the project navigator is visible and the UniversalTest project is open.

2. Click the `Main.storyboard` file.

➤ Add a label to the storyboard:

1. Ensure the Object Library is visible by selecting View ➪ Utilities ➪ Show Object Library.

2. Select a label from the Object Library and drag it onto the single scene of the storyboard. The position of the label does not matter at this point.

3. In the Attribute inspector, change the text of the label to "Hello World!" You can display the Attribute inspector by selecting View ➪ Utilities ➪ Show Attribute Inspector.

4. Use the Attribute inspector to change the alignment of the label to Centered.

5. Select Editor ➪ Size to Fit Content to resize the label so that its contents are not truncated. This option will not be visible in the menu if the label' contents are not truncated.

➤ Set up a few basic layout constraints to center the label on the screen regardless of the device family the app may be run on.

Ensure the label is selected. If it is not, simply click it once.

1. With the label selected, click the Align button located at the bottom right of the storyboard editor to bring up the alignment constraint editor.

2. Ensure the Horizontally In Container *and* Vertically In Container options are selected in the popup window.

3. Ensure the value of the Update Frames combo box is set to Items of New Constraints.

4. Click on the Add 2 Constraints button.

➤ Run the app on the iPhone Simulator.

1. Use the scheme/target selector buttons on the Xcode toolbar to select the iPhone6 simulator.

2. Run the application by selecting Product ➪ Run. Notice the label is centered in the simulator.

3. Go back to Xcode and stop the app in the simulator by selecting Product ➪ Stop.

➤ Run the app on the iPad Simulator.

1. Use the scheme/target selector buttons on the Xcode toolbar to select the iPad Air simulator.

2. Run the application by selecting Product ⇨ Run. Notice the label is centered in the simulator.

3. Go back to Xcode and stop the app in the simulator by selecting Product ⇨ Stop.

REFERENCE *To see some of the examples from this lesson, watch the Lesson 8 video online at* www.wrox.com/go/swiftiosvid.

Introduction to UIKit and Adaptive Layout

With the launch of iOS8, Apple has made it possible to build an application that can run on any device with a single storyboard. In Apple's terminology, the application adapts to the device it is running on. Prior to iOS8, it was common to have different storyboards for each device family.

Instead of specifying explicit sizes and positions for UI elements, with adaptive layout you specify constraints between the user interface elements of your view and have iOS apply these constraints at run time to work out the size and position the elements. A *constraint* is a mathematical description of the relationship between elements.

Most of the time, you apply these constraints using Interface Builder, but it is possible to specify these constraints programmatically in your code by creating instances of NSLayoutConstraint. Creating NSLayoutConstraint instances programmatically is outside the scope of this book. If you are interested in learning more about creating layout constraints programmatically, refer to the NSLayoutConstraint Class Reference at:

    https://developer.apple.com/library/ios/documentation/AppKit/Reference/
    NSLayoutConstraint_Class/

INTRODUCING THE UIKIT FRAMEWORK

A *framework* is a collection of classes that you can use to write your apps. Apple provides a large number of frameworks that enforce consistent implementation of features across applications from different developers. All the familiar user interface features such as navigation bars, toolbars, back buttons, and so on that you commonly use in iOS apps are, in fact, classes in one of the frameworks provided by Apple.

Although the idea of sticking to user interface elements that only appear in an Apple framework may seem limiting, it is in fact not the case. Apple's frameworks have a large number of classes; in fact, some frameworks do not have any user interface–specific classes at all. You must always try to use classes from one of the standard frameworks when possible; this will ensure that you do not spend time reinventing the wheel.

The frameworks are grouped together into layers, with frameworks in higher layers building upon frameworks found in lower layers. Figure 9-1 shows the different layers with examples of some of the frameworks they contain. In general, using a class from a framework in a lower layer requires you to write more code than using one from a higher layer.

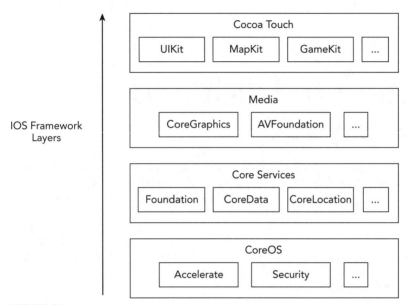

FIGURE 9-1

The top-most layer is known as Cocoa Touch and contains a large number of classes distributed within multiple frameworks that handle the most common aspects of iOS applications, including but not limited to processing events, touches, gestures, multithreading, map support, and accelerometer.

Every Xcode project that is created from one of the standard iOS application templates includes three key frameworks: `CoreGraphics`, `Foundation`, and `UIKit`. Most simple apps do not need to use classes from any other framework.

Of all the Cocoa Touch frameworks, perhaps the most important and commonly used is `UIKit`. The name `UIKit` may lead you to conclude that it contains only user interface–specific classes. This is, however, not true. Besides user interface–specific classes, `UIKit` contains classes for handling events, touches, gestures, and general application support.

Classes that are part of `UIKit` always begin with the `UI` prefix. Thus, the `UIApplication`, `UIWindow`, `UIView`, and `UIViewController` classes that you have encountered earlier in this lesson are all part of `UIKit`.

The UIButton Class

The UIButton class is part of the UIKit framework and encapsulates the functionality of a button on a touch screen. A UIButton object sends a message to a target object when it intercepts one or more touch events.

UIButton objects can intercept different types of touch events; some of the most common ones are briefly summarized in Table 9-1.

TABLE 9-1: UIButton Touch Events

EVENT	DESCRIPTION
Touch Up Inside	The user has lifted his finger from the touch screen inside the area of the button.
Touch Up Outside	The user had pressed this button but has lifted his finger outside the area of the button (that is, dragged his finger outside the button before lifting it).
Touch Down	The user has just pressed this button and hasn't yet lifted his finger, or moved it.
Touch Drag Enter	The user has pressed this button, then dragged his finger outside the button, and has just entered the area of the button again (without lifting the finger).
Touch Drag Exit	The user has pressed this button, then dragged his finger and, as a consequence of dragging, has just left the area of the button.
Touch Drag Inside	The user has pressed this button and is dragging his finger within the area of the button.
Touch Drag Outside	The user has pressed this button and is now dragging his finger outside the area of the button. The user would have had to move his finger out of the button and continued to drag without lifting his finger to receive this event.

By and large, the most common event that you will use in your code is the Touch Up Inside event.

Adding a UIButton to the view is a simple matter of dragging a Button object from the Object library onto the client area of the scene. You can use the Attributes inspector to set up some common properties of the new button. However, keep in mind that each of these properties can also be set up using Objective-C code. If you just want to add a title to a button quickly, simply double-click the button and type in a suitable title.

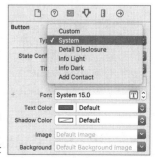

The default button created by Xcode is, in fact, quite boring. To make it more interesting you can change its appearance using use the Attribute inspector (View ⇨ Utilities ⇨ Show Attributes Inspector). You can select from common button types using the Type drop-down (see Figure 9-2).   **FIGURE 9-2**

The standard button types are:

➤ **Custom:** A button without any specific appearance, invisible unless you set up an image. Typically used to create hotspots or graphical buttons.

➤ **System:** This is the default.

➤ **Detail Disclosure:** A button with an arrow; usually indicates that tapping it will reveal additional information.

➤ **Info Light:** The standard "i" icon, intended to be used over dark backgrounds.

➤ **Info Dark:** The standard "i" icon, intended to be used over light backgrounds.

➤ **Add Contact:** The standard + icon.

A `UIButton` object can be in one of four states:

➤ **Default:** The button is visible on the screen; the user is not interacting with it.

➤ **Highlighted:** The user is currently pressing down the button.

➤ **Selected:** A `UIButton` object does not ordinarily move into this state as a result of user interaction, but this state can be set up programmatically.

➤ **Disabled:** The button is visible on the screen, but the user cannot interact with it.

For each state you can provide a different background color, title, and background image. You can use the Attribute inspector's State Config drop-down to select a state and set up attributes for that state. This is shown in Figure 9-3.

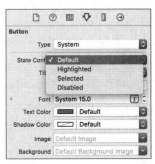

FIGURE 9-3

To assign an image for your button, you will need to create a PNG image for each state and import the images into your Xcode project. When applying an image to a button, you can assign the image to either the `Image` attribute or the `Background` attribute. There is a slight difference between the two. The background image is scaled to fill the entire area of the button and is displayed behind the title. The foreground image is displayed beside the title.

> **NOTE** *To learn more about the* `UIButton` *class, read the UIButton Class Reference documentation available at* `http://developer.apple.com/library/IOs/#documentation/UIKit/Reference/UIButton_Class/UIButton/UIButton.html`.

The UILabel Class

The `UILabel` class allows you to draw one or multiple lines of static text onto your view. The `UILabel` class does not normally generate touch events but provides several properties that allow you to customize its appearance. The most common ones are described in Table 9-2.

TABLE 9-2: UILabel Properties

PROPERTY	DESCRIPTION
text	Sets the text displayed by the label using the current font.
numberOfLines	The maximum number of lines of text to be drawn.
textAlignment	Defines the horizontal alignment of text in the label. Permissible values are UITextAlignmentLeft, UITextAlignmentRight, and UITextAlignmentCenter.
textColor	Sets the color used to display the text. You can set the color by providing a UIColor object. The UIColor class is discussed later in this lesson.
font	Sets the font that is used to display the text.

> **NOTE** *To learn more about the* UILabel *class, read the UILabel Class reference documentation available at* http://developer.apple.com/library/IOs/#documentation/UIKit/Reference/UILabel_Class/Reference/UILabel.html.

BASIC CONSTRAINTS

If you have developed iOS applications in the past, the first change you will notice when you open a nib or a storyboard is that each view is now represented using a square canvas instead of a rectangular one (see Figure 9-4).

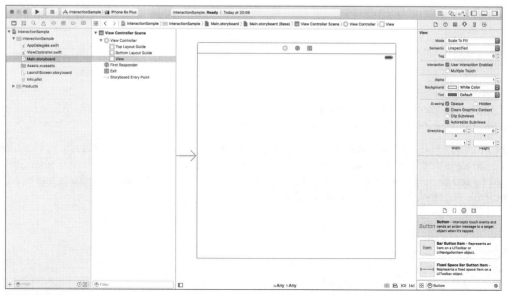

FIGURE 9-4

This may seem a little odd at first because the iPhones and iPads all have rectangular form factors. Apple has introduced a square canvas because they do not want you to think in terms of a specific device when designing your UI. Instead, you build your user interface for a generic square canvas and iOS will adapt it to fit the specific device based on the constraints you have specified.

The fundamental building block of this new layout system is the constraint. A constraint is a mathematical rule that helps lay out UI elements. Constraints can specify an element's height, width, horizontal position, or vertical position from another element. Constraints can be added, removed, and edited to affect the layout of your application's UI.

For instance, to position a label centered (horizontally and vertically) in the screen, you will need to add a few constraints. Start by dragging a Label object from the Object Library and placing it at an arbitrary location on the storyboard canvas (see Figure 9-5).

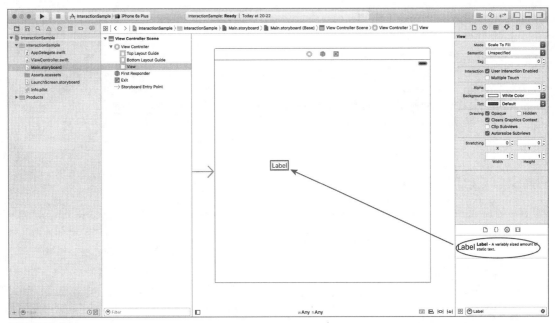

FIGURE 9-5

With the Label selected, you bring up the alignment constraint editor by clicking the Align button located at the bottom-right corner of the storyboard editor (see Figure 9-6).

In the alignment constraint editor, ensure the Horizontally in Container *and* Vertically in Container options are enabled and their corresponding values are both zero. Click on the Add 2 Constraints button to add these constraints. When you do this, you will notice two new constraints has been added between the label and the view (see Figure 9-7).

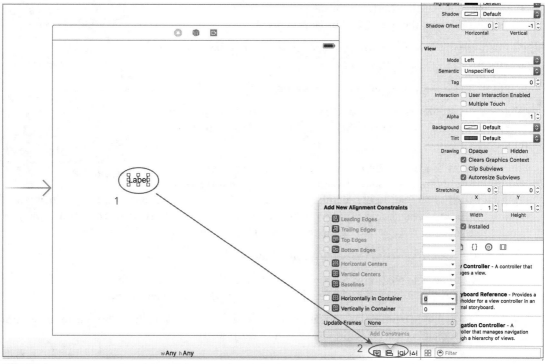

FIGURE 9-6

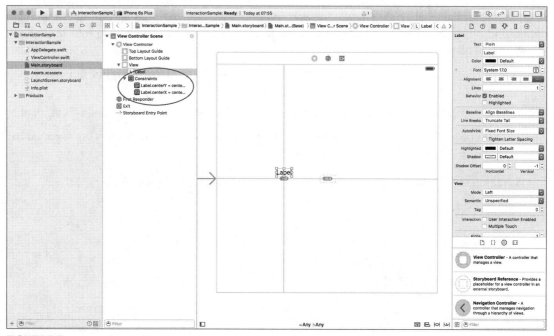

FIGURE 9-7

If you select one of the constraint in the view hierarchy, you can update its properties using the size inspector (see Figure 9-8).

Mathematically, any constraint can be expressed using the following equation:

$$Y = multiplier * X + Constant$$

X and Y are attributes of views and can be either `left`, `right`, `top`, `bottom`, `leading`, `trailing`, `width`, `height`, `centerX`, `centerY`, or `baseline`.

The attributes `leading` and `trailing` are the same as `left` and `right`

FIGURE 9-8

for left-to-right languages such as English. However, in a right-to-left language such as Arabic, `leading` and `trailing` are interpreted as `right` and `left`. When you create constraints, you should usually use `leading` and `trailing` (instead of `left` and `right`) to make sure your interface is laid out appropriately in all languages.

Some of the other properties relevant to constraints are:

➤ **Relation:** The relationship between the attributes represented in a constraint can be one of equality (=), greater than or equal to (>=), or less than or equal to (<=)

➤ **Priority:** When multiple constraints are defined for a given attribute, those with higher priority levels are satisfied before those with lower priority.

At this point, even though you have added constraints to center the label horizontally and vertically, the label is still where you left it on the storyboard. If you were to run the application now, you would find that the label is indeed centered as you would expect.

If you select the label on the storyboard, you will notice that it has an orange outline. An orange outline implies that there is an adaptive layout problem. There are three typical problems that you will encounter:

➤ The constraints are correct, but the size/position of the UI elements will be different from what you see on the storyboard in Interface Builder

➤ You don't have enough constraints to specify both the size and position of a UI element

➤ You have ambiguous constraints, i.e. either none or too many constraints are specified for the same attribute, with the same priority level.

You can find out what the problem is by switching to the Issue Navigator (see Figure 9-9).

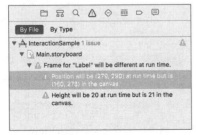

FIGURE 9-9

In this particular case there is just one issue with the constraints on this storyboard scene, and is listed as

➤ Frame for "Label" will be different at run time.

To fix this particular issue, select the label and then select Editor ➪ Resolve Auto Layout Issues ➪ Update Frames.

The storyboard should now resemble Figure 9-10.

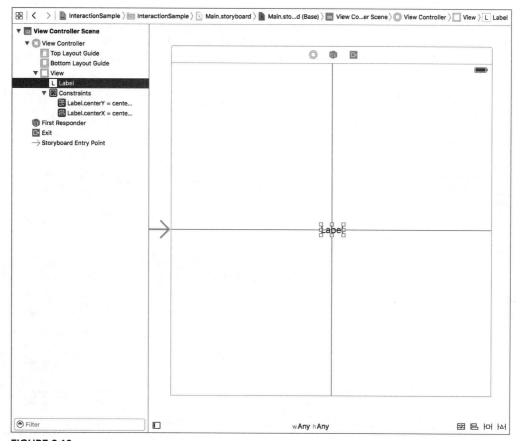

FIGURE 9-10

If you pay attention to the bottom-right corner of the storyboard, you will notice four auto layout–specific buttons (see Figure 9-11):

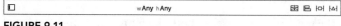

FIGURE 9-11

➤ **Stack:** This button is only enabled if one or more items are selected in a storyboard scene. When this option is available, using it will embed the selected items into a UIStackView.

➤ **Align:** This button enables you to add an alignment constraint to the selected UI element relative to another element in the scene. Clicking this button will bring up a popup that contains various alignment options.

➤ **Pin:** This button enables you to set the position of a UI element relative to other elements and to apply size constraints.

➤ **Resolve Auto Layout Issues:** This button enables you to correct layout problems. Clicking this button will bring up a popup menu that is identical to the Editor ➪ Resolve Auto Layout Issues menu item.

If you now wanted to add a button to the right of the label, you could do this by first dragging a Button object from the object library and placing it in the approximate location on the scene (see Figure 9-12).

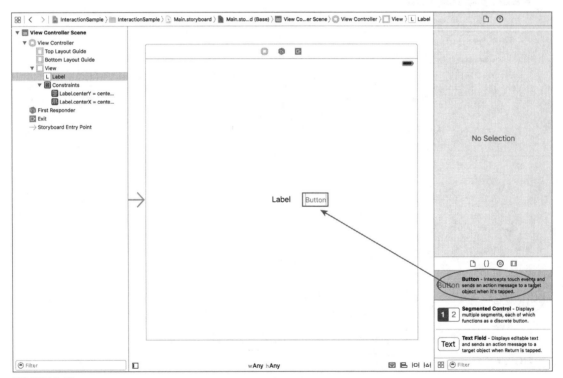

FIGURE 9-12

You can then use the Pin button to create constraints that fix the size of the button and its horizontal distance from the label, as shown in Figure 9-13.

To align the top of the button with the top of the label, select both the button and label (in that order), and then use the alignment constraint editor to add a new alignment constrained for Top Edges (see Figure 9-14).

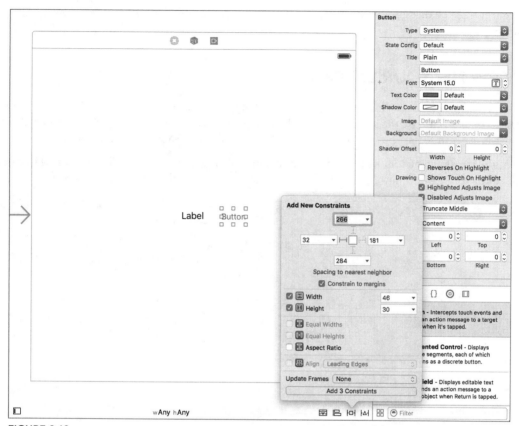

FIGURE 9-13

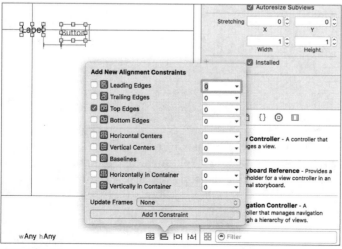

FIGURE 9-14

To reflect these changes on the storyboard, select Editor ➪ Resolve Auto Layout Issues ➪ Update Frames.

PREVIEWING YOUR LAYOUT

If you would like to know how your storyboard will appear on a specific device without running the application, you can use the assistant editor. First, ensure a scene is selected in your storyboard and show the assistant editor by selecting View ➪ Assistant Editor ➪ Show Assistant Editor.

Next, use the assistant editor's jump bar to switch to the layout preview (see Figure 9-15). The assistant editor will now display a preview of the storyboard in one of the standard iOS screen sizes.

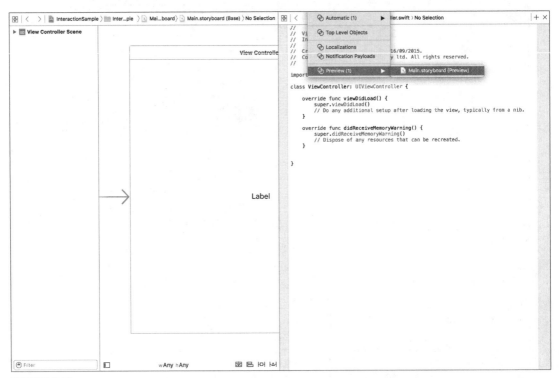

FIGURE 9-15

You can add additional screen sizes to the preview area by clicking the plus sign (+) button at the bottom-left corner of the preview window (see Figure 9-16). You can also toggle the orientation of the preview between portrait and landscape by clicking the device name (see Figure 9-17).

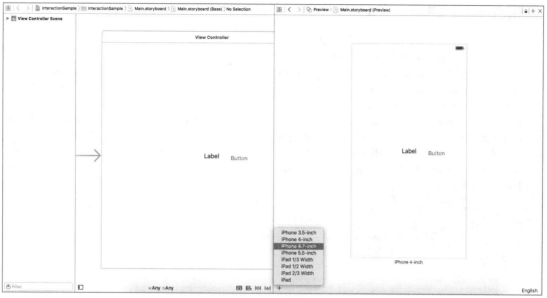

FIGURE 9-16

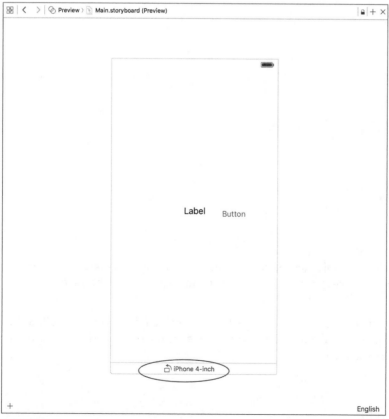

FIGURE 9-17

CREATING OUTLETS

User interface elements are usually defined in storyboards, and even though you can set their properties graphically using Interface Builder, there will be times when you will need to read or change a property from your code while your application is running. To do so, you need to create an appropriate instance variable in the `view controller` class and connect it to the user interface element in the `scene`. These connections are known as outlets, and can be created quickly using the assistant editor. To display the assistant editor, select View ➪ Assistant Editor ➪ Show Assistant Editor. If the assistant editor is in Automatic mode, selecting a user interface element in one of the scenes of the storyboard file automatically opens the Swift code (`.swift`) file of the corresponding view controller class. You can switch the assistant editor into Automatic mode using the jump bar. This is shown in Figure 9-18.

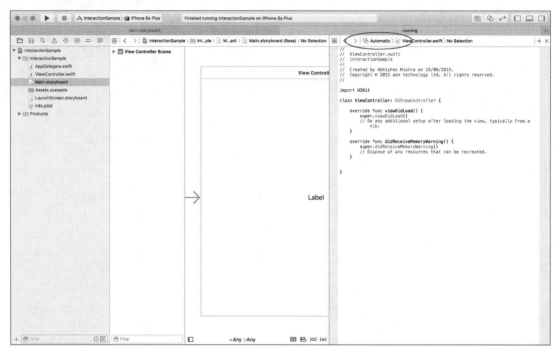

FIGURE 9-18

To create an outlet for the button object, right-click the button to bring up a context menu and drag from the circle beside the `New Referencing Outlet` line to an empty line in the Swift class (see Figure 9-19).

Release the mouse button on an empty line in the header file to open a dialog box that allows you to type in a name for the outlet (see Figure 9-20). Type a name for the outlet variable—for our purposes here, let's name it `someButton`.

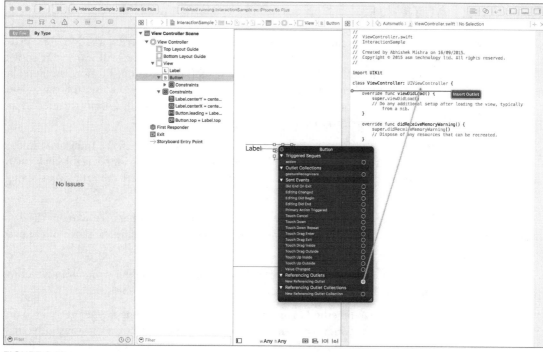

FIGURE 9-19

FIGURE 9-20

Click the Connect button in the popup dialog box to finish creating the outlet. Notice how Xcode has created an optional `var` of type `UIButton` in your class.

```
@IBOutlet weak var someButton: UIButton!
```

To signify that the variable refers to an object defined in the `storyboard` file, Xcode adds the `@IBOutlet` keyword to the variable declaration.

CREATING ACTIONS

Most user interface elements generate a variety of events as a result of user interaction. As a programmer, you will be interested in some of these user-generated events and will want your code to be executed when these events occur. To achieve this, you need to create one or more methods in the view controller class and wire them up to appropriate events generated by the user interface element. These methods in the view controller class that are called when an event has been triggered as a result of user interaction are referred to as *actions*.

As you might expect, both of these steps can be performed graphically with the Interface Builder. To show a list of events that can be intercepted by a user interface object, simply right-click the user interface element in Interface Builder and browse through the entries under the Sent Events category of the context menu.

You will see all the familiar touch events listed there along with a few others. To wire up the Touch Up Inside event to a method in your class, simply drag from the circle beside the name of the event to an empty line in your view controller class.

When you release the mouse on the view controller, Xcode presents a popup window in which you can provide a name for the new method. Call the new method `onButtonPressed`.

Note that the `onButtonPressed` method takes in a single argument of type `AnyObject` called `sender`. This parameter always contains a reference to the object that sent this message to your view controller. In this particular case, the sender would be the user interface object that generated the corresponding event.

Once you have an action method wired up to the button's Touch Up Inside event, you can write Swift code that will be executed when the user interacts with this button. This is examined in this lesson's Try It.

TRY IT

In this Try It, you launch Xcode and create a new Xcode project using the Single View Application template called `InteractionSample`. You use the Interface Builder to create an instance of a `UIButton` and a `UILabel` class and then write code to update the text displayed in the label when the button is pressed.

Lesson Requirements

➤   Launch Xcode.

➤   Create a new project based on the Single View Application template.

➤   Edit the storyboard with Interface Builder.

➤   Add a `UILabel` and a `UIButton` object to the default scene in the storyboard.

➤ Create and connect the `UILabel` to an outlet in the view controller class.

➤ Create and connect the Touch Up Inside event of the `UIButton` instance to an action method in the view controller class.

➤ Change the text of the label when the button is clicked.

> **REFERENCE** *The code for this Try It is available at* `www.wrox.com/go/ swiftios`.

Hints

➤ To show the Object library, select View ➪ Utilities ➪ Show Object Library.

➤ To show the assistant editor, select View ➪ Assistant Editor Show Assistant Editor.

➤ To show the source editor, select View ➪ Source Editor ➪ Show Standard Editor.

Step-by-Step

➤ Create a Single View Application in Xcode called `InteractionSample`:

1. Launch Xcode and create a new application by selecting File ➪ New ➪ Project.

2. Select the Single View Application template from the list of iOS project templates.

3. In the project options screen, use the following values:

➤ **Product name:** InteractionSample

➤ **Organization name:** your company

➤ **Organization identifier:** com.yourcompany

➤ **Language:** Swift

➤ **Devices:** iPhone

➤ **Use Core Data:** Unchecked

➤ **Include Unit Tests:** Unchecked

➤ **Include UI Tests:** Unchecked

4. Save the project to your hard disk.

➤ Open the `Main.storyboard` file in the Xcode editor:

1. Ensure the project navigator is visible and the InteractionSample project is open.

2. Click the `Main.storyboard` file.

➤ Add a label to the storyboard:

1. Ensure the Object Library is visible by selecting View ⇨ Utilities ⇨ Show Object Library.

2. Select a label from the Object Library and drag it onto the single scene of the storyboard. The position of the label does not matter at this point.

3. Use the Attribute inspector to change the alignment of the label to Centered.

4. Select Editor ⇨ Size to Fit Content to resize the label so that its contents are not truncated. This option is only visible if the text in the label is currently truncated.

➤ Set up a few basic layout constraints to center the label on the screen:

1. Ensure the label is selected; if it is not, simply click it once.

2. Center the label horizontally and vertically by using the alignment constraint editor popup window.

3. Update the storyboard to display the new position of the label accurately by selecting Editor ⇨ Resolve Auto Layout Issues ⇨ Update Frames.

➤ Add a button to the storyboard:

1. From the Object library, select a Button and drop it onto the scene.

2. Double-click the button and change the text displayed in it to `Greet Me!`

3. Drag the button to sit a short distance below the label. The precise position does not matter.

4. Ensure the button is selected; if it is not, simply click it once.

5. Center the button horizontally by using the alignment constraint editor popup window.

6. Use the pin button to add the following constraints (see Figure 9-21)

   ➤ Pin the distance between the top of the button and its nearest neighbor in the storyboard (the label).

   ➤ Pin the height of the button.

   ➤ Pin the width of the button.

➤ Create an outlet in the view controller class and connect it to the label.

1. Ensure the assistant editor is visible. To show it, select View ⇨ Assistant Editor ⇨ Show Assistant Editor. Ensure the `ViewController.swift` file is open in the assistant editor. If it's not, use the jump bars to select it.

2. Right-click the label to show the context menu. Ensure you have right-clicked the label and not the layout constraint.

3. Drag from the circle beside `New Referencing Outlet` to an empty line in the `ViewController.swift` file in the assistant editor.

4. Name the new connection `textLabel` in the popup dialog that appears and click the Connect button. The code in the assistant editor should now resemble the following:

```swift
import UIKit

class ViewController: UIViewController {

    @IBOutlet weak var textLabel: UILabel!

    override func viewDidLoad() {
        super.viewDidLoad()
        // Do any additional setup after loading the view,
        // typically from a nib.
    }

    override func didReceiveMemoryWarning() {
        super.didReceiveMemoryWarning()
        // Dispose of any resources that can be recreated.
    }

}
```

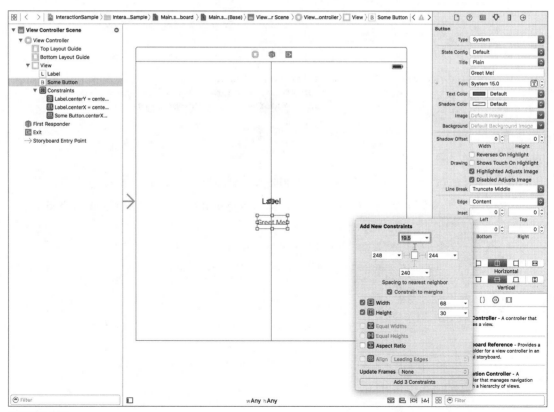

FIGURE 9-21

➤ Create an action method in the view controller class and connect it to the Touch Up Inside event of the button:

1. Right-click the button to show the context menu.

2. Drag from the circle beside the Touch Up Inside event to an empty line in the `ViewController.swift` file in the assistant editor.

3. Name the new method `onButtonPressed` in the popup dialog that appears and click the Connect button. The code in the assistant editor should now resemble the following:

```swift
import UIKit

class ViewController: UIViewController {

    @IBOutlet weak var textLabel: UILabel!

    @IBAction func onButtonPressed(sender: AnyObject) {

    }

    override func viewDidLoad() {
        super.viewDidLoad()
        // Do any additional setup after loading the view,
        // typically from a nib.
    }

    override func didReceiveMemoryWarning() {
        super.didReceiveMemoryWarning()
        // Dispose of any resources that can be recreated.
    }

}
```

➤ Write code to update the text of the label when the button is pressed:

1. Scroll down and locate the implementation of the `onButtonPressed` method in the Assistant Editor.

2. Replace it with the following code to change the text of the label:

```swift
@IBAction func onButtonPressed(sender: AnyObject) {
        textLabel.text = "Greetings mighty coder!"
}
```

➤ Run the app on the iOS Simulator:

1. Use the scheme/target selector buttons on the Xcode toolbar to select an iOS simulator.

2. Run the application by selecting Product ⇨ Run. Tap the button and observe the text in the label change.

3. Go back to Xcode and stop the app in the simulator by selecting Product ⇨ Stop.

REFERENCE *To see some of the examples from this lesson, watch the Lesson 9 video online at* `www.wrox.com/go/swiftiosvid`.

10

Introduction to Storyboards

Most iOS applications are made up of several screens of content with the user typically navigating from one screen to another. A storyboard is a feature in Xcode that lets you view all the screens as well as the connections between them in a single place. In general, storyboards provide a better high-level overview of all the screens in your application and the relationships between them.

Storyboards involve two key concepts, scenes and segues. A *scene* is defined by a view controller and is the major visual component of a storyboard. It represents one screen of content in your application.

If you have been programming iOS applications prior to iOS5, everything you know about Interface Builder applies to scenes. When you create a new project from any of the iOS Application templates, Xcode creates a single storyboard file for you called `Main.storyboard` (see Figure 10-1).

Figure 10-2 shows the scenes that make up the storyboard of a simple iOS application. As you can see, each scene contains familiar `UIKit` controls like image views, buttons, and labels. Clicking one of the scenes in the storyboard selects it. The selected scene has a dark gray outline around it.

Toward the upper portion of the selected scene you will notice three icons (see Figure 10-3) in a white strip. This strip is called the dock and the three icons represent the top-level items in the scene. The first two of these represent the view controller class associated with the scene, the second represents the first responder, and the third icon represents the exit item.

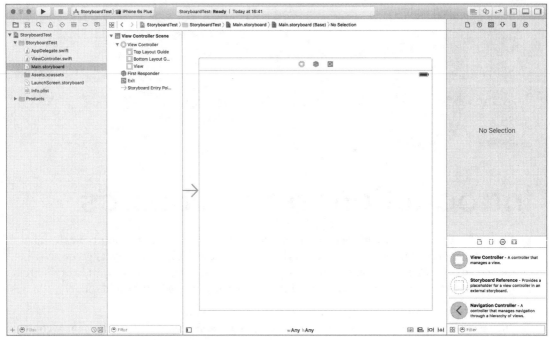

FIGURE 10-1

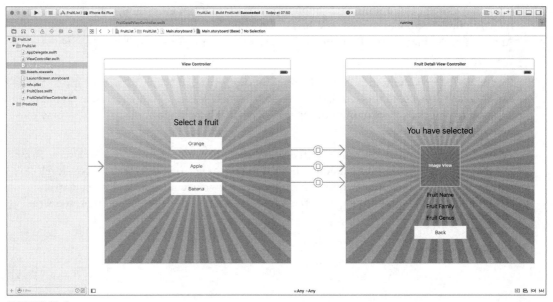

FIGURE 10-2

FIGURE 10-3

The actual user-interface elements in the view controller are not top-level objects because they are contained by the view controller and hence do not appear in the dock. These appear in the document outline, which can be expanded using the Document Outline button at the bottom-left corner of the storyboard (see Figure 10-4).

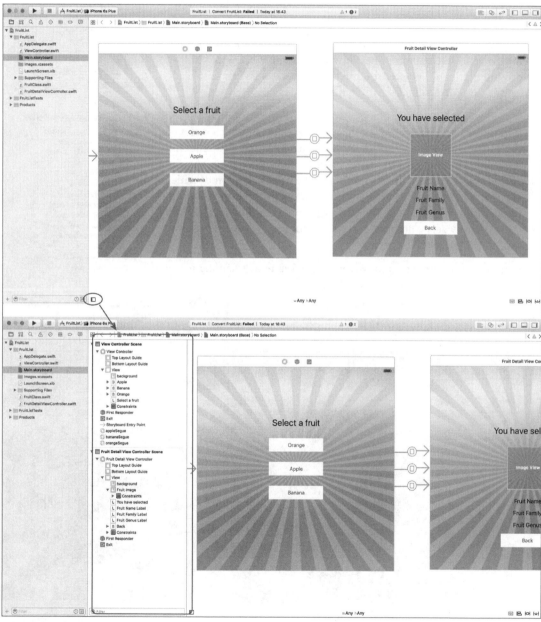

FIGURE 10-4

Objects contained within the scene are shown hierarchically (see Figure 10-5). Clicking an object in the hierarchy selects it in the corresponding scene.

To view the entire storyboard at a glance, simply double-click the canvas to zoom out. Double-click a scene to select and zoom in to the storyboard.

A *segue* represents the transition between one scene to another. It also represents the manner in which the new scene is presented. Segues are represented by arrows between scenes (see Figure 10-6). There can be multiple segues between scenes.

When using segues, there are four different ways in which a view can be presented: Push, Replace, Present Modally, Present As Popover. Modal segues are used to present modal content; they enable you to specify a transition style, the most common of which is one where the new scene slides up from the bottom of the screen. Push segues are used in conjunction with a navigation controller to slide a new scene onto the screen. Custom segues enable you to specify the presentation style.

You can set up the type and Attribute of a segue by selecting it and using the Attribute inspector (see Figure 10-7).

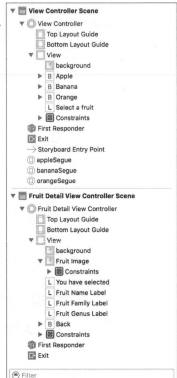

FIGURE 10-5

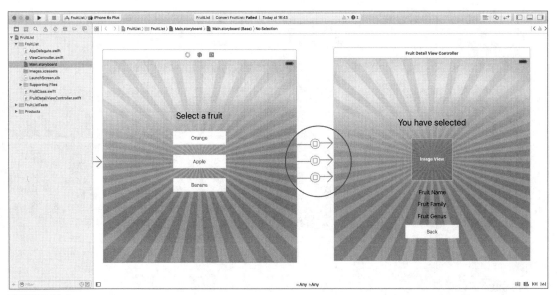

FIGURE 10-6

FIGURE 10-7

You can select a segue by clicking the circle in the middle of the arrow representing the segue on the storyboard (see Figure 10-8). Each segue in your application must be uniquely identified by a string. This identifier can also be set up using the Attribute inspector.

FIGURE 10-8

When you create a new Xcode project, the default storyboard file contains a single scene. To add a new scene to a storyboard, simply drag and drop a View Controller object from the Object library onto the canvas. You can add interface elements to the new scene by simply dragging and dropping objects from the Object library; to create outlets and actions for these elements you first need to create a UIViewController subclass that does not have an associated XIB file and link it to the new scene.

To create a new UIViewController subclass, simply right-click the project in the project navigator and select New File from the context menu. Select the Cocoa Touch Class template (under the iOS ⇨ Source group) in the dialog box that appears and click Next (see Figure 10-9).

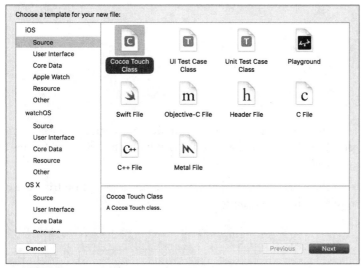

FIGURE 10-9

In the file options dialog box for the new class, ensure you have subclassed `UIViewController` and have cleared the Also create XIB file option (see Figure 10-10).

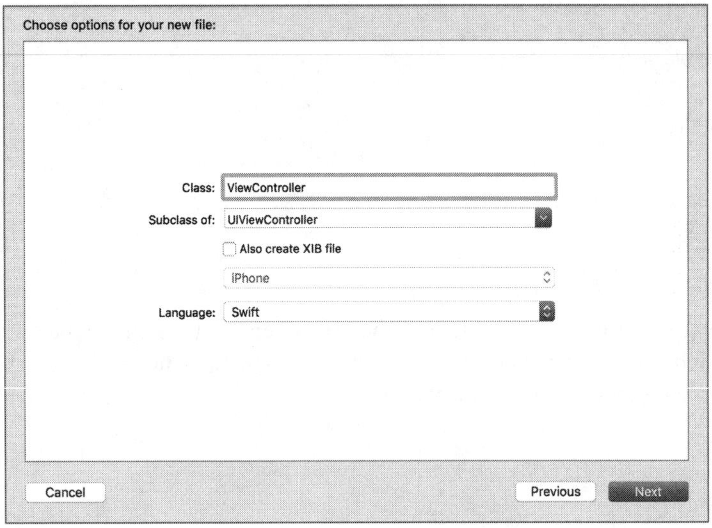

Choose options for your new file:

Class: ViewController

Subclass of: UIViewController

☐ Also create XIB file

iPhone

Language: Swift

Cancel   Previous   Next

FIGURE 10-10

After you create your `UIViewController` subclass, you need to associate it with the new scene in the storyboard. To do so, simply select the scene in the storyboard, select the view controller object (the yellow box) in the dock, and choose the appropriate class name in the Identity inspector (see Figure 10-11).

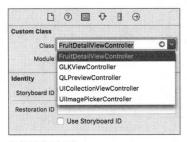

Custom Class

Class: FruitDetailViewController

Module: FruitDetailViewController
      GLKViewController
Identity   QLPreviewController
Storyboard ID   UICollectionViewController
      UIImagePickerController
Restoration ID
☐ Use Storyboard ID

FIGURE 10-11

To create a segue from an object in one scene to another scene, simply right-click the object to display a context menu and drag from the circle beside the action entry under the Triggered Segues category to the target scene (see Figure 10-12).

Alternately, you can Ctrl+drag from the object to the target scene and select an option from the context menu that appears when you release the mouse button.

Click the new segue to select it, and use the Attribute inspector to give it a unique string identifier. To perform some tasks in the source view controller when a segue is about to be performed, override the `prepareForSegue` method in the source view controller class.

```
override func prepareForSegue(segue: UIStoryboardSegue, sender: AnyObject?) {

}
```

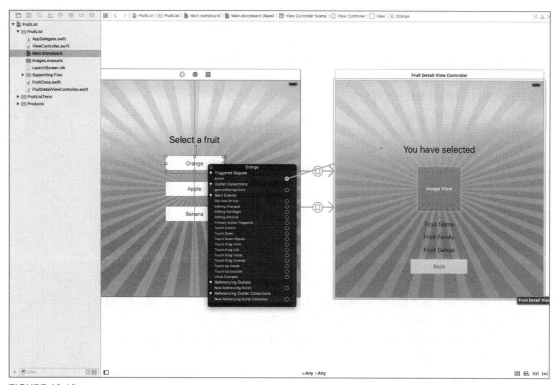

FIGURE 10-12

You could potentially have several buttons in the source view controller, each going to different scenes of the storyboard with individual segues. If you override the `prepareForSegue` method in the source view controller, your version of this method will be called regardless of which segue is in action. Within this method, you need to provide code to determine which segue is in action and take appropriate steps.

The first argument of this method is a `UIStoryboardSegue` object that represents the segue about to be performed. The second parameter is a reference to the object that initiated the segue.

The `UIStoryboardSegue` object provides the `identifier` variable, which contains the unique string identifier specified using the Attribute inspector. The `UIStoryboardSegue` object also provides the `sourceViewController` and `destinationViewController` variables that you can use to retrieve a reference to the source and target view controllers involved in the transition. You can use this information to set up properties in the destination view controller before it is displayed.

TRY IT

In this Try It, you launch Xcode and create a new Xcode project using the Single View Application template called `FruitList`. In the default scene, you present the user with a short list of fruits, and in the second scene you show detailed information on the fruit selected in the first scene. The user will be able to get back to the first scene from the second scene.

Lesson Requirements

➤ Launch Xcode.

➤ Create a new project based on the Single View Application template.

➤ Add image resources to your project.

➤ Add a new `NSObject` subclass to your project `FruitClass`.

➤ Add an array to the `FruitListViewController` class and add three instances of `FruitClass` to this array.

➤ Edit the storyboard with Interface Builder.

➤ Add a `UILabel` and three `UIButton` objects to the default scene in the storyboard.

➤ Create an additional scene in the storyboard and a new `UIViewController` subclass called `FruitDetailViewController` in the project.

➤ Use the Identity inspector to change the Custom class of the new scene to `FruitDetailViewController`.

➤ Create segues from the four buttons in the first scene to the second scene.

➤ Override the `prepareForSegue:sender` method in the `ViewController` class to pass information on the selected fruit to the second scene.

➤ Add user interface elements and code to the second scene to display information on a fruit.

➤ Add a `UIButton` to the second scene to dismiss it.

> **REFERENCE** *The code for this Try It is available at* www.wrox.com/go/ swiftios.

Hints

➤ To show the Object library, select View ➪ Utilities ➪ Show Object Library.

➤ To show the assistant editor, select View ➪ Assistant Editor ➪ Show Assistant Editor.

Step-by-Step

➤ Create a Single View Application in Xcode called `FruitList`.

1. Launch Xcode and create a new application by selecting File ➪ New ➪ Project.

2. Select the Single View Application template from the list of iOS project templates.

3. In the project options screen, use the following values:

   ➤ **Product Name:** FruitList

   ➤ **Organization Name:** your company

   ➤ **Organization Identifier:** com.yourcompany

   ➤ **Language:** Swift

   ➤ **Devices:** iPhone

   ➤ **Use Core Data:** Unchecked

   ➤ **Include Unit Tests:** Unchecked

   ➤ **Include UI Tests:** Unchecked

4. Save the project to your hard disk.

➤ Add image resources to your project.

1. Ensure the project navigator is visible. To show it, select View ➪ Navigators ➪ Show Project Navigator.

2. Open the `Assets.xcassets` file by clicking on it in the project navigator.

3. Navigate to the `Images` folder in this chapter's resources from the website.

4. Create a new image set by selecting Editor ➪ New Image Set, and name this new image set apple.

5. Drag the `apple1x.png`, `apple2x.png`, and `apple3x.png` images from this chapter's resources into the appropriate placeholders in the image set.

6. Create a new image set by selecting Editor ➪ New Image Set, and name this new image set banana.

7. Drag the `banana1x.png`, `banana2x.png`, and `banana3x.png` images from this chapter's resources into the appropriate placeholders in the image set.

8. Create a new image set by selecting Editor ➪ New Image Set, and name this new image set orange.

9. Drag the `orange1x.png`, `orange2x.png`, and `orange3x.png` images from this chapter's resources into the appropriate placeholders in the image set.

10. Create a new image set by selecting Editor ➪ New Image Set and name this new image set background.

11. Drag the `background1x.png`, `background2x.png`, and `background3x.png` images from this chapter's resources into the appropriate placeholders in the image set.

➤ Open the `Main.storyboard` file in the Xcode editor.

1. Ensure the project navigator is visible and the FruitList project is open.

2. Click the `Main.storyboard` file.

➤ Add a background image to the default scene of the storyboard.

1. Ensure the Object library is visible by selecting View ➪ Utilities ➪ Show Object Library.

2. Select an Image View from the Object library and drag it onto the single scene of the storyboard. The size and position of the image view does not matter at this point.

3. Use the Attribute inspector to set the Image attribute of the image view to `background`.

4. Ensure the image view is selected; if it is not, simply click it once.

5. Use the Pin button to display the constraints editor popup.

   ➤ Uncheck the Constrain to margins option.

   ➤ Pin the distance between the top of the image view and its nearest neighbor to 0.

   ➤ Pin the distance between the bottom of the image view and its nearest neighbor to 0.

   ➤ Pin the distance between the left edge of the image view and its nearest neighbor to 0.

   ➤ Pin the distance between the right edge of the image view and its nearest neighbor to 0.

   ➤ Click the Add 4 Constraints button to dismiss the constraints editor popup.

➤ Add a button to the storyboard.

1. From the Object library, select a button and drop it onto the scene.

2. Double-click the button and change the text displayed in it to `Apple`.

3. Drag the button to position it near the center of the scene. The precise size or position does not matter.

4. Use the Attribute inspector to change the background color of the button to White Color. The background color attribute is located in the View subsection of the Attribute inspector; you may need to scroll down a little to access it.

5. Ensure the button is selected; if it is not, simply click it once.

6. Use the Align button to display the alignment constraint editor and add two constraints to center the button both horizontally and vertically.

7. Ensure the button is selected and use the Pin button to display the constraints editor popup.

   ➤ Pin the width of the button to 165.

   ➤ Pin the height of the button to 40.

   ➤ Click the Add 2 Constraints button to dismiss the constraints editor popup.

➤ Update the frames to match the constraints you have set.

1. Click the View controller item in the dock above the storyboard scene. This is the first of the three icons located directly above the selected storyboard scene.

2. Select Editor ➪ Resolve Auto Layout Issues ➪ Update Frames.

➤ Add a second button to the storyboard.

1. From the Object library, select a button and drop it onto the scene.

2. Double-click the button and change the text displayed in it to `Banana`.

3. Drag the button to position it a short distance below the Apple button. The precise size or position does not matter.

4. Use the Attribute inspector to change the background color of the button to White Color. The background color attribute is located in the View subsection of the Attribute inspector. You may need to scroll down a little to access it.

5. Ensure the button is selected; if it is not, simply click it once.

6. Use the Align button to display the alignment constraint editor and add a constraint to center the button horizontally.

7. Ensure the button is selected and use the Pin button to display the constraints editor popup. While setting these constraints ensure the Constrain to margins option is unchecked.

   ➤ Pin the width of the button to 165.

   ➤ Pin the height of the button to 40.

   ➤ Pin the distance between the top of the button and its nearest neighbor to 30.

   ➤ Click the Add 3 Constraints button to dismiss the constraints editor popup.

8. Update the frames to match the constraints you have set.

➤ Click the View controller item in the dock above the storyboard scene. This is the first of the three icons located directly above the selected storyboard scene.

➤ Select Editor ➪ Resolve Auto Layout Issues ➪ Update Frames.

➤ Add a third button to the storyboard.

1. From the Object library, select a button and drop it onto the scene.

2. Double-click the button and change the text displayed in it to `Orange`.

3. Drag the button to position it a short distance above the Apple button. The precise size or position does not matter.

4. Use the Attribute inspector to change the background color of the button to White Color. The background color attribute is located in the View subsection of the Attribute inspector. You may need to scroll down a little to access it.

5. Ensure the button is selected. If it is not, simply click it once.

6. Use the Align button to display the alignment constraint editor and add a constraint to center the button horizontally.

7. Ensure the button is selected and use the pin button to display the constraints editor popup. While setting these constraints ensure the Constrain to margins option is unchecked.

➤ Pin the width of the button to 165.

➤ Pin the height of the button to 40.

➤ Pin the distance between the bottom of the button and its nearest neighbor to 30.

➤ Click the Add 3 Constraints button to dismiss the constraints editor popup.

8. Update the frames to match the constraints you have set.

➤ Click on the View controller item in the dock above the storyboard scene. This is the first of the three icons located directly above the selected storyboard scene.

➤ Select Editor ➪ Resolve Auto Layout Issues ➪ Update Frames.

➤ Add a label to the storyboard.

1. Ensure the Object library is visible by selecting View ➪ Utilities ➪ Show Object Library.

2. Select a label from the Object library and drag it onto the single scene of the storyboard. Place the label a short distance above the Orange button.

3. Use the Attribute inspector to change the alignment of the label to Centered.

4. Double-click the label and change the text displayed in it to `Select a fruit`.

5. Use the Attribute inspector to change the font size of the label to 36.

6. Select Editor ⇨ Size to Fit Content to resize the label so that its contents are not truncated.

7. Center the label horizontally by selecting Editor ⇨ Align ⇨ Horizontal Center in Container.

8. Ensure the label is selected and use the Pin button to display the constraints editor popup.

   ➤ Pin the distance between the bottom of the label and its nearest neighbor to 30.

   ➤ Click the Add 1 Constraint button to dismiss the constraints editor popup.

9. Update the frames to match the constraints you have set.

   ➤ Click on the View controller item in the dock above the storyboard scene. This is the first of the three icons located directly above the selected storyboard scene.

   ➤ Select Editor ⇨ Resolve Auto Layout Issues ⇨ Update Frames.

➤ Create an NSObject subclass called FruitClass.

1. Ensure the project navigator is visible.

2. Right-click the FruitList group and select New File from the context menu.

3. Select the Cocoa Touch Class template and click Next.

4. Call the new class FruitClass and ensure that the new class is a subclass of NSObject by selecting NSObject in the drop-down combo box, and click Next.

5. Select a folder where files should be created. It is best to accept the default location provided by Xcode.

6. Modify the FruitClass.swift file to resemble the following:

```
import UIKit
import Foundation

class FruitClass: NSObject {

    var fruitName:String!
    var fruitImage:String!
    var fruitFamily:String!
    var fruitGenus:String!

    init (fruitName:String,
          fruitImage:String,
          fruitFamily:String,
          fruitGenus:String) {
        self.fruitName = fruitName;
        self.fruitImage = fruitImage;
        self.fruitFamily = fruitFamily;
        self.fruitGenus = fruitGenus;
    }
}
```

➤ Add an Array variable to the `ViewController` class and populate it with three `FruitClass` instances. Do this by modifying the `ViewController.swift` file to resemble the following:

```
import UIKit


class ViewController: UIViewController {

    var arrayOfFruits:[FruitClass] = [FruitClass]()

    override func viewDidLoad() {
        super.viewDidLoad()

            let apple:FruitClass = FruitClass(fruitName: "Apple",
                                              fruitImage: "apple",
                                              fruitFamily: "Rosacae",
                                              fruitGenus: "Malus")

            let banana:FruitClass = FruitClass(fruitName: "Banana",
                                               fruitImage: "banana",
                                               fruitFamily: "Musacae",
                                               fruitGenus: "Musa")

            let orange:FruitClass = FruitClass(fruitName: "Orange",
                                               fruitImage: "orange",
                                               fruitFamily: "Rutacae",
                                               fruitGenus: "Citrus")

    override func didReceiveMemoryWarning() {
        super.didReceiveMemoryWarning()
        // Dispose of any resources that can be recreated.
    }

    }
```

➤ Add a new subclass of `UIViewController` called `FruitDetailViewController`.

1. Ensure the project navigator is visible.

2. Right-click the `FruitList` group and select New File from the context menu.

3. Select the Cocoa Touch Class template and click Next.

4. Call the new class `FruitDetailViewController` and ensure that the new class is a subclass of `UIViewController` by selecting `UIViewController` in the drop-down combo box.

5. Ensure that Also create XIB file option is not selected, and click Next.

6. Select a folder where files should be created. It is best to accept the default location provided by Xcode.

➤ Create a new scene in the storyboard.

1. Ensure the `Main.storyboard` file is open. If it is not, then select it in the project navigator.

2. Drag a View Controller object from the Object library onto the storyboard canvas.

3. Double-click the canvas to zoom out.

4. Position the new scene alongside the original scene.

5. Select the new scene in the storyboard, select the View Controller object from the dock, and use the Identity inspector to change its Custom class attribute to `FruitDetailViewController`. To show the Identity inspector, select View ➪ Utilities ➪ Show Identity inspector.

➤ Add user interface elements to the new scene.

1. Select the Fruit Detail View Controller scene to select it, and use the scroll bars to center it in the view area.

2. Add a background image to the new scene.

   ➤ Ensure the Object library is visible by selecting View ➪ Utilities ➪ Show Object Library.

   ➤ Select an image view from the Object library and drag it onto the single scene of the storyboard. The size and position of the image view does not matter at this point.

   ➤ Use the Attribute inspector to set the Image attribute of the image view to `background`.

   ➤ Ensure the image view is selected; if it is not, simply click it once.

   ➤ Use the Pin button to display the constraints editor popup:

   a. Clear the Constrain to margins option.

   b. Pin the distance between the top of the image view and its nearest neighbor to 0.

   c. Pin the distance between the bottom of the image view and its nearest neighbor to 0.

   d. Pin the distance between the left edge of the image view and its nearest neighbor to 0.

   e. Pin the distance between the right edge of the image view and its nearest neighbor to 0.

   f. Click the Add 4 Constraints button to dismiss the constraints editor popup.

3. Add an additional image view to the new scene. This will be used to display a picture of the fruit selected in the first scene.

   ➤ Ensure the Object library is visible by selecting View ➪ Utilities ➪ Show Object Library.

   ➤ Select an Image View from the Object library and drag it onto the single scene of the storyboard. The size and position of the image view does not matter at this point.

   ➤ Use the Align button to display the alignment constraint editor and add constraints to center the button horizontally and vertically.

➤ Use the Pin button to display the constraints editor popup.

a. Pin the height of the image view to 128.

b. Pin the width of the image view to 128.

c. Click the Add 2 Constraints button to dismiss the constraints editor popup.

➤ Update the frames to match the constraints you have set.

a. Click the View controller item in the dock above the storyboard scene. This is the first of the three icons located directly above the selected storyboard scene.

b. Select Editor ➪ Resolve Auto Layout Issues ➪ Update Frames.

➤ Create an outlet in the `FruitDetailViewController` class and connect it to the image view.

a. Ensure the assistant editor is visible. To show it, select View ➪ Assistant Editor ➪ Show Assistant Editor. Ensure the `FruitDetailViewController.swift` file is open in the assistant editor; if not, then use the jump bars to select it.

b. Right-click the image view to show the context menu. Ensure you have right-clicked the image view and not the layout constraint.

c. Drag from the circle beside `New Referencing Outlet` to an empty line in the `FruitDetailViewController.swift` file in the assistant editor.

d. Name the new outlet `fruitImage` in the popup dialog that appears and click the Connect button. The code in the assistant editor should now resemble the following:

```
import UIKit

class FruitDetailViewController: UIViewController {

    @IBOutlet weak var fruitImage: UIImageView!

    override func viewDidLoad() {
        super.viewDidLoad()

        // Do any additional setup after loading the view.
    }

    override func didReceiveMemoryWarning() {
        super.didReceiveMemoryWarning()
```

```
                                  // Dispose of any resources that can be recreated.
                    }
          }
```

4. Add a label to the storyboard.

    ➤ Ensure the Object library is visible by selecting View ⇨ Utilities ⇨ Show Object Library.

    ➤ Select a label from the Object library and drag it onto the single scene of the storyboard. Place the label a short distance above the image view added in the previous step.

    ➤ Use the Attribute inspector to change the alignment of the label to Centered.

    ➤ Double-click the label and change the text displayed in it to You have selected.

    ➤ Use the attribute editor to change the font size of the label to 26.

    ➤ Select Editor ⇨ Size to Fit Content and resize the label so that its contents are not truncated.

    ➤ Use the Align button to display the alignment constraint editor and add a constraint to center the button horizontally.

    ➤ Ensure the label is selected and use the pin button to display the constraints editor popup.

        a. Pin the distance between the bottom of the label and its nearest neighbor to 30.

        b. Click the Add 1 Constraint button to dismiss the constraints editor popup.

    ➤ Update the frames to match the constraints you have set.

5. Add three additional labels to the scene below the image view.

    ➤ Repeat the steps.

    ➤ Ensure the Text Alignment attribute of each label is Centered.

    ➤ Place them one below the other, and all of them below the image view.

    ➤ Ensure the labels are centered horizontally in the scene and are at an even distance of 15 units from each other.

    ➤ Change the caption of the labels to Fruit Name, Fruit Family, Fruit Genus.

    ➤ When complete, your scene should resemble Figure 10-13.

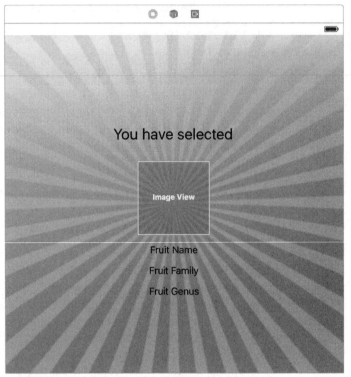

FIGURE 10-13

➤ Create three outlets in the FruitDetailViewController class and connect them to the three labels you have just created on the storyboard scene. Name these outlets fruitNameLabel, fruitFamilyLabel, and fruitGenusLabel. The code in the assistant editor should now resemble the following:

```
import UIKit

class FruitDetailViewController: UIViewController {

    @IBOutlet weak var fruitImage: UIImageView!
    @IBOutlet weak var fruitNameLabel: UILabel!
    @IBOutlet weak var fruitFamilyLabel: UILabel!
    @IBOutlet weak var fruitGenusLabel: UILabel!

    override func viewDidLoad() {
        super.viewDidLoad()

        // Do any additional setup after loading the view.
    }

    override func didReceiveMemoryWarning() {
```

```
                    super.didReceiveMemoryWarning()
                    // Dispose of any resources that can be recreated.
            }

        }
```

6. Add a button to the scene.

    ➤   From the Object library, select a Button object and drop it onto the scene.

    ➤   Double-click the button and change the text displayed in it to `Back`.

    ➤   Drag the button to position it a short distance below the Fruit Genus label. The precise size or position does not matter.

    ➤   Use the Attribute Editor to change the background color of the button to White Color. The background color attribute is located in the View subsection of the Attribute Editor; you may need to scroll down a little to access it.

    ➤   Ensure the button is selected. If it is not, simply click it once.

    ➤   Center the button horizontally by selecting Editor ⇨ Align ⇨ Horizontal Center in Container.

    ➤   Ensure the button is selected and use the pin button to set up the following constraints:

    a.   Pin the width of the button to 165.

    b.   Pin the height of the button to 40.

    c.   Pin the distance between the top of the button and its nearest neighbor to 15.

    ➤   Click the Add 3 Constraints button to dismiss the constraints editor popup.

    ➤   Update the frames to match the constraints you have set.

    a.   Click on the View controller item in the dock above the storyboard scene. This is the first of the three icons located directly above the selected storyboard scene.

    b.   Select Editor ⇨ Resolve Auto Layout Issues ⇨ Update Frames.

    ➤   Create an action method in the view controller class and connect it to the button.

    a.   Ensure the assistant editor is visible. To show it, select View ⇨ Assistant Editor ⇨ Show Assistant Editor. Ensure the `FruitDetailViewController.swift` file is open in the assistant editor; if not, then use the jump bars to select it.

    b.   Right-click the button to show the context menu. Ensure you have right-clicked the label and not the layout constraint.

c.   Drag from the circle beside `Touch Up Inside` to an empty line in the `FruitDetailViewController.swift` file in the assistant editor.

d.   Name the new action method `onBack` in the popup dialog that appears and click the Connect button.

e.   Add the following line of code to the implementation of the `onBack` method in the `FruitDetailViewController.swift` file:

```
self.dismissViewControllerAnimated(true, nil);
```

The code in the assistant editor should now resemble the following:

```
import UIKit

class FruitDetailViewController: UIViewController {

    @IBOutlet weak var fruitImage: UIImageView!
    @IBOutlet weak var fruitNameLabel: UILabel!
    @IBOutlet weak var fruitFamilyLabel: UILabel!
    @IBOutlet weak var fruitGenusLabel: UILabel!

    override func viewDidLoad() {
        super.viewDidLoad()

        // Do any additional setup after loading the view.
    }

    override func didReceiveMemoryWarning() {
        super.didReceiveMemoryWarning()
        // Dispose of any resources that can be recreated.
    }

    @IBAction func onBack(sender: AnyObject) {
        self.dismissViewControllerAnimated(true, completion: nil);
    }
}
```

➤ Create segues in the storyboard.

1.   Open the `Main.storyboard` file in Interface Builder

2.   Double-click the canvas to zoom out. Position the two scenes sufficiently apart on the canvas by dragging them.

3.   Double-click the first scene to activate it.

4.   Right-click the Orange button to bring up a context menu. Drag from the circle beside the action item under the `Triggered Segues` category in the context menu to the Fruit Detail View Controller scene (see Figure 10-14).

5.   When you release the mouse button, you will be asked to select the segue type. Select `Present Modally`.

6. Select the segue by clicking the circle along the line joining the two scenes and use the Attribute inspector to change the identifier to orangeSegue (see Figure 10-15).

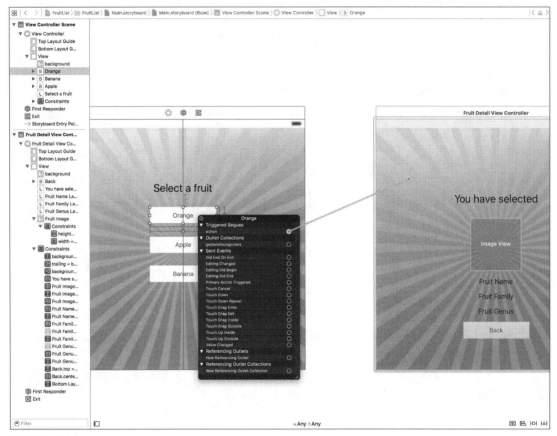

FIGURE 10-14

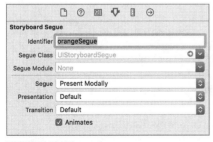

FIGURE 10-15

7. Similarly, create segues from each of the other two buttons (Apple, Banana) in the first scene to the second scene. Name these segues `appleSegue` and `bananaSegue` respectively. Your storyboard canvas should resemble Figure 10-16.

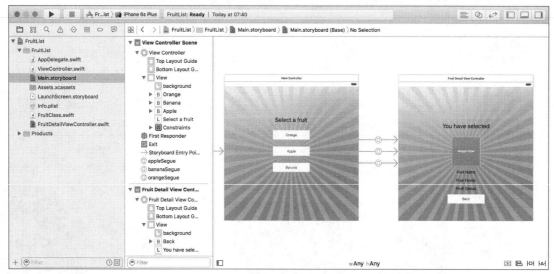

FIGURE 10-16

➤ Modify the implementation of the `ViewController` class by adding the following implementation for the `prepareForSegue:sender:` method in `ViewController.swift`:

```
override func prepareForSegue(segue: UIStoryboardSegue, sender: AnyObject?) {

        if (segue.identifier == "appleSegue") {
            var objectData:FruitClass = self.arrayOfFruits[0]
            let destination = segue.destinationViewController
                            as! FruitDetailViewController

            destination.dataObject = objectData;
        }
        else if (segue.identifier == "bananaSegue") {
            var objectData:FruitClass = self.arrayOfFruits[1]
            let destination = segue.destinationViewController
                            as! FruitDetailViewController

            destination.dataObject = objectData;
        }
        else if (segue.identifier == "orangeSegue") {
            var objectData:FruitClass = self.arrayOfFruits[2]
            let destination = segue.destinationViewController
                            as! FruitDetailViewController

            destination.dataObject = objectData;
        }
    }
```

When you finish typing these lines, you may notice the compiler complaining about the line:

```
destination.dataObject = objectData;
```

Ignore the issue momentarily as we will address it in the next step.

➤ Modify the interface of the `FruitDetailViewController` class.

1. Add the following variable directive to the top of the `FruitDetailViewController` `.swift` file:

```
var dataObject:FruitClass?
```

2. Modify the implementation of the `viewDidLoad` method as follows:

```
override func viewDidLoad() {
    super.viewDidLoad()
        guard let dataObject = dataObject else {
          return
         }

        fruitImage.image = UIImage(named: dataObject.fruitImage)
        fruitNameLabel.text = "Name: \(dataObject.fruitName)"
        fruitFamilyLabel.text = "Family: \(dataObject.fruitFamily)"
        fruitGenusLabel.text = "Genus: \(dataObject.fruitGenus)"
}
```

➤ Test your app in the iOS Simulator by clicking the Run button in the Xcode toolbar. Alternatively, you can select Project ➪ Run.

REFERENCE *To see some of the examples from this lesson, watch the Lesson 10 video online at* www.wrox.com/go/swiftiosvid.

SECTION II
More iOS Development

11

Handling User Input

In Lesson 9 you were introduced to the UIButton and UILabel classes. The UILabel class enables you to display static text on the screen. In this lesson, you learn to use text fields and text views to accept input from users. Text fields enable users to type a single line of text and are instances of the UITextField class. Text views, on the other hand, enable users to type in multiple lines of text and are instances of the UITextView class. Both classes are part of the UIKit framework.

TEXT FIELDS

To create a text field, simply drag and drop a Text Field object from the Object library onto a storyboard scene (see Figure 11-1).

You can use the Attribute inspector to set up several attributes of the text field, including the Placeholder, Alignment, Border Style, Text Color, Font, and the type of keyboard that is displayed when the user taps on the text field (see Figure 11-2).

A *placeholder* is some text that is displayed in the text field when it is empty, typically prompting the user to enter some information in the field. You can choose from seven different keyboards to associate with a text field; the choice you make will depend on the type of data you expect. These keyboard styles can be selected using the Attribute inspector and are displayed in Figure 11-3.

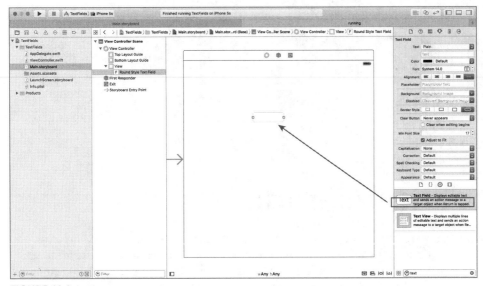

FIGURE 11-1

FIGURE 11-2

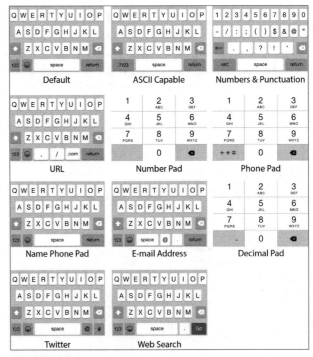

FIGURE 11-3

The text displayed in a text field is an instance of a `String` object. The `String` class is defined in the Foundation framework, and its instances represent sequences of characters (alphabets, numbers, punctuation marks).

To be able to access the text displayed in a text field object from code, you first need to create an outlet in the view controller class and then read the value of the `text` property in your code. For example, if `usernameField` is an outlet created using the assistant editor, you can use the following code to get the text displayed in the field:

```
let text:String = usernameField.text;
```

Tapping on a text field signifies that the user wants to interact with it, and as a result makes it the *active user interface element*. The active user interface element is formally known as the "first responder." When a text field receives first responder status, it automatically displays a keyboard.

To dismiss a keyboard when the Done button is pressed on the keypad, you will have to use the assistant editor to create a method in the view controller class and connect it to the `Did End On Exit` event of the text field (see Figure 11-4). A method in a view controller class that is wired to one of the events generated by a user interface element is commonly referred to as an action method.

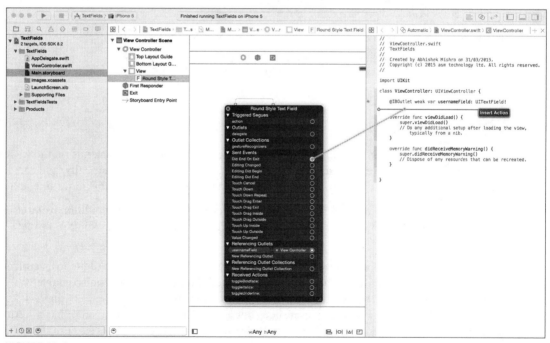

FIGURE 11-4

In your action method, you need to ask the text field to resign from first responder status. You can do this by calling the `resignFirstResponder` method of the text field object as shown in the following snippet:

```
@IBAction func onDismissKeyboard(sender: AnyObject) {
        self.usernameField.resignFirstResponder();
    }
```

Note that the `sender` parameter will contain a reference to the source of the event that triggered this method (which will be the text field).

This method of dismissing the keypad works for most keyboard styles, except for the numeric key-pads, which don't have a Done button. It is common practice for applications to allow the user to tap the background of the screen (outside the keypad or any other text field) to dismiss the keypad. One way to achieve this is by using a `UITapGestureRecognizer` object. Gesture recognizers are covered in detail in Lesson 21. For the moment, you can add a gesture recognizer to the view controller class by following these simple steps.

1. Add the following method declaration to the view controller class:

   ```
   func handleBackgroundTap(sender: UITapGestureRecognizer) {

   }
   ```

2. Add the following code to the `viewDidLoad` method of the view controller class:

   ```
   let tapRecognizer = UITapGestureRecognizer(target:self ,
              action: Selector("handleBackgroundTap:"))

   tapRecognizer.cancelsTouchesInView = false
   self.view.addGestureRecognizer(tapRecognizer)
   ```

3. Implement the `handleBackgroundTap:` method as follows:

   ```
   func handleBackgroundTap(sender: UITapGestureRecognizer) {
        self.usernameField.resignFirstResponder();
   }
   ```

TEXT VIEWS

Text views are similar to text fields in many respects. The key difference, however, is that text views can handle multiple lines of text. Text views handle the scrolling of text automatically, and can also be used as a read-only view, thus providing a convenient way to display scrollable multi-line text.

To create a text view, simply drag and drop a Text View element from the Object library onto the view (see Figure 11-5). By default a text view is sized to fit the entire screen, but you can resize/reposition it as needed.

To create a read-only text view, simply uncheck its Editable property in the Attribute inspector. A read-only text view does not display a keypad when tapped. Editable text views also enable you to select from one of seven different keypad types that will appear when the user taps them. The keypad associated with a text view, however, does not have a Done button; instead, it has a Return button that adds a new line to the text. Thus, to dismiss the keypad you will have to use the gesture recognizer technique discussed for text fields.

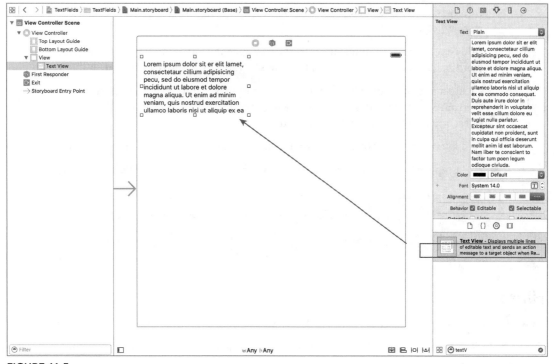

FIGURE 11-5

TRY IT

In this Try It, you create a new Xcode project based on the Single View Application template called `LoginSample` that presents a simple user interface to collect a username and password combination from the user. The user interface will also contain a Login button that displays a customized greeting to the user when it is tapped.

Lesson Requirements

➤   Launch Xcode.

➤   Create a new project based on the Single View Application template.

➤   Edit the storyboard with Interface Builder.

➤ Add two `UILabel` instances to the default scene, with the text `User name:` and `Password:`, respectively.

➤ Add two `UITextField` instances to the same scene, corresponding to the username and password fields, and create appropriate outlets in the view controller for them.

➤ Create an action method called `dismissKeyboard()` in the view controller class that calls the `resignFirstResponder` method on each text field, and connect the Did End On Exit event of each text field to this action method.

➤ Add a `UIButton` instance to the scene that, when tapped, displays a message in an alert view.

➤ Use a tap gesture recognizer to dismiss the keyboard when the background is tapped.

> **REFERENCE** *The code for this Try It is available at* www.wrox.com/go/ swiftios.

Hints

➤ To show the Object library, use the View ➪ Utilities ➪ Show Object Library menu item.

➤ To show the assistant editor, use the View ➪ Assistant Editor ➪ Show Assistant Editor menu item.

Step-by-Step

➤ Create a Single View Application in Xcode called `LoginSample`.

1. Launch Xcode and create a new application by selecting File ➪ New Project.

2. Select the Single View Application template from the list of iOS project templates.

3. In the project options screen, use the following values:

➤ **Product Name:** LoginSample

➤ **Organization Name:** your company

➤ **Organization Identifier:** com.yourcompany

➤ **Language:** Swift

➤ **Devices:** iPhone

➤ **Use Core Data:** Unchecked

➤ **Include Unit Tests:** Unchecked

➤ **Include UI Tests:** Unchecked

4. Save the project to your hard disk.

➤ Open the `Main.storyboard` file in the Xcode editor.

1. Ensure the project navigator is visible and the LoginSample project is open.

2. Click the `Main.storyboard` file.

➤ Add two `UILabel` instances to the default scene.

1. Ensure the Object library is visible. To show it, select View ➪ Utilities ➪ Show Object Library.

2. From the Object library, drag and drop two Label objects onto the scene.

3. Use the Attribute inspector to set the `text` attribute of the first label to `User name:`. To show the Attribute inspector, select View ➪ Utilities ➪ Show Attributes Inspector.

4. Change the `text` attribute of the second label to `Password:`.

5. Select both labels in the scene and select Editor ➪ Size to Fit Contents to ensure the labels are large enough to show their contents.

6. Add the following constraints using the pin constraints dialog box for the user name label:

   ➤ Ensure the Constrain to margins option is unchecked.

   ➤ The distance from the left edge of the label to the view is 10.

   ➤ The distance from the top of the label to the view is 15.

   ➤ The width of the label is 91.

   ➤ The height of the label is 21.

7. Add the following constraints using the pin constraints dialog box for the password label:

   ➤ Ensure the Constrain to margins option is unchecked.

   ➤ The distance from left edge of the label to the view is 10.

   ➤ The vertical distance between the two labels is 15.

   ➤ The width of the label is 91.

   ➤ The height of the label is 21.

8. Update the frames to match the constraints you have set.

   ➤ Click on the View controller item in the dock above the storyboard scene. This is the first of the three icons located directly above the selected storyboard scene.

   ➤ Select Editor ➪ Resolve Auto Layout Issues ➪ Update Frames.

➤ Add two `UITextField` instances to the scene.

1. From the Object library, drag and drop two Text Field objects onto the scene and position them beside the two labels created in the previous step.

2. Use the Attribute inspector to set the Placeholder attribute of the first text field to `Enter user name`.

3. Use the Attribute inspector to set the Placeholder attribute of the second text field to `Enter password`.

4. Select both text fields in the scene and select Editor ➪ Size to Fit Contents to ensure the labels are large enough to show their contents.

5. Select the user name field in the scene and click the Pin button to display the constraints editor. Set the following constraints.

    ➤ Ensure that Constrain to margins is unchecked.

    ➤ The distance between the text field and the label should be 15.

    ➤ The distance from the top of the text field to the view should be 10.

    ➤ The width of the text field should be 200.

    ➤ The height of the text field should be 30.

6. Add the following constraints for the password field:

    ➤ Ensure the Constrain to margins option is unchecked.

    ➤ The distance between the text field and the label should be 15.

    ➤ The vertical distance between the two text fields should be 10.

    ➤ The width of the text field should be 200.

    ➤ The height of the text fields should be 30.

7. Update the frames to match the constraints you have set.

    ➤ Click on the View controller item in the dock above the storyboard scene. This is the first of the three icons located directly above the selected storyboard scene.

    ➤ Select Editor ➪ Resolve Auto Layout Issues ➪ Update Frames.

➤ Add a `UIButton` instance to the scene.

1. From the Object library, drag and drop a Button object onto the scene.

2. Double-click it and set the text in the button to `Login`.

3. Select the button in the scene and click the Pin button to display the constraints editor. Set the following constraints:

➤ Ensure the Constrain to margins option is unchecked.

➤ The horizontal distance between the button and the view should be 116.

➤ The vertical distance between the button and the password field should be 10.

➤ The width of the button should be 64.

➤ The height of the button should be 40.

4. Change the background color for the button to a dark gray color so that it is visible against a white background.

5. Update the frames to match the constraints you have set.

➤ Click on the View controller item in the dock above the storyboard scene. This is the first of the three icons located directly above the selected storyboard scene.

➤ Select Editor ⇨ Resolve Auto Layout Issues ⇨ Update Frames.

Your storyboard should resemble Figure 11-6.

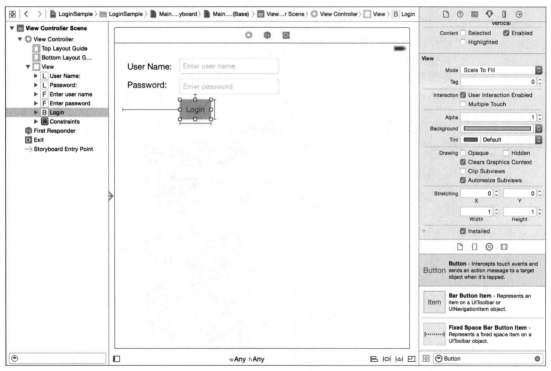

FIGURE 11-6

➤ Create outlets in the `ViewController` class and connect these outlets to the text fields in the scene.

1. Ensure the assistant editor is visible. To show it, select View ⇨ Editor ⇨ Show Assistant Editor.

2. Right-click the `UITextField` object corresponding to the user name to display a context menu. Drag from the circle beside the New Referencing Outlet option in the context menu to an empty line in the `ViewController.swift` file.

3. Name the new outlet `usernameField`.

4. Repeat this procedure for the password text field, and name the corresponding outlet `passwordField`.

➤ Create an action method in the `ViewController` class and associate it with the Did End On Exit events of the two text fields.

1. Right-click the `UITextField` object corresponding to the username to display its context menu, and drag from the circle beside the Did End On Exit item to an empty line in the `ViewController.swift` file.

2. Name the new Action `onDismissKeyboard`.

3. Right-click the `UITextField` object corresponding to the password to display its context menu, and drag from the circle beside the Did End On Exit item to the icon representing the view controller in the dock (see Figure 11-7).

FIGURE 11-7

4. Release the mouse button over the yellow view controller icon in the dock to present a list of existing action methods in the view controller. Select the `onDismissKeyboard` method.

5. Click the `ViewController.swift` file in the project navigator to open it.

6. Add the following code to the implementation of the `onDismissKeyboard` method:

```
usernameField.resignFirstResponder()
passwordField.resignFirstResponder()
```

➤ Create an action in the `ViewController.swift` file and connect it with the Touch Up Inside event of the login button.

1. Select the storyboard in the project navigator.

2. Right-click the Login button in the scene to display its context menu, and drag from the circle beside the Touch Up Inside item to an empty line in the `ViewController.swift` file.

3. Name the new action method `onLogin`.

4. Click the `ViewController.swift` file in the project navigator to open it.

5. Add the following code to the implementation of the `onLogin` method:

```
usernameField.resignFirstResponder()
passwordField.resignFirstResponder()

let userName:String = usernameField.text!
let length:Int = userName.characters.count

if length == 0 {
    return
}

let alert = UIAlertController(title: "",
    message: "Login succesfull",
    preferredStyle: UIAlertControllerStyle.Alert)

alert.addAction(UIAlertAction(title: "Ok",
    style: UIAlertActionStyle.Default,
    handler: nil))

self.presentViewController(alert,
    animated: true,
    completion: nil)
```

➤ Add a tap gesture recognizer and use it to dismiss the keyboard when the background area of the view is tapped.

1. Add the following code to the `viewDidLoad` method of the `ViewController.Swift` file, after the `super.viewDidLoad()` line:

```
let tapRecognizer = UITapGestureRecognizer(target:self ,
                action: Selector("handleBackgroundTap:"))
```

```
tapRecognizer.cancelsTouchesInView = false
self.view.addGestureRecognizer(tapRecognizer)
```

2. Implement the `handleBackgroundTap()` method in the `ViewController.swift` file as follows:

```
func handleBackgroundTap(sender: UITapGestureRecognizer) {
    usernameField.resignFirstResponder()
    passwordField.resignFirstResponder()
}
```

➤ Test your app in the iOS Simulator.

Click the Run button in the Xcode toolbar. Alternatively, you can use the Project ➪ Run menu item.

REFERENCE *To see some of the examples from this lesson, watch the Lesson 11 video online at* www.wrox.com/go/swiftiosvid.

12

Alert Views and Action Sheets

The user interface elements you have encountered so far have all been created by dragging and dropping from the Object library. In this lesson you are introduced to alert views and action sheets, two user interface elements that are created only with code. Prior to iOS 8, alert views and action sheets were represented by the `UIAlertView` and `UIActionSheet` classes. This is no longer the case with iOS 8; both of these are now handled by a single class `UIAlertController`.

ALERT VIEWS

An alert view is a special modal view that is used to display a short message to the user and typically enables the user to choose from a small number of options. The most common use of an alert view is to display information on success or failure of an operation; for example, on success a typical login operation may display an alert view, as shown in Figure 12-1.

FIGURE 12-1

When an alert view is displayed, the screen is dimmed automatically for you. You can specify a title, a message, and one or more buttons to present the user with options. When multiple options are presented to the user, it is common to designate one of the buttons to act as the cancel button. You can change the text displayed in the cancel button, but it is always displayed at the bottom of the alert view with a boldface font, as shown in Figure 12-2.

FIGURE 12-2

An alert view is managed by an instance of the `UIAlertController` class, which is part of the `UIKit` framework and is created in code as follows:

```
let alert = UIAlertController(title: "This is the title",
            message: "This is the message text",
            preferredStyle: UIAlertControllerStyle.Alert)
```

The first parameter is the title of the alert view. This is followed by the message. The third parameter should be `UIAlertControllerStyle.Alert` if you want an alert view.

Once you have created an alert view, you need to add buttons to it. This is achieved by creating instances of the `UIAlertAction` class and adding them to the alert view using the `addAction` method. The following code snippet creates two buttons, one of them being the Cancel button.

```
alert.addAction(UIAlertAction(title: "Ok",
style: UIAlertActionStyle.Default,
handler: nil))

alert.addAction(UIAlertAction(title: "Cancel",
style: UIAlertActionStyle.Cancel,
handler: nil))
```

The first parameter to the UIAlertAction constructor is the title that appears on the button; this is followed by the type of button (Default or Cancel). The final parameter is an optional closure that is executed when the button is pressed.

The following code snippet creates an alert view with two actions. The first action has a closure associated with it that will display another alert view:

```
let alert = UIAlertController(title: "Help",
        message: "Would you like to call customer services?",
        preferredStyle: UIAlertControllerStyle.Alert)

let dialActionHandler = { (action:UIAlertAction!) -> Void in
        let alertMessage = UIAlertController(title: "Error",
            message: "Sorry, unable to make a call at the moment.",
            preferredStyle: UIAlertControllerStyle.Alert)

        alertMessage.addAction(UIAlertAction(title: "OK",
            style: .Default,
            handler: nil))

        self.presentViewController(alertMessage,
            animated: true,
            completion: nil)
    }

alert.addAction(UIAlertAction(title: "Call +44 7922 394132",
        style: UIAlertActionStyle.Default,
        handler: dialActionHandler))

alert.addAction(UIAlertAction(title: "Cancel",
        style: UIAlertActionStyle.Cancel,
        handler: nil))
```

To show the alert view, simply use the presentViewController method of UIViewController as follows:

```
self.presentViewController(alert, animated: true, completion: nil)
```

The alert view object enables you to add up to two text fields, in addition to buttons. This comes in handy when you want to collect username and password information from the user (see Figure 12-3).

To do this, you can use the addTextFieldWithConfigurationHandler method of the UIAlertController class. The following code snippet creates an alert view with a text field:

```
let alert = UIAlertController(title: "Enter name",
        message: "",
        preferredStyle: UIAlertControllerStyle.Alert)
```

```
alert.addAction(UIAlertAction(title: "Ok",
         style: UIAlertActionStyle.Default,
         handler: nil))

alert.addTextFieldWithConfigurationHandler({(textField: UITextField!) in
         textField.placeholder = "What is your name?"
      })

self.presentViewController(alert, animated: true, completion: nil)
```

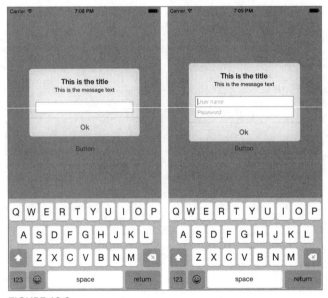

FIGURE 12-3

To retrieve the value typed by the user when the alert view is dismissed, you need to retrieve a reference to the `UITextField` object within the alert controller and read its text as follows:

```
let alert = UIAlertController(title: "Enter name",
         message: "",
         preferredStyle: UIAlertControllerStyle.Alert)


let okActionHandler = { (action:UIAlertAction!) -> Void in

      var nameField = alert.textFields![0] as UITextField

      let alertMessage = UIAlertController(title: "Hello",
      message: "\(nameField.text)",
      preferredStyle: UIAlertControllerStyle.Alert)

      alertMessage.addAction(UIAlertAction(title: "OK",
      style: .Default,
      handler: nil))
```

```
            self.presentViewController(alertMessage,
            animated: true,
            completion: nil)
        }

    alert.addAction(UIAlertAction(title: "Ok",
            style: UIAlertActionStyle.Default,
            handler: okActionHandler))

    alert.addTextFieldWithConfigurationHandler({(textField: UITextField!) in
            textField.placeholder = "What is your name?"
        })

    self.presentViewController(alert, animated: true, completion: nil)
```

ACTION SHEETS

An action sheet is another user interface component that is created through code and can be used to present a list of choices to a user. Action sheets are similar to alert views in many respects, but they have several important differences. To start with, action sheets look significantly different from alert views, and they look different on an iPhone and an iPad (see Figure 12-4).

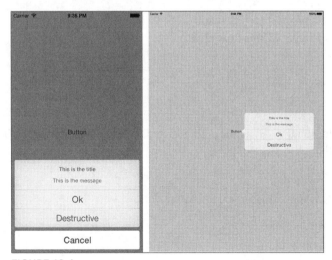

FIGURE 12-4

On an iPhone, they slide up from the bottom of the screen, and on the iPad they display as popover windows. On an iPad, the cancel button is not visible. If the user taps outside the action sheet on an iPad, the action sheet is dismissed.

Action sheets enable you to highlight one of the buttons in red—this button is referred to as the *destructive* button. The following code snippet shows how to create an action sheet on an iPhone:

```
let alert = UIAlertController(title: "This is the title",
        message: "This is the message",
        preferredStyle: UIAlertControllerStyle.ActionSheet)


alert.addAction(UIAlertAction(title: "Ok",
        style: UIAlertActionStyle.Default,
        handler: nil))

alert.addAction(UIAlertAction(title: "Cancel",
        style: UIAlertActionStyle.Cancel,
        handler: nil))

alert.addAction(UIAlertAction(title: "Destructive",
        style: UIAlertActionStyle.Destructive,
        handler: nil))

self.presentViewController(alert, animated: true, completion: nil)
```

As you can see, the parameters are very similar to those of an alert view, with the main difference being that the third argument to the `UIAlertController` constructor is now `UIAlertControllerstyle.ActionSheet`.

The destructive button is created by instantiating a `UIAlertAction` object with the style parameter set to `UIAlertActionStyle.Destructive`.

```
alert.addAction(UIAlertAction(title: "Destructive",
        style: UIAlertActionStyle.Destructive,
        handler: nil))
```

Showing an action sheet on an iPhone is identical to alert views:

```
self.presentViewController(alert, animated: true, completion: nil)
```

However, on an iPad you will need additional code, as the action sheet is presented in a popover. To show an action sheet on an iPad, use the following snippet:

```
alert.modalPresentationStyle = UIModalPresentationStyle.Popover

if let popoverController = alert.popoverPresentationController {
    popoverController.sourceView = sender as UIView;
    popoverController.sourceRect = sender.bounds;
}

self.presentViewController(alert, animated: true, completion: nil)
```

You cannot display an action sheet in the `viewDidLoad` method of a view controller class on the iPad. Another important distinction between action sheets and alert views is that the former cannot have text fields in them.

TRY IT

In this Try It, you create a new Xcode project based on the Single View Application template called `ActionSheetSample` that presents an action sheet with a list of colors when a button is tapped. When the user selects a color from the action sheet, the background color of the scene will be updated to match the selected color.

Lesson Requirements

➤ Launch Xcode.

➤ Create a new project based on the Single View Application template.

➤ Edit the storyboard with Interface Builder.

➤ Add UIButton instance to the default scene.

➤ Write code to display a list of colors to the user when the button is tapped.

➤ Write code to update the background color of the scene to reflect the selected color.

> **REFERENCE** *The code for this Try It is available at* `www.wrox.com/go/swiftios`.

Hints

➤ To show the Object library, select View ➪ Utilities ➪ Show Object Library.

➤ To show the assistant editor, select View ➪ Assistant Editor ➪ Show Assistant Editor.

Step-by-Step

➤ Create a Single View Application in Xcode called `ActionSheetSample`.

1. Launch Xcode and create a new application by selecting File ➪ New ➪ Project.

2. Select the Single View Application template from the list of iOS project templates.

3. In the project options screen, use the following values:

    ➤ **Product Name:** ActionSheetSample

    ➤ **Organization Name:** your company

    ➤ **Organization Identifier:** com.yourcompany

➤   **Language:** Swift

➤   **Devices:** iPhone

➤   **Use Core Data:** Unchecked

➤   **Include Unit Tests:** Unchecked

➤   **Include UI Tests:** Unchecked

4.   Save the project to your hard disk.

➤   Open the `Main.storyboard` file in the Xcode editor.

1.   Ensure the project navigator is visible and the ActionSheetSample project is open.

2.   Click the `Main.storyboard` file.

➤   Add a `UIButton` instance to the scene.

1.   From the Object library, drag and drop a Button object onto the scene.

2.   Double-click it and set the text in the button to `Change Background Color`.

3.   Select the button in the scene and click the Pin button to display the constraints editor. Set the following constraints:

➤   The width of the button should be 210.

➤   The height of the button should be 40.

4.   Change the background color for the button to a dark gray color so that it is visible against a white background.

5.   Select the button in the scene and click the Align button to display the alignment constraint editor. Add two constrains to center the button both horizontally and vertically (see Figure 12-5).

6.   Update the frames to match the constraints you have set.

➤   Click on the View controller item in the dock above the storyboard scene. This is the first of the three icons located directly above the selected storyboard scene.

➤   Select Editor ➪ Resolve Auto Layout Issues ➪ Update Frames.

Your storyboard should resemble Figure 12-6.

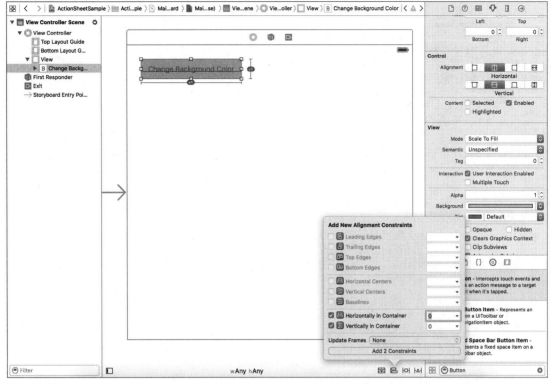

FIGURE 12-5

➤ Create an action in the `ViewController.swift` file and connect it with the Touch Up Inside event of the Change Background Color button.

1. Select the storyboard in the project navigator.

2. Right-click the Change Background Color button in the scene to display its context menu, and drag from the circle beside the Touch Up Inside item to an empty line in the `ViewController.swift` file.

3. Name the new action method `onPresentActionSheet`.

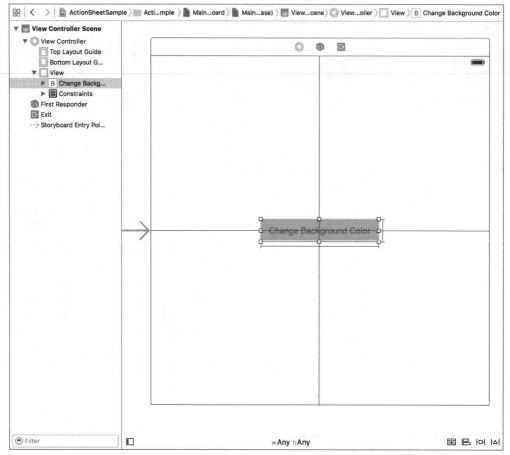

FIGURE 12-6

4. Click the `ViewController.swift` file in the project navigator to open it.

5. Add the following code to the implementation of the `onPresentActionSheet` method:

```
let alert = UIAlertController(title: "Change background color",
        message: "Select a color",
        preferredStyle: UIAlertControllerStyle.ActionSheet)

    alert.addAction(UIAlertAction(title: "Red",
        style: UIAlertActionStyle.Default,
        handler: { (action: UIAlertAction) -> Void in
        self.view.backgroundColor = UIColor.redColor()
}))

    alert.addAction(UIAlertAction(title: "Green",
        style: UIAlertActionStyle.Default,
        handler: { (action: UIAlertAction) -> Void in
            self.view.backgroundColor = UIColor.greenColor()
```

```
    }))

    alert.addAction(UIAlertAction(title: "Blue",
        style: UIAlertActionStyle.Default,
        handler: { (action: UIAlertAction) -> Void in
            self.view.backgroundColor = UIColor.blueColor()
    }))

    alert.addAction(UIAlertAction(title: "Yellow",
        style: UIAlertActionStyle.Default,
        handler: { (action: UIAlertAction) -> Void in
            self.view.backgroundColor = UIColor.yellowColor()
    }))

    alert.addAction(UIAlertAction(title: "Cancel",
        style: UIAlertActionStyle.Cancel,
        handler:nil))


    self.presentViewController(alert, animated: true, completion: nil)
```

➤ Test your app in the iOS Simulator.

Click the Run button in the Xcode toolbar. Alternatively, you can use the Project ➪ Run menu item.

REFERENCE *To see some of the examples from this lesson, watch the Lesson 12 video online at* www.wrox.com/go/swiftiosvid.

13

Adding Images to Your View

The UIKit framework provides classes that enable you to represent and display images. In this lesson, you learn how to use the `UIImage` and `UIImageView` classes.

THE UIIMAGE CLASS

A `UIImage` object represents image data that has either been read from a file or created using Quartz primitives. Instances are immutable. Thus, their properties can't be changed once they have been created. `UIImage` instances do not provide access to the underlying image data, but do enable you to retrieve a PNG or JPEG image representation in an `NSData` object.

Images generally require large amounts of memory to store, and you should avoid creating image objects larger than 4096 x 4096 pixels. To load an image from a file into a `UIImage` object, you first need to ensure the file is in one of the formats listed in Table 13-1.

TABLE 13-1: UIImage Supported File Formats

DESCRIPTION	FILE EXTENSIONS
Portable Network Graphics	`.png`
Joint Photographic Experts Group	`.jpeg`, `.jpg`
Graphics Interchange Format	`.gif`
Windows Device Independent Bitmap	`.bmp`
Tagged Image File Format	`.tif`, `.tiff`

You also need to ensure that the file is part of the project's asset catalog. To access the asset catalog for your project, simply click on the `Assets.xcassets` file in the Project Explorer (see Figure 13-1).

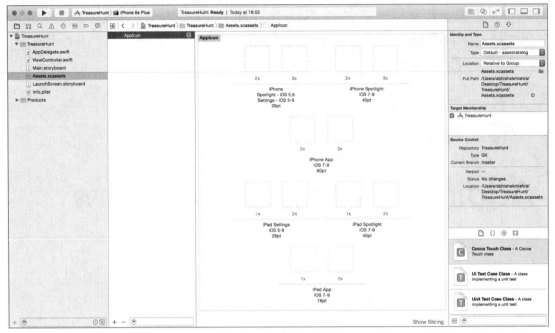

FIGURE 13-1

An asset catalog lets you keep all the images in your project in one place and access them conveniently. An asset catalog can contain the following:

➤ **Image sets:** An image set contains all the versions of an image, at different sizes to support different device scale factors.

➤ **App icons:** An app icon contains the application icon in different sizes. The application icon is used to represent the application on the iOS home screen, settings app, spotlight results, and the app store.

➤ **Launch images:** A launch image is a placeholder image used by iOS to stand in place of an application while the application is being loaded in the background. Once the application is loaded, iOS swaps the static launch image with the application's first screen. You will need to provide the launch image in different sizes.

Each image set in an asset catalog has a unique name that can be used to refer to the asset from both the Interface editor and code. To add a new image set to an asset catalog, select Editor ➪ New Image Set. Double-click the new image set entry within the asset catalog to rename it.

For any given image set, you must provide at least one image. It is highly recommended that you provide multiple versions at different sizes. When you create a new image asset, you can provide three sizes of the image (see Figure 13-2).

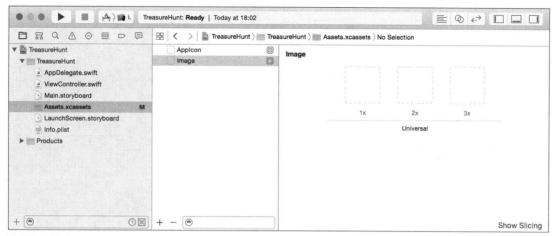

FIGURE 13-2

The base version of the image is called the 1x version, and is used when your app is running on a non-retina device. The only non-retina devices that are supported under iOS9 are the early generation iPads. To support retina devices, you provide an image that is twice the size of the base (non-retina) version. This larger image is called the 2x version. When the iPhone 6Plus was introduced with its larger screen size, a third larger image size was introduced into the mix to support this device. This larger image size, which is only used with the iPhone 6 Plus, is called the 3x version and is three times as large as the base 1x version.

Alternately, you can provide device-specific sizes by selecting Device Specific in the Devices dropdown of the Attribute Editor (see Figure 13-3).

If you have an image set called `cat` and want to load it into a `UIImage` object, you use the following code:

```
let catImage:UIImage! = UIImage(named: "cat")
```

This code uses one of the constructors of the `UIImage` class, which in turn implements an internal system cache. Thus, if you were to use this method to repeatedly load the same image file, the image data would be loaded only once and shared between the `UIImage` instances.

Loading images from your application bundle is not the only way to use `UIImage` objects. You can also create one from an online data source by downloading the data available at the URL into an `NSData` object and then instantiating a `UIImage` using an overloaded constructor that takes an `NSData` variable as input.

The following code snippet shows how to do this synchronously, but in production code, you should try and download any data from the web, including images, asynchronously. Downloading images asynchronously is an advanced topic and is not covered in this book.

```
let url = NSURL(string:"http://...")
let data = NSData(contentsOfURL: url!)
let image:UIImage! = UIImage(data: data!)
```

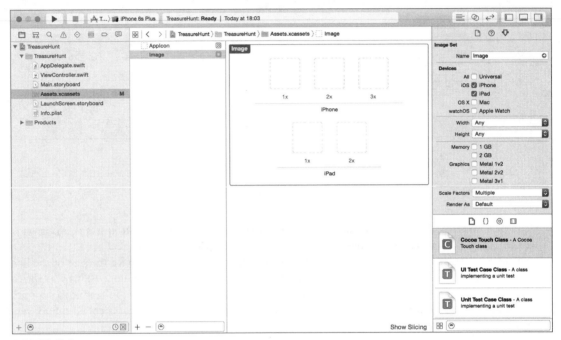

FIGURE 13-3

THE UIIMAGEVIEW CLASS

A `UIImageView` object provides a container for displaying either a single `UIImage` object or an animated series of `UIImage` objects. To add a `UIImageView` object to a view controller or storyboard scene, simply drag an Image View object from the Object library (see Figure 13-4).

To set up the default image displayed in the image view, simply select an image from the project's asset catalog for the `image` property in the Attribute inspector (see Figure 13-5).

If you wish to display a `UIImage` object in an image view programmatically, you need to create an outlet for the image view in the view controller class and set up its `image` property as follows:

```
imageView.image = UIImage(named: "cat")
```

To use a `UIImageView` object to perform simple frame animation, simply provide an array of `UIImage` objects in the image view's `animationImages` property as follows:

```
let animationImageList:[AnyObject] = [
    UIImage(named: "frame1")!,
```

```
        UIImage(named: "frame2")!,
        UIImage(named: "frame3")!,
        UIImage(named: "frame4")!
]

imageView.animationImages = animationImageList
```

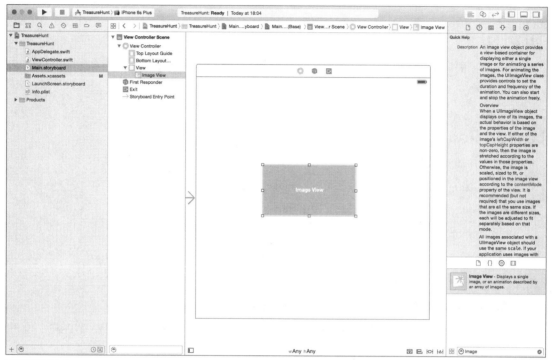

FIGURE 13-4

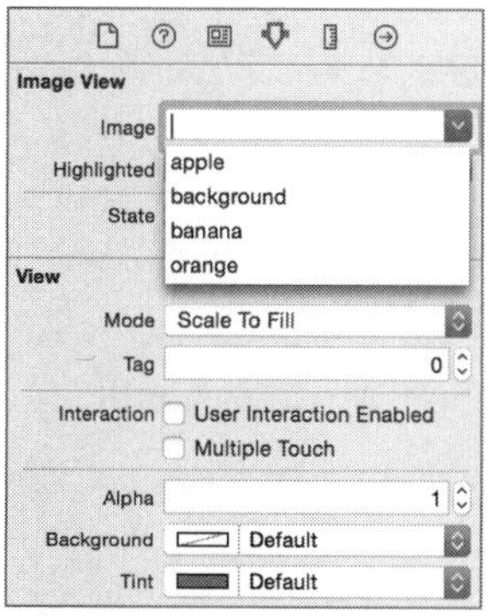

FIGURE 13-5

To kick off the animation, call the `startAnimating` method of the image view:

```
imageView.startAnimating()
```

Specify the duration of the animation in seconds, using the `animationDuration` property:

```
imageView.animationDuration = 2
```

TRY IT

In this Try It, you create a new Xcode project based on the Single View Application template called `TreasureHunt` that displays an image and asks the user to find an object in the image. When the user taps the object, a short congratulatory animation sequence is displayed.

Lesson Requirements

➤ Launch Xcode.

➤ Create a new project based on the Single View Application template.

➤ Edit the storyboard with Interface editor.

➤ Import image resources into the project.

➤ Add a `UILabel` instance to the default scene.

➤ Add two `UIImageView` instances to the default scene.

➤ Use a gesture recognizer to detect a tap on the image and display an alert view.

➤ If the tap occurs over a specific region of the image, display a congratulatory frame animation.

> **REFERENCE** *The code for this Try It is available at* www.wrox.com/go/ swiftios.

Hints

➤ To show the Object library, select View ⇨ Utilities ⇨ Show Object Library.

➤ To show the assistant editor, select View ⇨ Assistant Editor ⇨ Show Assistant Editor.

Step-by-Step

➤ Create a Single View Application in Xcode called `TreasureHunt`.

1. Launch Xcode and create a new application by selecting File ⇨ New ⇨ Project.

2. Select the Single View Application template from the list of iOS project templates.

3. In the project options screen, use the following values:

   ➤ **Product Name:** TreasureHunt

   ➤ **Organization Name:** your company

   ➤ **Organization Identifier:** com.yourcompany

   ➤ **Language:** Swift

   ➤ **Devices:** iPhone

   ➤ **Use Core Data:** Unchecked

   ➤ **Include Unit Tests:** Unchecked

   ➤ **Include UI Tests:** Unchecked

4. Save the project onto your hard disk.

➤ Add image resources to your project.

1. Ensure the project navigator is visible. To show it, select View ➪ Navigators ➪ Show Project Navigator.

2. Open the `Assets.xcassets` file by clicking on it in the project navigator.

3. Navigate to the `Images` folder in this chapter's resources from the website.

4. Create a new image set by selecting Editor ➪ New Image Set and name this new image set `beads`.

5. Drag the `beads1x.png`, `beads2x.png`, and `beads3x.png` images from this chapter's resources into the appropriate placeholders in the image set.

6. Create a new Image set by selecting Editor ➪ New Image Set and name this new image set `animframe1`.

7. Drag the `animframe1_1x.png`, `animframe1_2x.png`, and `animframe1_3x.png` images from this chapter's resources into the appropriate placeholders in the image set.

8. Similarly, create new image sets called `animframe2`, `animframe3`, `animframe4`, `anim-frame5`, and `animframe6`, and use the appropriate images from this chapter's resources folder.

➤ Add a `UILabel` instance to the default scene.

1. Open the `MainStoryboard.storyboard` file in Interface Builder.

2. Ensure the Object library is visible. To show it, select View ➪ Utilities ➪ Show Object Library.

3. From the Object library, drag and drop a Label object onto the scene.

4. Use the Attribute inspector to set the Text attribute of the label to `Tap the blue bead!` To show the Attribute inspector, select View ➪ Utilities ➪ Show Attributes Inspector.

5. Select the label in the scene, and select Editor ⇨ Size to Fit Contents to ensure the label is large enough to show its contents.

6. Select the label in the scene and click the Align button to display the alignment constraint editor. Add a constraint to center the label horizontally.

7. Select the label in the scene and click the Pin button to display the constraints editor. Ensure the Constrain to margins options is unchecked and set the following constraint:

   ➤ The distance from the top of the label to the view should be 10.

8. Update the frames to match the constraints you have set.

   ➤ Click on the View controller item in the dock above the storyboard scene. This is the first of the three icons located directly above the selected storyboard scene.

   ➤ Select Editor ⇨ Resolve Auto Layout Issues ⇨ Update Frames.

➤ Add two `UIImageView` instances to the default scene.

1. From the Object library, drag and drop an Image View object onto the scene, and place it below the label.

2. Use the Attribute inspector to set the Image attribute of the image view to `bead`. To show the Attribute inspector, select View ⇨ Utilities ⇨ Show Attributes Inspector.

3. Using the Attribute inspector, set the View Mode attribute to Aspect Fill.

4. Select the image view in the scene, and select Editor ⇨ Size to Fit Contents to ensure the image view is large enough to show its image.

5. Select the image view in the scene and click the Align button to display the alignment constraint editor. Add a constraint to center the image view horizontally.

6. Select the image view in the scene and click the Pin button to display the constraints editor. Ensure the Constrain to margins options is unchecked and set the following constraint:

   ➤ The vertical distance between the label and the image view should be 10.

7. Update the frames to match the constraints you have set.

   ➤ Click on the View controller item in the dock above the storyboard scene. This is the first of the three icons located directly above the selected storyboard scene.

   ➤ Select Editor ⇨ Resolve Auto Layout Issues ⇨ Update Frames.

8. Use the assistant editor to create an outlet in the view controller class called `large Image` and connect the image view to it.

9. From the Object library, drag and drop a second Image View object to the scene.

10. Use the Attribute inspector to set the Image attribute of the image view to `animframe1`. To show the Attribute inspector, select View ⇨ Utilities ⇨ Show Attributes Inspector.

11. Using the Attribute inspector, set the View Mode attribute to Aspect Fill.

12. Select the image view in the scene and click the Align button to display the alignment constraint editor. Add a couple of constrains to center the image view horizontally and vertically.

13. Update the frames to match the constraints you have set.

14. Use the Assistant editor to create an outlet in the view controller class called `animated Image` and connect the image view to it.

➤ Add a tap gesture recognizer and use it to show an animated image sequence when the blue bead is tapped. Gesture recognizers are covered in detail in Lesson 21.

1. Update the `viewDidLoad` method of the view controller class to resemble the following:

```
override func viewDidLoad() {

super.viewDidLoad()

// install tap gestue recognizer.
let tapRecognizer = UITapGestureRecognizer(target: self,
                    action:"handleTap:")

tapRecognizer.cancelsTouchesInView = false
self.view.addGestureRecognizer(tapRecognizer)

// setup animatedImage
let frameArray:[UIImage] = [
    UIImage(named: "animframe1")!,
    UIImage(named: "animframe2")!,
    UIImage(named: "animframe3")!,
    UIImage(named: "animframe4")!,
    UIImage(named: "animframe5")!,
    UIImage(named: "animframe6")!
]

animatedImage.animationImages = frameArray
animatedImage.animationDuration = 0.5
animatedImage.animationRepeatCount = 1
animatedImage.userInteractionEnabled = false
animatedImage.hidden = true
}
```

2. Add the following method to the `ViewController.swift` file:

```
func handleTap(sender:UITapGestureRecognizer) {

    let startLocation:CGPoint =
```

```
        sender.locationInView(self.largeImage)

        let scaleFactor = self.largeImage.frame.size.height / 430.0;

        if ((startLocation.y >= 211 * scaleFactor) &&
            (startLocation.y <= (211 + 104) * scaleFactor))
        {
            animatedImage.hidden = false
            animatedImage.startAnimating()
        }
    }
}
```

➤   Test your app in the iOS Simulator.

Click the Run button in the Xcode toolbar. Alternatively, you can select Project ⇨ Run.

REFERENCE *To see some of the examples from this lesson, watch the Lesson 13 video online at* www.wrox.com/go/swiftiosvideo.

14

Pickers

A picker view is a user interface component that enables a user to pick a value from a set of related values using a slot machine–style interface. An example is shown in Figure 14-1.

Mountain View
Sunnyvale
Cupertino
Santa Clara
San Jose

FIGURE 14-1

Each wheel of the picker view is called a component, and it is fairly common to have picker view with multiple components. Each component can have a different number of items in it (see Figure 14-2).

A picker view is encapsulated by the UIPickerView class, which is part of the UIKit framework. Apple provides a special picker for allowing the user to select date and time. This component is called the date picker.

A picker requires a data source object and a delegate object. The data source object is one that implements the UIPickerViewDataSource protocol and provides information on the number of components, and rows-per-component, of the picker.

New York	Hotels
London	Cinemas
Paris	**Theaters**
Chicago	Airports
	Museums

FIGURE 14-2

The delegate object implements the UIPickerViewDelegate protocol and has methods that are called when the current selection in a component has changed.

The delegate and data source objects could both be the same object, and in many cases the duties of these objects are performed by the view controller. However, it is very possible for them to be independent objects.

Creating a picker view is a simple matter of dragging the Picker View component from the Object library onto your storyboard or XIB file (see Figure 14-3) and then creating an appropriate outlet in your view controller class using the assistant editor.

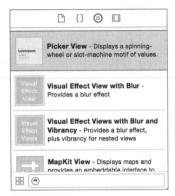

FIGURE 14-3

The delegate and data source objects can be set up using the Interface editor (see Figure 14-4) or by setting up the `delegate` and `dataSource` properties in code.

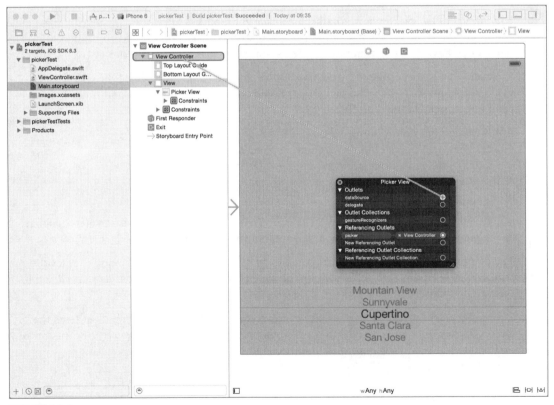

FIGURE 14-4

The following code snippet assumes `pickerView` is an outlet that is connected to a `UIPickerView` instance and sets up the view controller to be the delegate and the data source object:

```
override func viewDidLoad() {

    super.viewDidLoad()

    pickerView.delegate = self
    pickerView.dataSource = self
}
```

The `UIPickerViewDataSource` protocol defines two methods:

```
func numberOfComponentsInPickerView(pickerView: UIPickerView) -> Int

func pickerView(pickerView: UIPickerView,
    numberOfRowsInComponent component: Int) -> Int
```

You must return the number of components in the picker view from the `numberOfComponents InPickerView` method. The number of rows in each component should be returned by the `pickerView(pickerView, numberOfRowsInComponent)` method. For example, a two-component picker can be set up as follows:

```
// returns the number of 'columns' to display.
func numberOfComponentsInPickerView(pickerView: UIPickerView) -> Int
{
    return 2
}

// returns the # of rows in each component..
func pickerView(pickerView: UIPickerView,
    numberOfRowsInComponent component: Int) -> Int
{
    if component == 0
    {
        return cities.count
    }
    else
    {
        return placesOfInterest.count
    }
}
```

The following are the most commonly used `UIPickerViewDelegate` methods:

```
func pickerView(pickerView: UIPickerView,
    titleForRow row: Int,
     forComponent component: Int) -> String!

func pickerView(pickerView: UIPickerView,
    didSelectRow row: Int,
    inComponent component: Int)
```

The text to be displayed in each row of each component is to be returned by the `pickerView` (`pickerView`, `titleForRow`, `forComponent`) delegate method. When the user selects a row in any component of the picker, your delegate object's `pickerView`(`pickerView`, `didSelectRow`, `inComponent`) method will be called.

Typically, the data for each component of a picker view is stored in an array. Assuming that `cities` and `placesOfInterest` are arrays of `String` objects that contain the data for the two components of a picker view, the `pickerView`(`pickerView`, `titleForRow`, `forComponent`) delegate method can be implemented as follows:

```
var cities = ["New York","London","Paris","Chicago"]

var placesOfInterest = ["Hotels","Cinemas","Theaters","Airports","Museums","Clubs"]

func pickerView(pickerView: UIPickerView,
    titleForRow row: Int,
    forComponent component: Int) -> String!
{
    if component == 0
    {
        return cities[row]
    }
    else
    {
        return placesOfInterest[row]
    }
}
```

ARRAYS IN SWIFT

Arrays are one of two collection types provided in Swift (the other being the dictionary). An array is an ordered collection of similar objects, and each object in the array has an index. The index of the first object is zero.

If you create an array and assign it to a constant using the `let` keyword, that array will be *immutable*. This means that you cannot change the contents of that array after you have created it.

If, however, you create an array and assign it to a variable using the `var` keyword, then this array will have no such restriction. However, you must keep in mind that inserting/deleting objects from an array can be a time-consuming operation, and thus you should aim to use mutable arrays wherever possible.

To create an array variable instance, and add four string objects to it in the same step, you can use code similar to the following:

```
var cities:[String] = ["New York","London","Paris","Chicago"]
```

To retrieve an object at a specific index position, you can use the subscript operator (`[]`). Index numbers start from zero.

```
var someCity:String! = cities[0]
```

To retrieve the number of objects in an array, you can use the `count` method:

```
var arrayCount:int = cities.count
```

To add an element to the back of a mutable array, you can use the `append()` method:

```
cities.append("Tokyo")
```

To remove an object at a specific index position from a mutable array, you can use the `removeAtIndex` method.

DATE PICKERS

Although it is possible to create a picker view with several components to allow your user to enter a date, Apple provides a special user interface component for precisely this purpose. The date picker is a special picker that can be used to select dates and times. You can configure it to display only time, only date, or both date and time as shown in Figure 14-5.

FIGURE 14-5

The `UIDatePicker` class provides the functionality of a date picker, which is part of the UIKit framework. The `UIDatePicker` class privately uses a `UIPickerView` instance, but you cannot access this instance directly.

A date picker is much simpler to use than a picker view. For starters, it does not require you to provide a delegate or data source object. Creating a date picker is a simple matter of dragging the Date Picker component from the Object library onto a scene in your storyboard.

The *mode* of the date picker refers to whether it displays date, time, or both date and time. You can also specify the range of values that should be displayed by the date picker. Both these tasks can be accomplished by using the assistant editor (see Figure 14-6).

FIGURE 14-6

You can read the date currently selected in the picker by accessing the date picker's `date` property. The result is returned as an `NSDate` instance:

```
// get date from date picker
var pickerDate:NSDate! = datePicker.date
```

The date picker provides a `Value Changed` event that is fired when the user changes the selection in the picker. You can use the assistant editor to create and associate an action method in your view controller class with this event.

DATES IN SWIFT

Swift provides an `NSDate` class, instances of which represent a combined date and time value. To create an `NSDate` object that has the current date and time, use the following code:

```
let todaysDate:NSDate = NSDate()
```

To create an `NSDate` object dated at a specific interval of time from the current date, you can use the `NSDate(timeIntervalSinceNow)` method. This method requires a single argument, which is the number of seconds in the past or future from the current date. A positive number indicates a future date.

Thus, to create an `NSDate` object exactly 24 hours from the current date, you can use the following code:

```
let tomorrowsDate:NSDate = NSDate(timeIntervalSinceNow: 24 * 3600)
```

If you want to create an `NSDate` without reference to the current date, you can use the `NSDate(timeIntervalSinceReferenceDate)` method to create a date that is at a specified interval from January 1, 1970. The interval is specified in seconds.

`NSDate` instances also provide several useful methods to compare dates, including:

➤   `isEqualToDate`: Returns `true` if two `NSDate` instances are equal

➤   `earlierDate`: Returns the earlier of two `NSDate` objects

➤   `laterDate`: Returns the later of two `NSDate` objects

The following examples contain these methods:

```
let comparisonResult:Bool = pickerDate.isEqualToDate(todaysDate)

let firstDate:NSDate = pickerDate.earlierDate(todaysDate)
```

For information on `NSDate` objects, refer to the NSDate Class Reference at

```
https://developer.apple.com/library/prerelease/ios//
documentation/Cocoa/Reference/Foundation/Classes/NSDate_Class/
index.html
```

Creating a formatted representation of the contents of an `NSDate` object requires the use of another class: `NSDateFormatter`.

To use an `NSDateFormatter`, you need to first instantiate it and use the `setLocalizedDateFormatFromTemplate` method on the instance to specify the internal format used by the date formatter object. This internal format is specified as a string. Once a date formatter is instantiated, you can use it to create a textual representation of an `NSDate` object using the `stringFromDate` method. This is demonstrated in the following code:

```
let todaysDate:NSDate = NSDate()

var dateFormatter:NSDateFormatter = NSDateFormatter()
dateFormatter.setLocalizedDateFormatFromTemplate("MMMM d, yyyy")

let textualRepresentation:String = dateFormatter.stringFromDate
(todaysDate)
```

The format string consists of a series of characters that represent parts of a date and time. The characters themselves are case-sensitive. Some of the most common format strings are:

➤ `MMMM`: The full name of the month

➤ `d`: The day of the month

➤ `yyyy`: The four-digit year

➤ `hh`: Two-digit hour of the day

➤ `mm`: Two-digit minute

➤ `ss`: Two-digit second

➤ `a`: AM

➤ `p`: PM

continues

continued

For a complete list of format strings, refer to the Data Formatting Guide, available at

```
https://developer.apple.com/library/ios/documentation/Cocoa/
Conceptual/DataFormatting/Articles/dfDateFormatting10_4.html#//
apple_ref/doc/uid/TP40002369-SW1
```

For more information on the NSDateFormatter class, refer to the NSDateFormatter Class Reference, available at

```
https://developer.apple.com/library/ios/documentation/Cocoa/
Reference/Foundation/Classes/NSDateFormatter_Class/
```

CUSTOM PICKERS

Picker views do not have to be restricted to displaying text; in fact, they can just as easily display images, or a combination of images and text. In this section, you learn how to provide your own `UIView` subclasses for individual elements of a picker view, thus creating pickers that have images instead of text, as shown in Figure 14-7.

FIGURE 14-7

The key to implementing this functionality lies in three optional methods of the `UIPickerViewDelegate` protocol:

```
func pickerView(pickerView: UIPickerView,
    widthForComponent component: Int) -> CGFloat

func pickerView(pickerView: UIPickerView,
    rowHeightForComponent component: Int) -> CGFloat

func pickerView(pickerView: UIPickerView,
    viewForRow row: Int,
    forComponent component: Int,
    reusingView view: UIView!) -> UIView
```

You can customize the width of each picker component by returning an appropriate value from the `pickerView(pickerView, widthForComponent)` delegate method. If you do not implement this method, the picker view distributes the available width equally between its components.

The `pickerView(pickerView, rowHeightForComponent)` delegate method enables you to specify the height of each row in a given component. All rows in a component must have the same height.

You need to return a `UIView` subclass in the `pickerView(pickerView, viewForRow, forComponent, reusingView)` delegate method. This method's arguments include a reference to the picker view, the row, and the component number.

The view returned by this method can be an instance of an existing UIKit class such as `UIImageView` or `UILabel`. You can also provide instances of your own `UIView` subclass in which you have implemented custom drawing logic. Subclassing `UIView` is outside the scope of this book.

The last argument of this delegate method is a reference to an existing `UIView` object. If this argument is not nil, it will refer to one of the view objects provided by this method on a previous occasion. You should try to reuse it instead of creating one from scratch.

When you scroll a row in one of the components off the screen, the picker does not immediately destroy the corresponding view; instead it adds it to an internal cache of "reusable views." When it is time to display a new row in the same component, the picker provides one of these cached views to your delegate method, encouraging you to reuse it instead of instantiating a fresh copy.

TRY IT

In this Try It, you create a new Xcode project based on the Single View Application template called `CustomPickerTest`, which displays three-component custom picker view with images of fruits.

Lesson Requirements

➤ Launch Xcode.

➤ Create a new project based on the Single View Application template.

➤ Edit the storyboard with Interface Builder.

➤ Import image resources into the project.

➤ Add a picker view and create an outlet for it in the view controller class.

➤ Add three data arrays with the names of fruits to be displayed for each picker component in the view controller class and populate them in the `viewDidLoad` method.

➤ Add a `Dictionary` object that maps names of fruits to image filenames.

➤ Implement the `UIPickerViewDataSource` and `UIPickerViewDelegate` protocols in your view controller class.

Hints

➤ To show the Object library, select View ➪ Utilities ➪ Show Object Library.

➤ To show the assistant editor, select View ➪ Assistant Editor ➪ Show Assistant Editor.

➤ A `Dictionary` object contains a list of mappings between keys and values. Each key in a dictionary is unique.

➤ Use the `let` keyword to create an array whose contents will not change.

> **REFERENCE** *The code for this Try It is available at* `www.wrox.com/go/`
> `swiftios.`

Step-by-Step

➤ Create a Single View Application in Xcode called `CustomPickerTest`.

1. Launch Xcode and create a new application by selecting File ➪ New ➪ Project.

2. Select the Single View Application template from the list of iOS project templates.

3. In the project options screen, use the following values:

 ➤ **Product Name:** CustomPickerTest

 ➤ **Organization Name:** your company

 ➤ **Organization Identifier:** com.yourcompany

 ➤ **Language:** Swift

 ➤ **Devices:** iPhone

 ➤ **Use Core Data:** Unchecked

 ➤ **Include Unit Tests:** Unchecked

 ➤ **Include UI Tests:** Unchecked

4. Save the project onto your hard disk.

➤ Add image resources to your project.

1. Ensure the project navigator is visible. To show it, select View ➪ Navigators ➪ Show Project Navigator.

2. Open the `Assets.xcassets` file by clicking on it in the project navigator.

3. Navigate to the `Images` folder in this chapter's downloads from the website.

4. Create a new Image set by selecting Editor ➪ New Image Set and name this new image set `appleImages`.

5. Drag the `apple1x.png`, `apple2x.png`, and `apple3x.png` images from this chapter's resources into the appropriate placeholders in the image set.

6. Similarly, create new image sets called `bananaImages`, `lemonImages`, `orangeImages`, `peachImages`, `pearImages`, and `pineappleImages` and use the appropriate images from this chapter's resources folder.

➤ Add a `UIPickerView` instance to the default scene.

1. Open the `MainStoryboard.storyboard` file in Interface Builder.

2. Ensure the Object library is visible. To show it, select View ➪ Utilities ➪ Show Object Library.

3. From the Object library, drag and drop a Picker View object onto the scene.

4. Select the picker view in the scene and click the Align button to display the alignment constraint editor. Add a constraint to center the picker view horizontally.

5. Select the picker view in the scene and click the Pin button to display the constraints editor. Ensure the Constrain to margins options is unchecked, and set the following constraints:

➤ The distance from the top of the picker to the view should be 0.

➤ The height of the picker should be 162.

6. Update the frames to match the constraints you have set.

➤ Click on the View controller item in the dock above the storyboard scene. This is the first of the three icons located directly above the selected storyboard scene.

➤ Select Editor ➪ Resolve Auto Layout Issues ➪ Update Frames.

7. Use the assistant editor to create an outlet in the view controller class called `pickerView` and connect the picker to it.

8. Set up the view controller as the delegate and data source of the picker.

➤ Ctrl+Click on the picker object in the storyboard scene to reveal a popup menu.

➤ Drag from the circle beside the `delegate` item in the popup menu onto the view controller object in the dock (see figure 14-8).

➤ Drag from the circle beside the `dataSource` item in the popup menu onto the view controller object in the dock.

➤ Add a `UILabel` instance to the default scene.

1. From the Object library, drag and drop a Label object onto the scene and position it beneath the picker.

2. Select the label and center it horizontally in the storyboard by selecting Editor ➪ Align ➪ Horizontal Center In Container.

3. Select the label in the scene and select Editor ➪ Size to Fit Contents to ensure the label is large enough to show its contents.

4. Add the following constraints using the pin constraints dialog box for the label:

➤ Ensure the Constrain to margins option is unchecked.

➤ The distance from the top of the label to the view = 32.

5. Update the frames to match the constraints you have set.

➤ Click on the View controller item in the dock above the storyboard scene. This is the first of the three icons located directly above the selected storyboard scene.

➤ Select Editor ⇨ Resolve Auto Layout Issues ⇨ Update Frames.

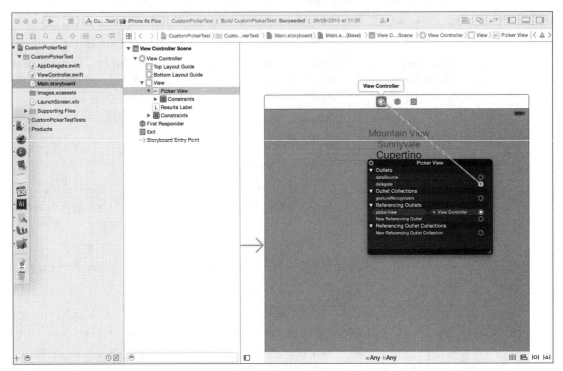

FIGURE 14-8

6. Use the assistant editor to create an outlet in the view controller class called `results-Label` and connect the label to it.

➤ Add three arrays called `dataForComponent1`, `dataForComponent2`, and `dataForComponent3` to the view controller class.

```
let dataForComponent1:[String] = ["Apple", "Banana", "Lemon",
                                  "Orange", "Peach", "Pear",
                                  "Pineapple"]

let dataForComponent2:[String] = ["Banana", "Orange", "Pear",
                                  "Apple", "Pineapple", "Lemon",
                                  "Peach"]

let dataForComponent3:[String] = ["Pear", "Peach", "Lemon",
                                  "Pineapple", "Apple", "Banana",
                                  "Orange"]
```

➤ Add a dictionary `nameToImageMapping` to the view controller class.

```
let nameToImageMapping:[String:String] = ["Apple":"appleImages",
                                          "Banana":"bananaImages",
                                          "Lemon":"lemonImages",
                                          "Orange":"orangeImages",
                                          "Peach":"peachImages",
                                          "Pear":"pearImages",
                                          "Pineapple":"pineappleImages"]
```

➤ Add the following code to your view controller's `viewDidLoad` method to set up the initial text of the `UILabel` instance `resultsLabel`:

```
resultsLabel.text = "Match the fruits in each row!";
```

➤ Have your view controller class conform to the `UIPickerViewDataSource` and `UIPickerViewDelegate` protocols by modifying its declaration to the following:

```
class ViewController: UIViewController,
                      UIPickerViewDataSource,
                      UIPickerViewDelegate {
```

At this point, your compiler will issue an error that the view controller does not conform to the `UIPickerViewDataSource` and `UIPickerViewDelegate` protocols. This is because these protocols contain mandatory methods that must be implemented by a conforming class. We will implement these methods over the next few steps; for the moment ignore this error.

➤ Your view controller class should now resemble the following:

```
class ViewController: UIViewController,
                      UIPickerViewDataSource,
                      UIPickerViewDelegate {

    @IBOutlet weak var pickerView: UIPickerView!
    @IBOutlet weak var resultsLabel: UILabel!

    let dataForComponent1:[String] = ["Apple", "Banana", "Lemon",
                                      "Orange", "Peach", "Pear",
                                      "Pineapple"]

    let dataForComponent2:[String] = ["Banana", "Orange", "Pear",
                                      "Apple", "Pineapple", "Lemon",
                                      "Peach"]

    let dataForComponent3:[String] = ["Pear", "Peach", "Lemon",
                                      "Pineapple", "Apple", "Banana",
                                      "Orange"]


    let nameToImageMapping:[String:String] = ["Apple":"appleImages",
                                              "Banana":"bananaImages",
                                              "Lemon":"lemonImages",
                                              "Orange":"orangeImages",
                                              "Peach":"peachImages",
                                              "Pear":"pearImages",
                                              "Pineapple":"pineappleImages"]
```

```
override func viewDidLoad() {
    super.viewDidLoad()
}

override func didReceiveMemoryWarning() {
    super.didReceiveMemoryWarning()
}
```

}

➤ Implement the `numberOfComponentsInPickerView()` delegate method in your view controller as follows:

```
func numberOfComponentsInPickerView(pickerView: UIPickerView) -> Int
{
    return 3
}
```

This delegate method must return the number of columns in the picker view. In this project, you return 3 as the project builds a three-column picker.

➤ Implement the `pickerView(pickerView, numberOfRowsInComponent)` data source method in your view controller as follows:

```
func pickerView(pickerView: UIPickerView,
numberOfRowsInComponent component: Int) -> Int
{
    if component == 0
    {
        return dataForComponent1.count
    }
    else if component == 1
    {
        return dataForComponent2.count
    }
    else
    {
        return dataForComponent3.count
    }
}
```

This data source method must return the number of rows in each component of the picker. In this project, since the data for each component is stored in an array, the snippet simply returns the number of elements in the array for the each component.

➤ Implement the `pickerView(pickerView, rowHeightForComponent)` delegate method in your view controller as follows:

```
func pickerView(pickerView: UIPickerView,
rowHeightForComponent component: Int) -> CGFloat
{
    return 50
}
```

This delegate method must return the height of each row in a given component of the picker. In this project, you return 50 as the row height is the same for all three components of the picker.

➤ Implement the `pickerView(pickerViewm viewForRow, forComponent, reusingView)` delegate method in your view controller as follows:

```swift
func pickerView(pickerView: UIPickerView,
viewForRow row: Int,
forComponent component: Int,
reusingView view: UIView!) -> UIView
{
    // get the fruit name
    var keyString:String? = nil

    if component == 0
    {
        keyString = dataForComponent1[row]
    }
    else if component == 1
    {
        keyString = dataForComponent2[row]
    }
    else if component == 2
    {
        keyString = dataForComponent3[row]
    }

    var imageFileName:String? = nameToImageMapping[keyString!]

    if view == nil
    {
        return UIImageView(image:UIImage(named: imageFileName!));
    }

    var imageView:UIImageView = view as! UIImageView

    imageView.image = UIImage(named: imageFileName!)

    return view;
}
```

This delegate method is called by the picker view when it needs a view for a specific column and row position. The column and row position for which a view is required are passed in as parameters to the delegate method.

In this snippet you query the underlying data array for the requested component to retrieve the name of the fruit that should be displayed in the specified column and row position. Once you have the name of the fruit, you obtain the name of an image in the asset bundle that corresponds to the fruit by using the `nameToImageMapping` dictionary.

The third parameter to this delegate method is a `UIView` optional. If this parameter is not `nil`, then you need to reuse it (modify its contents in some way) and return it to the picker. If the parameter is `nil` you need to create a new view and return the new view to the picker. This is achieved in the final part of the code snippet:

```swift
if view == nil{
    return UIImageView(image:UIImage(named: imageFileName!));
}

var imageView:UIImageView = view as! UIImageView
```

```
        imageView.image = UIImage(named: imageFileName!)
        return view;
```

➤ Implement the `pickerView:didSelectRow:inComponent:` delegate method in your view
controller as follows:

```
func pickerView(pickerView: UIPickerView,
didSelectRow row: Int,
inComponent component: Int)
{
    // get selected fruit in each component
    var selectedRowInComponent1 = pickerView.selectedRowInComponent(0)
    var fruitInComponent1:String! =
dataForComponent1[selectedRowInComponent1]

    var selectedRowInComponent2 = pickerView.selectedRowInComponent(1)
    var fruitInComponent2:String! =
dataForComponent2[selectedRowInComponent2]

    var selectedRowInComponent3 = pickerView.selectedRowInComponent(2)
    var fruitInComponent3 = dataForComponent3[selectedRowInComponent3]

    // if the same fruit is selected in
    // each row, then show a message
    if fruitInComponent1 == fruitInComponent2 &&
       fruitInComponent2 == fruitInComponent3
    {
        resultsLabel.text = "Jackpot!";
    }
    else
    {
        resultsLabel.text = "Match the fruits in each row!";
    }
}
```

This delegate method is called when the user moves one of the wheels of the picker to
update the current selection in the picker. The picker passes the row and column whose
value has been changed as parameters to this delegate method.

In this snippet you retrieve the name of the fruit selected in each component of the picker.
If the same fruit has been selected in each component of the picker, you display a message
on the screen.

➤ Test your app in the iOS Simulator.

1. Click the Run button in the Xcode toolbar. Alternatively, you can select Project ➪ Run.

2. Change the selection in the components of the picker. If you get three fruits of the same
   kind in the central row, you should see the *Jackpot!* message.

REFERENCE To see some of the examples from this lesson, watch the Lesson 14
video online at www.wrox.com/go/swiftiosvideo.

15

Navigation Controllers

A navigation controller is a class that manages the presentation of a stack of view controllers one at a time. The topmost item on the stack is visible, and users can navigate down the stack one view controller at a time. Whenever a view controller is pushed on—or off the navigation controller's stack—iOS applies an appropriate slide animation automatically. Navigation controllers are implemented in the UINavigationController class in the UIKit framework and can be found in several standard applications such as the iOS Mail, and Settings apps.

ADDING A NAVIGATION CONTROLLER TO A STORYBOARD

To create a navigation controller using the interface editor, simply select the storyboard scene that you want to use as the root view controller of the navigation stack and select Editor ⇨ Embed In ⇨ Navigation Controller. You can optionally drag a Navigation Controller object from the Object library to the storyboard. When you create a navigation controller in this manner, Xcode creates a default scene that is set up to act as the root view controller for the navigation controller (see Figure 15-1).

In most cases, you will want to use one of the existing scenes in the storyboard as the root view controller. To do this, first select the Relationship Segue between the navigation controller and the default root view controller and delete it (see Figure 15-2).

Now select the navigation controller scene, hold down the Ctrl key, and drag from the navigation controller scene to whatever scene you want to use as the root view controller. When you release the mouse pointer you will be presented with a list of segue types to use; select Relationship Segue (see Figure 15-3).

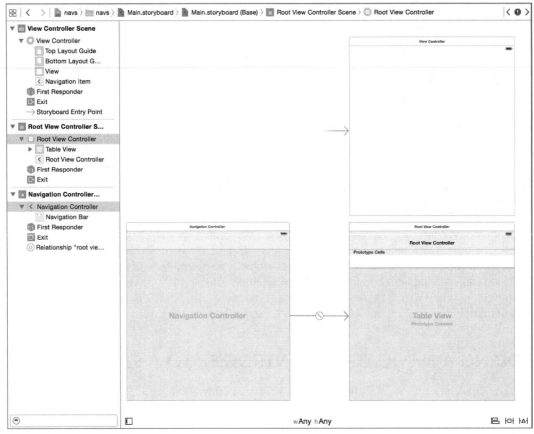

FIGURE 15-1

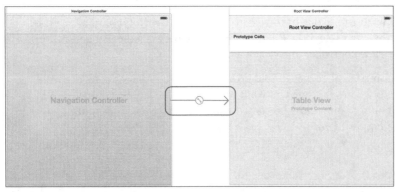

FIGURE 15-2

You can now delete the previous root view controller scene, which is now unused if you wish. If the navigation controller is going to be the primary view controller of your application, then you must ensure that the Is Initial View Controller option in the Attribute Editor is selected for the navigation controller (see Figure 15-4).

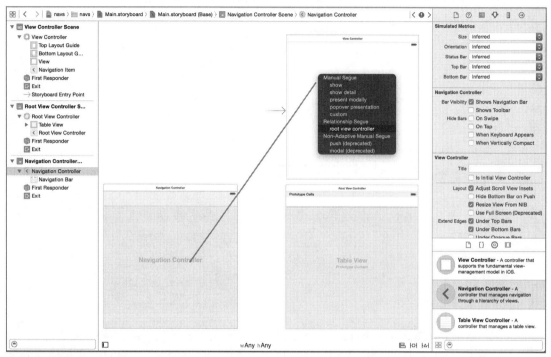

FIGURE 15-3

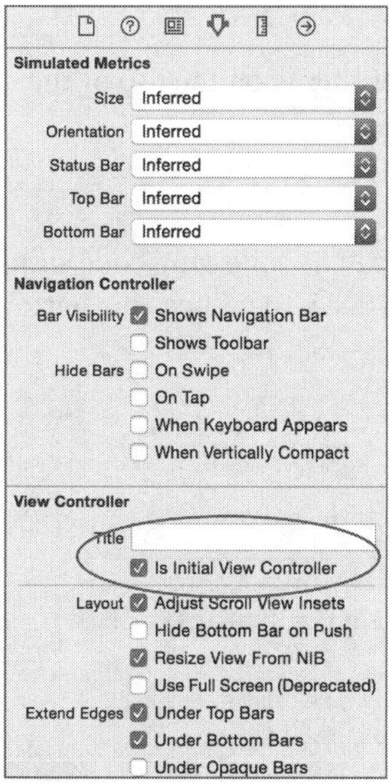

FIGURE 15-4

THE NAVIGATION CONTROLLER INTERFACE

A navigation controller contains two key components, as shown in Figure 15-1.

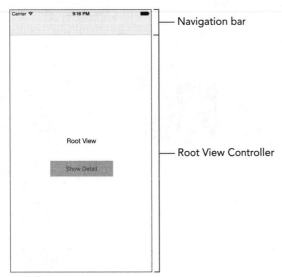

— Navigation bar

— Root View Controller

FIGURE 15-5

➤   **Navigation bar:** This is the horizontal header on the top of the view, just below the status bar; it typically contains the title of the view being displayed and an optional back button.

➤   **Root view controller:** This is the base view controller at the bottom of the navigation stack; it cannot be removed from the navigation controller. When this view controller is visible, there is no back button available to the user.

To set the title that is displayed in the navigation bar when a view controller is on the top of the stack, you can set up the view controller's title property as follows:

```
self.title = "Root View";
```

You can add buttons to the navigation bar that perform custom actions. The following code snippet adds a Share button to the right side of the navigation bar (see Figure 15-6). When this button is tapped, the onShare method will be called.

```
override func viewDidLoad()
{
    super.viewDidLoad()

    self.title = "Root View";

    let shareButton:UIBarButtonItem = UIBarButtonItem(barButtonSystemItem:
        UIBarButtonSystemItem.Action,
        target: self,
        action: "onShare:")
```

```
        self.navigationItem.setRightBarButtonItem(shareButton, animated: false)

    }

    func onShare(sender: UIBarButtonItem) {

    }
```

FIGURE 15-6

You can add and remove view controllers onto the navigation stack by using the following methods:

```
pushViewController(viewController, animated)
popViewControllerAnimated(animated)
```

The `UINavigationController` class provides the following two additional methods that enable you to pop all view controllers down to a specific view controller:

```
popToRootViewControllerAnimated(animated: Bool)
popToViewController(viewController, animated)
```

TRY IT

In this Try It, you create a new Xcode project based on the Single View Application template called `NavigationControllerTest` that uses a navigation controller to manage a hierarchy of views.

> **REFERENCE** *The code for this Try It is available at* www.wrox.com/go/ swiftios.

Lesson Requirements

➤ Launch Xcode.

➤ Create a new project based on the Single View Application template.

➤ Edit the storyboard with Interface Builder.

➤ Embed the default storyboard scene in a navigation controller.

➤ Add a button to the default scene.

➤ Add a second scene to the storyboard.

➤ Create a segue from the button in the first scene to the second scene.

Hints

➤ To show the Object library, select View ➪ Utilities ➪ Show Object Library.

➤ To show the assistant editor, select View ➪ Assistant Editor Show Assistant Editor.

Step-by-Step

➤ Create a Single View Application in Xcode called `NavigationControllerTest`.

1. Launch Xcode and create a new application by selecting File ➪ New ➪ Project.

2. Select the Single View Application template from the list of iOS project templates.

3. In the project options screen, use the following values:

    ➤ **Product Name:** NavigationControllerTest

    ➤ **Organization Name:** your company

    ➤ **Organization Identifier:** com.yourcompany

    ➤ **Language:** Swift

    ➤ **Devices:** iPhone

    ➤ **Use Core Data:** Unchecked

    ➤ **Include Unit Tests:** Unchecked

    ➤ **Include UI Tests:** Unchecked

4. Save the project onto your hard disk.

➤ Add a `UILabel` instance to the default scene.

1. From the Object library, drag and drop a Label object onto the scene and position it beneath the picker.

2. Edit the text displayed in the label to Root View.

3. Select the label in the scene and click the Align button to display the alignment constraint editor. Add a constraint to center the label horizontally.

4. Select the label in the scene and click the Align button to display the alignment constraint editor. Add a constraint to center the label vertically.

5. Select the label in the scene and select Editor ⇨ Size to Fit Contents to ensure the label is large enough to show its contents.

6. Update the frames to match the constraints you have set.

   ➤ Click on the View controller item in the dock above the storyboard scene. This is the first of the three icons located directly above the selected storyboard scene.

   ➤ Select Editor ⇨ Resolve Auto Layout Issues ⇨ Update Frames.

➤ Add a button to the storyboard.

   1. From the Object library, select a button and drop it onto the scene.

   2. Double-click the button and change the text displayed in it to `Show Detail`.

   3. Drag the button to position it near the center of the scene, beneath the label. The precise size or position does not matter.

   4. Use the Attribute inspector to change the background color of the button to a shade of gray. The background color attribute is located in the View subsection of the Attribute inspector; you may need to scroll down a little to access it.

   5. Ensure the button is selected; if it is not, simply click it once.

   6. Center the button horizontally by selecting Editor ⇨ Align ⇨ Horizontal Center in Container.

   7. Ensure the button is selected and use the Pin button to display the constraints editor popup.

      ➤ Pin the width of the button to 165.

      ➤ Pin the height of the button to 40.

      ➤ Pin the distance between the button and the label to 50.

      ➤ Click the Add 3 Constraints button to dismiss the constraints editor popup.

   8. Update the frames to match the constraints you have set.

      ➤ Click on the View controller item in the dock above the storyboard scene. This is the first of the three icons located directly above the selected storyboard scene.

      ➤ Select Editor ⇨ Resolve Auto Layout Issues ⇨ Update Frames.

➤ Embed the default scene in a navigation controller.

1. Click on the View controller item in the dock above the storyboard scene. This is the first of the three icons located directly above the selected storyboard scene.

2. Select Editor ⇨ Embed In ⇨ Navigation Controller to embed the default scene as the root view controller of a navigation controller. Your storyboard should resemble Figure 15-7.

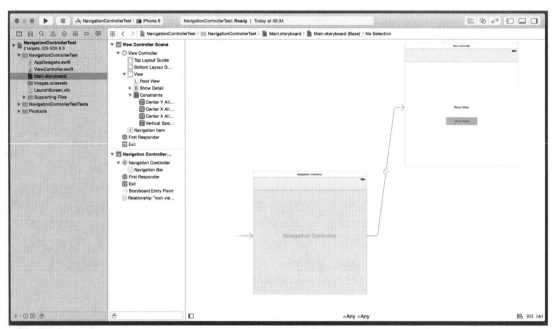

FIGURE 15-7

➤ Add a new subclass of `UIViewController` called `DetailViewController`.

1. Ensure the project navigator is visible.

2. Right-click the `NavigationControllerTest` group and select New File from the context menu.

3. Select the Cocoa Touch Class template and click Next.

4. Call the new class `DetailViewController` and ensure that the new class is a subclass of `UIViewController` by selecting `UIViewController` in the drop-down combo box.

5. Ensure that the Also create XIB file option is unchecked and click Next.

6. Select a folder where files should be created. It is best to accept the default location provided by Xcode.

➤ Create a new scene in the storyboard.

1. Ensure the `Main.storyboard` file is open. If it is not, then select it in the project navigator.

2. Drag a View Controller object from the Object library onto the storyboard canvas.

3. Double-click the canvas to zoom out.

4. Position the new scene alongside the original scene.

5. Select the new scene in the storyboard, select the View Controller object from the dock, and use the Identity inspector to change its Custom Class to DetailViewController. To show the Identity inspector, select View ⇨ Utilities ⇨ Show Identity inspector.

➤ Add a UILabel instance to the new scene.

1. From the Object library, drag and drop a Label object onto the scene and position it beneath the picker.

2. Edit the text displayed in the label to Detail View.

3. Select the label in the scene and click the Align button to display the alignment constraint editor. Add a constraint to center the label horizontally.

4. Select the label in the scene and click the Align button to display the alignment constraint editor. Add a constraint to center the label vertically.

5. Select the label in the scene and choose Editor ⇨ Size to Fit Contents to ensure the label is large enough to show its contents.

6. Update the frames to match the constraints you have set.

➤ Click on the View controller item in the dock above the storyboard scene. This is the first of the three icons located directly above the selected storyboard scene.

➤ Select Editor ⇨ Resolve Auto Layout Issues ⇨ Update Frames.

➤ Create a segue from the button in the first scene to the new scene.

1. Double-click the canvas to zoom out. Position the two scenes sufficiently apart on the canvas by dragging them.

2. Double-click the first scene to activate it.

3. Right-click the Show detail button in the first scene to bring up a context menu. Drag from the circle beside the action item under the Triggered Segues category in the context menu to the second scene.

4. When you release the mouse button, you will be asked to select the segue type. Select Show.

➤ Test your app in the iOS Simulator.

1. Click the Run button in the Xcode toolbar. Alternatively, you can select Project ⇨ Run.

2. Tap on the Show Detail button and observe the second scene pushed onto the navigation controller stack.

REFERENCE *To see some of the examples from this lesson, watch the Lesson 15 video online at* www.wrox.com/go/swiftiosvid.

16

Table Views

A table view is a user interface component used to present a list of items to the user. Table views are instances of the UITableView class and are part of the UIKit framework. Table views are one of the most versatile user interface components in UIKit and can be found in several apps, including Apple's own contacts, and mail applications. In this lesson, you learn to use table views in your applications.

TABLE VIEW APPEARANCE

A table view allows you to present a single column of values. Each value is presented vertically in its own row. A user can scroll through the rows vertically. Vertical scrolling is automatically managed by the table view and is enabled when the number of rows exceed the visible height of the table view.

Each row in a table view is an instance of another UIKit class called UITableViewCell. The table view has a mechanism in place that allows you to reuse table view cells instead of creating a new one for each row.

Data in table views are presented in sections. Sections are numbered from zero and run vertically down the table (see Figure 16-1).

Each section can have an optional header and footer. The default table view has just one section with no visible header or footer (see Figure 16-2).

Rows within each section are also numbered from 0 and run vertically down the table, within the section.

Additionally, a table view has one of two presentation styles, plain and grouped (see Figure 16-3). A plain table view is a continuous list; a grouped table view has gaps between sections.

FIGURE 16-1

FIGURE 16-2

FIGURE 16-3

CREATING A TABLE VIEW WITH INTERFACE BUILDER

To add a new scene in your storyboard that contains a table view, simply drag and drop a Table View Controller object into your scene. A table view controller is an object that manages a table view (see Figure 16-4).

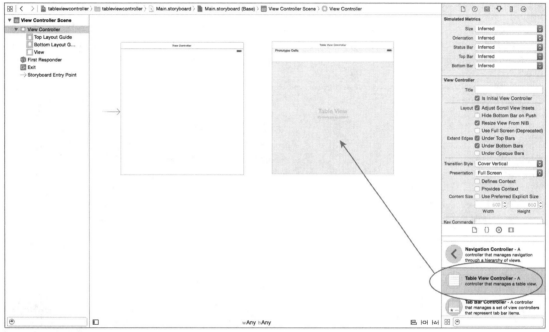

FIGURE 16-4

If, however, you want to add a table view to an existing scene, drag and drop a table view object onto the scene. When using a table view, your view controller class will be responsible for managing the table view, and will need to implement the `UITableViewDataSource` and `UITableViewDelegate` protocols. You can use the Attribute inspector to set up the table views style as plain or grouped (see Figure 16-5).

FIGURE 16-5

You can set up your table view to show static or dynamic content by using the Content property in the Attribute inspector.

Static Table Views

A table view with static content has a fixed number of rows that are configured at design time in the storyboard. Static cells can only be used with table view controllers.

If you are using a table view controller and wish to populate it with static content, simply use the Attribute inspector to set the Content property of the table view to Static Cells.

You can then use the Sections attribute to configure the number of sections in the table view. To edit the number of rows, section header, or section footer for each section, simply select the section from the document outline and use the Attribute inspector (see Figure 16-6).

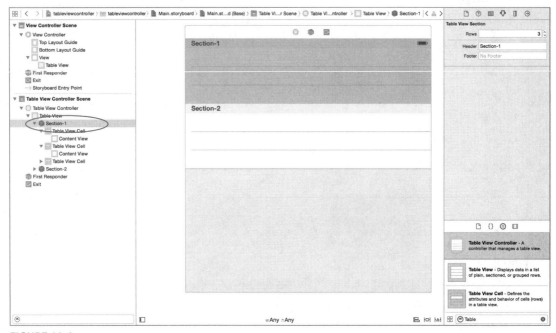

FIGURE 16-6

To edit the content of each row, select a row in the document outline and drag standard components, such as labels and image views, into the cell. You will need to set up the constraints for each cell individually (see Figure 16-7).

If the layout for your cell is simple, you can optionally use a standard cell style for each row. This can be done by selecting the row in the document outline and using the Attribute inspector to change the cell style to one of four options:

➤ Basic

➤ Right Detail

➤ Left Detail

➤ Subtitle

Selecting one of these options will add one or more labels into the cell at fixed positions; you can simply edit the text in these labels by double-clicking the label (see Figure 16-8).

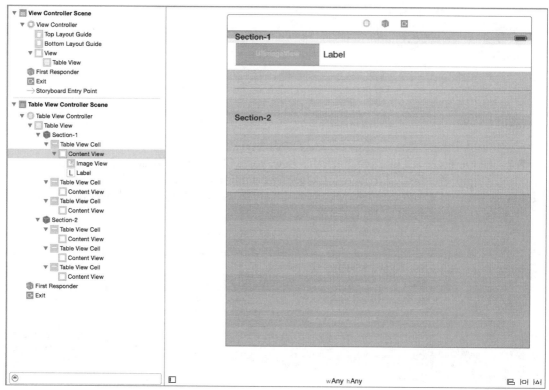

FIGURE 16-7

FIGURE 16-8

Dynamic Table Views

If the contents of your table view are to be managed at runtime, you need to set the Content attribute to Dynamic Prototype. When using dynamic table views, you will first need to design a template cell in the storyboard. This template cell is known as a *prototype cell* and will be instantiated programmatically at runtime and populated with content for each row.

It is possible to register multiple prototype cells with a table view, but this is not often used as the rows in a table view generally share the same visual layout, differing only in content.

To set up the number of prototype cells in a dynamic table view, select the table view and change the value of the Prototype Cells property in the Attribute inspector (see Figure 16-9)

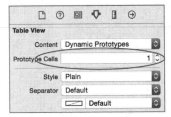

FIGURE 16-9

For each prototype cell in a dynamic table view, you will need to provide a unique string for the Identifier property in the Attribute inspector By default, each prototype cell is an instance of `UITableViewCell`. `UITableViewCell` provides an image view and a text label, accessed via the `imageView` and `textLabel` properties.

If, however, your prototype cell contains more than just a single line of text and an image view, you will need to first create a subclass of `UITableViewCell` and associate it with the cell using the Identity inspector (see Figure 16-10).

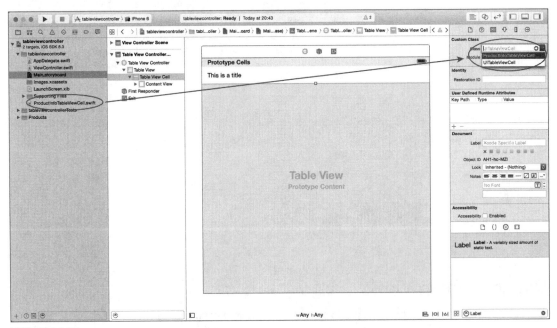

FIGURE 16-10

You can then drag and drop standard user interface elements onto the prototype cell and create outlets/actions in the associated `UITableViewCell` subclass.

Dynamic table views require a data source and a delegate object. A data source object must implement the UITableViewDataSource protocol, and the delegate object must implement the UITableViewDelegate protocol.

If the table view was added to an existing scene, then the data source and delegate are both usually set to be the view controller, with the view controller implementing the relevant methods from both protocols (see Figure 16-11).

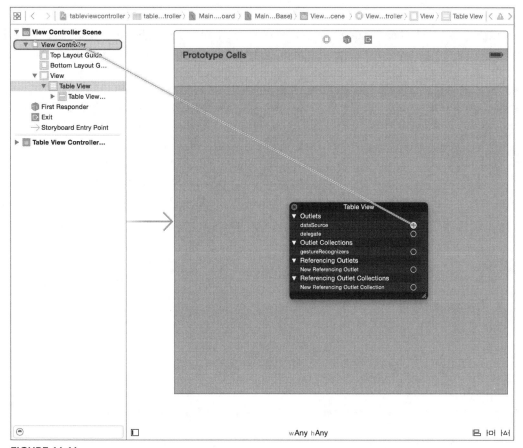

FIGURE 16-11

The UITableViewDataSource and UITableViewDelegate protocols define several methods, most of which are optional. The most common UITableViewDataSource methods you are likely to implement are:

```
func numberOfSectionsInTableView(tableView: UITableView) -> Int

func tableView(tableView: UITableView,
numberOfRowsInSection section: Int) -> Int

func tableView(tableView: UITableView,
cellForRowAtIndexPath indexPath: NSIndexPath) -> UITableViewCell
```

You should return the number of sections in your table view from the `numberOfSectionsInTableView` method. If this method is not implemented, the table view assumes a single section. The number of rows in each section are to be returned from `numberOfRowsInSection` and a `UITableViewCell` instance for each row within each section is to be returned from `cellForRowAtIndexPath`.

The most common `UITableViewDelegate` method that you are likely to implement is:

```
func tableView(tableView: UITableView,
didSelectRowAtIndexPath indexPath: NSIndexPath)
```

This method is called when the user selects a row in your table view. If, however, you have created segues in your storyboard from your table view to another scene, then `prepareForSegue` is called instead.

If on the other hand, you are using a table view controller in your storyboard, then you will need to associate a custom `UITableViewController` subclass with the table view controller in the Identity Inspector and implement the data source and delegate methods in this subclass.

The following code snippet shows how these data source and delegate methods are implemented in a view controller:

```
class ViewController: UIViewController, UITableViewDataSource,
UITableViewDelegate {

    var fruits:Array<String> = ["Apple", "Banana",
"Mango", "Pear",
"Peach", "Plum",
"Grape", "Melon",
"Orange"]

    override func viewDidLoad() {
        super.viewDidLoad()
    }

    override func didReceiveMemoryWarning() {
        super.didReceiveMemoryWarning()
    }

    func numberOfSectionsInTableView(tableView: UITableView) -> Int
    {
        return 1
    }

    func tableView(tableView: UITableView,
    numberOfRowsInSection section: Int) -> Int
    {
        return fruits.count
    }

    func tableView(tableView: UITableView,
        cellForRowAtIndexPath indexPath: NSIndexPath) -> UITableViewCell
    {
        var cell:UITableViewCell =
```

```
tableView.dequeueReusableCellWithIdentifier("cellPrototype1")
as! UITableViewCell

        cell.textLabel?.text = fruits[indexPath.row]

        return cell

    }

}
```

TRY IT

In this Try It, you create a new Xcode project based on the Single View Application template called `TableViewTest` that adds a grouped table view with multiple sections to an existing scene of the default storyboard.

Lesson Requirements

➤ Launch Xcode.

➤ Create a new project based on the Single View Application template.

➤ Edit the storyboard with Interface Builder.

➤ Add a table view to the default scene.

➤ Set up a prototype cell.

➤ Set up table view attributes with the Attribute inspector.

➤ Set up the data source and delegate property of the table view.

➤ Implement `UITableViewDataSource` and `UITableViewDelegate` methods.

> **REFERENCE** *The code for this Try It is available at* www.wrox.com/go/
> swiftios.

Hints

➤ To show the Object library, select View ⇨ Utilities ⇨ Show Object Library.

➤ To show the assistant editor, select View ⇨ Assistant Editor Show Assistant Editor.

Step-by-Step

➤ Create a Single View Application in Xcode called `TableViewTest`.

1. Launch Xcode and create a new application by selecting File ⇨ New ⇨ Project.

2. Select the Single View Application template from the list of iOS project templates.

3. In the project options screen, use the following values:

    ➤ **Product Name:** TableViewTest

    ➤ **Organization Name:** your company

    ➤ **Organization Identifier:** com.yourcompany

    ➤ **Language:** Swift

    ➤ **Devices:** iPhone

    ➤ **Use Core Data:** Unchecked

    ➤ **Include Unit Tests:** Unchecked

    ➤ **Include UI Tests:** Unchecked

4. Save the project onto your hard disk.

➤ Add a `UITableView` instance to the default scene.

1. From the Object library, drag and drop a Table View object onto the scene.

2. Ensure the table view is selected and use the Pin button to display the constraints editor popup.

    ➤ Ensure the Constrain to margins option is unchecked.

    ➤ Pin the distance between the left edge of the view and the table view to 0.

    ➤ Pin the distance between the right edge of the view and the table view to 0.

    ➤ Pin the distance between the bottom of the view and the table view to 0.

    ➤ Pin the distance between the top of the view and the table view to 20.

    ➤ Click the Add 4 Constraints button to dismiss the constraints editor popup.

3. Update the frames to match the constraints you have set.

    ➤ Click on the View controller item in the dock above the storyboard scene. This is the first of the three icons located directly above the selected storyboard scene.

    ➤ Select Editor ➪ Resolve Auto Layout Issues ➪ Update Frames.

4. Set up the data source and delegate properties.

    ➤ Right-click the table view to bring up a context menu. Drag from the item labeled "dataSource" in the context menu to the item labeled "View Controller" in the document outline.

    ➤ Right-click the table view to bring up a context menu. Drag from the item labeled "delegate" in the context menu to the item labeled "View Controller" in the document outline.

➤ Set up the table view's appearance:

1. Select the table view and ensure the Attribute inspector is visible.

2. Ensure the Content attribute is set to Dynamic Prototypes.

3. Ensure the value of the Prototype Cells attribute is 1.

4. Ensure the Style attribute is set to Grouped.

➤ Set up the prototype cell:

1. Expand the table view in the document outline; this will reveal the table view cell.

2. Select the table view cell.

3. Use the attribute editor to ensure that the value of the identifier attribute is prototypeCell1.

4. Ensure the Style attribute is set to Basic.

➤ Implement the data source and delegate methods in the view controller.

1. Add the following code snippet to the ViewController.swift file to declare five arrays of strings:

```swift
var continents:Array<String> = ["Asia", "North America",
                                "Europe", "Australia"]

var citiesInAsia:Array<String> = ["Bangkok", "New Delhi",
                                  "Singapore", "Tokyo"]

var citiesInNorthAmerica:Array<String> = ["San Francisco","Cupertino"]
var citiesInEurope:Array<String> = ["London", "Paris", "Rome", "Athens"]
var citiesInAustralia:Array<String> = ["Sydney", "Melbourne", "Cairns"]
```

2. Implement the numberOfSectionsInTableView data source method as follows:

```swift
func numberOfSectionsInTableView(tableView: UITableView) -> Int
{
    return continents.count;
}
```

3. Implement the numberOfRowsInSection data source method as follows:

```swift
func tableView(tableView: UITableView,
               numberOfRowsInSection section: Int) -> Int
{
    if section == 0
    {
        return citiesInAsia.count
    }
    else if section == 1
    {
        return citiesInNorthAmerica.count
    }
```

```
        else if section == 2
        {
            return citiesInEurope.count
        }
        else if section == 3
        {
            return citiesInAustralia.count
        }

        return 0
    }
```

4. Implement the `titleForHeaderInSection` data source method as follows:

```
func tableView(tableView: UITableView,
               titleForHeaderInSection section: Int) -> String?
{
    return continents[section];
}
```

5. Implement the `cellforRowAtIndexPath` data source method as follows:

```
func tableView(tableView: UITableView, cellForRowAtIndexPath indexPath:
NSIndexPath) -> UITableViewCell
{
    var cell:UITableViewCell =
tableView.dequeueReusableCellWithIdentifier("prototypeCell1") as!
 UITableViewCell

        if indexPath.section == 0
        {
            cell.textLabel?.text = citiesInAsia[indexPath.row]
        }
        else if indexPath.section == 1
        {
            cell.textLabel?.text = citiesInNorthAmerica[indexPath.row]
        }
        else if indexPath.section == 2
        {
            cell.textLabel?.text = citiesInEurope[indexPath.row]
        }
        else if indexPath.section == 3
        {
            cell.textLabel?.text = citiesInAustralia[indexPath.row]
        }

        return cell
    }
```

6. Modify the declaration of the `ViewController` class to inherit from `UIViewController`, `UITableViewDataSource`, and `UITableViewDelegate`:

```
class ViewController: UIViewController, UITableViewDataSource,
UITableViewDelegate {
```

➤ Test your app in the iOS Simulator.

Click the Run button in the Xcode toolbar. Alternatively, you can select Project ➪ Run.

REFERENCE *To see some of the examples from this lesson, watch the Lesson 16 video online at* www.wrox.com/go/swiftiosvid.

17

Collection Views

In the previous lesson, you learned about table views. Collection views are similar to table views in many respects; the primary difference between them is that collection views are not restricted to single column layouts. A collection views layout can be customized programmatically, allowing collection views to present data in grid layouts, circular layouts, and cover-flow layouts (see Figure 17-1).

FIGURE 17-1

Collection views are instances of the `UICollectionView` class and are part of the UIKit framework. Data in a collection view is referred to as *Items* that are grouped into sections. Each section can have an optional header and a footer view.

CREATING A COLLECTION VIEW WITH INTERFACE BUILDER

To add a new scene in your storyboard that contains a collection view, simply drag and drop a Collection View Controller object into your scene. A collection view controller is an object that manages a collection view (see Figure 17-2).

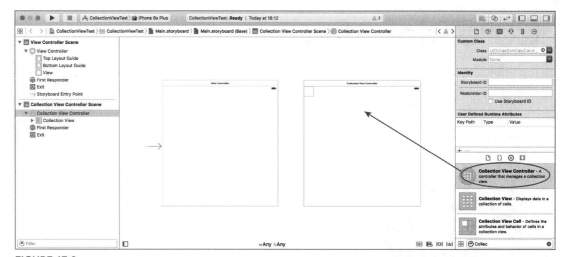

FIGURE 17-2

If, however, you want to add a collection view to an existing scene, drag and drop a collection view object onto the scene. When using a collection view your view controller class will be responsible for managing the collection view and will need to implement relevant methods from the `UICollectionViewDataSource` and `UICollectionViewDelegate` protocols. You will also need to set the view controller to act as both the data source and delegate object for the collection view (see Figure 17-3). The data source and delegate will be discussed in more detail later in this lesson.

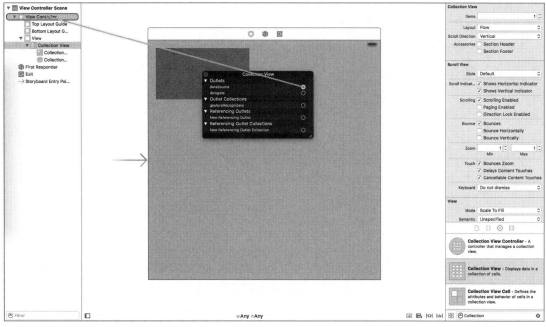

FIGURE 17-3

COLLECTION VIEW CELLS

Each item in a collection view is an instance of another UIKit class called UICollectionViewCell. The collection view has a mechanism in place that allows you to reuse collection view cells instead of creating one for each item.

When you add a collection view to your storyboard, the collection view has a default cell of dimensions 50 x 50 units. Select the collection view in the document outline, and use the Size Inspector to edit the dimensions of the cell and the spacing between cells (see Figure 17-4).

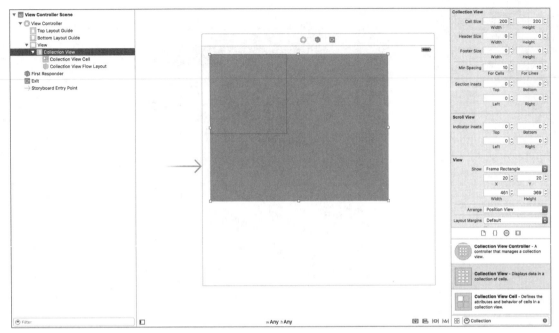

FIGURE 17-4

Select the collection view cell (not the collection view) in the document outline and switch to the Attribute inspector to set up a unique identifier that will be used to access this cell programmatically (see Figure 17-5).

You will also need to create a custom `UICollectionViewCell` subclass and associate it with the collection view cell using the Identity Inspector (see Figure 17-6).

Unlike table view cells, the default collection view cell is empty. You will need to build a layout using standard `UIKit` elements such as labels and image views, and set up layout constraints within the cell.

Once a custom `UICollectionViewCell` subclass is associated with the collection view cell in the storyboard, you can create outlets and actions for the elements within the cell in this class.

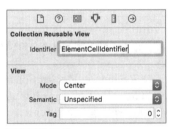

FIGURE 17-5

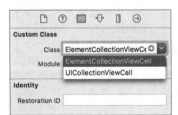

FIGURE 17-6

COLLECTION VIEW DELEGATE AND DATA SOURCE

The `UICollectionViewDataSource` and `UICollectionViewDelegate` protocols define several methods, most of which are optional. The most common `UICollectionViewDataSource` methods you are likely to implement are:

```
func collectionView(collectionView: UICollectionView,
numberOfItemsInSection section: Int) -> Int

func collectionView(collectionView: UICollectionView,
cellForItemAtIndexPath indexPath: NSIndexPath) ->
UICollectionViewCell

func numberOfSectionsInCollectionView(collectionView: UICollectionView) -> Int
```

You should return the number of sections in your collection view from the `numberOfSectionsIn CollectionView` method. If this method is not implemented, the collection view assumes a single section. The number of items in each section are to be returned from `collectionView(collectionView, numberOfItemsInSection)`, and a `UICollectionViewCell` instance for each row within each section is to be returned from `collectionView(collectionView, cellForItemAtIndexPath)`.

The most common `UICollectionViewDelegate` method that you are likely to implement is:

```
func collectionView(collectionView: UICollectionView,
didSelectItemAtIndexPath indexPath: NSIndexPath)
```

This method is called when the user selects an item in your collection view. If, however, you have created segues in your storyboard from your table view to another scene, then `prepareForSegue` is called instead.

If, on the other hand, you are using a collection view controller in your storyboard, then you will need to associate a custom `UICollectionViewController` subclass with the collection view controller in the Identity Inspector and implement the data source and delegate methods in this subclass.

The following code snippet shows how these data source and delegate methods are implemented in a view controller; this snippet assumes that `ElementCollectionViewCell` is a custom `UICollectionViewCell` subclass:

```
class ViewController: UIViewController,
                      UICollectionViewDataSource,
                      UICollectionViewDelegate {

    var elements:Array<String> = ["Hi", "He", "Li", "Be", "B", "C",
                                  "N", "O", "F" ,"Ne", "Na", "Mg",
                                  "Al", "Si", "P", "S", "Cl", "Ar",
                                  "K", "Ca"]

    override func viewDidLoad() {
        super.viewDidLoad()
    }

    override func didReceiveMemoryWarning() {
        super.didReceiveMemoryWarning()
    }
```

```
    func collectionView(collectionView: UICollectionView,
        numberOfItemsInSection section: Int) -> Int
    {
        return elements.count;
    }


    func collectionView(collectionView: UICollectionView,
                    cellForItemAtIndexPath indexPath: NSIndexPath) ->
                    UICollectionViewCell
    {
        var cell: ElementCollectionViewCell =
    collectionView.dequeueReusableCellWithReuseIdentifier("ElementCell",
    forIndexPath:indexPath) as! ElementCollectionViewCell

        var elementName:String = elements[indexPath.row]
        cell.elementImage.image = UIImage(named: elementName)

        return cell
    }

    func numberOfSectionsInCollectionView(collectionView: UICollectionView) -> Int
    {
        return 1;
    }

}
```

TRY IT

In this Try It, you create a new Xcode project based on the Single View Application template called `CollectionViewTest` that adds a collection view with three sections to an existing scene of the default storyboard. The sections display a few elements from the periodic table sorted into solids, liquids, and gases.

Lesson Requirements

➤   Launch Xcode.

➤   Create a new project based on the Single View Application template.

➤   Edit the storyboard with Interface Builder.

➤   Add a collection view to the default scene.

➤   Set up a collection view cell.

➤   Set up collection view attributes with the Attribute inspector.

➤   Set up the data source and delegate property of the table view.

➤   Implement `UICollectionViewDataSource` and `UICollectionViewDelegate` methods.

> **REFERENCE** *The code for this Try It is available at* www.wrox.com/go/
> swiftios.

Hints

➤ To show the Object library, select View ➪ Utilities ➪ Show Object Library.

➤ To show the assistant editor, select View ➪ Assistant Editor ➪ Show Assistant Editor.

Step-by-Step

➤ Create a Single View Application in Xcode called `CollectionViewTest`.

1. Launch Xcode and create a new application by selecting File ➪ New ➪ Project.

2. Select the Single View Application template from the list of iOS project templates.

3. In the project options screen, use the following values:

   ➤ **Product Name:** CollectionViewTest

   ➤ **Organization Name:** your company

   ➤ **Organization Identifier:** com.yourcompany

   ➤ **Language:** Swift

   ➤ **Devices:** iPhone

   ➤ **Use Core Data:** Unchecked

4. Save the project onto your hard disk.

➤ Add image resources to your project.

1. Ensure the project navigator is visible. To show it, select View ➪ Navigators ➪ Show Project Navigator.

2. Open the `Assets.xcassets` file by clicking it in the project navigator.

3. Navigate to the `Images` folder in this chapter's resources from the website.

4. Create a new Image set by selecting Editor ➪ New Image Set, and name this new image set `Al`.

5. Drag the `Al_1x.png`, `Al_2x.png`, and `Al_3x.png` images from this chapter's resources into the appropriate placeholders in the image set.

6. Similarly, create new image sets called `F`, `Hg`, `Li`, `N`, `O`, and `Si`, and use the appropriate images from this chapter's resources folder.

➤ Add a `UICollectionView` instance to the default scene.

1. From the Object library, drag and drop a Collection View object onto the scene.

2. Ensure the collection view is selected and use the Pin button to display the constraints editor popup.

   ➤ Ensure the Constrain to margins option is unchecked.

   ➤ Pin the distance between the left edge of the view and the table view to 0.

   ➤ Pin the distance between the right edge of the view and the table view to 0.

   ➤ Pin the distance between the bottom of the view and the table view to 0.

   ➤ Pin the distance between the top of the view and the table view to 20.

   ➤ Click the Add 4 Constraints button to dismiss the constraints editor popup.

3. Update the frames to match the constraints you have set.

   ➤ Click on the View controller item in the dock above the storyboard scene. This is the first of the three icons located directly above the selected storyboard scene.

   ➤ Select Editor ⇨ Resolve Auto Layout Issues ⇨ Update Frames.

4. Set up the data source and delegate properties.

   ➤ Right-click the collection view to bring up a context menu. Drag from the item labeled "dataSource" in the context menu to the item labeled "View Controller" in the document outline.

   ➤ Right-click the collection view to bring up a context menu. Drag from the item labeled "delegate" in the context menu to the item labeled "View Controller" in the document outline.

➤ Set up the collection view's appearance.

1. Select the collection view and ensure the Attribute inspector is visible.

2. Ensure the Layout attribute is set to Flow.

3. Ensure the Scroll Direction attribute is set to Vertical.

4. Ensure the Section Header check box is unchecked.

5. Ensure the collection view is selected, and switch to the Size Inspector to set the height and width of the collection view cell to 150 units each.

6. Set the Top Section Inset to 10 units.

➤ Add a `UICollectionViewCell` subclass.

1. Option-click the `CollectionViewTest` group in the project explorer and select New File from the context menu.

2. Select Swift File under the iOS Templates section.

3. Name the file `ElementCollectionViewCell.swift` and click Create.

4. Modify the contents of the `ElementCollectionViewCell.swift` file to subclass `UICollectionViewCell`. The modified contents of this file should resemble the following:

```
import UIKit

class ElementCollectionViewCell: UICollectionViewCell {

}
```

➤ Set up the collection view cell.

1. Expand the collection view in the document outline; this will reveal the collection view cell.

2. Select the collection view cell.

3. Use the attribute editor to ensure that the value of the identifier attribute is `ElementCellIdentifier`.

4. Drag and drop an Image view onto the collection view cell.

5. Ensure the image view is selected and use the pin button to display the constraints editor popup.

   ➤ Ensure the Constrain to margins option is unchecked.

   ➤ Pin the distance between the left edge of the view and the table view to 0.

   ➤ Pin the distance between the right edge of the view and the table view to 0.

   ➤ Pin the distance between the bottom of the view and the table view to 0.

   ➤ Pin the distance between the top of the view and the table view to 0.

   ➤ Click the Add 4 Constraints button to dismiss the constraints editor popup.

6. Update the frames to match the constraints you have set.

   ➤ Select the collection view cell in the document outline. This will now be listed as `ElementCellIdentifier`.

   ➤ Select Editor ⇨ Resolve Auto Layout Issues ⇨ Update Frames.

7. Select the collection view cell, and use the Identity Inspector to change the custom class of the cell to `ElementCollectionViewCell`.

8. Ensure the assistant editor is visible and the `ElementCollectionViewCell.Swift` file is open in it.

9. Select the image view in the document outline and create an outlet for the image view in the `ElementCollectionViewCell.Swift` file. Name the outlet `imageView`.

➤ Implement the data source and delegate methods in the view controller.

1. Add the following code snippet to the `ViewController.swift` file to declare four arrays of strings:

```
var statesOfMatter:Array<String> = ["Solid", "Liquid", "Gas"]
```

```
var solids:Array<String> = ["Li", "Al", "Si"]

var liquids:Array<String> = ["Hg"]

var gasses:Array<String> = ["N", "O", "F"]
```

2. Implement the `numberOfSectionsInCollectionView` data source method as follows:

```
func numberOfSectionsInCollectionView(collectionView: UICollectionView)
    -> Int
{
    return statesOfMatter.count;
}
```

3. Implement the `collectionView(collectionView, numberOfItemsInSection)` data source method as follows:

```
func collectionView(collectionView: UICollectionView,
numberOfItemsInSection section: Int) -> Int
{
    if section == 0
    {
        return solids.count
    }
    else if section == 1
    {
        return liquids.count
    }
    else if section == 2
    {
        return gasses.count
    }

    return 0
}
```

4. Implement the `collectionView(collectionView, cellForItemAtIndexPath)` data source method as follows:

```
func collectionView(collectionView: UICollectionView,
cellForItemAtIndexPath indexPath: NSIndexPath) ->
UICollectionViewCell
{
    var section =  indexPath.section
    var row = indexPath.row

    var cell: ElementCollectionViewCell =
collectionView.dequeueReusableCellWithReuseIdentifier
("ElementCellIdentifier", forIndexPath:indexPath)
as! ElementCollectionViewCell

    if section == 0
    {
        var elementName:String = solids[indexPath.row]
        cell.imageView.image = UIImage(named: elementName)
    }
```

```
            else if section == 1
            {
                var elementName:String = liquids[indexPath.row]
                cell.imageView.image = UIImage(named: elementName)
            }
            else if section == 2
            {
                var elementName:String = gasses[indexPath.row]
                cell.imageView.image = UIImage(named: elementName)
            }

            return cell
        }
```

5. Modify the declaration of the `ViewController` class to inherit from `UIViewController`, `UICollectionViewDataSource`, and `UICollectionViewDelegate`:

```
class ViewController: UIViewController,
                      UICollectionViewDataSource,
                      UICollectionViewDelegate {
```

➤   Test your app in the iOS Simulator.

Click the Run button in the Xcode toolbar. Alternatively, you can select Project ➪ Run.

REFERENCE *To see some of the examples from this lesson, watch the Lesson 17 video online at* www.wrox.com/go/swiftiosvid.

18

Tab Bars and Toolbars

Lesson 15 discussed navigation controllers, which allowed your application to present a hierarchy of views one at a time. A tab bar controller, on the other hand, allows you to display multiple view controllers at the same time (see Figure 18-1).

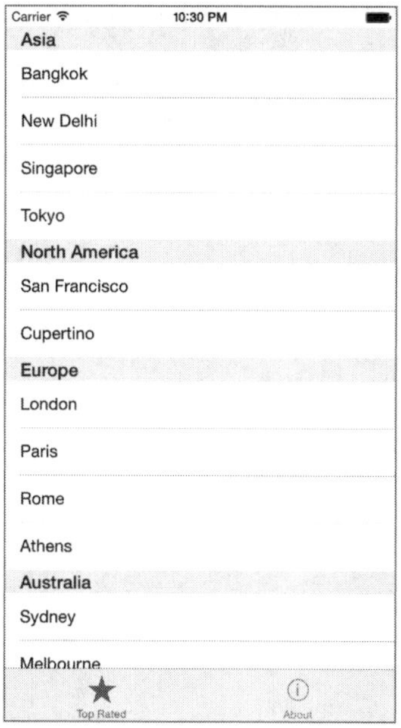

FIGURE 18-1

Navigation controllers are well suited to a hierarchical app structure, where users navigate one screen at a time to reach their destination. A tab bar controller is handy when it comes to creating a flat app structure where users can navigate directly from one primary category to another (see Figure 18-2). Examples of such apps include the Clock and the App store apps on iOS devices.

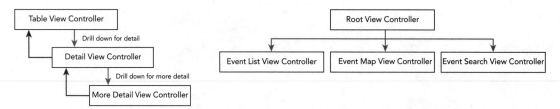

Hierarchical structure, works well with navigation controllers   Flat structure, works well with tab bar controllers

FIGURE 18-2

View controllers provide the content of tabs within a tab bar controller. It is quite common to combine tab bar controllers and navigation controllers to create an app that provides the best of both. The tab bar sits at the top of the view controller hierarchy and some of the tabs could have a navigation controller within them that provides a drill-down interface for the content within that tab. The Phone app on the iPhone is an example of such an app, with the Contacts tab containing a navigation controller that allows you to drill down into a contact's details.

A tab bar represents a single tab within a tab bar controller. Tab bars are located at the bottom of the screen and consist of an icon and text to describe the content it represents. Each tab can also have a badge, which is a red oval with a number in it (see Figure 18-3).

FIGURE 18-3

On an iPhone, a tab bar controller can only display five tabs at a time. If there are more than five, then the first four are displayed and the tab bar controller adds a More tab that reveals a list of additional tabs. The iPad can display more than five tabs because it has a larger screen.

CREATING A TAB BAR CONTROLLER

Xcode contains a template specifically for applications that want to present a tabbed interface. This template is called the Tabbed Application template and can be selected when creating a new project (see Figure 18-4).

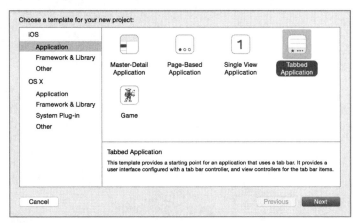

FIGURE 18-4

The template adds a tab bar controller to the default storyboard scene and configures the tab bar to present two tabs, the contents of which are provided by two view controllers, called `FirstViewController` and `SecondViewController` respectively (see Figure 18-5).

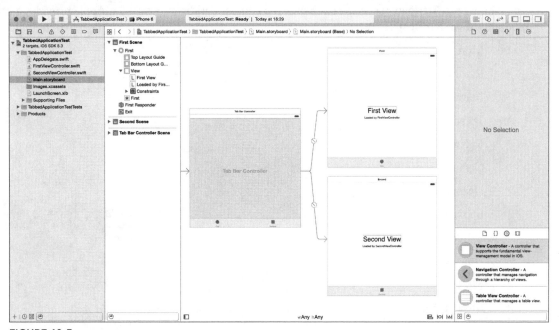

FIGURE 18-5

Inspecting the storyboard in the document outline reveals that each view controller contains a view and a tab bar item. The tab bar item is used to represent the view controller within the parent tab bar controller (see Figure 18-6).

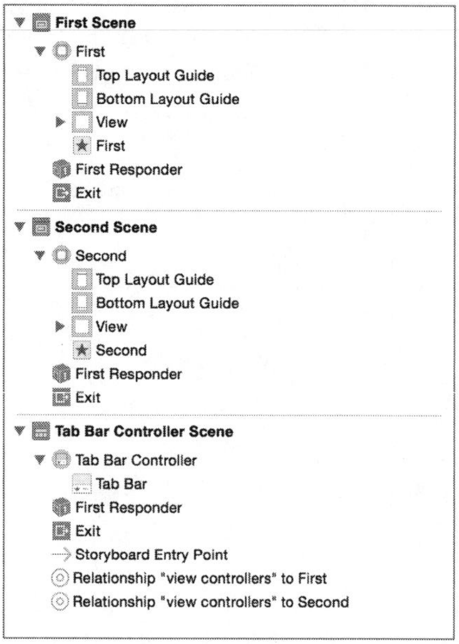

FIGURE 18-6

You can use the Attribute inspector to change the contents of the tab bar item. Apple provides a list of standard tab bar items:

➤ More

➤ Favorites

➤ Featured

➤ Top rated

➤ Recents

➤ Contacts

➤ History

➤ Bookmarks

➤ Search

➤ Downloads

➤ Most recent

➤ Most visited

You can choose one of these using the System Item drop-down combo in the Attribute inspector (see Figure 18-7).

FIGURE 18-7

If you choose one of the standard tab bar items, then Xcode will provide a suitable icon and caption for you. If, however, you wish to use your own icon and caption, set the System Item to Custom. Astute readers will note that the default setting for the tab bar items created by the Tabbed Application template is Custom, with appropriate icons in the project's asset bundle.

To add a new tab to the tab bar controller, you must first add a new view controller scene to the storyboard. To do this, drag and drop a View Controller from the Object library onto the storyboard scene (see Figure 18-8).

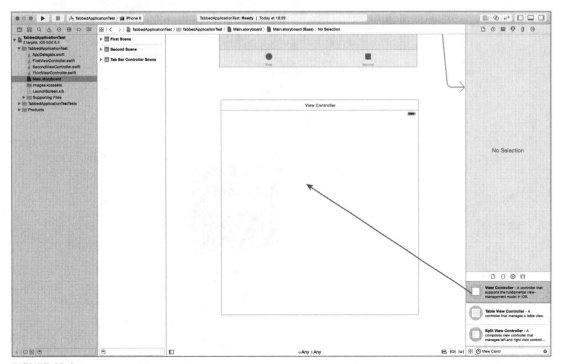

FIGURE 18-8

Next, create a new Swift class that subclasses `UIViewController` and use the Identity Inspector to associate this class with the view controller you have just dropped onto the storyboard.

To add a tab bar item to the new scene, ensure the scene is selected, and then drag and drop a Tab Bar Item from the Object library anywhere onto the scene. The tab bar item will automatically snap to the bottom of the scene regardless of where you drop it. To configure the tab bar item, simply select it and use the attribute editor.

Finally, to add the new view controller to the tab bar, simply hold down the Ctrl key on your keyboard and drag from the tab bar onto the new view controller scene (you are creating a segue). When you release the mouse button, select Relationship Segue from the popup menu (see Figure 18-9).

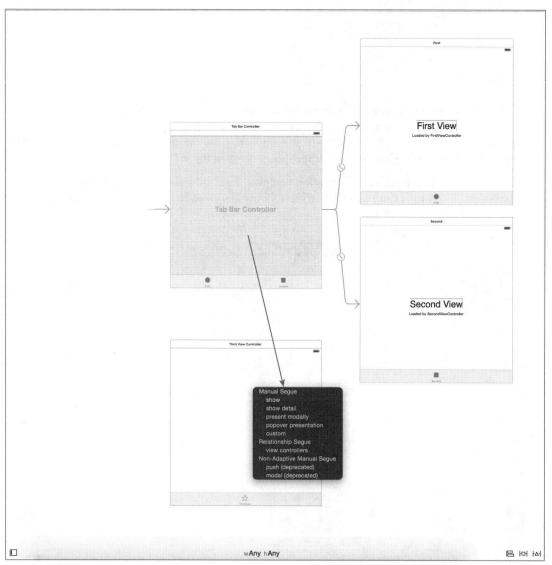

FIGURE 18-9

TOOLBARS

Toolbars look similar to tab bars in that both of them appear at the bottom of the screen, but the similarity ends there. A tab bar is used when you want to present multiple view controllers on the screen simultaneously. A toolbar is used to present a menu of options related to the content presented in a view controller. The two are not usually used together. The Maps application uses a toolbar to present options related to the map being displayed (see Figure 18-10). Tapping the info button brings up a modal view with options that will change the way in which data is displayed on the map.

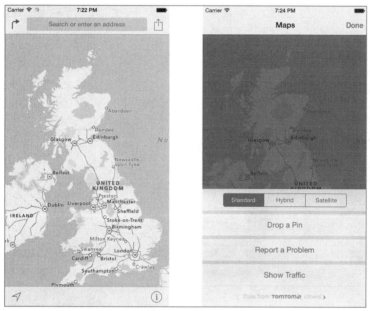

FIGURE 18-10

Typically, the buttons on a tab bar represent command functions that would be used on the current view. To add a toolbar to a view controller scene, simply drag and drop a Toolbar from the Object library. Unlike tab bar items, toolbars do not automatically snap to the bottom of the screen. You will need to provide appropriate constraints to anchor the toolbar to the bottom of the screen (see Figure 18-11).

Options within a toolbar are instances of the `UIBarButtonItem` class. You can add to the options displayed in a toolbar by dragging and dropping a Bar Button Item from the Object library (see Figure 18-12).

Configuring a bar button item is similar to configuring a tab bar item. You simply select it and bring up the Attribute inspector to change appropriate properties. Xcode provides a set of standard bar button item styles that can be selected using the Identifier drop-down combo box in the Attribute inspector (see Figure 18-13).

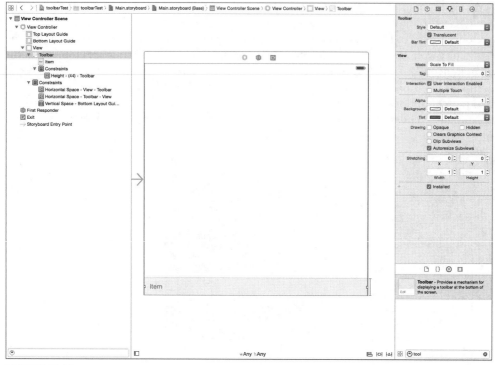

FIGURE 18-11

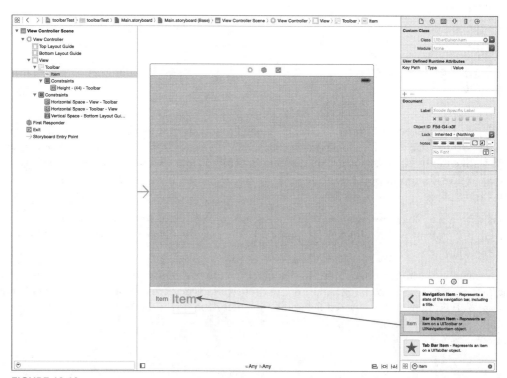

FIGURE 18-12

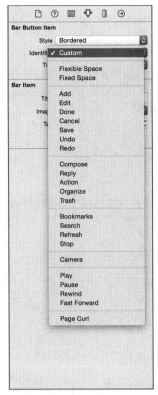

FIGURE 18-13

Two styles are worth special mention. The first is the Fixed Space style. When applied, the bar button item renders as empty space (of fixed width) between its neighboring bar button items. Figure 18-14 shows a toolbar that starts with three bar button items. The Fixed Space style is then applied to the one in the middle. Note how it changes to represent whitespace. You can edit the width of a bar button item (even fixed spaces) by using the Size inspector.

FIGURE 18-14

The second style is the Flexible Space style. The toolbar distributes the available free space across all bar button items that have this style applied to them. In a toolbar with three items, if this style were to be applied to the middle item, the neighboring items would be placed at ends of the toolbar because the width of the flexible spacebar button item would equal all the free space in the toolbar (see Figure 18-15).

FIGURE 18-15

For a toolbar with five items in which the second and fourth items are given the Flexible Space style, the remaining three items would be spaced apart evenly (see Figure 18-16) because the free space in the toolbar would be split equally between the two flexible space items.

FIGURE 18-16

Last but not least, you will need to associate action methods in your view controller class with each bar button item. To do this simply use the assistant editor to create a method and associate it with the bar button item (see Figure 18-17).

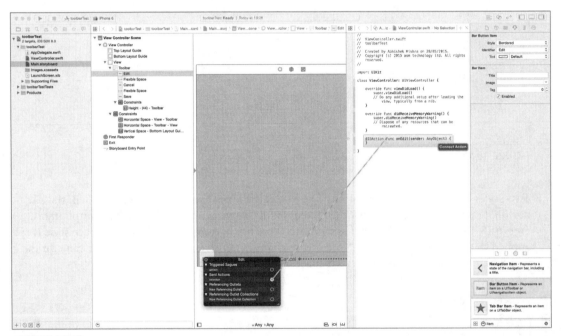

FIGURE 18-17

TRY IT

In this Try It, you create a simple application based on the Tabbed Application template, called TabbedApplication, that contains two tabs. The first tab contains a list of cities; the second tab serves as an About page for the app.

Lesson Requirements

➤ Launch Xcode.

➤ Create a new project based on the Tabbed Application template, with two tabs.

➤ Add a Table View to the first tab.

➤ Use Interface Builder to add several user interface elements to the second tab.

➤ Add code to the view controller class for the first tab to populate the table view.

> **REFERENCE** *The code for this Try It is available at* www.wrox.com/go/
> swiftios.

Hints

➤ When creating a new project, you can use your website's domain name as the Company Identifier in the Project Options dialog box.

➤ To show the Object library, select View ➪ Utilities ➪ Show Object Library menu item.

➤ To show the assistant editor, select View ➪ Assistant Editor ➪ Show Assistant Editor.

Step-by-Step

➤ Create a Tabbed Application in Xcode called TabbedApplicationTest.

1. Launch Xcode and create a new application by selecting File ➪ New ➪ Project.

2. Select the Tabbed Application template from the list of iOS project templates.

3. In the project options screen use the following values:

   ➤ **Product Name:** TabbedApplicationTest

   ➤ **Organization Name:** your company

   ➤ **Organization Identifier:** com.yourcompany

   ➤ **Language:** Swift

   ➤ **Devices:** iPhone

   ➤ **Include UI Tests:** Unchecked

   ➤ **Include Unit Tests:** Unchecked

4. Save the project onto your hard disk.

➤   Add image resources to the project.

1.   Open the `Assets.xcassets` asset bundle by clicking it in the project explorer.

2.   Add a new image set called `aboutImage` by selecting Editor ➪ Add Assets ➪ New Image Set menu item.

3.   Select the new image set and use the Attribute inspector to change the value of the Scale Factors property to Single Vector.

4.   Drag and drop the `about.pdf` file from this lesson's resources folder onto the placeholder in the image set.

➤   Add user interface elements to the first tab.

1.   Open the `Main.storyboard` file and locate the scene called First Scene.

2.   Delete the two labels that are present on the scene. These should have the captions "First View" and "Loaded by FirstViewController" respectively.

3.   Add a `UITableView` instance to the scene using the Object library.

4.   Ensure the table view is selected and use the Pin button to display the constraints editor popup.

   ➤   Ensure the Constrain to margins option is unchecked.

   ➤   Pin the distance between the left edge of the view and the table view to 0.

   ➤   Pin the distance between the right edge of the view and the table view to 0.

   ➤   Pin the distance between the bottom of the view and the table view to 0.

   ➤   Pin the distance between the top of the view and the table view to 20.

   ➤   Click the Add 4 Constraints button to dismiss the constraints editor popup.

5.   Update the frames to match the constraints you have set.

   ➤   Click on the View controller item in the dock above the storyboard scene. This is the first of the three icons located directly above the selected storyboard scene.

   ➤   Select Editor ➪ Resolve Auto Layout Issues ➪ Update Frames.

6.   Using the assistant editor, create an outlet for the table view in the view controller class, and call the outlet `tableView`.

7.   Set up the data source and delegate properties.

   ➤   Right-click the table view to bring up a context menu. Drag from the item labeled "dataSource" in the context menu to the item labeled "First" in the document outline.

   ➤   Right-click the table view to bring up a context menu. Drag from the item labeled "delegate" in the context menu to the item labeled "First" in the document outline.

8. Set up the table view's appearance.

    ➤   Select the table view and ensure the Attribute inspector is visible.

    ➤   Ensure the Content attribute is set to Dynamic Prototypes.

    ➤   Ensure the value of the Prototype Cells attribute is 1.

    ➤   Ensure the Style attribute is set to Grouped.

9. Set up the prototype cell.

    ➤   Expand the table view in the document outline; this will reveal the table view cell.

    ➤   Select the table view cell.

    ➤   Use the attribute editor to ensure that the value of the identifier attribute is `prototypeCell1`.

    ➤   Ensure the Style attribute is set to Basic.

➤   Update the tab bar item for the first tab.

    1. Select the Tab bar item on the scene called First.

    2. Use the Attribute inspector to set the value of the System Item property to Top Rated.

➤   Add user interface elements to the second tab.

    1. Open the `Main.storyboard` file and locate the scene called Second Scene.

    2. Edit the contents of the "Second View" label to "City Index."

    3. Edit the contents of the "Loaded by SecondViewController" label to "Cities listed by continent."

➤   Update the tab bar item for the second tab.

    1. Select the Tab bar item on the scene called Second.

    2. Use the Attribute inspector to set the value of the Title property to About.

    3. Set the value of the Image attribute to `aboutImage`.

➤   Ensure the `FirstViewController` class implements the `UITableViewDataSource` and `UITableViewDelegate` protocols.

    Modify the declaration of the `FirstViewController` class from

    ```
    class FirstViewController: UIViewController
    ```
    to
    ```
    class FirstViewController: UIViewController,
                               UITableViewDataSource,
                               UITableViewDelegate
    ```

➤   Implement the data source and delegate methods in the view controller.

1. Add the following code snippet to the FirstViewController.swift file to declare five arrays of strings:

    ```
    let continents:Array<String> = ["Asia", "North America",
                                    "Europe", "Australia"]
    ```

    ```
    let citiesInAsia:Array<String> = ["Bangkok", "New Delhi",
                                      "Singapore", "Tokyo"]
    let citiesInNorthAmerica:Array<String> = ["San Francisco","Cupertino"]
    let citiesInEurope:Array<String> = ["London", "Paris", "Rome", "Athens"]
    let citiesInAustralia:Array<String> = ["Sydney", "Melbourne", "Cairns"]
    ```

2. Implement the numberOfSectionsInTableView data source method as follows:

    ```
    func numberOfSectionsInTableView(tableView: UITableView) -> Int
    {
        return continents.count;
    }
    ```

3. Implement the numberOfRowsInSection data source method as follows:

    ```
    func tableView(tableView: UITableView,
    numberOfRowsInSection section: Int) -> Int
    {
        if section == 0
        {
            return citiesInAsia.count
        }
        else if section == 1
        {
            return citiesInNorthAmerica.count
        }
        else if section == 2
        {
            return citiesInEurope.count
        }
        else if section == 3
        {
            return citiesInAustralia.count
        }

        return 0
    }
    ```

4. Implement the titleForHeaderInSection data source method as follows:

    ```
    func tableView(tableView: UITableView,
    titleForHeaderInSection section: Int) -> String?
    {
        return continents[section];
    }
    ```

5. Implement the cellforRowAtIndexPath data source method as follows:

    ```
    func tableView(tableView: UITableView,
    cellForRowAtIndexPath indexPath: NSIndexPath) ->
    UITableViewCell
    {
    ```

```
        let cell =
        tableView.dequeueReusableCellWithIdentifier("prototypeCell1",
        forIndexPath: indexPath)

        if indexPath.section == 0
        {
            cell.textLabel?.text = citiesInAsia[indexPath.row]
        }
        else if indexPath.section == 1
        {
            cell.textLabel?.text = citiesInNorthAmerica[indexPath.row]
        }
        else if indexPath.section == 2
        {
            cell.textLabel?.text = citiesInEurope[indexPath.row]
        }
        else if indexPath.section == 3
        {
            cell.textLabel?.text = citiesInAustralia[indexPath.row]
        }

        return cell
    }
```

➤ Test your app in the iOS Simulator.

Click the Run button in the Xcode toolbar. Alternatively, you can select Project ⇨ Run.

REFERENCE *To see some of the examples from this lesson, watch the Lesson 18 video online at* www.wrox.com/go/swiftiosvid.

19

Creating Views That Scroll

When your apps start to get more complex, sooner or later you will need to develop a strategy to scroll to off-screen content when a user swipes on a view in your app. This is particularly true if your app requires a user to fill a large form on a device with limited screen size.

You can either try to break up the content of your application and present it across multiple views using tab bars or navigation controllers, or you could still keep all the content in a single view but allow the user to scroll through the content of the view.

UIKit provides the UIScrollView class specifically designed to help you create scrollable views. In this lesson, you learn to use UIScrollView instances in your applications.

THE UISCROLLVIEW CLASS

To create a UIScrollView instance using the Xcode Interface Builder, simply drag and drop a Scroll View object from the Object library onto a scene, and create an outlet using the assistant editor (see Figure 19-1).

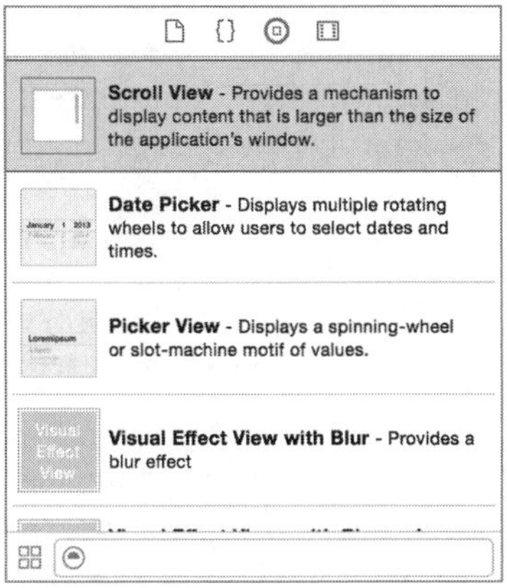

FIGURE 19-1

You can add one or more instances of UIView subclasses as subviews of the scroll view. The collective dimensions of these subviews can be much larger than the dimensions of the scroll view itself (see Figure 19-2).

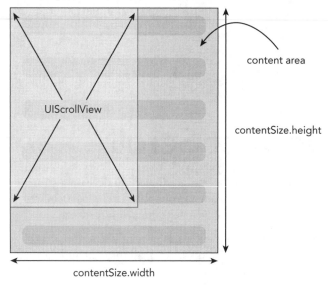

FIGURE 19-2

The dimensions of the content managed by a scroll view can be read (or set) using the contentSize property. The contentSize property is a CGSize structure and contains two float members, height and width. Thus, if scrollView is a UIScrollView instance, the following code could be used to read the height and width of the content area:

```
var contentHeight = scrollView.contentSize.height
var contentWidth = scrollView.contentSize.width
```

When you create a scroll view instance with Interface Builder, the size of the content area is exactly the same as the size of the scroll view. Thus, scroll views, by default, do not scroll. To enable the scrolling behavior, you need to set up the contentSize property programmatically. You can do this at any point after the scroll view is instantiated. If you created the scroll view with Interface Builder, you may want to set it up in the viewDidLoad method of the view controller class that contains the scroll view, using code similar to the following:

```
scrollView.contentSize = CGSizeMake(320, 4200);
```

Another property related to the scrolling behavior is the contentOffset property. This property is a CGPoint structure and contains two float members, x and y, that represent the distance scrolled by the user along the horizontal and vertical axes (see Figure 19-3).

You can add user interface elements to a scroll view with Interface Builder by simply dragging and dropping them from the Object library onto the scroll view. Positioning elements that are not initially visible in the scroll view can be a bit tricky. One way to solve this problem is to drag and drop elements onto the scroll view and then provide precise numeric values for the X and Y positions using the Attribute inspector (see Figure 19-4). If you do this though, you will also need to set up the appropriate constraints to ensure that the user elements occupy the current positions on the screen at runtime.

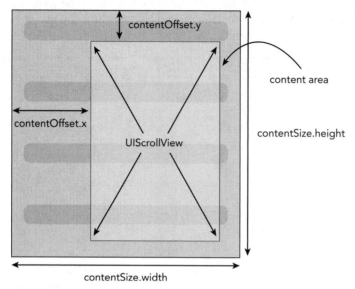

FIGURE 19-3

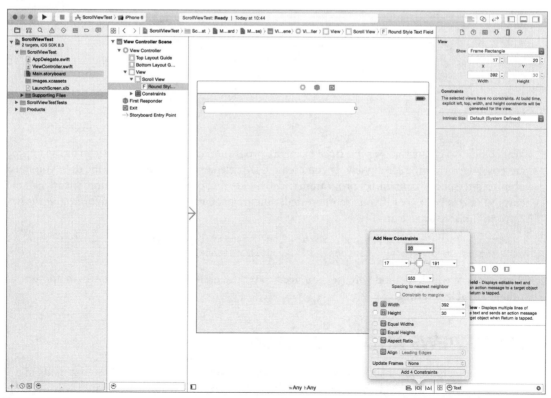

FIGURE 19-4

Another way is to resize/reposition the scroll view within the scene and create the user interface elements visually in their correct positions. Once the elements are in their correct positions, you can then set up constraints. This approach requires you to move the scroll view about in the scene a few times until you get the results you want (see Figure 19-5). Don't forget to reset the scroll view's position and size to their initial values after you are done.

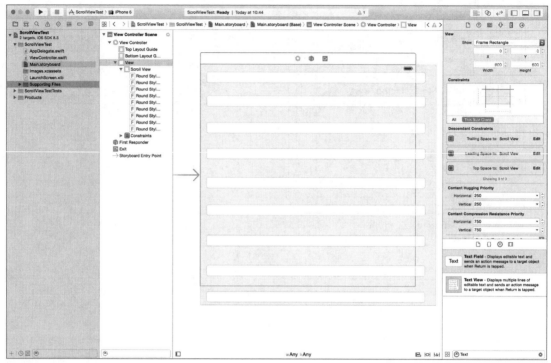

FIGURE 19-5

You could also create the user interface elements programmatically and insert them at the appropriate position within the scroll view. If you create UIKit elements programmatically, then you must also need to specify constraints programmatically. Creating constraints programmatically is not covered in this book, but if you are interested, you are encouraged to read the *Working with Auto Layout Guide* available at:

```
https://developer.apple.com/library/ios/documentation/UserExperience/Conceptual/
AutolayoutPG/AutoLayoutinCode/AutoLayoutinCode.html
```

Regardless of which method you use, you need to set the `contentSize` property to an appropriate value to enable scrolling.

SCROLL VIEWS AND TEXT FIELDS

A common scenario in which you are likely to use a scroll view involves multiple text fields in a scene. If you tap a text field closer to the bottom of the screen, a keyboard automatically pops up and covers part of the user interface. This is illustrated in Figure 19-6; when a user taps on the

Address (Line 1): field, the keyboard comes up and covers the text field, thus making it impossible for the user to see what is being typed.

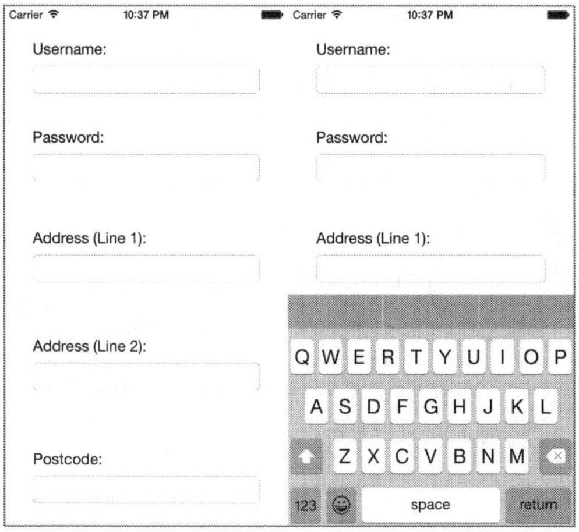

FIGURE 19-6

Scroll views provide a simple and elegant solution to this problem; you can change the Y offset of the content area within the scroll view when a specific text field is tapped, thus moving the content toward the top by a small amount. This solution is explored next, in this lesson's Try It section.

TRY IT

In this Try It, you create a simple application based on the Single View Application template called ScrollingForms that contains several text fields and a scroll view. When a text field is tapped on, the content of the scroll view is moved up by a small amount to ensure that the iOS keyboard will not cover the text field.

Lesson Requirements

➤ Launch Xcode.

➤ Create a new project based on the Single View Application template.

➤ Add a scroll view to the default scene of the storyboard.

➤ Use Interface Builder to add several user interface elements to the scroll view.

➤ Add code to the view controller class to move the content in the scroll view when a text field is tapped, thus ensuring the text field is always visible.

> **REFERENCE** *The code for this Try It is available at* www.wrox.com/go/
> swiftios.

Hints

➤ When creating a new project, you can use your website's domain name as the Company Identifier in the Project Options dialog box.

➤ To show the Object library, select View ⇨ Utilities ⇨ Show Object Library.

➤ To show the assistant editor, select View ⇨ Assistant Editor ⇨ Show Assistant Editor.

Step-by-Step

➤ Create a Single View Application in Xcode called `ScrollingForms`.

1. Launch Xcode and create a new application by selecting File ⇨ New ⇨ Project.

2. Select the Single View Application template from the list of iOS project templates.

3. In the project options, screen use the following values:

   ➤ **Product Name:** ScrollingForms

   ➤ **Organization Name:** your company

   ➤ **Organization Identifier:** com.yourcompany

   ➤ **Language:** Swift

   ➤ **Devices:** iPhone

   ➤ **Use Core Data:** Unchecked

   ➤ **Include Unit Tests:** Unchecked

   ➤ **Include UI Tests:** Unchecked

4. Save the project onto your hard disk.

➤ Add user interface elements to your storyboard's scene.

1. Add a `UIScrollView` instance to the default scene.

   Using the Object library, add a Scroll View to the default scene of the storyboard.

2. Ensure the scroll view is selected and use the Pin button to display the constraints editor popup (see Figure 19-7).

   ➤ Ensure the Constrain to margins option is unchecked.

   ➤ Pin the distance between the left edge of the view and the table view to 0.

   ➤ Pin the distance between the right edge of the view and the table view to 0.

   ➤ Pin the distance between the bottom of the view and the table view to 0.

   ➤ Pin the distance between the top of the view and the table view to 20.

   ➤ Click the Add 4 Constraints button to dismiss the constraints editor popup.

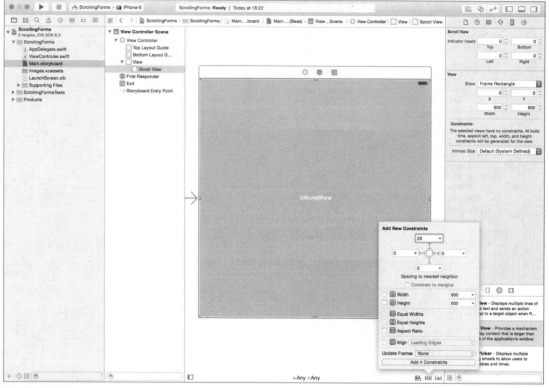

FIGURE 19-7

3. Update the frames to match the constraints you have set.

➤ Click on the View controller item in the dock above the storyboard scene. This is the first of the three icons located directly above the selected storyboard scene.

➤ Use the Editor ➪ Resolve Auto Layout Issues ➪ Update Frames menu item.

4. Using the assistant editor, create an outlet for the scroll view in the view controller class called `scrollView`.

➤ Add user interface elements to the scroll view.

1. Use the Object library to add five Label instances and five Text Field instances to the scroll view. Position them to resemble Figure 19-8.

2. Create layout constraints for each of elements on the storyboard scene using the information in Table 19-1. When creating layout constraints using the pin constraints dialog box, ensure the Constrain to margins option is unchecked.

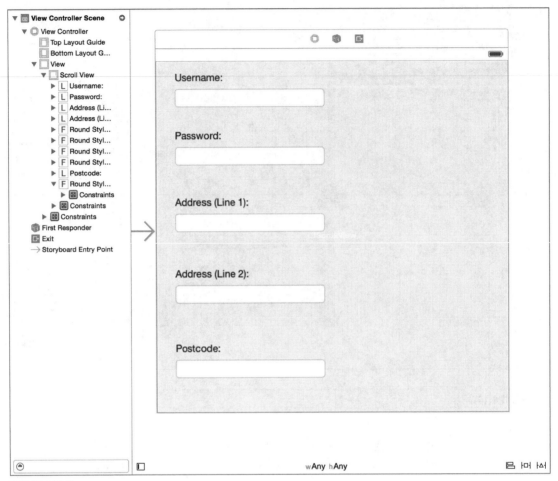

FIGURE 19-8

TABLE 19-1: Layout Constraints

ELEMENT	LEFT	TOP	WIDTH	HEIGHT
Username (Label)	32	17	84	21
Username (Text field)	32	8	256	30
Password (Label)	32	38	81	21
Password (Text field)	32	8	256	30
Address 1 (Label)	32	59	129	21
Address 1 (Text Field)	32	8	256	30

ELEMENT	LEFT	TOP	WIDTH	HEIGHT
Address 2 (Label)	32	59	129	21
Address 2 (Text Field)	32	8	256	30
Postcode (Label)	32	64	79	21
Postcode (Text Field)	32	8	256	30

3. Update the frames to match the constraints you have set.

➤ Click on the View controller item in the dock above the storyboard scene. This is the first of the three icons located directly above the selected storyboard scene.

➤ Use the Editor ➪ Resolve Auto Layout Issues ➪ Update Frames menu item.

4. Use the assistant editor to create outlets for each of the text fields in the view controller class. Name the outlets `usernameField`, `passwordField`, `addressField1`, `address-Field2`, and `postcodeField`.

➤ Ensure the view controller class implements the `UITextFieldDelegate` protocol.

Modify the declaration of the view controller class from

```
class ViewController: UIViewController
```

to

```
class ViewController: UIViewController, UITextFieldDelegate
```

➤ Add additional variable declarations to the `ViewController.swift` file.

1. Add the following variable declarations to the `ViewController.swift` file:

```
var keyboardHeight:Float
var currentTextField:UITextField!
```

2. The code in the `ViewController.swift` file should now resemble the following:

```
import UIKit

class ViewController: UIViewController, UITextFieldDelegate {

    @IBOutlet weak var usernameField: UITextField!
    @IBOutlet weak var passwordField: UITextField!
    @IBOutlet weak var addressField1: UITextField!
    @IBOutlet weak var addressField2: UITextField!
    @IBOutlet weak var postcodeField: UITextField!

    var keyboardHeight:Float = 0.0
    var currentTextField:UITextField!

    override func viewDidLoad() {
        super.viewDidLoad()
    }
```

```
override func didReceiveMemoryWarning() {
    super.didReceiveMemoryWarning()
}

}
```

➤ Set up the delegate for the text field instances.

Set up the view controller instance to be the `delegate` object for the text field instances by modifying the implementation of the `viewDidLoad` method to the following:

```
override func viewDidLoad() {
    super.viewDidLoad()

    usernameField.delegate = self
    passwordField.delegate = self
    addressField1.delegate = self
    addressField2.delegate = self
    postcodeField.delegate = self

}
```

➤ Set up your view controller class to be notified when the keyboard is displayed and dismissed.

1. You need to tell iOS to call the `keyboardDidShow` and `keyboarDidHide` methods in your view controller class when the keyboard becomes visible/hidden, respectively. To do this, you need to register these methods as observers for the `UIKeyboardDidShowNotification` and `UIKeyboardDidHideNotification` events. Add the following code to your view controller class to override the `viewWillAppear` method:

```
override func viewWillAppear(animated: Bool) {

    super.viewWillAppear(animated)

    NSNotificationCenter.defaultCenter().addObserver(self,
    selector: Selector("keyboardDidShow:"),
    name: UIKeyboardDidShowNotification ,
    object: self.view.window)

    NSNotificationCenter.defaultCenter().addObserver(self,
    selector: Selector("keyboardDidHide:"),
    name: UIKeyboardDidHideNotification ,
    object: nil)
}
```

2. When your view controller is dismissed, you need to tell iOS that your code is not interested in the notifications previously registered by overriding the `viewDidDisappear` method as follows:

```
override func viewDidDisappear(animated: Bool) {

    super.viewDidDisappear(animated)
```

```
NSNotificationCenter.defaultCenter().removeObserver(self,
name: UIKeyboardDidShowNotification,
object: nil)

NSNotificationCenter.defaultCenter().removeObserver(self,
name: UIKeyboardDidHideNotification,
object: nil)
}
```

> **NOTE** *The preceding code snippet removes individual observers one by one. If you want to remove all observers in one line, you can alternately implement the* viewDidDisappear *method as:*
>
> ```
> override func viewDidDisappear(animated: Bool) {
>
>     super.viewDidDisappear(animated)
>
>     NSNotificationCenter.defaultCenter().removeObserver(self)
> }
> ```

3. Implement the keyboardDidShow method in your view controller class as follows:

```
func keyboardDidShow(sender: NSNotification!)
{
    // get height of keyboard
    let info: NSDictionary = sender.userInfo!

    let value: NSValue =
    info.valueForKey(UIKeyboardFrameEndUserInfoKey) as! NSValue

    let keyboardFrame: CGRect = value.CGRectValue()

    // convert from Core Graphics CGFloat to Swift Float
    let cgFloatKeyboardHeight:CGFloat = keyboardFrame.size.height

    keyboardHeight = Float(cgFloatKeyboardHeight)

    // ensure current text field is visible,
    // if not adjust the contentOffset
    // of the scrollView appropriately.
    let textFieldTop:Float = Float(currentTextField.frame.origin.y)
    let textFieldBottom:Float = textFieldTop +
        Float(currentTextField.frame.size.height)

    if (textFieldBottom > keyboardHeight)
    {
        scrollView.setContentOffset(CGPointMake(0,
                CGFloat(textFieldBottom - keyboardHeight)),
                animated: true)
    }
}
```

The preceding code snippet stores the height of the keyboard in a member variable `keyboardHeight`. It then tests to see if the currently active text field is partly or wholly covered by the keyboard. If it is, it updates the `contentOffset` property of the scroll view to rectify the situation.

4. Implement the `keyboardDidHide` method in your view controller class as follows:

```
func keyboardDidHide(sender: NSNotification!)
{
    scrollView.setContentOffset(CGPointMake(0, 0), animated: false)
}
```

The preceding code snippet resets the `contentOffset` property of the scroll view to X = 0, and Y = 0.

➤ Implement `UITextFieldDelegate` methods in your view controller class.

1. Implement the `textFieldShouldReturn` method of the `UITextFieldDelegate` protocol as follows:

```
func textFieldShouldReturn(textField: UITextField) -> Bool {
    textField.resignFirstResponder()
    return true;
}
```

2. Implement the `textFieldDidBeginEditing` method of the `UITextFieldDelegate` protocol as follows:

```
func textFieldDidBeginEditing(textField: UITextField)
{
    currentTextField = textField

    var textFieldTop:Float = Float(currentTextField.frame.origin.y)
    var textFieldBottom:Float = textFieldTop +
        Float(currentTextField.frame.size.height)

    if textFieldBottom > keyboardHeight && keyboardHeight != 0.0
    {
        scrollView.setContentOffset(CGPointMake(0,
                CGFloat(textFieldBottom - keyboardHeight)),
                animated: true)
    }
}
```

The preceding code snippet is called when the user taps on a text field. It first saves a reference to the text field in the variable `currentTextField`. It then checks to see if the field is wholly/partially obscured by the keyboard. If this is the case, it updates the `contentOffset` property of the scroll view to rectify this situation.

➤ Test your app in the iOS Simulator.

Click the Run button in the Xcode toolbar. Alternatively, you can select Project ➪ Run.

REFERENCE *To see some of the examples from this lesson, watch the Lesson 19 video online at* www.wrox.com/go/swiftiosvid.

20

Popovers and Modal Views

Popovers and modal views provide ways to temporarily display some information to users. The information that is displayed is usually contextual and related to an action performed by the user.

Both popovers and modal views interrupt the user's journey through your application; the user must interact with the popover/modal view before using the rest of the application. Popovers are dismissed by tapping outside the bounds of the popover; modal views are dismissed by using a user-defined cancel button located in the modal view. Popovers are only available on iPads, whereas modal views are available on both the iPad and iPhone.

POPOVERS

A popover view is one that is revealed when a control is tapped. A popover appears attached to the control that was tapped to reveal it (see Figure 20-1).

Popovers are only supported on the iPad, and should be used to display additional information related to the control that displays it. When presenting a popover, you do not provide a Done or Cancel button; popovers are dismissed when the user taps outside the popover.

To present a scene in your storyboard in a popover, simply create a popover presentation segue from a button in one of the other scenes of your view controller to the scene you wish to use within the popover (see Figure 20-2).

FIGURE 20-1

You can use the Attribute inspector to configure the popover presentation segue (see Figure 20-3). The Anchor attribute references a button (or bar button item) in the presenting view controller. The popover will be anchored to this control. By default, popovers are dismissed as soon as the user taps outside them. If you do not want the popover to be dismissed when some controls are tapped, you can set up the Passthrough attribute to reference them.

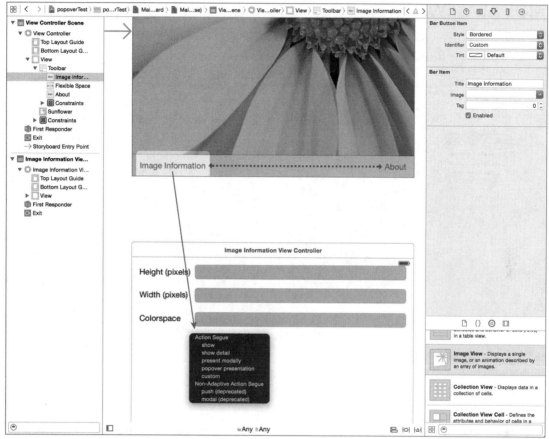

FIGURE 20-2

FIGURE 20-3

MODAL VIEWS

A modal view can be created in a couple of different ways; the most common is to use a Present Modally segue from a button in a scene to another scene (see Figure 20-4).

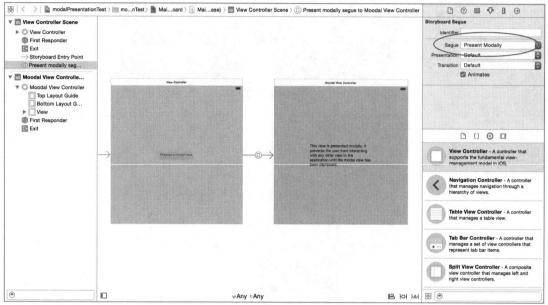

FIGURE 20-4

The Present Modally segue has a few presentation styles that can be set up using the Attribute inspector:

➤ Full Screen

➤ Current Context

➤ Form Sheet

➤ Page Sheet

The default setting is to present the modal view so that it takes up the entire screen. A commonly used presentation style is form sheet. On an iPhone, the form sheet presentation style and the full screen presentation style achieve identical effects. However, on the iPad, the form sheet presentation style causes the modal view to appear as a self-contained form centered in the presenting view (see Figure 20-5).

When a view is presented modally, there is no system-provided means to dismiss it and return back to the presenting view. If you do not provide a way to dismiss the modal view, then your user will be unable to use the rest of your application (see Figure 20-6).

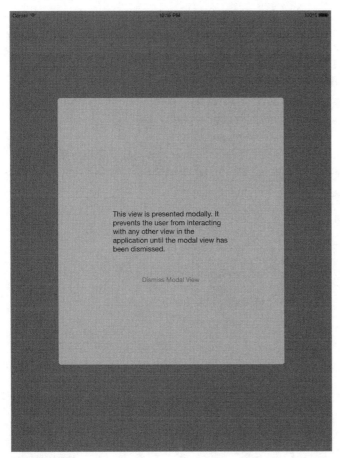

FIGURE 20-5

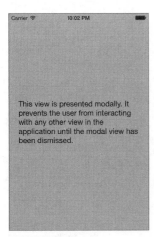

FIGURE 20-6

Modal views are used when your app needs to collect some vital information before proceeding. Typically you add a close button in the modal view that, when tapped, will dismiss it. You cannot use a segue to dismiss a modal view; instead you must call the `dismissViewControllerAnimated` method on the modal view controller. This method allows you to provide an optional completion handler that is executed when the modal view is dismissed.

```
@IBAction func onDismissModalView(sender: AnyObject) {
        self.dismissViewControllerAnimated(true, completion: nil);
    }
```

If you do not wish to use a segue, you can alternately present a scene in your storyboard modally by using the following code snippet attached to a `UIButton` instance in the presenting view controller:

```
@IBAction func onPresentModalView(sender: AnyObject) {

        let modalViewController:ModalViewController =

(self.storyboard!.instantiateViewControllerWithIdentifier
("ModalViewController") as? ModalViewController)!
        modalViewController.modalPresentationStyle =
UIModalPresentationStyle.FormSheet
        self.presentViewController(modalViewController,
animated: true, completion: nil)

    }
```

TRY IT

In this Try It, you create a simple iPad-only application based on the Single View Application template called PopoverTest, which displays an image and some information on the image in a popover.

Lesson Requirements

➤   Launch Xcode.

➤   Create a new iPad-only project based on the Single View Application template.

➤   Create a storyboard with multiple scenes.

➤   Use Interface Builder to create segues between scenes.

➤   Present a scene in a popover.

> **REFERENCE** *The code for this Try It is available at* www.wrox.com/go/ swiftios.

Hints

➤ When creating a new project, you can use your website's domain name as the Company Identifier in the Project Options dialog box.

➤ To show the Object library, select View ➩ Utilities ➩ Show Object Library.

➤ To show the assistant editor, select View ➩ Assistant Editor ➩ Show Assistant Editor.

Step-by-Step

➤ Create a Single View Application in Xcode called PopoverTest.

1. Launch Xcode and create a new application by selecting File ➩ New ➩ Project.

2. Select the Single View Application template from the list of iOS project templates.

3. In the project options screen, use the following values:

   ➤ **Product Name:** PopoverTest

   ➤ **Organization Name:** your company

   ➤ **Organization Identifier:** com.yourcompany

   ➤ **Language:** Swift

   ➤ **Devices:** iPad

   ➤ **Use Core Data:** Unchecked

   ➤ **Include Unit Tests:** Unchecked

   ➤ **Include UI Tests:** Unchecked

4. Save the project onto your hard disk.

➤ Add image resources to your project.

1. Ensure the project navigator is visible. To show it, select View ➩ Navigators ➩ Show Project Navigator.

2. Open the Assets.xcassets file by clicking on it in the project navigator.

3. Navigate to the Images folder in this chapter's download from the book website.

4. Create a new image set using Editor ➩ New Image Set and name this new image set Sunflower.

5. Drag the Sunflower_1x.jpg, sunflower_2x.jpg, and Sunflower_3x.jpg images from this chapter's resources into the appropriate placeholders in the image set.

➤ Add user interface elements to your storyboard's scene.

1. Add a toolbar to the bottom of the scene.

   Using the Object library, add a Toolbar to the bottom of the storyboard scene.

2. Ensure the toolbar is selected and use the Pin button to display the constraints editor popup.

   ➤ Ensure the Constrain to margins option is unchecked.

   ➤ Pin the distance between the left edge of the view and the toolbar to 0.

   ➤ Pin the distance between the right edge of the view and the toolbar to 0.

   ➤ Pin the distance between the bottom of the view and the toolbar to 0.

   ➤ Pin the height of the toolbar to 44.

   ➤ Click the Add 4 Constraints button to dismiss the constraints editor popup.

3. Update the frames to match the constraints you have set.

   ➤ Click on the View controller item in the dock above the storyboard scene. This is the first of the three icons located directly above the selected storyboard scene.

   ➤ Select Editor ⇨ Resolve Auto Layout Issues ⇨ Update Frames.

4. Edit the toolbar.

   Select the default bar button item in the toolbar and rename it to Image Information.

5. Add a UIImageView instance to the default scene.

   Use the Object library to add an Image View to the default scene of the storyboard. Place it above the tab bar.

6. Ensure the image view is selected and use the Pin button to display the constraints editor popup.

   ➤ Ensure the Constrain to margins option is unchecked.

   ➤ Pin the distance between the left edge of the view and the image view to 0.

   ➤ Pin the distance between the right edge of the view and the image view to 0.

   ➤ Pin the distance between the bottom of the image view and the tab bar to 0.

   ➤ Pin the distance between the top of the view and the image view to 20.

   ➤ Click the Add 4 Constraints button to dismiss the constraints editor popup.

7. Update the frames to match the constraints you have set.

   ➤ Click on the View controller item in the dock above the storyboard scene. This is the first of the three icons located directly above the selected storyboard scene.

   ➤ Select Editor ⇨ Resolve Auto Layout Issues ⇨ Update Frames.

8. Using the assistant editor, create an outlet for the image view in the view controller class called `imageView`.

➤ Add code to the view controller class.

1. Add a variable declaration to the view controller class.

```
var image:UIImage!
```

2. Add the following snippet to the end of the view controller's `viewDidLoad` method to load an image and set up the image view:

```
image = UIImage(named: "Sunflower")

imageView.image = image
imageView.contentMode = UIViewContentMode.ScaleAspectFit
```

3. Add the following implementation of the `prepareForSegue(segue: sender:)` to the view controller class.

```
override func prepareForSegue(segue: UIStoryboardSegue, sender: AnyObject?) {

        if segue.identifier == "imageInformationSegue" {
            let viewController:ImageInformationViewController =
    segue.destinationViewController as!
    ImageInformationViewController
                viewController.imageBeingDisplayed = self.image
        }


    }
```

➤ Create an additional view controller scene.

1. Use the Object library to drag and drop a new View Controller scene onto the storyboard.

2. Create a new Cocoa Touch class called `ImageInformationViewController` by selecting File ➪ New. Ensure the class is a subclass of `UIViewController` (see Figure 20-7).

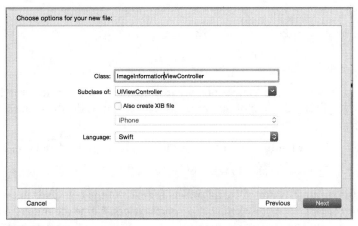

FIGURE 20-7

3. Select the new scene in the storyboard and switch to the Identity Inspector (View ⇨ Utilities ⇨ Show Identity Inspector).

4. Change the Class attribute of the scene to `ImageInformationViewController`.

➤ Add user interface elements to your new scene.

1. Add three labels to the scene.

   Using the Object Library, drag and drop three labels onto the scene, position them one below the other, and name them Height (pixels), Width (pixels), and Colorspace.

2. Add three text fields to the scene.

   ➤ Using the Object Library, drag and drop three text fields onto the scene; position them one below the other and beside the three labels you have created in the previous step.

   ➤ Use the Attribute inspector to change the background color of the three text fields to a shade of dark gray.

3. Create layout constraints for each of elements on the storyboard scene using the information in Table 20-1. When creating layout constraints using the pin constraints dialog box, ensure the Constrain to margins option is unchecked.

TABLE 20-1: Layout Constraints

ELEMENT	LEFT	TOP	RIGHT	WIDTH	HEIGHT
Height (label)	16	20		115	21
Height (text field)	24	0	16		30
Width (label)	16	26		115	21
Width (text field)	24	18	16		30
Colorspace (label)	16	26		115	21
Colorspace (text field)	24	18	16		30

4. Update the frames to match the constraints you have set.

   ➤ Click on the View controller item in the dock above the storyboard scene. This is the first of the three icons located directly above the selected storyboard scene.

   ➤ Select Editor ⇨ Resolve Auto Layout Issues ⇨ Update Frames.

   ➤ Your scene should resemble Figure 20-8.

5. Use the assistant editor to create outlets for each of the text fields in the `ImageInformationViewController.swift` class. Name the outlets `imageHeight`, `imageWidth`, and `imageColorSpace`.

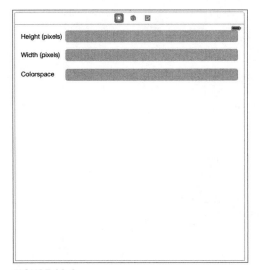

FIGURE 20-8

➤ Update the `ImageInformationViewController.swift` file to display information on the image file.

1. Add the following variable declarations to the file:

```
var imageBeingDisplayed:UIImage!
```

2. Update the `viewDidLoad` method in the `ImageInformationViewController.swift` file to resemble the following:

```
override func viewDidLoad() {
        super.viewDidLoad()

        let imageSize = imageBeingDisplayed.size
        let height = imageSize.height
        let width = imageSize.width

        imageHeight.text = "\(height)"
        imageWidth.text = "\(width)"
        imageColorSpace.text = "RGB"
    }
```

➤ The code in the `ImageInformationViewController.swift` file should now resemble the following:

```
import UIKit

class ImageInformationViewController: UIViewController {

    @IBOutlet weak var imageHeight: UITextField!
    @IBOutlet weak var imageWidth: UITextField!
    @IBOutlet weak var imageColorSpace: UITextField!
```

```
var imageBeingDisplayed:UIImage!

override func viewDidLoad() {
    super.viewDidLoad()

    let imageSize = imageBeingDisplayed.size
    let height = imageSize.height
    let width = imageSize.width

    imageHeight.text = "\(height)"
    imageWidth.text = "\(width)"
    imageColorSpace.text = "RGB"
}

override func didReceiveMemoryWarning() {
    super.didReceiveMemoryWarning()
}

}
```

➤ Create a segue from the Image Information bar button item in the first scene to the Image Information View Controller scene.

1. Select the Image Information bar button item in the first scene.

2. Ctrl+drag from the bar button item to the second scene. On releasing the mouse button, you will be presented with a context menu that lets you select the segue type. Select `Popover Presentation` from the list.

3. Select the segue in the scene and use the Attribute inspector to set its identifier attribute to `imageInformationSegue`.

➤ Test your app in the iOS Simulator.

Click the Run button in the Xcode toolbar. Alternatively, you can select Project ➪ Run.

REFERENCE *To see some of the examples from this lesson, watch the Lesson 20 video online at* www.wrox.com/go/swiftiosvid.

21

Touches and Gestures

Your users interact with your iOS applications using touches and gestures, as opposed to a keyboard and mouse. While touches and gestures aren't the only ways users could interact with your apps, they are definitely the most common, with touches being more prevalent than gestures. Both touches and gestures are UIEvent instances and are managed by the UIApplication class.

TOUCH EVENTS

When the user begins a touch sequence, the system generates a touch event and packages information into this event. A touch event is represented by an instance of the UIEventTypeTouches object; individual touches themselves are represented by UITouch instances.

Touch events are placed by UIKit in an application-level event queue and dispatched by your application's run loop to the window that initiated the event. From there they are forwarded to the first responder, which is usually the view where the touch occurred. If that view cannot handle the touch event, then the event is forwarded to the next responder in the chain, which could be the view controller that manages the view.

To place a UIView subclass at the front of the responder chain, you send it the becomeFirst Responder() message. Some views such as UITextView display a keyboard when they are sent this message.

If you want to process touch events in your own UIView subclass, you must first override can-BecomeFirstResponder and return true from this method.

To handle touch events, you need to override one or more of the following methods:

```
func touchesBegan(_ touches: Set<UITouch>, withEvent event: UIEvent?)
func touchesMoved(_ touches: Set<UITouch>, withEvent event: UIEvent?)
func touchesEnded(_ touches: Set<UITouch>, withEvent event: UIEvent?)
func touchesCancelled(_ touches: Set<UITouch>?, withEvent event: UIEvent?)
```

The `touchesBegan` method is called to inform your view when one or more fingers touch down in a view, `touchesMoved` is called when the user drags one or more fingers across your view, and `touchesEnded` is called when the user lifts one or more fingers off your view. The first parameter is a set of `UITouch` instances, one for each finger. Multi-touch is disabled by default; to enable it, you must call `multipleTouchEnabled` on the view in question.

The last method in the list, `touchesCancelled`, is called if the system cancels the touch event in response to a low memory warning or an incoming call.

> **NOTE** *If you override any of these four methods without calling* super *in your implementation, you must also override the other methods, even if you provide empty implementations.*

GESTURE RECOGNIZERS

Touch events provide low-level information on touches as they happen; sometimes they can provide too much detail, and interpreting a sequence of touches to represent a gesture can be a complex task. This is where gesture recognizers come it.

A gesture recognizer is a subclass of `UIGestureRecognizer` and can be used to interpret low-level touch event data into meaningful gestures. Apple provides the following subclasses of `UIGestureRecognizer` to recognize specific types of gestures:

➤ `UITapGestureRecognizer`: For single and multiple taps

➤ `UIPinchGestureRecognizer`: For pinch in, pinch out gestures

➤ `UIPanGestureRecognizer`: For dragging

➤ `UISwipeGestureRecognizer`: For swipes

➤ `UIRotationGestureRecognizer`: For rotation

➤ `UILongPressGestureRecognizer`: For touch and hold (long press)

To use a gesture recognizer in your view, you can either add one or more appropriate gesture recognizers programmatically, or through the interface editor.

To add a gesture recognizer to a view using the interface editor, simply drag and drop the appropriate gesture recognizer from the Object Library onto your view (see Figure 21-1).

To create a gesture recognizer programmatically, simply instantiate one using the appropriate initializer and add it to the view using the views `addGestureRecognizer` method.

Regardless of which method you use to add a gesture recognizer to your view, you will need to provide a method in your class that will be called when the gesture recognizer has detected an appropriate gesture.

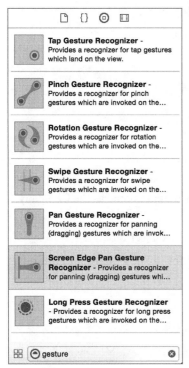

FIGURE 21-1

The following snippet shows how to add a tap gesture recognizer to a view:

```
let tapRecognizer = UITapGestureRecognizer(target:self ,
action: Selector("handleBackgroundTap:"))

tapRecognizer.cancelsTouchesInView = false
self.view.addGestureRecognizer(tapRecognizer)
```

If you would like your gesture recognizer to forward the underlying touch events to your view after it has processed them, ensure the `cancelsTouchesInViews` property is set to false.

TRY IT

In this Try It, you create a simple iPhone application based on the Single View Application template called GestureTest that adds a tap gesture recognizers to the main scene of the storyboard and updates a label when a gesture is interpreted.

Lesson Requirements

➤   Launch Xcode.

➤   Create a new iPhone project based on the Single View Application template.

➤ Add user interface elements to the default scene of the storyboard.

➤ Add gesture recognizers to the scene using the Interface Editor.

> **REFERENCE** *The code for this Try It is available at* www.wrox.com/go/
> swiftios.

Hints

➤ When creating a new project, you can use your website's domain name as the Company Identifier in the Project Options dialog box.

➤ To show the Object library, select View ➪ Utilities ➪ Show Object Library.

➤ To show the assistant editor, select View ➪ Assistant Editor ➪ Show Assistant Editor.

Step-by-Step

➤ Create a Single View Application in Xcode called GestureTest.

1. Launch Xcode and create a new application by selecting File ➪ New ➪ Project.

2. Select the Single View Application template from the list of iOS project templates.

3. In the project options screen use the following values:

   ➤ **Product Name:** Gesture

   ➤ **Organization Name:** your company

   ➤ **Organization Identifier:** com.yourcompany

   ➤ **Language:** Swift

   ➤ **Devices:** iPhone

   ➤ **Use Core Data:** Unchecked

   ➤ **Include UI Tests:** Unchecked

4. Save the project onto your hard disk

➤ Add a UILabel instance to the default scene.

1. From the Object library, drag and drop a Label object onto the scene.

2. Ensure the label is selected and use the Pin button to display the constraints editor popup.

➤ Ensure the Constrain to margins option is unchecked.

➤ Pin the distance between the left edge of the view and the table view to 20.

➤ Pin the distance between the right edge of the view and the table view to 20.

➤ Pin the height of the label to 21.

➤ Pin the distance between the top of the view and the table view to 20.

➤ Ensure the value of the Update Frames combo box is set to All Frames In Container. Using this option will automatically update the frames for all objects in the scene as soon as you finish adding the constraints. The alternative is to use the Editor ➪ Resolve Auto Layout Issues ➪ Update Frames menu item after adding the constraints.

➤ Click the Add 4 Constraints button to dismiss the constraints editor popup.

3. Add an outlet in the view controller class and connect it to the label in the scene.

➤ Ensure the Assistant editor is visible. To show it, select View ➪ Assistant Editor ➪ Show Assistant Editor.

➤ Right-click the `label` to display a context menu. Drag from the circle beside the New Referencing Outlet option in the context menu to an empty line in the `ViewController` class.

➤ Name the new outlet `gestureType`.

➤ Add a tap gesture recognizer to the default scene.

1. From the Object library, drag and drop a Tap Gesture Recognizer object onto the scene.

2. Ensure the Assistant editor is visible. To show it, select View ➪ Assistant Editor ➪ Show Assistant Editor.

3. Right-click the tap gesture recognizer to display a context menu. Drag from the circle beside the first item under the Sent Actions group to an empty line in the `ViewController` class (see Figure 21-2).

4. Name the new action `onTapGestureDetected`.

➤ Add code to the view controller class.

1. Open the `ViewController.swift` file in the project explorer.

2. Replace the stub implementation of the `onTapGestureDetected` method to resemble with following:

```
@IBAction func onTapGestureDetected(sender: AnyObject) {
    gestureType.text = "Tap gesture detected"
}
```

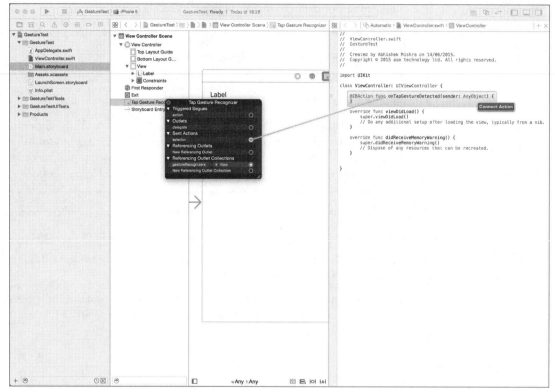

FIGURE 21-2

➤ Test your app in the iOS Simulator.

Click the Run button in the Xcode toolbar. Alternatively, you can select Project ⇨ Run.

> **REFERENCE** *To see some of the examples from this lesson,* watch the Lesson 21 *video online at* www.wrox.com/go/swiftiosvid.

SECTION III
Storing Data and Network Programming

22

Property Lists

A property list is an XML key-value store that allows applications to store small amounts of data locally. Property lists are best suited to storing small amounts of data (less than a few hundred kilobytes). It is quite common for applications to use property lists to store application configuration information, such as server addresses and URLs.

CREATING PROPERTY LISTS

A property list can be created using the property list editor, or programmatically. The GUI property list editor that is integrated with XCode displays a property list file as a hierarchy of nodes and elements, all contained under a root node (see Figure 22-1). The root node can be either an array or a dictionary.

Key	Type	Value
▼ Root	Array	(3 items)
▼ Item 0	Dictionary	(3 items)
name	String	Bob
age	Number	21
address	String	117 Bilton Road
▼ Item 1	Dictionary	(3 items)
name	String	Jane
age	Number	45
address	String	11 Stucley Avenue
▼ Item 2	Dictionary	(3 items)
name	String	Paul
age	Number	25
address	String	17 Leicester Square

FIGURE 22-1

To create a property list, add a new file to the project and select Property List from the iOS Resource section in the file options dialog box (see Figure 22-2).

FIGURE 22-2

This will add an empty property list file to your project, with a single dictionary element called Root (see Figure 22-3).

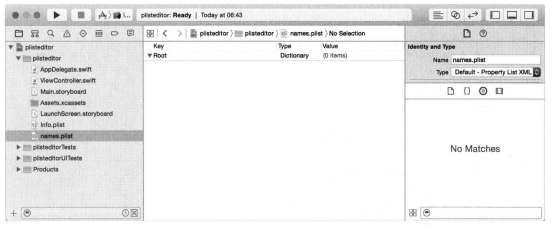

FIGURE 22-3

To add a new entry to the property list, select the parent node and select Editor ➪ Add Item (see Figure 22-4).

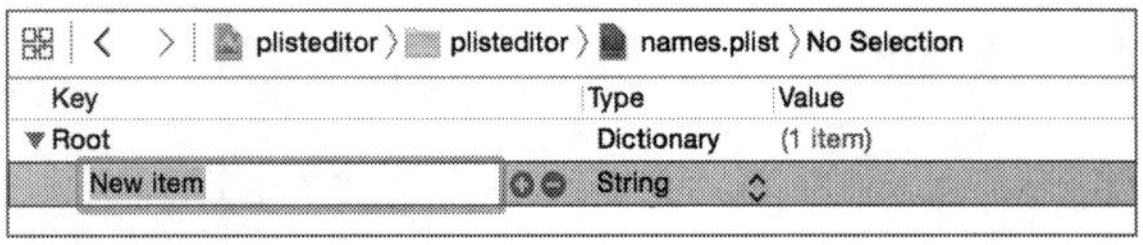

Key	Type	Value
▼ Root	Dictionary	(1 item)
New item	String	

FIGURE 22-4

The default data type for new items is String; you can change that using the drop-down picker in the second column. If the parent node is a dictionary, then each child is treated as a key-value pair with keys being unique Strings.

To create a property list programmatically, you need to build a dictionary or array with data you wish to save and write it to a file in your application's documents directory. The following code snippet shows how you can achieve this:

```
func writeToPlist(fileName:String!, data:NSMutableDictionary!)
{
    let paths = NSSearchPathForDirectoriesInDomains(.DocumentDirectory,
            .UserDomainMask, true)[0] as String
    let path = paths.stringByAppendingPathComponent(fileName)
        data.writeToFile(path, atomically: true)
}
```

If all the data you wish to write to a property list file can be represented using a combination of NSNumber, NSString, NSArray, NSDictionary, and NSData instances, then your task is straightforward. If, however, you wish to write instances of your own classes to a property list file, you must implement the NSCoding protocol.

NSCoding defines two methods encodeWithCoder(aCoder: NSCoder) and a designated initializer init?(coder aDecoder: NSCoder).

The following code snippet lists a class Employee that is NSCoding-compliant and can be inserted into a property list.

```
import UIKit

class Employee: NSObject, NSCoding {

    var name:String?
    var address:String?

    func encodeWithCoder(aCoder: NSCoder)
    {
        // write to plist here.
        aCoder.encodeObject(name)
        aCoder.encodeObject(address)
    }

    required init?(coder aDecoder: NSCoder)
    {
      // read from plist here
      name = aDecoder.decodeObjectForKey("name") as? String
      address = aDecoder.decodeObjectForKey("address") as? String }
}
```

READING PROPERTY LISTS

To read a property list file, you need to load its contents into an array or dictionary. The following code snippet assumes you have added a property list file called Config.plist to the project:

```
var plistDictionary: NSDictionary?
if let path = NSBundle.mainBundle().pathForResource("Config", ofType: "plist") {
    plistDictionary = NSDictionary(contentsOfFile: path)
}

if let unwrappedDictionary = pListDictionary {
    // Use unwrappedDictionary here
}
```

TRY IT

In this Try It, you create a simple iPhone application based on the Single View Application template called PropertyListTest that populates a table view with contents read off a plist file. The contents of the plist file will be generated programmatically.

Lesson Requirements

➤ Launch Xcode.

➤ Create a new iPhone project based on the Single View Application template.

➤ Create a storyboard with a single scene.

➤ Add code to the application delegate object to create the plist file when the application is launched.

➤ Read the plist file in the view controller and display its contents in a table view.

> **REFERENCE** *The code for this Try It is available at* www.wrox.com/go/
> swiftios.

Hints

➤ When creating a new project, you can use your website's domain name as the Company Identifier in the Project Options dialog box.

➤ To show the Object library, select View ➪ Utilities ➪ Show Object Library.

➤ To show the Assistant editor, select View ➪ Assistant Editor ➪ Show Assistant Editor.

Step-by-Step

➤ Create a Single View Application in Xcode called PropertyListTest.

1. Launch Xcode and create a new application by selecting File ➪ New ➪ Project menu item.

2. Select the Single View Application template from the list of iOS project templates.

3. In the project options screen, use the following values:

> ➤ **Product Name:** PropertyListTest

> ➤ **Organization Name:** your company

> ➤ **Organization Identifier:** com.yourcompany

> ➤ **Language:** Swift

> ➤ **Devices:** iPhone

> ➤ **Use Core Data:** Unchecked

> ➤ **Include Unit Tests:** Unchecked

> ➤ **Include UI Tests:** Unchecked

4. Save the project onto your hard disk.

➤ Add a `UITableView` instance to the default scene.

1. From the Object library, drag and drop a Table View object onto the scene.

2. Ensure the table view is selected and use the Pin button to display the constraints editor popup.

> ➤ Ensure the Constrain to margins option is unchecked.

> ➤ Pin the distance between the left edge of the view and the table view to 0.

> ➤ Pin the distance between the right edge of the view and the table view to 0.

> ➤ Pin the distance between the bottom of the view and the table view to 0.

> ➤ Pin the distance between the top of the view and the table view to 20.

> ➤ Click the Add 4 Constraints button to dismiss the constraints editor popup.

3. Update the frames to match the constraints you have set.

> ➤ Click on the View controller item in the dock above the storyboard scene. This is the first of the three icons located directly above the selected storyboard scene.

> ➤ Select Editor ⇨ Resolve Auto Layout Issues ⇨ Update Frames.

4. Set up the data source and delegate properties

> ➤ Right-click the table view to bring up a context menu. Drag from the item labeled "dataSource" in the context menu to the item labeled "View Controller" in the document outline.

> ➤ Drag from the item labeled "delegate" in the context menu to the item labeled "View Controller" in the document outline.

➤ Set up the table view's appearance.

1. Select the table view and ensure the Attributes inspector is visible.

2.   Ensure the Content attribute is set to Dynamic Prototypes.

3.   Ensure the value of the Prototype Cells attribute is 1.

4.   Ensure the Style attribute is set to Grouped.

➤ Set up the prototype cell.

1.   Expand the table view in the document outline; this will reveal the table view cell.

2.   Select the table view cell.

3.   Use the attribute editor to ensure that the value of the identifier attribute is `prototypeCell1`.

4.   Ensure the Style attribute is set to Basic.

➤ Add code to the application delegate to create a plist file.

1.   Open the `AppDelegate.swift` file in the project explorer.

2.   Replace the implementation of `application(application, didFinishLaunching-WithOptions) -> Bool` with

```
func application(application: UIApplication, didFinishLaunchingWithOptions
launchOptions: [NSObject: AnyObject]?) -> Bool {

    // create contacts.plist in the documents directory, if it does not
exist
    let fileManager:NSFileManager! = NSFileManager.defaultManager()

    let documentsDirectory:String =
NSSearchPathForDirectoriesInDomains(
NSSearchPathDirectory.DocumentDirectory, NSSearchPathDomainMask.
UserDomainMask,
true)[0] as String

    let plistPath = documentsDirectory + "/contacts.plist"

    if fileManager.fileExistsAtPath(plistPath) == false {

        let contacts:NSMutableArray = NSMutableArray()
        contacts.addObject("Elana")
        contacts.addObject("Sonam")
        contacts.addObject("Jane")
        contacts.addObject("Paul")
        contacts.addObject("Abhishek")
        contacts.addObject("Nick")
        contacts.addObject("Steve")

        contacts.writeToFile(plistPath, atomically: true)
    }

    return true
}
```

➤ Load the plist file in the view controller class.

1. Open the `ViewController.swift` file in the project explorer.

2. Add the following variable declaration to the view controller class:

    ```
    var arrayOfContacts:NSArray? = nil
    ```

3. Replace the implementation of the `viewDidLoad` method with the following:

    ```
    override func viewDidLoad() {

        super.viewDidLoad()

        // load contacts.plist into arrayOfContacts
        let documentsDirectory:String =
    NSSearchPathForDirectoriesInDomains(
    NSSearchPathDirectory.DocumentDirectory, NSSearchPathDomainMask.
    UserDomainMask,
    true)[0] as String

        let plistPath = documentsDirectory + "/contacts.plist"

        arrayOfContacts = NSArray(contentsOfFile: plistPath)
    }
    ```

➤ Implement the data source and delegate methods in the view controller.

1. Implement the `numberOfSectionsInTableView` data source method as follows:

    ```
    func numberOfSectionsInTableView(tableView: UITableView) -> Int
    {
        return 1;
    }
    ```

2. Implement the `numberOfRowsInSection` data source method as follows:

    ```
    func tableView(tableView: UITableView,
        numberOfRowsInSection section: Int) -> Int
    {
        return arrayOfContacts!.count
    }
    ```

3. Implement the `cellforRowAtIndexPath` data source method as follows:

    ```
    func tableView(tableView: UITableView,
       cellForRowAtIndexPath indexPath: NSIndexPath) -> UITableViewCell
    {
        let cell = tableView.dequeueReusableCellWithIdentifier("prototypeCell1",
            forIndexPath: indexPath) as UITableViewCell

        let contactName:String =
        arrayOfContacts!.objectAtIndex(indexPath.row)
        as! String

        cell.textLabel?.text = contactName
        return cell
    }
    ```

4. Modify the declaration of the `ViewController` class to inherit from `UIViewController`, `UITableViewDataSource`, and `UITableViewDelegate`:

```
class ViewController: UIViewController,
                      UITableViewDataSource,
                      UITableViewDelegate {
```

➤ Test your app in the iOS Simulator.

Click the Run button in the Xcode toolbar. Alternatively, you can select Project ➪ Run.

> **REFERENCE** *To see some of the examples from this lesson, watch the Lesson 22 video online at* www.wrox.com/go/swiftiosvid.

23

Application Settings

Most applications that perform complex tasks will at some point need to allow users to customize the applications' operation to suit their specific needs. These customizable options are usually referred to as *application preferences* or *application settings*. iOS applications can either expose their preferences within Apple's Settings application, or provide a user interface within the application where the user can customize them appropriately.

To integrate your application's preferences with Apple's Settings application, your application must include a `Settings.bundle` file. A settings bundle file enables you to declare the preferences in your application as a property list, and the Settings application provides the user interface for editing those preferences.

Keep in mind that to access the Settings application your users will have to first exit your application if they were using it. You should always refresh settings data when the application is activated so that your application can learn about the changes made by the user via the settings app. In this lesson, you learn to create this file and use it to expose system preferences.

ADDING A SETTINGS BUNDLE

To add a `Settings.bundle` file to your application, right-click your application's group in the project navigator and select New File from the context menu. Select the Settings Bundle file type from the iOS Resource section of the dialog box (see Figure 23-1).

FIGURE 23-1

When the Settings application is launched on an iOS device, every third-party application is checked to see if it has a `Settings.bundle` file. For each application on the iOS device that has this file, its name and icon are added to a list on the main page of the Settings application (see Figure 23-2).

FIGURE 23-2

Tapping on the icon will take the user to the particular application's settings page. By default, the Settings application will use an application's standard icon file when listing it. If you want to provide a custom icon to be used for your application in the Settings application, include the appropriate 2x and 3x images for the `AppIcon` asset in the project's asset catalog.

The Settings application can display application preferences in a series of hierarchical pages. Creating hierarchical settings pages is not covered in this lesson, but if you are interested in this topic, you should read the Preferences and Settings Programming Guide available at `https://developer.apple.com/library/ios/documentation/Cocoa/Conceptual/UserDefaults/Introduction/Introduction.html`.

A settings bundle is actually a collection of files. To see the contents of the bundle, simply click the triangle beside the `Settings.bundle` file in the project navigator (see Figure 23-3).

FIGURE 23-3

Inside the settings bundle, you will find a file named `Root.plist`. This file controls how your application's preferences will appear within the Settings application. Clicking the file opens it in the property list editor. When you do this, you will see a table with three columns—`Key`, `Type`, and `Value`. This file contains two properties: an array called `Preference Items` and a string called `Strings Filename` (see Figure 23-4).

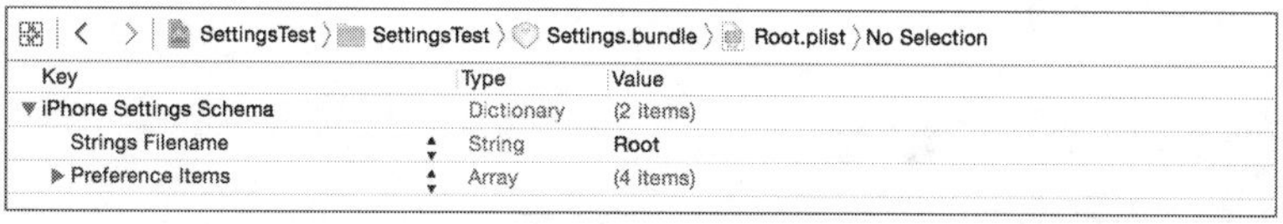

Key	Type	Value
▼ iPhone Settings Schema	Dictionary	(2 items)
Strings Filename	String	Root
▶ Preference Items	Array	(4 items)

FIGURE 23-4

Each preference that you want to expose to your users will be an entry in the `Preference Items` array. To see the contents of the `Preference Items` array, simply expand it within the property list editor. When you create a new settings bundle, this array contains four items by default (see

Figure 23-5). Each entry in the array is a dictionary of key-value pairs. Technically speaking, the `Preference Items` property is an array of dictionaries.

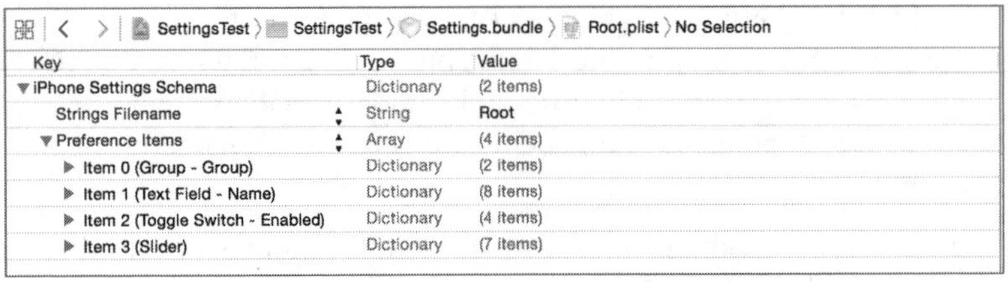

FIGURE 23-5

Each entry within the `Preference Items` array, given that it's a dictionary, can have several key-value pairs, but you will always find four keys in each entry—`Title`, `Type`, `Identifier`, and `DefaultValue`.

The value of the `Title` key is used by the Settings application to label the preference when it is presented to the user. The value of the `Type` key determines what kind of preference value it is and thus what user interface component will be used by the Settings application when presenting it. The value of the `Identifier` key contains a string that you can use to read the value of the preference in your Objective-C code. The value of the `DefaultValue` key contains the default value for the preference.

The default settings bundle created by Xcode contains four entries in the `Preference Items` array:

➤ Group

➤ Text Field

➤ Toggle Switch

➤ Slider

If you were to run this app on an iOS device, and look at its settings page in the Settings application, you would see something similar to that shown in Figure 23-6.

Table 23-1 describes the element types that can be used in the settings bundle.

TABLE 23-1: Preference Types

TYPE	DESCRIPTION
Text Field	An editable text field
Toggle Switch	On/Off toggle button
Title	A read-only text string
Slider	A slider to allow the user to select from a range of values
Multi Value	A list of values

TYPE	DESCRIPTION
Group	A logical group of preferences
Child Pane	Child preferences page, used to implement hierarchical preference pages

FIGURE 23-6

READING PREFERENCES WITH CODE

To read the value of a preference in a settings bundle from your code, you need to use an NSUserDefaults object. NSUserDefaults is part of the Core Foundation framework and provides a set of methods that allow you to manage application preferences. NSUserDefaults is a singleton class, and thus only one object should exist during the lifetime of an application. To get access to this one instance, use the following code:

```
let userDefaults = NSUserDefaults()
```

Recall that each preference within a settings bundle is represented by a dictionary of key-value pairs, and one of the four keys that each dictionary must contain is Identifier. To retrieve the value of a preference that has the identifier user_name, use the following code:

```
let userName = userDefaults.valueForKey("user_name") as? String
```

This code assumes that the value being retrieved is a string. The NSUserDefaults class provides several methods that allow you to retrieve preference values of different data types, including:

➤   boolForKey

➤   floatForKey

> ➤ `doubleForKey`

> ➤ `integerForKey`

Although you have provided default values for the preferences in the settings bundle, these values will not be applied until the users launch the Settings application on their device after installing your application. To get around this problem, you should specify a default value for each of your preferences in code as well as the settings bundle.

You can then use methods in the `NSUserDefaults` class to ensure that the default values are applied only once regardless of whether your user launches the Settings application or your application first. To do this, you need to create a dictionary with the default values of each preference and use the `registerDefaults` and `synchronize` methods of the `NSUserDefaults` object as follows:

```
let registrationDictionary:[String: String] = ["user_name":"Paul Woods",
  "user_age":"28"]

userDefaults.registerDefaults(registrationDictionary)
userDefaults.synchronize()
```

TRY IT

In this Try It, you create a simple iPhone application based on the Single View Application template called `SettingsTest` that allows the user to specify a name and age value within the Settings application. Your application, when launched, will display this name and age.

Lesson Requirements

> ➤ Launch Xcode.

> ➤ Create a new iPhone project based on the Single View Application template.

> ➤ Add a settings bundle to the application.

> ➤ Add user interface elements to the default scene of the storyboard.

> ➤ In the `viewDidLoad` method, read the preference values and display them in the labels.

> **REFERENCE** *The code for this Try It is available at* www.wrox.com/go/ swiftios.

Hints

> ➤ To display your application's preferences in the Settings application, you must include a `Settings.bundle` file.

> ➤ To access the preference values specified by the user in the settings page from within your code, each preference must have a unique string identifier.

➤ When creating a new project, you can use your website's domain name as the Company Identifier in the Project Options dialog box.

➤ To show the Object library, select View ➪ Utilities ➪ Show Object Library.

➤ To show the Assistant editor, select View ➪ Assistant Editor ➪ Show Assistant Editor.

Step-by-Step

➤ Create a Single View Application in Xcode called `SettingsTest`.

1. Launch Xcode and create a new application by selecting File ➪ New ➪ Project menu item.

2. Select the Single View Application template from the list of iOS project templates.

3. In the project options screen, use the following values:

   ➤ **Product Name:** SettingsTest

   ➤ **Organization Name:** your company

   ➤ **Organization Identifier:** com.yourcompany

   ➤ **Language:** Swift

   ➤ **Devices:** iPhone

   ➤ **Use Core Data:** Unchecked

   ➤ **Include UI Tests:** Unchecked

4. Save the project onto your hard disk.

➤ Add a settings bundle to the project.

1. Ensure the project navigator is visible.

2. Right-click the `Settings Test` group and select New File from the context menu.

3. Select the Settings Bundle template from the iOS Resources section. Save the file as `Settings.bundle`.

➤ Edit the `Settings.bundle` file.

1. Expand the `Settings.bundle` file in the project navigator and click the `Root.plist` file to edit it with the property editor.

2. Expand the `Preference Items` property.

3. Delete items 2 and 3. These are the Toggle Switch and Slider items, respectively. To delete an item, select it and hit the backspace key.

4. Edit the Text Field preference.

   ➤ Expand the `Item 1 (Text Field - Name)` dictionary.

   ➤ Set the `Title` to **User Name**, `Identifier` to **user_name**, and `Default Value` to **Paul Woods** (see Figure 23-7).

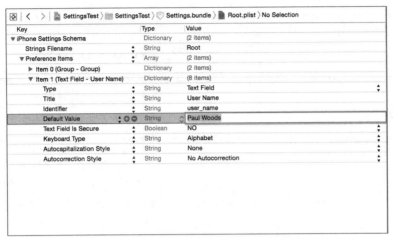

FIGURE 23-7

5.   Add a new Text Field preference.

➤   Ensure the `Item 1 (Text Field - User Name)` dictionary is collapsed.

➤   Right-click the row corresponding to the `Item 1 (Text Field - User Name)` dictionary and select Add Row from the context menu (see Figure 23-8).

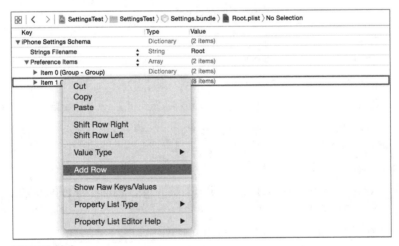

FIGURE 23-8

➤   Expand the newly added preference dictionary.

➤   Ensure the `Type` key is set to **Text Field**, `Title` is set to **Age**, and `Identifier` is set to **user_age**.

➤ Add a new key to the dictionary by right-clicking the last key (`Identifier`) and selecting Add Row from the context menu.

➤ Ensure the name of the new key is `Default Value` and the value of the key is 28 (see Figure 23-9).

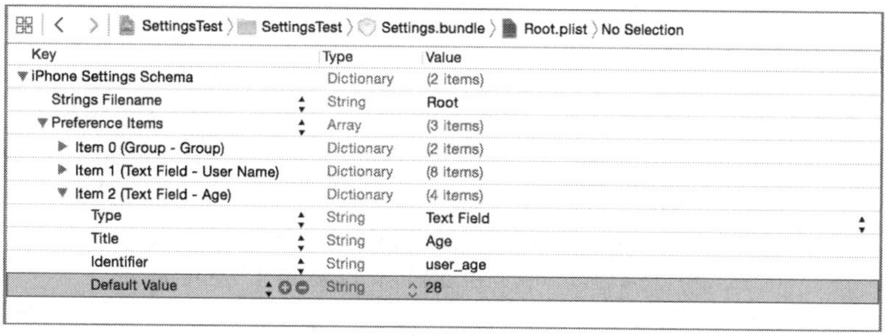

Key	Type	Value
▼ iPhone Settings Schema	Dictionary	(2 items)
Strings Filename	String	Root
▼ Preference Items	Array	(3 items)
▶ Item 0 (Group - Group)	Dictionary	(2 items)
▶ Item 1 (Text Field - User Name)	Dictionary	(8 items)
▼ Item 2 (Text Field - Age)	Dictionary	(4 Items)
Type	String	Text Field
Title	String	Age
Identifier	String	user_age
Default Value	String	28

FIGURE 23-9

➤ Add two `UILabel` instances to the default scene.

1. Open the `Main.storyboard` file in the Interface Editor.

2. From the Object library, drag and drop two Label objects onto the scene and place them one below the other.

3. Create layout constraints for each of elements on the storyboard scene using the information in Table 23-2. When creating layout constraints using the pin constraints dialog box, ensure the Constrain to margins option is unchecked and the value of the Update Frames combo box is set to Items of New Constraints.

TABLE 23-2: Layout Constraints

ELEMENT	LEFT	TOP	RIGHT	HEIGHT
Label 1	20	20	20	21
Label 2	20	20	20	21

4. Use the assistant editor to create outlets for each of the labels in the view controller class. Name the outlets **nameLabel** and **ageLabel**.

➤ Read and display the preference values provided by the user in the Settings application.

1. Open the `ViewController.swift` file in the project explorer.

2. Replace the implementation of the `viewDidLoad` method to resemble the following:

```
override func viewDidLoad() {
        super.viewDidLoad()

        let userDefaults = NSUserDefaults()
        let registrationDictionary:[String: String] =
```

```
        ["user_name":"Paul Woods", "user_age":"28"]

    userDefaults.registerDefaults(registrationDictionary)
    userDefaults.synchronize()

    nameLabel.text = userDefaults.valueForKey("user_name") as? String
    ageLabel.text = userDefaults.valueForKey("user_age") as? String
}
```

➤ Test your app in the iOS Simulator.

1. Click the Run button in the Xcode toolbar. Alternatively, you can use the Project ⇨ Run menu item.

2. After changing preferences in the Settings application, ensure your application is not running in the background before launching it again.

REFERENCE *To see some of the examples from this lesson, watch the Lesson 23 video online at* www.wrox.com/go/swiftiosvid.

24

Introduction to iCloud Storage

iCloud Storage is a set of classes and services that enable you to share data between instances of your application running across different devices. In this lesson, you learn to use the iCloud Storage APIs in your apps.

BASIC CONCEPTS

Apple's iCloud is a service that allows applications to synchronize data across devices. Your data is stored across a set of servers maintained by Apple and is made available to copies of your app across all iCloud-compatible devices. Changes made to this data by one instance of your application are automatically propagated to other instances.

From a developer's perspective, you need to use Apple's iCloud Storage APIs to interact with the iCloud service. These APIs enable you to store both documents and small amounts of key-value data.

> **NOTE** *This lesson does not cover key-value data storage. For more information on storing key-value data with iCloud, refer to the Designing for Key-Value Data in iCloud section of the iCloud Design Guide, available at:*
>
> https://developer.apple.com/library/ios/documentation/General/
> Conceptual/iCloudDesignGuide/Chapters/DesigningForKey-ValueDataIn-
> iCloud.html#//apple_ref/doc/uid/TP40012094-CH7-SW1.

iCloud applications cannot be tested on the iOS Simulator, and to make the most of this lesson you should ideally have two iOS devices to test on. iCloud Storage APIs are available to both iOS and MacOS X developers.

Your iOS applications always execute in a restricted environment on the device known as the *application sandbox*. Some of these restrictions affect where and how your application can store data.

Each application is given a directory on the device's file system. The contents of this directory are private to the application and cannot be read by other applications on the device.

Each application's directory has four locations into which you can store data:

➤   Preferences

➤   Documents

➤   Caches

➤   tmp

The first of these, Preferences, is not intended for direct file manipulation; however, the other three are. The most commonly used directories are the Documents and the tmp directories.

The Documents directory is the main location for storing application data. The contents of this directory can also be manipulated within iTunes. The Caches directory is used to store temporary files that need to persist between application launches. The tmp directory is used to store temporary files that do not need to persist between application launches.

Applications are responsible for cleaning up the contents of these directories because storage space on a device is limited. The contents of the Caches and tmp directories are not backed up by iTunes.

iCloud Storage conceptually extends this model and allows your applications to upload your data from its private directory to Apple's servers. This data then filters down to other iCloud-compatible devices on which copies of your application are running. Your application also receives notifications when a document has been created or updated by another copy of the application.

This synchronization is achieved by a background process (also known as a daemon) that runs on all iCloud-compatible devices. Figure 24-1 illustrates the iCloud architecture.

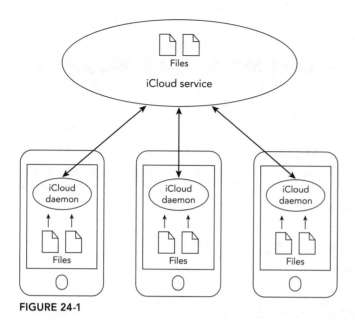

FIGURE 24-1

PREPARING TO USE THE ICLOUD STORAGE APIS

To use the iCloud Storage APIs in an application, you need to perform three steps:

1. Create an iCloud-enabled App ID.
2. Create an appropriate provisioning profile.
3. Enable appropriate entitlements in your Xcode project.

Creating an iCloud-Enabled App ID

To create an appropriate App ID, log in to your iOS developer account at `https://developer.apple.com/ios`. Click the Member Center link on the right side to navigate to the member center. Within the member center click, the Certificates, Identifiers & Profiles link (see Figure 24-2).

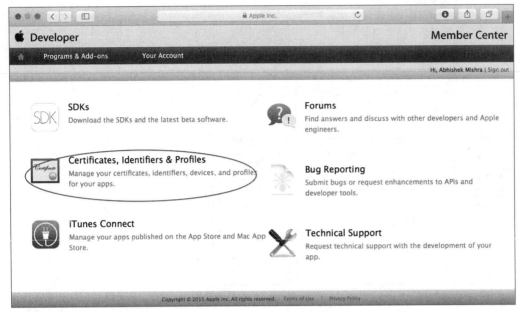

FIGURE 24-2

Next, click the Identifiers link in the iOS Apps category on the left side of the page (see Figure 24-3).

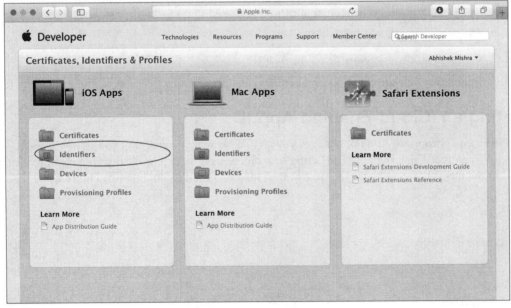

FIGURE 24-3

To create a new App ID, click the New App ID button on the top-right side (see Figure 24-4).

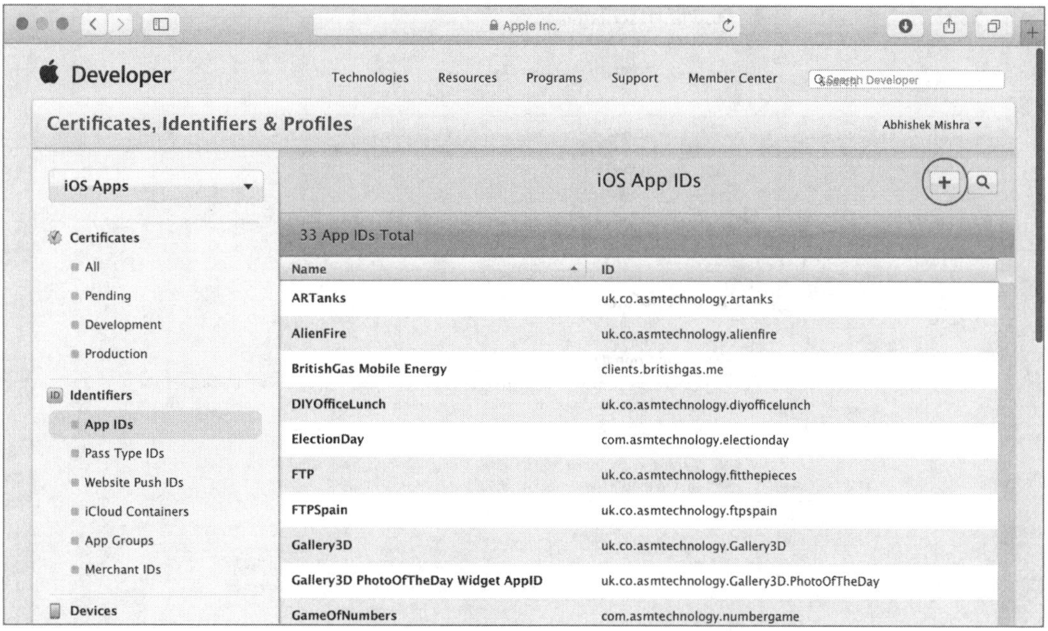

FIGURE 24-4

Provide a descriptive name of the new App ID in the Name field and select Team ID in the App ID prefix drop-down. Select the Explicit App ID radio button under the App ID suffix section and provide a unique identifier in the Bundle ID field that ends in the name of the Xcode project you are going to create (or have created).

Typically, you create this identifier by combining the reverse-domain name of your website and the name of your Xcode project. For example, the project created in this lesson is called `SwiftCloudTest` and the bundle identifier specified is `com.wileybook.CloudTest`. Your browser window should resemble Figure 24-5.

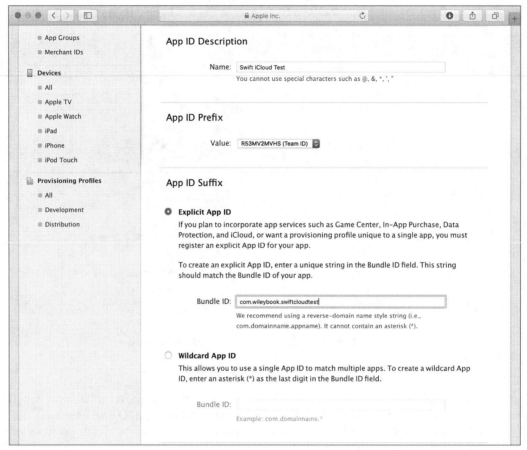

FIGURE 24-5

Scroll down to reveal the App Services section and ensure the iCloud checkbox is selected and the Compatible with Xcode 5 option is selected (see Figure 24-6).

FIGURE 24-6

Click the Continue button to proceed. You will be presented with a summary of the App ID information (see Figure 24-7). Click on Submit to finish creating the App ID.

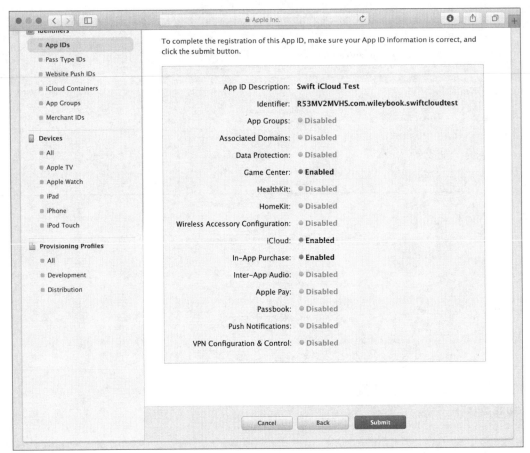

FIGURE 24-7

Creating an Appropriate Provisioning Profile

To create a provisioning profile for an iCloud-enabled App ID, click the All link (under the Provisioning category) in the menu on the left side of the iOS Provisioning Portal window (see Figure 24-8).

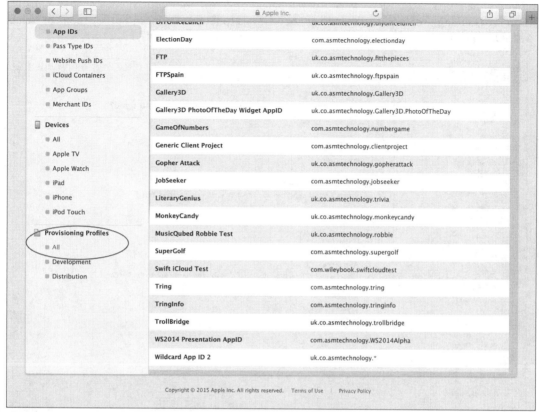

FIGURE 24-8

Click the New Profile button on the top-right side (see Figure 24-9).

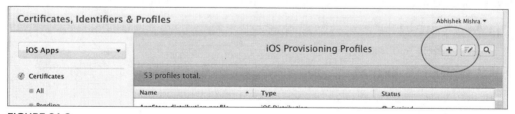

FIGURE 24-9

You will be asked to choose between a development or distribution provisioning profile. A distribution provisioning profile is used to submit applications to iTunes Connect. For the moment, select the iOS App Development option and click Continue (see Figure 24-10).

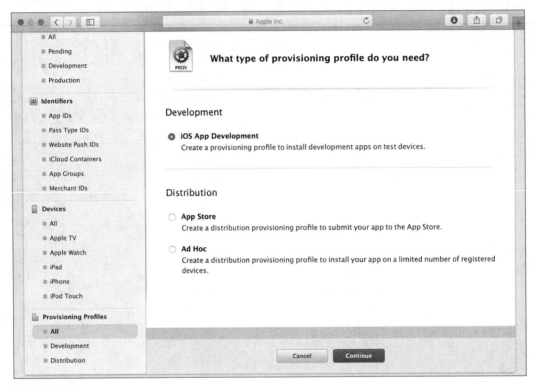

FIGURE 24-10

A development provisioning profile ties together three pieces of information:

➤   A single App ID

➤   One or more public keys

➤   A list of test device IDs

The next step requires you to select an App ID that will be associated with this provisioning profile. Select the iCloud-enabled App ID you have created (see Figure 24-11) and click Continue.

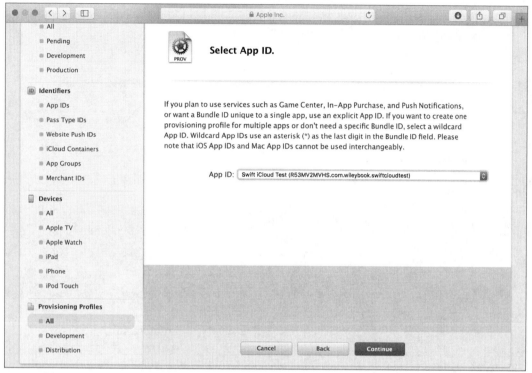

FIGURE 24-11

Select one or more development certificates that will be included in the profile. You must make sure to sign the app in Xcode using one of the certificates you select here. Select a suitable certificate and click Continue (see Figure 24-12).

FIGURE 24-12

Next, you must select one or more devices that will be included in this provisioning profile. The corresponding identifiers for these devices must be registered with your development account. Your app will only be testable on these devices (see Figure 24-13).

FIGURE 24-13

The final step involves providing a suitable name for the profile and clicking the Generate button. When the profile is created, you will be provided an option to download it onto your computer (see Figure 24-14).

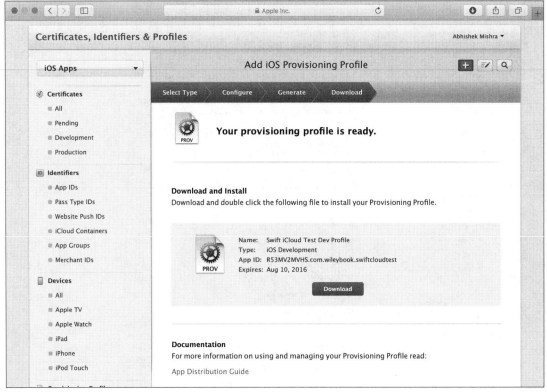

FIGURE 24-14

If you were to now click the All link under the Provisioning section on the left side menu, you should see an entry for the new profile in the list of available profiles. You can also download a provisioning profile from this list.

Once the profile has been downloaded, simply locate it in the Downloads folder on your Mac and double-click it to install it in Xcode.

Enabling Appropriate Entitlements in Your Xcode Project

Create a new project in Xcode using one of the standard iOS application templates. In the Project Options dialog box, make sure you provide the correct value for the Product Name and Organization Identifier fields so as to create the same App ID that was registered on the iOS Provisioning Portal. If, for instance, the App ID you registered was com.wileybook.swiftcloud-test, use swiftcloudtest for the Product Name field and com.wileybook for the Company Identifier field.

Applications that use iCloud must be signed with iCloud-specific entitlements. These entitlements ensure that only your applications can access the documents that they create. To enable entitlements, select the project's root node in the project navigator and the appropriate build target. Ensure the

Capabilities tab is selected. Locate the iCloud node and enable it. You may be asked to provide your iOS developer accounts credentials when you enable the iCloud entitlement. Because this lesson is about iCloud document storage, ensure the iCloud Documents checkbox is checked (see Figure 24-15).

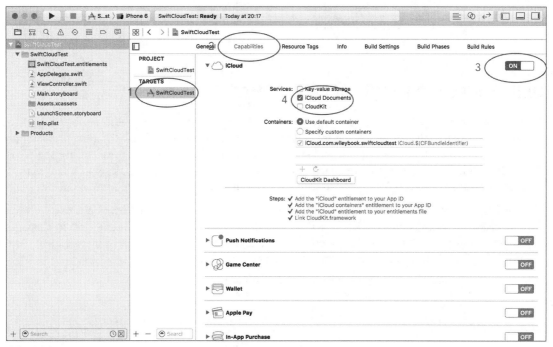

FIGURE 24-15

CHECKING FOR SERVICE AVAILABILITY

If your application intends to make use of the iCloud Storage APIs, you must ensure that the service is available to the application. This may not necessarily be the case if, for example, the user has not set up iCloud on the device.

To check for service availability, use the URLForUbiquityContainerIdentifier() method of the NSFileManager class. This method requires one String parameter that specifies a container identifier that your application uses.

If this method succeeds, the return value is an NSURL instance that identifies the container directory. If the method fails, the return value is nil.

If your application uses only one container identifier, or you want to use the main container identifier for the application, pass nil for the parameter. If your application accesses multiple containers, you must call this method for each container identifier to ensure you have access to each container. The following code snippet shows how to use this method for the main container identifier:

```
let folderURL =
NSFileManager.defaultManager().URLForUbiquityContainerIdentifier(nil)

if let unwrappedFolderURL = folderURL {
    // cloud access is available
}
else {
    // cloud access is not available.
}
```

USING ICLOUD DOCUMENT STORAGE

Any file stored by your application on iCloud must be managed by a file presenter object. A file presenter is an object that implements the NSFilePresenter protocol. Essentially, a file presenter acts as an agent for a file. Before an external source can change the file, the file presenter for the file is notified. When your app wants to change the file, it must lock the file by making its changes through a file coordinator object. A file coordinator object is an instance of the NSFileCoordinator class.

The simplest way to incorporate file presenters and coordinators in your application is to have your data classes (also known as model classes) subclass UIDocument. The UIDocument class implements the methods of the NSFilePresenter protocol and handles all of the file-related management. At the most basic level, you will need to override two UIDocument methods:

```
public func loadFromContents(contents: AnyObject,
        ofType typeName: String?) throws

public func contentsForType(typeName: String) throws -> AnyObject
```

The loadFromContents(contents, ofType) method is overridden by your UIDocument subclass and is called when the application needs to read data into its data model.

The first parameter of this method, contents, encapsulates the document data to be read. In the case of flat files, contents is an instance of an NSData object. It can also be an NSFileWrapper instance if the data being read corresponds to a file package. The typeName parameter indicates the file type of the document.

If you cannot load the document for some reason, you should throw an exception encapsulating the reason for failure.

The contentsForType() method is also overridden by your UIDocument subclass and is called when the application saves data to a file. This method must return an NSData instance that will be written to the file. If you cannot return an NSData instance for some reason, you throw an exception that encapsulates the reason for failure.

The following code presents a simple UIDocument subclass called SwiftCloudTestDocument. The example assumes that the application where this class is used has a rather simple data model consisting of a single String instance.

```
import UIKit

enum DocumentReadError: ErrorType {
```

```
        case InvalidInput
    }

    enum DocumentWriteError: ErrorType {
        case NoContentToSave
    }

    class SwiftCloudTestDocument: UIDocument {

        var documentContents:String?

        override init(fileURL url: NSURL) {
            super.init(fileURL: url)
        }

        override func loadFromContents(contents: AnyObject,
                    ofType typeName: String?) throws {

            if let castedContents = contents as? NSData {
                documentContents = NSString(data: castedContents,
                encoding: NSUTF8StringEncoding) as? String

            }
            else {
                documentContents = nil
                throw DocumentReadError.InvalidInput
            }
        }

        override func contentsForType(typeName: String) throws -> AnyObject {

            if documentContents == nil {
                throw DocumentWriteError.NoContentToSave
            }

            return documentContents!.dataUsingEncoding(NSUTF8StringEncoding)!
        }
    }
}
```

Creating a New iCloud Document

To create a new document, initialize an instance of your `UIDocument` subclass by using the
`init(fileURL url: NSURL)` initializer and then call `saveToURL(url, saveOperation, comple-
tionHandler)` on the instance.

The initializer requires a single `NSURL` parameter that identifies the location where document data is
to be written. This URL is usually composed by appending a filename in the `Documents` subdirec-
tory to the path to an iCloud container. For instance, to create a new document on iCloud called
`phoneNumber.txt`, you could use the following snippet:

```
let containerURL =
NSFileManager.defaultManager().URLForUbiquityContainerIdentifier(nil)
```

```
let documentDirectoryURL = containerURL!.URLByAppendingPathComponent("Documents")

let documentURL =
documentDirectoryURL.URLByAppendingPathComponent("phoneNumber.txt")

let cloudDocument:SwiftCloudTestDocument =
    SwiftCloudTestDocument(fileURL: documentURL)

cloudDocument.saveToURL(cloudDocument.fileURL,
forSaveOperation: UIDocumentSaveOperation.ForCreating) {
    (Bool success) -> Void in
    if (success) {
        // document was created successfully.
    }
}
```

The `saveToURL(url, saveOperation, completionHandler)` method is described later in this lesson.

Opening an Existing Document

To open an existing document, allocate and initialize an instance of your `UIDocument` subclass and call `openWithCompletionHandler()` on the instance. For example, you could open a file called `phoneNumbers.txt` from iCloud using the following snippet:

```
let containerURL =
NSFileManager.defaultManager().URLForUbiquityContainerIdentifier(nil)

let documentDirectoryURL = containerURL!.URLByAppendingPathComponent("Documents")

let documentURL =
documentDirectoryURL.URLByAppendingPathComponent("phoneNumber.txt")

let cloudDocument:SwiftCloudTestDocument =
SwiftCloudTestDocument(fileURL: documentURL)

cloudDocument.openWithCompletionHandler {
        (BOOL success) -> Void in
        if (success)
        {
            // cloud document opened successfully!
        }
}
```

Saving a Document

Once you have an instance of a `UIDocument` subclass, saving it to iCloud is simply a matter of calling the `saveToURL(url, saveOperation, completionHandler)` method on it. The first parameter to this method is an `NSURL` instance that contains the target URL. You can compose this URL in the same manner as when you instantiated your `UIDocument` subclass.

If, however, you want to retrieve the URL corresponding to an existing `UIDocument` subclass, simply use the `fileURL` property of the subclass. Thus, if `cloudDocument` is an instance of a `UIDocument` subclass, you can retrieve the URL used when it was instantiated using the following code:

```
Let documentURL = cloudDocument.fileURL
```

The second parameter is a constant that is used to indicate whether the document contents are being saved for the first time, or overwritten. It can be either of:

➤   `UIDocumentSaveOperation.ForCreating`

➤   `UIDocumentSaveOperation.ForOverwriting`

The third parameter is a block completion handler.

> **NOTE** *For more information on the* `UIDocument` *class, refer to the UIDocument Class reference, available at:*
>
> ```
> https://developer.apple.com/library/prerelease/ios/documentation/
> UIKit/Reference/UIDocument_Class/index.html.
> ```

Searching for Documents on iCloud

Often, you will need to search iCloud container directories for documents. To do this, you need to create a search query using an `NSMetadataQuery` instance, set up an appropriate search filter, and execute the query.

Queries have two phases: an initial search phase and a second live-update phase. During the live-update phase, updated results are typically available once every second. The following code snippet builds a search query:

```
let searchQuery:NSMetadataQuery = NSMetadataQuery()
searchQuery.searchScopes = [NSMetadataQueryUbiquitousDocumentsScope];
```

The `searchScopes` property allows you to specify an array of directory strings over which the search should execute. To specify the iCloud container folder as the search target, you provide an `Array` instance with a single object:

```
NSMetadataQueryUbiquitousDocumentsScope
```

Before you can execute the query, you need to specify a search filter. Search filters are also known as predicates and are instances of the `NSPredicate` class. The following code snippet creates an `NSPredicate` instance that filters out a file with a specific name:

```
let documentFileName = "cloudDocument.txt"
let predicate = NSPredicate(format: "%K == %@",
argumentArray: [NSMetadataItemFSNameKey, documentFileName])
```

To apply the predicate to the search query, use the `predicate` property on the `NSMetadataQuery` instance:

```
searchQuery.predicate = predicate
```

Search queries execute asynchronously. When the query has finished gathering results, your application will receive the `NSMetadataQueryDidFinishGatheringNotification` notification message. Use the following code snippet to set up a method in your code called `queryDidFinish()` to be called when this notification is received:

```
NSNotificationCenter.defaultCenter().addObserver(self,
selector: "queryDidFinish:",
name: NSMetadataQueryDidFinishGatheringNotification ,
object: searchQuery)
```

Finally, to start the query, call the `startQuery` method of the `NSMetadataQuery` instance:

```
searchQuery.startQuery()
```

When you receive the notification message, you can find out the number of results returned by the search by querying the `resultCount` property of the `NSMetadataQuery` instance:

```
let numResults = searchQuery.resultCount
```

To retrieve an `NSURL` instance for each result returned by the search query, you can use a simple `for` loop:

```
for (var resultIndex = 0; resultIndex < numResults; resultIndex++)
{
    let item:NSMetadataItem? = searchQuery.results[resultIndex] as?
                             NSMetadataItem

    if let unwrappedItem = item {
        let url = unwrappedItem.valueForAttribute(NSMetadataItemURLKey)
    }
}
```

If you do not want the search query to continue returning results, use the following code snippet to stop it:

```
searchQuery.disableUpdates()
searchQuery.stopQuery()
```

The Try It section for this lesson contains a simple project that uses an `NSMetadataQuery` instance to find a document on iCloud and then proceeds to open it.

> **NOTE** *For more information on the* NSMetadataQuery *class, refer to the* NSMetadataQuery Class Reference, *available at:*
>
> https://developer.apple.com/library/prerelease/ios/documentation/Cocoa/Reference/Foundation/Classes/NSMetadataQuery_Class/.
>
> *For more information on the* NSPredicate *class, refer to the NSPredicate Class Reference available at:*
>
> https://developer.apple.com/library/prerelease/mac/documentation/Cocoa/Reference/Foundation/Classes/NSPredicate_Class/index.html.

TRY IT

In this Try It, you build a new Xcode project based on the Single View Application template called SwiftCloudTest. In this application, you create a simple text document called cloudDocument .txt and store it on iCloud. This document can then be edited across multiple copies of the application running on different iOS devices.

Lesson Requirements

➤ Create a new Universal application project based on the Single View Application template.

➤ Register the App ID with the iOS Provisioning Portal.

➤ Create a development provisioning profile.

➤ Download and install the development provisioning profile.

➤ Create a simple user interface that consists of a UIButton instance, a UILabel instance, and a UITextView instance.

➤ Create a data class that subclasses UIDocument.

➤ Check iCloud service availability in the viewDidLoad method of the view controller class.

➤ Load an existing document stored on iCloud. If the document does not exist, create a new one.

➤ Implement code to save the document on iCloud when a button is tapped.

> **REFERENCE** *The code for this Try It is available at* www.wrox.com/go/swiftios.

Hints

➤   To make best use of this application, you will need at least two iOS devices set up to use the same iCloud account.

➤   You must ensure iCloud has been set up on each test device.

➤   Testing your apps on iOS devices is covered in Appendix A.

Step-by-Step

➤   Create a Single View Application in Xcode called `SwiftCloudTest`.

1.   Launch Xcode and create a new application by selecting File ➪ New ➪ Project.

2.   Select the Single View Application template from the list of iOS project templates.

3.   In the project options screen, use the following values:

   ➤   **Product Name:** SwiftCloudTest

   ➤   **Organization Name:** your company

   ➤   **Organization Identifier:** com.yourcompany

   ➤   **Language:** Swift

   ➤   **Devices:** Universal

   ➤   **Use Core Data:** Unchecked

   ➤   **Include UI Tests:** Unchecked

   ➤   **Include Unit Tests:** Unchecked

4.   Save the project onto your hard disk.

➤   Register an App ID with the iOS Provisioning Portal.

1.   Log in to the iOS Provisioning Portal, and register a new App ID with the following details:

   ➤   **Description:** SwiftCloudTest AppID

   ➤   **Bundle Seed ID:** Use Team ID

   ➤   **Bundle Identifier:** com.wileybook.SwiftCloudTest

2.   Enable the App ID to use with iCloud. This process is covered in the section titled "Creating an iCloud-Enabled App ID" earlier in this lesson.

➤   Create a development provisioning profile using the App ID created in the previous step.

1.   The process of creating the provisioning profile is covered in the section titled "Creating an Appropriate Provisioning Profile" earlier in this lesson. Follow those instructions to create a development provisioning profile called Swift Cloud Test Development Profile.

2.   Download and install the provisioning profile by double-clicking on the profile after it has been downloaded to your computer.

➤ Enable iCloud-specific entitlements for the application target.

1. Select the project's root node in the project navigator and select the appropriate build target. Ensure the Capabilities tab is selected. Scroll down to the iCloud option and enable it.

2. Once the iCloud entitlement has been enabled, ensure the iCloud Documents checkbox has been checked

➤ Create a `UIDocument` subclass.

1. Right-click your project's root node in the project navigator and select New File from the context menu.

2. Select the Swift file template and click Next.

3. Name the class `SwiftCloudTestDocument` and click Create.

4. Replace the contents of the `SwiftCloudTestDocument.swift` file with the following:

```swift
import UIKit

enum DocumentReadError: ErrorType {
    case InvalidInput
}

enum DocumentWriteError: ErrorType {
    case NoContentToSave
}

class SwiftCloudTestDocument: UIDocument {

    var documentContents:String?

    override init(fileURL url: NSURL) {
        super.init(fileURL: url)
    }

    override func loadFromContents(contents: AnyObject,
                ofType typeName: String?) throws {

        if let castedContents = contents as? NSData {
            documentContents = NSString(data: castedContents,
            encoding: NSUTF8StringEncoding) as? String

        NSNotificationCenter.defaultCenter().
        postNotificationName("refreshDocumentPreview",
        object: self)
        }
        else {
            documentContents = nil
            throw DocumentReadError.InvalidInput
        }
    }

    override func contentsForType(typeName: String)
```

```
                    throws -> AnyObject {

            if documentContents == nil {
                throw DocumentWriteError.NoContentToSave
            }

            return documentContents!.dataUsingEncoding(NSUTF8StringEncoding)!
        }
    }
```

Recall that the `loadFromContents()` method is called when a document must be loaded from a file. In case of iCloud documents, this method is also called automatically when the contents of the file have changed. This will typically happen when the file was edited by another copy of the application.

In the preceding implementation, in addition to loading the contents of the file into member variables of the `SwiftCloudTestDocument` class, you also send out an application-wide notification called `refreshDocumentPreview`.

The view controller class listens for these notifications, and treats the arrival of one as a cue to update the user interface.

➤ Create a simple user interface with Interface Builder.

1. Open the storyboard file and use the Object library to drag and drop a label, button, and text view onto the default scene.

2. Select the label and display the Pin constraints popup. Ensure the Constrain to margins options is unchecked and Update Frames is set to None. Create the following layout constraints:

   ➤ **Left:** 20

   ➤ **Right:** 20

   ➤ **Top:** 20

   ➤ **Height:** 21

3. Select the button and display the Pin constraints popup. Ensure the Constrain to margins options is unchecked and Update Frames is set to None. Create the following layout constraints:

   ➤ **Left:** 20

   ➤ **Right:** 20

   ➤ **Top:** 20

   ➤ **Height:** 30

4. Select the text view and the Pin constraints popup. Ensure the Constrain to margins options is unchecked and Update Frames is set to All Frames in Container. Create the following layout constraints:

   ➤ **Left:** 20

   ➤ **Right:** 20

➤ **Top:** 20

➤ **Bottom:** 20

5. Use the Attribute inspector to set the text property of the label to iCloud Service Status.

6. Use the Attribute inspector to set the Alignment property of the label to center.

7. Double-click the button in the scene and change its title to Save Document.

8. Change the background color of the button to a shade of gray.

9. Use the assistant editor to create an outlet called `serviceStatus` in the `ViewController` class and connect it to the `UILabel` instance in the default scene.

10. Use the assistant editor to create an outlet called `documentContentView` in the `ViewController` class and connect it to the `UITextView` instance in the default scene.

11. Use the assistant editor to create an action method called `onSaveDocument` in the `ViewController` class and connect it to the `Touch Up Inside` event of the `UIButton` instance in the default scene.

Your storyboard should resemble Figure 24-16.

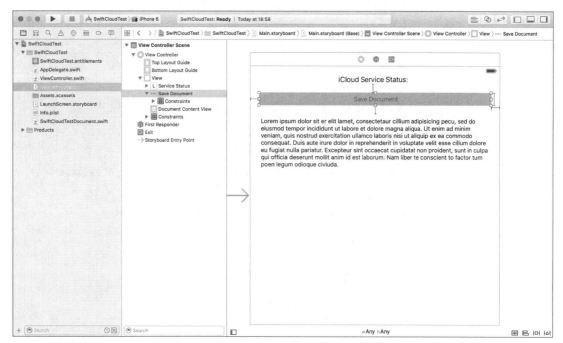

FIGURE 24-16

➤ Edit the `ViewController.swift` file.

1. Add the following member variable declarations to the class:

    ```
    var cloudServicesAreAvailable:Bool?
    var cloudDocument:SwiftCloudTestDocument?
    var searchQuery:NSMetadataQuery?
    ```

2. Update the implementation of the `viewDidLoad` method to resemble the following:

    ```
    override func viewDidLoad() {

        super.viewDidLoad()

        documentContentView.text = ""

        // register this class as an observer for the 'refreshDocumentPreview'
        // notification, this notification is sent by the document class when
        // the contents of the document have ben updated.
        NSNotificationCenter.defaultCenter().addObserver(self,
        selector: "refreshDocumentPreview:",
        name: "refreshDocumentPreview" ,
        object: nil)

        // check if cloud services are available.
        let containerURL =
        NSFileManager.defaultManager().URLForUbiquityContainerIdentifier(nil)

        if containerURL != nil  {
            self.cloudServicesAreAvailable = true
            serviceStatus.text = "Cloud Service Status: Available"

            // load existing document, or create a new document
            loadDocument()
        }
        else {
            self.cloudServicesAreAvailable = false
            serviceStatus.text = "Cloud Service Status: Not Available"

            let alert = UIAlertController(title: "Error",
            message: "iCloud has not been setup on this device!",
            preferredStyle: UIAlertControllerStyle.Alert)

            alert.addAction(UIAlertAction(title: "Ok",
            style: UIAlertActionStyle.Default,
            handler: nil))

            self.presentViewController(alert,
            animated: true,
            completion: nil)
        }
    }
    ```

    In this method, you check if the iCloud service is available, and if it is, then proceed to load a specific document from iCloud.

3. Implement the `deinit` method in your `ViewController` class as follows:

    ```
    deinit {
    ```

```
    if cloudDocument != nil {
        cloudDocument?.closeWithCompletionHandler(nil)
    }

    NSNotificationCenter.defaultCenter().removeObserver(self)
}
```

4. Add a new method called `loadDocument` method as follows:

```
func loadDocument() {
    // search for cloudDocument.txt
    searchQuery = NSMetadataQuery()
    searchQuery!.searchScopes = [NSMetadataQueryUbiquitousDocumentsScope];

    let documentFileName = "cloudDocument.txt"
    let predicate = NSPredicate(format: "%K == %@",
    argumentArray: [NSMetadataItemFSNameKey, documentFileName])

    searchQuery!.predicate = predicate

    NSNotificationCenter.defaultCenter().addObserver(self,
    selector: "queryDidFinish:",
    name: NSMetadataQueryDidFinishGatheringNotification ,
    object: searchQuery)

    UIApplication.sharedApplication().networkActivityIndicatorVisible = true

    searchQuery!.startQuery()
}
```

These statements instantiate an `NSMetadataQuery` object to search the Documents directory in the application's iCloud container for a file called `cloudDocument.txt`. When the query is complete, the `queryDidFinish()` method of the view controller class will be called.

5. Implement the `queryDidFinish()` method as follows:

```
func queryDidFinish(notifcation: NSNotification) {

    UIApplication.sharedApplication().networkActivityIndicatorVisible = false

    // stop the query to prevent it from running constantly
    searchQuery!.disableUpdates()
    searchQuery!.stopQuery()

    NSNotificationCenter.defaultCenter().removeObserver(self,
    name: NSMetadataQueryDidFinishGatheringNotification,
    object: nil)

    // this application expects this query to return a single
    // result. If no documents were found, then create a new
    // document and inform the user.
    if searchQuery!.resultCount == 0
    {
        let alert = UIAlertController(title: "",
```

```
            message: "iCloud document not found., creating new document!",
            preferredStyle: UIAlertControllerStyle.Alert)

            alert.addAction(UIAlertAction(title: "Ok",
            style: UIAlertActionStyle.Default,
            handler: nil))

            self.presentViewController(alert,
animated: true,
completion: nil)

            createDocument()
            return
    }

    // instantiate a SwiftCloudTestDocument instance and
    // open the cloud document
    if cloudDocument == nil
    {
        let item:NSMetadataItem? = searchQuery!.results[0] as?
            NSMetadataItem

        if let unwrappedItem = item {
            let url = unwrappedItem.valueForAttribute(NSMetadataItemURLKey)
                    as! NSURL
            cloudDocument = SwiftCloudTestDocument(fileURL: url)
        }
    }

    cloudDocument!.openWithCompletionHandler {
        (BOOL success) -> Void in
        if (success) {
            let alert = UIAlertController(title: "",
            message: "iCloud document loaded!",
            preferredStyle: UIAlertControllerStyle.Alert)

            alert.addAction(UIAlertAction(title: "Ok",
            style: UIAlertActionStyle.Default,
            handler: nil))

            self.presentViewController(alert,
            animated: true,
            completion: nil)
        }
        else {
            let alert = UIAlertController(title: "",
            message: "Could not load iCloud document!",
            preferredStyle: UIAlertControllerStyle.Alert)

            alert.addAction(UIAlertAction(title: "Ok",
            style: UIAlertActionStyle.Default,
            handler: nil))

            self.presentViewController(alert,
```

```
                animated: true,
                completion: nil)
        }
    }
}
```

The preceding implementation first stops the query from running constantly. If the query did not return any results, it calls the `createDocument` method of the view controller class to create a new document on iCloud; otherwise, it loads the existing document from iCloud.

6. Implement the `onSaveDocument()` method as follows:

```
@IBAction func onSaveDocument(sender: AnyObject) {

    if cloudDocument == nil {
        return
    }

    documentContentView.resignFirstResponder()

    cloudDocument!.documentContents = documentContentView.text

    cloudDocument!.saveToURL(cloudDocument!.fileURL,
    forSaveOperation: UIDocumentSaveOperation.ForCreating) {
        (Bool success) -> Void in
        if (success) {
            self.cloudDocument!.openWithCompletionHandler(nil)
        }
    }
}
```

This method dismisses the keypad, if it is visible, and saves the `SwiftCloudTestDocument` object to the iCloud document.

7. Implement the `createDocument()` method as follows:

```
func createDocument(){

    if self.cloudDocument == nil {
        let containerURL =
    NSFileManager.defaultManager().URLForUbiquityContainerIdentifier(nil)

        let documentDirectoryURL =
    containerURL!.URLByAppendingPathComponent("Documents")

        let documentURL =
    documentDirectoryURL.URLByAppendingPathComponent("cloudDocument.txt")

        cloudDocument = SwiftCloudTestDocument(fileURL: documentURL)
    }

    cloudDocument!.documentContents = documentContentView.text
    cloudDocument!.saveToURL(cloudDocument!.fileURL,
        forSaveOperation: UIDocumentSaveOperation.ForCreating) {
        (Bool success) -> Void in
```

```
            if (success) {
                self.cloudDocument!.openWithCompletionHandler(nil)
            }
        }
    }
```

This method is used to create an empty file called `cloudDocument.txt` on iCloud, and is used when the `loadDocument` method could not find a document to load.

8. Implement the `refreshDocumentPreview()` method as follows:

```
func refreshDocumentPreview(notifcation: NSNotification) {
    documentContentView.text = cloudDocument!.documentContents;
}
```

This method is received when the `CloudTestDocument` object loads data from the iCloud document `cloudDocument.txt`. Here, you simply refresh the user interface.

➤ Test your app on an iOS device.

1. Connect your iOS device to your Mac.

2. Select your device from the Target/Device selector in the Xcode toolbar.

3. Ensure the correct value has been selected for the Code Signing Entity build settings of the application target (see Figure 24-17).

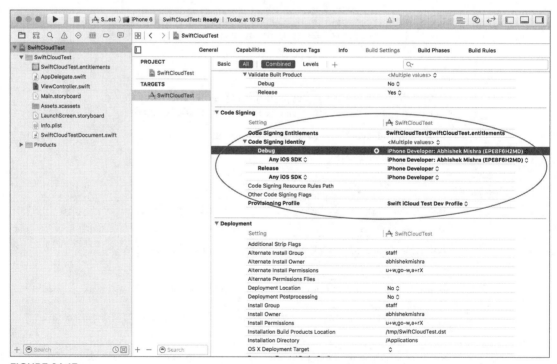

FIGURE 24-17

4. Click the Run button in the Xcode toolbar. Alternatively, you can use the Project ⇨ Run menu item.

5. When you run the application for the first time, you will see a message similar to Figure 25-16, telling you that a new iCloud document is going to be created for you.

6. Type some text into the text view and tap the Save Document button.

7. If you now run this application on a different device, you will get a message telling you that an existing iCloud document has been opened.

REFERENCE *To see some of the examples from this lesson, watch the Lesson 24 video online at* www.wrox.com/go/swiftiosvid.

25

Introduction to CloudKit

In Lesson 24, you learned how to create an app that could store documents on iCloud and access these documents across different devices. In this lesson, you learn about CloudKit, which is a set of APIs that allow you to move structured data between your app and iCloud. Whereas iCloud document storage operates on files, CloudKit operates on dictionaries of key-value pairs called *records*. To use a relational database analogy, a record is similar to a row in a table.

CloudKit also allows relationships between records. You may be tempted to use CloudKit to replace CoreData in your application, but these two technologies complement each other and are not meant to replace each other. CoreData is concerned with storing model objects locally; CloudKit is concerned with moving some of the data in these model objects to iCloud so that they can be accessed by other instances of your application.

When using CloudKit, your application decides when to move data to and from iCloud. The process is not automatic. It is possible to configure iCloud to inform your application when changes occur; your application will still need to fetch those changes. In this lesson, you will look at some of the key concepts involved in building iOS applications with CloudKit.

CONTAINERS, DATABASES, AND RECORDS

Data in iCloud is organized into containers. Containers are represented by instances of CKContainer objects and every iCloud enabled app has at least one container called the *default container*, the identifier of which is the same as that of the app. Conceptually, you can think of a container to represent storage space for your app on iCloud.

When you add iCloud entitlements in your Xcode project, Xcode adds the identifier for the app's default container to the project (see Figure 25-1).

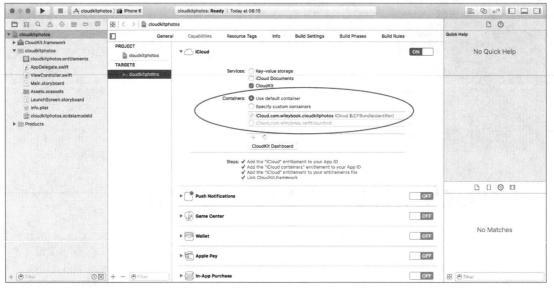

FIGURE 25-1

You have the option to add other container identifiers, which is something you would do if you wanted to perhaps share data between a group of applications you have developed. Multiple container identifiers are outside the scope of this lesson.

To obtain a reference to the default container for your app, simply use the `defaultContainer` class method of the `CKContainer` class:

```
let defaultContainer = CKContainer.defaultContainer()
```

Each Container contains a public database and multiple private databases (there is one private database per user of your app). Databases are represented by instances of `CKDatabase` objects. Data in a private database is only visible to the user who created it. Data in a public database is visible to all users of the app.

You can retrieve a `CKDatabase` instance for the public or private database using the `publicCloud-Database()` or `privateCloudDatabase()` instance methods of `CKContainer`:

```
let privateDatabase:CKDatabase = CKContainer.defaultContainer().
privateCloudDatabase

let publicDatabase:CKDatabase = CKContainer.defaultContainer().publicCloudDatabase
```

At runtime, all the data in the public database will always be readable by your app, even if there is no active iCloud account on the device. However, a user must set up an iCloud account in order to write to public databases or access private databases.

Within databases, your app's data is grouped into record types. In terms of a relational database analogy, record types are the equivalent of database tables. A record type contains a unique identifier, a collection of records, and some additional metadata required by CloudKit. A collection of record types is known as a schema.

A record is an instance of a `CKRecord` objects and is a dictionary of key-value pairs called fields. A record is similar to a row in a relational database system. CloudKit requires that a record not exceed 1MB in size, and because of this limitation you should save large files such as images in physical files, and simply store the file name in the record. Table 25-1 shows the commonly used field types.

TABLE 25-1: CloudKit Field Types

FIELD	CLASS	DESCRIPTION
Asset	CKAsset	A large file that is stored separately from the record
Bytes	NSData	Raw binary data stored within the record
Date/Time	NSDate	A date/time
Double	NSNumber	A double
Int	NSNumber	An integer
Location	CLLocation	A latitude and longitude pair
Reference	CKReference	A relationship to a field in another record type
String	NSString	An immutable string
List	NSArray	An array of any of the above types

The relationship between containers, databases, and records is shown in Figure 25-2.

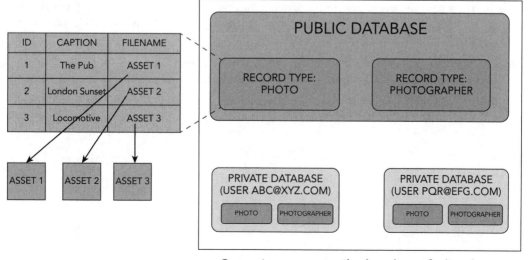

Container: com.wileybook.swiftcloudtest

FIGURE 25-2

DEVELOPMENT AND PRODUCTION ENVIRONMENTS

CloudKit provides separate development and production environments for your app's data. The development environment is only accessible to members of your development team. When you save a record to a database in the development environment, CloudKit automatically updates the database schema by creating the associated record type. This feature is called just-in-time schema and is only available in the development environment.

In the development environment, you can also use the CloudKit Dashboard to modify the schema and records. In the production environment, you cannot edit the schema but you can modify individual records in the public database.

If you decide to use CloudKit to generate the schema for you, keep in mind that once you add a field to a record, the data type associated with that field cannot be changed programmatically. It can, however, be changed from the CloudKit dashboard.

Typically, you use the development environment while developing and testing your app. In fact, when you run your app from Xcode on a simulator or device, it is automatically configured to use the development environment.

When you use Xcode to submit your app for review, Xcode will automatically configure the app to target the production environment prior to submission. When you export an app for testing, you will be asked to specify either the development or production environment.

Once your app appears to be working fine with the development environment, you will want to switch over to the production environment prior to submitting the app to the iTunes Store. Switching over to the production environment will require you to deploy the schema into the production environment. Deploying a scheme only copies the record types, and not the individual records themselves.

The first time you deploy the schema from the development environment to the production environment, the schema is copied over to the production environment. The next time you deploy the schema (because perhaps you modified the schema in the development environment), the schema is merged with the production schema.

To prevent merge conflicts, CloudKit does not allow you to delete fields or record types in a schema in the development environment that was previously deployed to the production environment.

THE CLOUDKIT DASHBOARD

The CloudKit dashboard (see Figure 25-3) is a web-based application that allows you to manage both the schema and the records stored on iCloud by your CloudKit-based applications. You can access it at `https://icloud.developer.apple.com/dashboard/`.

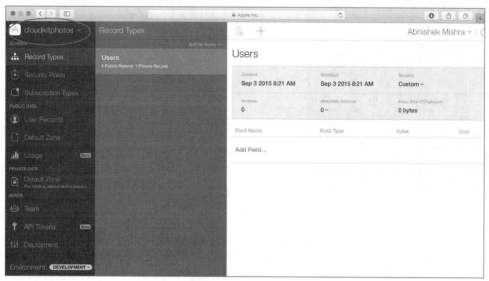

FIGURE 25-3

The features of the dashboard only apply to the currently selected container. You can use the drop-down combo box located at the top left of the dashboard to switch containers. The dashboard will only display containers that belong to your Apple developer account.

The rest of this section explores some of the common tasks you are likely to perform with the dashboard. Keep in mind that some of these tasks can be performed programmatically.

Creating a Record Type

A record type is the equivalent of a table in a relational database. To create a record type, first click on the Record Types option under the Schema group in the left-hand navigation menu. Next, click the Add (+) button in the upper-left corner of the detail area (see Figure 25-4).

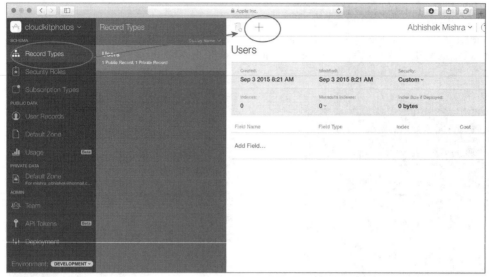

FIGURE 25-4

Enter a name for the new record type, and then proceed to add fields to the record type. There is no limit to the number of fields you can have in a record type. A record type must have at least one field, and to enforce this the dashboard creates one for you by default (see Figure 25-5).

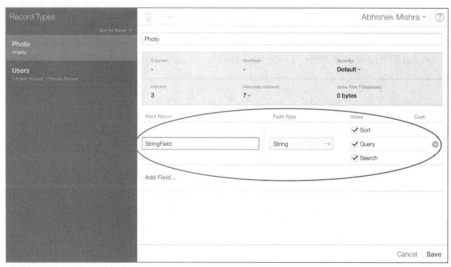

FIGURE 25-5

Every field must have a unique name, and can have one of the data types listed in Table 25-1. To add additional fields click the Add Field button. When you have finished creating all the fields, click the Save button on the bottom right side of the detail area to update the schema.

You can delete a field by clicking the delete (X) button located to the right of the field row (see Figure 25-6). Deleting a field will remove the field from the record type as well as any records.

FIGURE 25-6

Deleting a Record Type

To delete a record type, simply select it in the list of record types and click the trash icon in the upper-left corner of the detail area (see Figure 25-7). Deleting a record type will also delete all records that are based on the record type. Once a development schema has been deployed to the production environment, you cannot delete record types.

FIGURE 25-7

Creating Relationships Between Record Types

Relationships between record types are represented using fields that have the CKReference data type. Relationships can be used to express hierarchies in the data and can be both one-to-one or one-to-many.

A CKReference object encapsulates a record identifier of a target record and is added to the source record. To add a one-to-one relationship between a source and target record types, add the reference field to the source record type (see Figure 25-8).

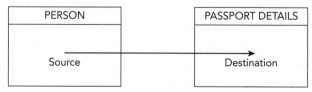

FIGURE 25-8

When adding a one-to-many relationship between record types in CloudKit, the child object is considered to be the source of the relationship and the CKReference object is added to the child. This is illustrated in Figure 25-9 where there is a one-to-many relationship between a record type called Photographer and a record type called Photo.

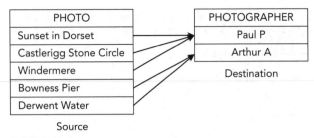

FIGURE 25-9

The actual process of adding the field from the CloudKit dashboard is a simple matter of selecting the correct record type and adding a field, whose type is Reference (see Figure 25-10).

FIGURE 25-10

While adding references between two record types, it is advisable to create inverse references from the destination record type to the source record type as well.

Adding Records

To add a new record to a container, you must first decide which database you want to add the record to. If you add the record to the public database, the record will be visible to all users of your application. If you add the record to the private database, then the record will be added to your private database (as you are accessing the CloudKit dashboard using your developer account).

Data within the database is grouped into *zones*. A zone is a logical grouping of the records in the database; every database starts out with a single zone called the *Default* zone. Additional zones can be added.

For certain types of applications, segregating the data in the database by zones may make sense (for example, zones could represent different business functions within an organization such as finance, marketing, development, and so on). In the examples created in this lesson, however, all databases use the default zone.

To add a new record using the dashboard, simply select the Default zone for the public or private database on the left-hand side navigation menu, select the record type, and click the Add (+) button in the detail area (see Figure 25-11).

FIGURE 25-11

Type in values for the fields and click the Save button to create the record. When you add a record from the dashboard, CloudKit automatically creates a unique record identifier for the record, which is visible in the Record Name attribute in Figure 25-12.

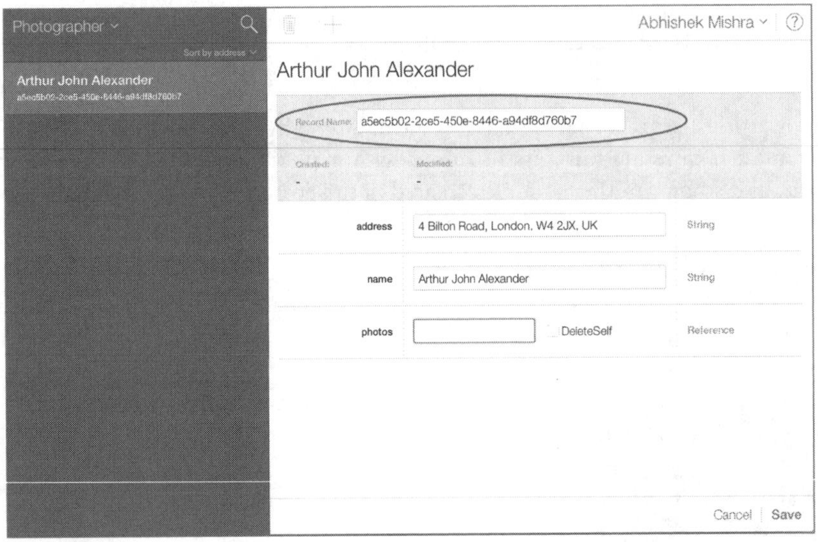

FIGURE 25-12

If the field type is a reference, then you will have a check box labeled `DeleteSelf` visible beside the field value (see Figure 25-13).

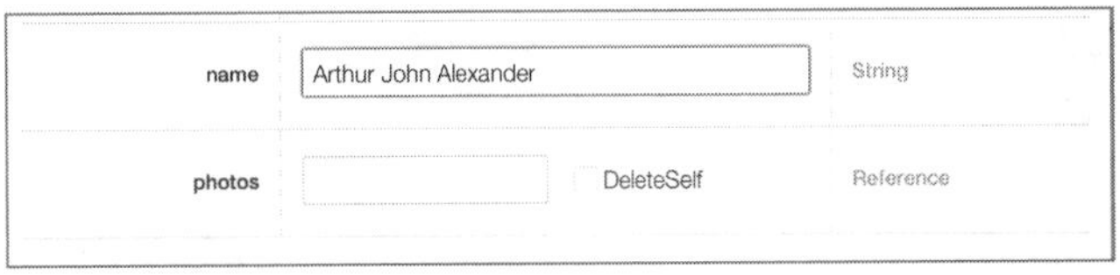

FIGURE 25-13

Enabling the `DeleteSelf` option implies that the record you are creating will be automatically deleted if the referenced record is deleted.

Modifying and Deleting Records

To edit a record, simply select the record from the list of records, enter new values for the fields, and click Save. To delete a record, use the trash icon located at the upper-left corner of the detail area (see Figure 25-14).

FIGURE 25-14

Resetting the Development Schema

You can reset the development schema to a previous state by using the Deployment ⇨ Reset Development Environment option (see Figure 25-15).

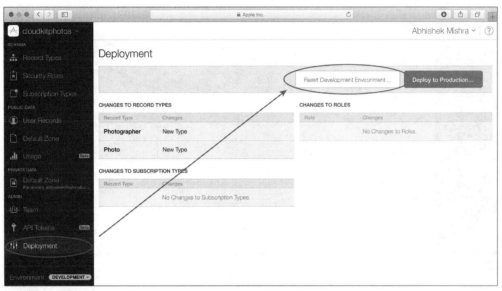

FIGURE 25-15

If you have never deployed your schema to the production environment, resetting the schema results in all records and record types being deleted from all databases.

If, however, you have deployed your schema previously, then resetting the schema in the development environment results in all records being deleted and the schema being restored to the production version.

The Deployment option is only available when you are working in the development environment. To find out which environment you are working in (or to switch to the other environment), use the environment drop-down option at the bottom-left of the dashboard (see Figure 25-16).

FIGURE 25-16

Deploying to Production

Once your app appears to be working fine with the development environment, you will want to switch over to the production environment prior to submitting the app to the iTunes Store. Switching over to the production environment will require you to deploy the schema into the production environment. Deploying a schema only copies the record types, not the individual records themselves.

To deploy a schema to production, click the Deployment option in the left-hand navigation menu and then click the Deploy to Production button in the detail area (see Figure 25-17).

FIGURE 25-17

If you have unused indexes, you may get a warning message asking you to either deploy unused indexes or optimize them. An Index helps to improve the speed of fetching records from the database.

When you add fields to a record type, CloudKit creates an index for the field. Depending on the type of field, CloudKid will create indexes for sorting, querying, and searching on that field. In production, it is wasteful to store indexes you do not use.

PREPARING TO USE CLOUDKIT

To use the CloudKit APIs in an application, you need to perform three steps:

1. Create an iCloud-enabled App ID.

2. Create an appropriate provisioning profile.

3. Enable appropriate entitlements in your Xcode project.

Create an iCloud-Enabled App ID

To create an appropriate App ID, log in to your iOS developer account at https://developer .apple.com/ios. Click the Member Center link on the right side to access the member center. Within the member center, click the Certificates, Identifiers & Profiles link (see Figure 25-18).

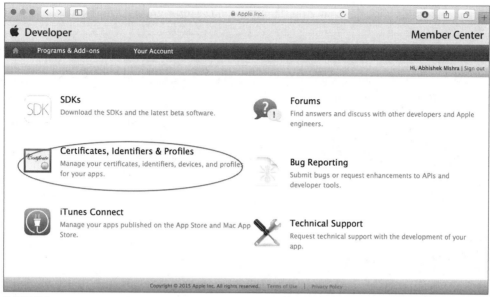

FIGURE 25-18

Next, click the Identifiers link in the iOS Apps category on the left side of the page (see Figure 25-19).

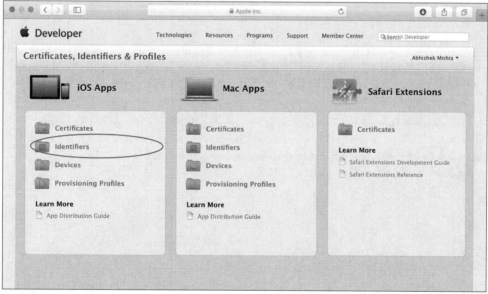

FIGURE 25-19

To create a new App ID, click the New App ID button on the top-right side (see Figure 25-20).

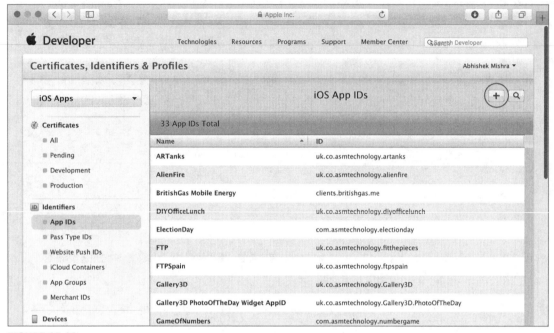

FIGURE 25-20

Provide a descriptive name of the new App ID in the Name field and select Team ID in the App ID prefix drop-down. Select the Explicit App ID radio button under the App ID suffix section and provide a unique identifier in the Bundle ID field that ends in the name of the Xcode project you are going to create (or have created).

Typically, you create this identifier by combining the reverse-domain name of your website and the name of your Xcode project. For example, the project created in this lesson is called CloudKitPhotos and the bundle identifier specified is com.wileybook.cloudkitphotos. Your browser window should resemble Figure 25-21.

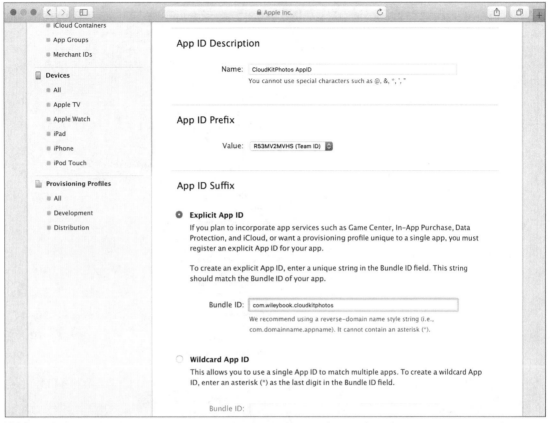

FIGURE 25-21

Scroll down to reveal the App Services section and ensure that both the iCloud checkbox and the Include CloudKit support option are selected (see Figure 25-22).

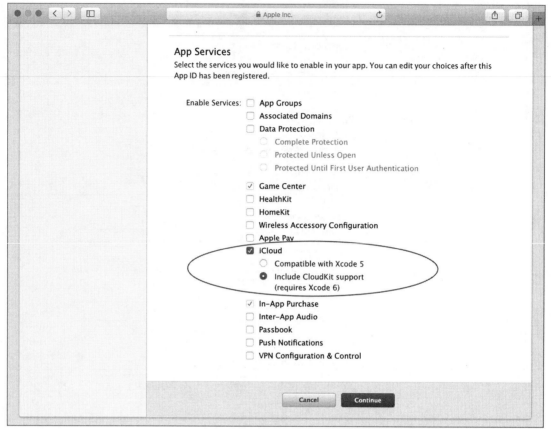

FIGURE 25-22

Click the Continue button to proceed. You will be presented with a summary of the App ID information (see Figure 25-23). Click Submit to finish creating the App ID.

FIGURE 25-23

Create an Appropriate Provisioning Profile

To create a provisioning profile for an iCloud-enabled App ID, click the All link (under the Provisioning category) in the menu on the left-hand side of the iOS Provisioning Portal window (see Figure 25-24).

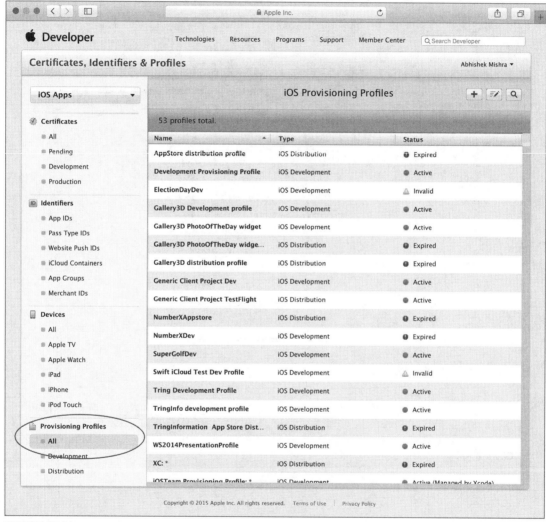

FIGURE 25-24

Click the New Profile button on the top-right side (see Figure 25-25).

FIGURE 25-25

You will be asked to choose between a development or distribution provisioning profile. A distribution provisioning profile is used to submit applications to iTunes Connect. For the moment, select the iOS App Development option and click Continue (see Figure 25-26).

FIGURE 25-26

A development provisioning profile ties together three pieces of information:

➤ A single App ID

➤ One or more public keys

➤ A list of test device IDs

The next step requires you to select an App ID that will be associated with this provisioning profile. Select the iCloud-enabled App ID you have created (see Figure 25-27) and click Continue.

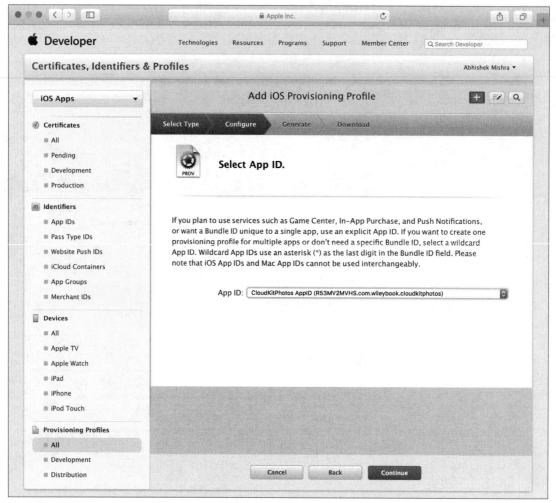

FIGURE 25-27

Select one or more development certificates that will be included in the profile. You must make sure to sign the app in Xcode using one of the certificates you select here. Select a suitable certificate and click Continue (see Figure 25-28).

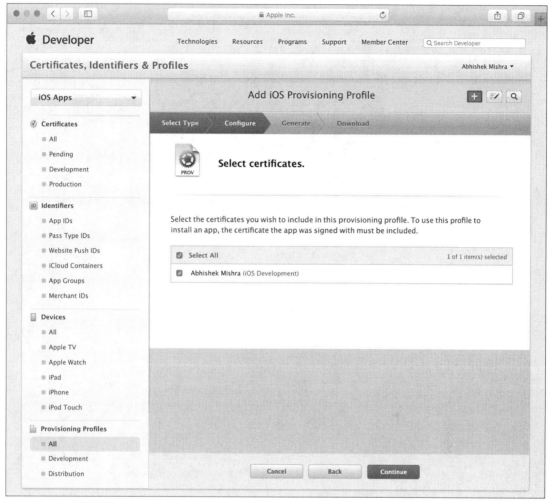

FIGURE 25-28

Next, you must select one or more devices that will be included in this provisioning profile. The corresponding identifiers for these devices must be registered with your development account. Your app will only be testable on these devices (see Figure 25-29).

FIGURE 25-29

The final step involves providing a suitable name for the profile and clicking the Generate button. When the profile is created, you will be provided an option to download it onto your computer (see Figure 25-30).

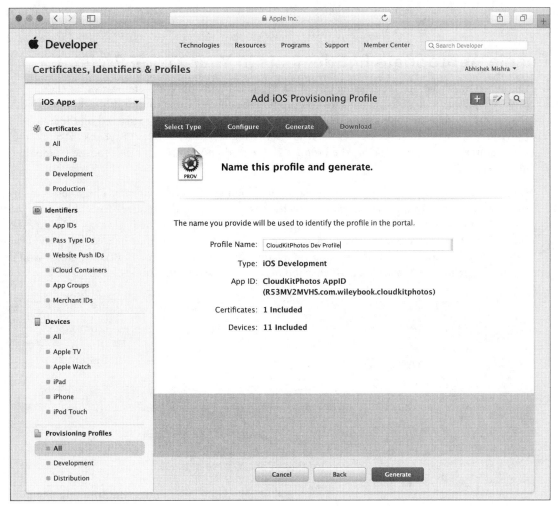

FIGURE 25-30

If you were to now click the All link under the Provisioning section of the left-hand side menu, you would see an entry for the new profile in the list of available profiles. You can also download a provisioning profile from this list.

Once the profile has been downloaded, simply locate it in the Downloads folder on your Mac and double-click it to install it in Xcode.

Enable Appropriate Entitlements in Your Xcode Project

Create a new project in Xcode using one of the standard iOS application templates. In the Project Options dialog box, make sure you provide the correct value for the Product Name and Organization Identifier fields so as to create the same App ID that was registered on the iOS Provisioning Portal. If, for instance, the App ID you registered was `com.wileybook.cloudkit-photos`, use `cloudkitphotos` for the Product Name field and `com.wileybook` for the Company Identifier field.

Applications that use iCloud must be signed with iCloud-specific entitlements. These entitlements ensure that only your applications can access the documents that they create. To enable entitlements, select the project's root node in the project navigator and the appropriate build target. Ensure the Capabilities tab is selected. Locate the iCloud node and enable it. You may be asked to provide your iOS developer accounts credentials when you enable the iCloud entitlement. Because this lesson is about CloudKit, ensure the CloudKit checkbox is checked (see Figure 25-31).

FIGURE 25-31

COMMON OPERATIONS

In this section, you learn how to perform common operations such as checking for service availability, adding/updating records, and retrieving records. While it is possible to create records using the iCloud dashboard, you will most likely need to be able to do this programmatically in response to some action taken by the user.

Checking for Service Availability

Before writing data to one of the CloudKit databases (private or public), the user must be signed in to iCloud. The following snippet uses the `accountStatusWithCompletionHandler` method of the `CKContainer` object to check if the user is signed in:

```
CKContainer.defaultContainer().accountStatusWithCompletionHandler {
(accountStatus, error) -> Void in

        if accountStatus == CKAccountStatus.NoAccount {

            let alert = UIAlertController(title: "Sign in to iCloud",
                message: "You need to sign in to iCloud to create records.",
                preferredStyle: UIAlertControllerStyle.Alert)

            alert.addAction(UIAlertAction(title: "Ok",
                style: UIAlertActionStyle.Default,
                handler: nil))

            self.presentViewController(alert,
                animated: true,
                completion: nil)
        }
        else {
            // show the view controller to allow the user to create a
new record.
        }
    }
```

Creating Records Programmatically

To create a record, you will first need to give it a unique record identifier. CloudKit only generates unique record identifiers for records created using the dashboard. To generate unique record identifiers, use the `UDIDString` method of the `NSUDID` class to generate a unique record name:

```
let uuid:String = NSUUID().UUIDString
```

and then create a `CKRecordID` instance with that name:

```
let photoRecordID = CKRecordID(recordName: uuid)
```

The next step is to create a `CKRecordInstance`. To create one, you will need to provide a string that represents the record type and the unique record identifier for the new record. This is shown in the following snippet:

```
let photoRecord:CKRecord = CKRecord(recordType: "Photo", recordID: photoRecordID)
```

You can set up the values of individual fields in the record using key-value coding:

```
photoRecord["photoCaption" ] = "By the lake"
photoRecord["photoDescription"] = "Photo by Andy Brown"
```

Finally, save the `CKRecord` instance to CloudKit by using the `saveRecord` method of a `CKDatabase` instance. The following snippet demonstrates how to save a record to the public database:

```
let publicDatabase:CKDatabase = CKContainer.defaultContainer().publicCloudDatabase

publicDatabase.saveRecord(photoRecord) { (newRecord, error) -> Void in

    if error != nil {
        // handle the error in some way.
    }
}
```

Retrieving Records

If you know the record identifier (listed as "record name" on the CloudKit dashboard) for the record you want to retrieve, you can create a CKRecordID instance with that identifier and then use the fetchRecordWithID() method of the CKDatabase instance. This is demonstrated in the following snippet:

```
let publicDatabase = CKContainer.defaultContainer().publicCloudDatabase

let someRecordID:CKRecordID = CKRecordID(recordName: "9181.a8d5xv26")

publicDatabase.fetchRecordWithID(someRecordID) { (record:CKRecord?,
error:NSError?) -> Void in
            // examine error, if no error then do something with record.
}
```

The fetchRecordWithID method requires two arguments. The first is a CKRecordID that contains the record identifier for the record you wish to retrieve; the second parameter is a completion block that will be called by CloudKit with the results of the fetch operation.

If you do not know the record identifier, then you will need to perform a query on the database to retrieve all records that satisfy some criteria and then iterate through the results. The following code snippet performs a query on the database to retrieve all records from the Photographer table that have the name field containing the value Arthur:

```
let publicDatabase:CKDatabase = CKContainer.defaultContainer().publicCloudDatabase

let predicate:NSPredicate = NSPredicate(format: "name = ",
    argumentArray: ["Arthur"])

let query:CKQuery = CKQuery(recordType: "Photographer",
    predicate: predicate)

publicDatabase.performQuery(query,
    inZoneWithID: nil,
    completionHandler: { (results:[CKRecord]?, error:NSError?) -> Void in
      // if error is nil, then examine the contents of the array results
})
```

TRY IT

In this Try It, you build a new Xcode project based on the Single View Application template called CloudKitPhotos. In this application, you use CloudKit to share photos with other users of your application using a public database. You also use Core Data to save these photos locally on your device.

Lesson Requirements

➤ Create a new Universal application project based on the Single View Application template.

➤ Register the App ID with the iOS Provisioning Portal.

➤ Create a development provisioning profile.

➤ Download and install the development provisioning profile.

➤ Create a Table View Controller based user interface.

➤ Create a data model with Core Data.

➤ Check iCloud service availability in the `viewDidLoad` method of the view controller class.

➤ Load previously downloaded content into the table view.

➤ Build a detail view to show information on a photo selected in the table view.

➤ Build a view controller that allows users to upload new pictures.

➤ Implement code to upload new images to the public CloudKit database.

> **REFERENCE** *The code for this Try It is available at* www.wrox.com/go/
> swiftios.

Hints

➤ To make best use of this application, you will need at least two iOS devices set up to use the same iCloud account.

➤ You must ensure iCloud has been set up on each test device.

➤ Testing your apps on iOS devices is covered in Appendix B.

Step-by-Step

➤ Create a Single View Application in Xcode called `CloudKitPhotos`.

1. Launch Xcode and create a new application by selecting File ➪ New ➪ Project.

2. Select the Single View Application template from the list of iOS project templates.

3. In the project options screen, use the following values:

   ➤ **Product Name:** cloudkitphotos (*in lowercase*)

   ➤ **Organization Name:** your company

   ➤ **Organization Identifier:** com.wileybook.cloudkitphotos

   ➤ **Language:** Swift

   ➤ **Devices:** Universal

➤ **Use Core Data:** Checked

➤ **Include Unit Tests:** Unchecked

➤ **Include UI Tests:** Unchecked

4. Save the project onto your hard disk.

➤ Register an App ID with the iOS Provisioning Portal.

1. Log in to the iOS Provisioning Portal, and register a new App ID with the following details:

➤ **Description:** CloudKitPhotos AppID

➤ **Bundle Seed ID:** Use Team ID

➤ **Bundle Identifier:** com.wileybook.cloudkitphotos

2. Enable the App ID to use with iCloud.

This process is covered in the section "Create an iCloud-Enabled App ID" earlier in this lesson.

➤ Create a development provisioning profile using the App ID created in the previous step.

1. The process of creating the provisioning profile is covered in the section "Creating an Appropriate Provisioning Profile" earlier in this lesson. Follow those instructions to create a development provisioning profile called "Swift Cloud Test Development Profile."

2. Download and install the provisioning profile by double-clicking on the profile after it has been downloaded to your computer.

➤ Enable iCloud-specific entitlements for the application target.

1. Select the project's root node in the project navigator and select the appropriate build target. Ensure the Capabilities tab is selected. Scroll down to the iCloud option and enable it.

2. Once the iCloud entitlement has been enabled, ensure the CloudKit checkbox has been selected.

➤ Build the user interface of the application.

1. Open the `Main.storyboard` file from the project explorer and drag-and-drop a Table View Controller object onto the storyboard. This will create a new scene in the storyboard (see Figure 25-32).

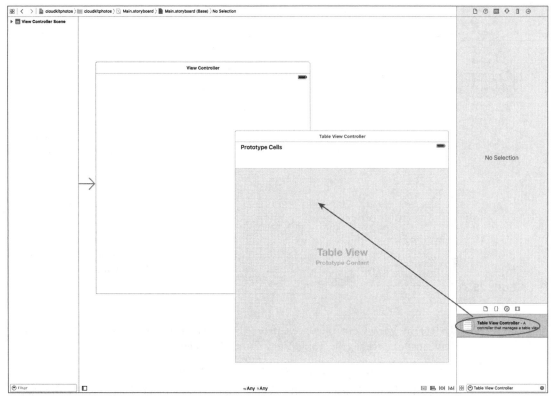

FIGURE 25-32

A table view controller is an instance of `UITableViewController` and is used to manage a table view. The table view in this application will be used to present a list of photos in the local database to the user.

2. Position the two scenes side by side, and zoom out of the storyboard a little if necessary. To zoom in/out, select Editor ➪ Canvas ➪ Zoom.

3. Set up the Table View Controller scene to replace the default scene of the storyboard.

   ➤ Select the Table View Controller scene in the storyboard.

   ➤ Ensure the Attribute inspector is visible and scroll down to the View Controller section.

   ➤ Ensure the Is Initial View Controller option is selected. When you select this option, the Storyboard Entry Point indicator will jump to the table view controller scene (see Figure 25-33).

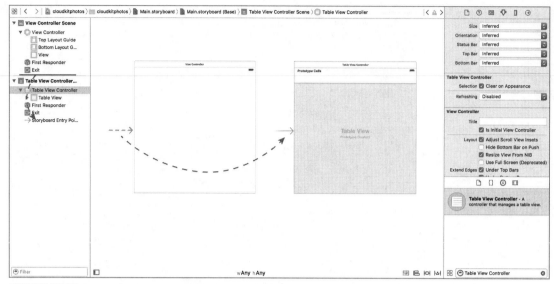

FIGURE 25-33

4. Delete the View Controller scene from the storyboard. Your storyboard should now have just one scene (the Table View Controller scene).

5. Embed the Table View Controller scene in a navigation controller.

   Select the Table View Controller scene from the document outline panel and then select Editor ➪ Embed In ➪ Navigation Controller.

   This action will add a Navigation Controller scene to the storyboard and make it the default scene of the storyboard. Your Table View Controller scene will now be embedded in the Navigation Controller (see Figure 25-34).

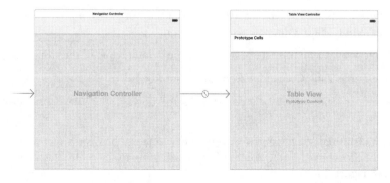

FIGURE 25-34

6. Set up the table view's appearance.

   ➤ Select the table view and ensure the Attribute inspector is visible.

   ➤ Ensure the Content attribute is set to Dynamic Prototypes.

   ➤ Ensure the value of the Prototype Cells attribute is 1.

   ➤ Ensure the Style attribute is set to Grouped.

7. Set up the prototype cell.

   ➤ Expand the table view in the document outline; this will reveal the table view cell.

   ➤ Select the table view cell.

   ➤ Use the attribute editor to ensure that the value of the identifier attribute is `prototypeCell1`.

   ➤ Ensure the Style attribute is set to Basic.

8. Set up the `ViewController` class (implemented in `ViewController.swift`) to inherit from `UITableViewController` instead of `UIViewController`.

   ➤ Open the `ViewController.Swift` file.

   ➤ Locate the following line in the file:

   ```
   class ViewController: UIViewController {
   ```

   ➤ Change it to

   ```
   class ViewController: UITableViewController {
   ```

9. Add a right bar button item to the navigation bar of the Table View Controller scene.

   ➤ Expand the document outline for the storyboard and select the Navigation Item under the Table View (see Figure 25-35).

FIGURE 25-35

   ➤ Drag and drop a Bar Button Item from the object library onto the right edge of the Navigation Item (see Figure 25-36).

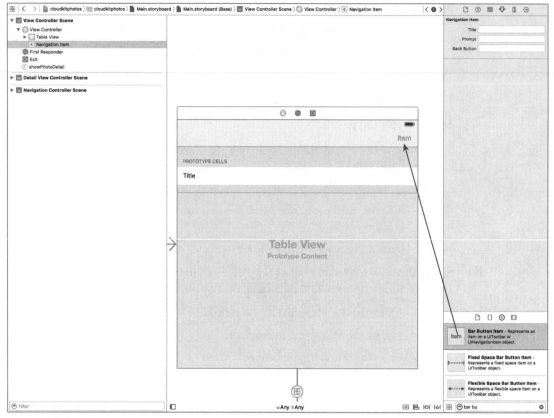

FIGURE 25-36

➤   Select the new Bar Button Item and use the Attribute inspector to set the value of its System Item attribute to Add (see Figure 25-37).

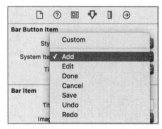

FIGURE 25-37

10. Link the Table View Controller scene in the storyboard to the `ViewController` class.

> ➤ Select the Table View Controller scene.

> ➤ Use the Identity Inspector to change the Custom Class to `ViewController`.

11. Add a detail view controller scene. This view controller will be used to show details on a photo selected in the table view.

> ➤ Drag and drop a View Controller object onto the storyboard. This will create a new scene.

> ➤ Create a Show detail segue between the table view cell and the new view controller. Hold down the Control key on your keyboard and drag from the prototype cell in the Table View Controller and drop onto the new scene you have added (see Figure 25-38).

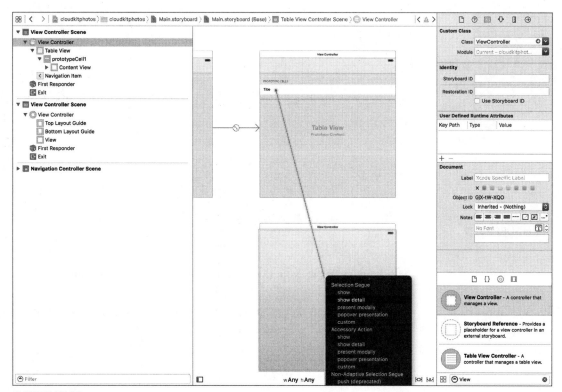

FIGURE 25-38

Your storyboard will now have three scenes and will resemble Figure 25-39.

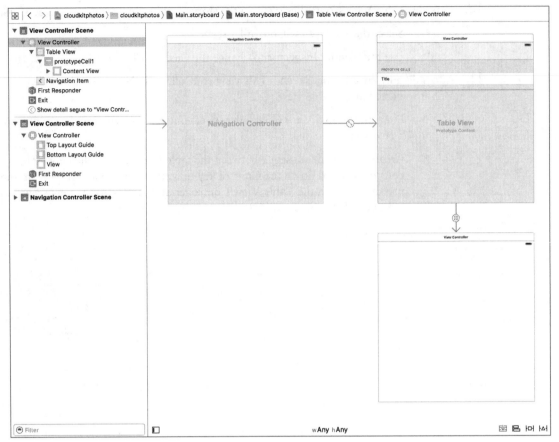

FIGURE 25-39

➤ Select the segue that you have just created, and use the Attribute inspector to set the identifier property of the segue to showPhotoDetail.

➤ Create a new Swift file called DetailViewController.swift and replace its contents with the following code:

```
import UIKit

class DetailViewController: UIViewController {

    override func viewDidLoad() {
        super.viewDidLoad()
    }

    override func didReceiveMemoryWarning() {
        super.didReceiveMemoryWarning()
    }

}
```

➤ Use the Identity Inspector to change the Custom Class of the new scene to `DetailViewController`.

12. Add user interface elements to the Detail View Controller scene.

➤ Drag-and-drop an image view and two label objects onto the Detail View Controller scene and position them to resemble Figure 25-40.

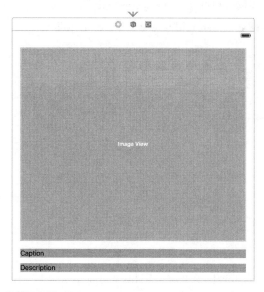

FIGURE 25-40

You will need to zoom in to 100 percent magnification to be able to add objects onto scenes.

➤ Create layout constraints for each of elements on the storyboard scene using the information in Table 25-2. When creating layout constraints using the pin constraints dialog box, ensure the Constrain to margins option is unchecked and Update Frames is set to None.

TABLE 25-2: Layout Constraints

ELEMENT	LEFT	TOP	RIGHT	BOTTOM
Image view	20	20	20	20
Caption label	20	20	20	20
Description label	20	20	20	20

➤ Select the Detail View Controller scene in the document outline and select Editor ➪ Resolve Auto Layout Issues ➪ All Views ➪ Update Frames to update the storyboard scene with the layout constraints you have just applied.

➤ Using the Assistant Editor, create an outlet in the `DetailViewController` class called `imageView` and connect it to the image view.

➤ Using the Assistant Editor, create an outlet in the `DetailViewController` class called `captionLabel` and connect it to the first label.

➤ Using the Assistant Editor, create an outlet in the `DetailViewController` class called `detailLabel` and connect it to the second label.

The code in `DetailViewController.swift` should now resemble the following:

```swift
import UIKit

class DetailViewController: UIViewController {

    @IBOutlet weak var imageView: UIImageView!
    @IBOutlet weak var captionLabel: UILabel!
    @IBOutlet weak var detailLabel: UILabel!

    override func viewDidLoad() {
        super.viewDidLoad()
    }

    override func didReceiveMemoryWarning() {
        super.didReceiveMemoryWarning()
    }
}
```

13. Add a new view controller scene to the storyboard scene. This will be used when the user wants to add a photo to iCloud using CloudKit.

➤ Drag-and-drop a View Controller object onto the storyboard. This will create a new scene.

➤ Create a Present modally segue between the right bar button item and the new view controller.

➤ Your storyboard will now have four scenes and will resemble Figure 25-41.

➤ Select the segue that you have just created and use the Attribute inspector to set the identifier property of the segue to `addPhoto`.

➤ Create a new Swift file called `AddPhotoViewController.swift` and replace its contents with the following code:

```swift
import UIKit

class AddPhotoViewController: UIViewController {

    override func viewDidLoad() {
        super.viewDidLoad()
```

```
        }

        override func didReceiveMemoryWarning() {
            super.didReceiveMemoryWarning()
        }

    }
```

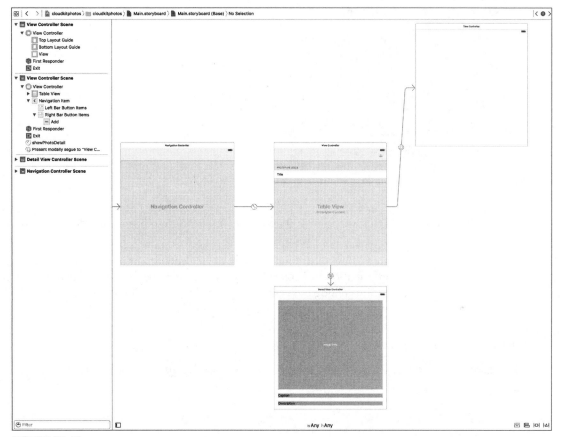

FIGURE 25-41

➤ Use the Identity inspector to change the Custom Class of the new scene to `AddPhotoViewController`.

14. Add user interface elements to the Add Photo View Controller scene.

➤ Drag-and-drop an image view, two text fields, and three buttons onto the Add Photo View Controller scene and position them to resemble Figure 25-42.

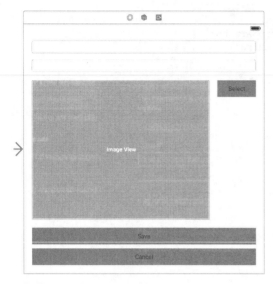

FIGURE 25-42

You will need to zoom in to 100 percent magnification to be able to add objects onto scenes.

➤ Create layout constraints for each of elements on the storyboard scene using the information in Table 25-3. When creating layout constraints using the pin constraints dialog box, ensure the Constrain to margins option is unchecked and Update Frames is set to None.

TABLE 25-3: Layout Constraints

ELEMENT	LEFT	TOP	RIGHT	BOTTOM	HEIGHT
Text field 1	20	20	20	20	30
Text field 2	20	20	20	20	30
Image view	20	20	20	20	
Select button	20	20	20		40
Save button	20	10	20	10	40
Cancel button	20	10	20	20	40

➤ Select the Add Photo View Controller scene in the document outline and select Editor ➪ Resolve Auto Layout Issues ➪ All Views ➪ Update Frames to update the storyboard scene with the layout constraints you have just applied.

➤ Using the Assistant editor, create outlets in the AddPhotoViewController class called imageView, captionField, and descriptionField and then connect the image view, first text field, and second text field respectively.

➤ Create action methods in the AddPhotoViewController class called on SelectPicture, onSaveRecord, and onCancel and connect them to the Select Picture, Save, and Cancel buttons respectively.

The code in AddPhotoViewController.swift should now resemble the following:

```
import UIKit

class AddPhotoViewController: UIViewController {

    @IBOutlet weak var imageView: UIImageView!
    @IBOutlet weak var captionField: UITextField!
    @IBOutlet weak var descriptionField: UITextField!

    override func viewDidLoad() {
        super.viewDidLoad()
    }

    override func didReceiveMemoryWarning() {
        super.didReceiveMemoryWarning()
    }

    @IBAction func onSelectPicture(sender: AnyObject) {

    }

    @IBAction func onSaveRecord(sender: AnyObject) {

    }

    @IBAction func onCancel(sender: AnyObject) {

    }
}
```

➤ Build the client-side data model using Core Data.

1. Select the cloudkitphotos.xcdatamodeld file in the project navigator to open it in the Xcode editor.

2. Add an Entity to the data model to represent photos.

➤ Select Editor ➪ Add Entity and name the new entity Photo.

➤ Add the following attributes to the Photo entity:

photoCaption: String

photoDescription: String

fileName: String

dateTaken: Date

ckRecordID: String

3. Use the Editor ➪ Create NSManagedObject subclass menu item to create an `NSManagedObject` subclass to represent the `Photo` entity. While creating the `NSManagedObject` subclass, ensure the language is set to Swift.

4. Ensure the `Photo.swift` file has the following import statements at the top:

```
import Foundation
import CoreData
import CloudKit
import UIKit
```

5. Add a method called `saveImageToDocumentsDirectory`, which saves a `UIImage` instance to a JPEG file in the documents directory and returns the path to the saved file:

```
static func saveImageToDocumentsDirectory(image: UIImage,
    _ fileName:String) -> NSURL {

    let documentsURL =
    NSFileManager.defaultManager().URLsForDirectory(
    .DocumentDirectory,        inDomains:.UserDomainMask)[0]

    let fileURL =
    documentsURL.URLByAppendingPathComponent(fileName)

    UIImageJPEGRepresentation(image, 0.5)?.
    writeToURL(fileURL,
    atomically: true)

    return fileURL
}
```

This method has been defined with the static keyword; therefore, you do not need an instance of Photo to use this method. You can simply call it on the class.

6. Add a static method called `addFromCKRecord`, which creates a `Photo` entity in Core Data from a `CKRecord` instance.

```
static func addFromCKRecord(record:CKRecord) {

    // read fields from CKRecord
    let recordIdentifier:String = record.recordID.recordName

    guard let
        dateTaken:NSDate = record["dateTaken"] as? NSDate,
        fileName:String = record["filename"] as? String,
        photoCaption:String = record["photoCaption"] as? String,
        photoDescription:String = record["photoDescription"] as? String,
        asset:CKAsset = record["photoAsset"] as? CKAsset else {
            return
    }

    // save asset to documents directory
    guard let image = UIImage(contentsOfFile:asset.fileURL.path!) else {
        print ("unable to download image")
        return
    }
```

```
        saveImageToDocumentsDirectory(image, fileName)

        // insert new record.
        let appDelegate = UIApplication.sharedApplication().delegate as!
                            AppDelegate

        let newItem =
        NSEntityDescription.insertNewObjectForEntityForName("Photo",
        inManagedObjectContext: appDelegate.managedObjectContext) as! Photo

        newItem.ckRecordID = recordIdentifier
        newItem.fileName = fileName
        newItem.dateTaken = dateTaken
        newItem.photoCaption = photoCaption
        newItem.photoDescription = photoDescription

        // save managed object context.
        do {
            try appDelegate.managedObjectContext.save()
        }
        catch {
            print("error saving managed object context")
        }
    }
}
```

The preceding code snippet extracts fields from the CKRecord instance, downloads the asset into the documents directory, and creates a managed object in the local data store.

➤ Build the server-side data model using the CloudKit Dashboard.

1. Log in to the CloudKit dashboard at https://icloud.developer.apple.com/dashboard/.

2. Ensure the dashboard is set to use the correct container. The cloudkitphotos container should be selected in the drop-down menu located at the top-left corner of the dashboard.

3. Ensure you are working with the development environment. The development environment should be selected in the drop-down menu located at the bottom-left corner of the dashboard.

4. Add a record type called Photo. To this record type, add the following fields:

   ➤ dateTaken: Date/Time

   ➤ fileName: String

   ➤ photoAsset: Asset

   ➤ owner: Reference

   ➤ photoCaption: String

   ➤ photoDescription: String

Adding record types using the CloudKit dashboard has been covered earlier in this lesson.

➤ Add code to the `ViewController.swift` file to Fetch initial data from CloudKit and save to the managed objects using Core Data.

1. Ensure both CloudKit and CoreData have been imported at the top of the `ViewController.swift` file:

```
import CloudKit
import CoreData
```

2. Declare a protocol called `CloudLoaderDelegate` as follows:

```
protocol CloudLoaderDelegate : NSObjectProtocol {

    func willProcessRecords(recordType:String, _ records:[CKRecord]?)

    func processCKRecord(recordType:String, _ record:CKRecord)

    func didProcessRecords(recordType:String, _ records:[CKRecord]?)

    func didReceiveError(recordType:String, _ error:NSError?)
}
```

3. Add the following variable declarations to the `ViewController.swift` file:

```
var photos:[Photo]?
var publicDatabase:CKDatabase?
var matchAllPredicate:NSPredicate?
```

4. Ensure the `ViewController` class implements the `CloudLoaderDelegate` protocol by changing the following line:

```
class ViewController: UITableViewController {
```

to

```
class ViewController: UITableViewController, CloudLoaderDelegate {
```

5. Declare a block called `recordDownloadBlock`, which takes as input a record type, `CKDatabase` instance, a predicate, and a delegate object that implements `CloudLoaderDelegate` as follows:

```
let recordDownloadBlock: (String,  CKDatabase, NSPredicate,
    CloudLoaderDelegate) -> Void =
{ (recordType, database, predicate, delegate) -> Void in

    let query = CKQuery(recordType: recordType, predicate: predicate)

    database.performQuery(query, inZoneWithID: nil) { results, error in

        if error != nil{
            delegate.didReceiveError(recordType, error)
            return
        }

        guard let results = results else {
```

```
            delegate.didProcessRecords(recordType, nil)
            return
        }

        // delete photographer records from Core Data
        delegate.willProcessRecords(recordType, results)

        for record in results {
            delegate.processCKRecord(recordType, record)
        }

        delegate.didProcessRecords(recordType, results)
    }
}
```

This block will perform a query on a CloudKit database to retrieve records of a specific record type and call methods on the delegate object when it has retrieved records.

The code in `ViewController.swift` should now resemble the following:

```swift
import UIKit
import CloudKit
import CoreData

protocol CloudLoaderDelegate : NSObjectProtocol {

    func willProcessRecords(recordType:String, _ records:[CKRecord]?)

    func processCKRecord(recordType:String, _ record:CKRecord)

    func didProcessRecords(recordType:String, _ records:[CKRecord]?)

    func didReceiveError(recordType:String, _ error:NSError?)
}

class ViewController: UITableViewController, CloudLoaderDelegate {

    var photos:[Photo]?
    var publicDatabase:CKDatabase?
    var matchAllPredicate:NSPredicate?

    let recordDownloadBlock: (String, CKDatabase, NSPredicate,
    CloudLoaderDelegate) -> Void = { (recordType, database, predicate,
    delegate) -> Void in

        let query = CKQuery(recordType: recordType, predicate: predicate)

        database.performQuery(query, inZoneWithID: nil) { results, error in

            if error != nil{
                delegate.didReceiveError(recordType, error)
                return
            }

            guard let results = results else {
                delegate.didProcessRecords(recordType, nil)
                return
```

```
        }

        // delete photographer records from Core Data
        delegate.willProcessRecords(recordType, results)

        for record in results {
            delegate.processCKRecord(recordType, record)
        }

        delegate.didProcessRecords(recordType, results)
    }
}


override func viewDidLoad() {
    super.viewDidLoad()
}

override func didReceiveMemoryWarning() {
    super.didReceiveMemoryWarning()
}
```

6. Get a reference to the public CloudKit database and create a predicate that will return all records in a record type in the `viewDidLoad` method:

```
override func viewDidLoad() {

    super.viewDidLoad()

    self.publicDatabase =
    CKContainer.defaultContainer().publicCloudDatabase

    self.matchAllPredicate = NSPredicate(value: true)
}
```

7. Override the `viewDidAppear` method in your `ViewController.swift` file as follows:

```
override func viewDidAppear(animated: Bool) {

    super.viewDidAppear(animated)

    fetchListOfPhotos()
    tableView.reloadData()

    downloadPhotosFromCloud(recordDownloadBlock)
}
```

This method fetches all `Photo` entities from the CoreData store and then reloads the contents of the table view. It then attempts to download `Photo` records from CloudKit if the user has signed into the device with a CloudKit account.

8. Implement the `fetchListOfPhotos` methods in the `ViewController.swift` file as follows:

```
func fetchListOfPhotos() {
```

```
    let fetchRequest = NSFetchRequest(entityName: "Photo")

    let appDelegate = UIApplication.sharedApplication().delegate as!
                AppDelegate

    do {
        self.photos = try
        appDelegate.managedObjectContext.executeFetchRequest(fetchRequest)
        as? [Photo]
    }
    catch {
        print ("error retrieving list of photos from local database.")
    }

}
```

9. Implement the `downloadPhotosFromCloud` method as follows:

```
func downloadPhotosFromCloud(completionBlock : (String, CKDatabase,
                            NSPredicate, CloudLoaderDelegate) -> Void) {

    CKContainer.defaultContainer().accountStatusWithCompletionHandler {
        (accountStatus, error) -> Void in

        if accountStatus == CKAccountStatus.NoAccount {
            // user has not signed in to iCloud, show an alert.
            let alert = UIAlertController(title: "Sign in to iCloud",
                message: "You need to sign in to iCloud to create records.",
                preferredStyle: UIAlertControllerStyle.Alert)

            alert.addAction(UIAlertAction(title: "Ok",
                style: UIAlertActionStyle.Default,
                handler: nil))

            self.presentViewController(alert,
                animated: true,
                completion: nil)
        }
        else {
        // user has signed in to iCloud, download Photo from server
            completionBlock("Photo", self.publicDatabase!,
                        self.matchAllPredicate!, self);
        }
    }
}
```

This method takes as input, a block that will be called to fetch data from CloudKit. However, this block will only be called if the user has signed in to iCloud on the device.

10. Implement the `CloudLoaderDelegate` methods as follows:

```
func willProcessRecords(recordType:String, _ records:[CKRecord]?)
{
    // delete all Photos from core data before
    // processing new ones in CloudKit
```

```swift
        let fetchRequest = NSFetchRequest(entityName: "Photo")
        let appDelegate = UIApplication.sharedApplication().delegate
                        as! AppDelegate

var results:[Photo]? = nil

        do {
            results = try
            appDelegate.managedObjectContext.executeFetchRequest(fetchRequest)
            as? [Photo]

            guard let results = results else {
                return
            }

            for photo in results {
                appDelegate.managedObjectContext.deleteObject(photo)
            }

            try appDelegate.managedObjectContext.save()
        }
        catch {
            print ("error retrieving list of photos from local database.")
        }
}


func processCKRecord(recordType:String, _ record:CKRecord)
{
    if recordType.compare("Photo") == NSComparisonResult.OrderedSame {
        Photo.addFromCKRecord(record)
    }
}


func didProcessRecords(recordType:String, _ records:[CKRecord]?)
{
    if recordType.compare("Photo") == NSComparisonResult.OrderedSame {
        fetchListOfPhotos()
        tableView.reloadData()
    }
}

func didReceiveError(recordType:String, _ error:NSError?)
{
    print ("received error \(error) for record type \(recordType)")
}
```

11. Override the `prepareforSegue` methods in the ViewController.swift file to pass the selected item in the table view to the photo detail view controller:

```swift
override func prepareForSegue(segue: UIStoryboardSegue,
            sender: AnyObject?) {

        guard let identifier = segue.identifier else {
```

```
                return
            }

            if identifier.compare("showPhotoDetail") ==
                NSComparisonResult.OrderedSame {

                guard let
                    detailViewController =
                    segue.destinationViewController as?
                    DetailViewController else {
                    return
                }

                guard let indexPath =
                    tableView.indexPathForSelectedRow,
                    arrayOfPhotos = self.photos else {
                        return
                }

                let modelObject:Photo = arrayOfPhotos[indexPath.row]
                detailViewController.modelObject = modelObject
            }
        }
```

➤ Implement `UITableViewDataSource` methods in the `ViewController.swift` file.

1. Implement the `tableView(tableView, numberOfRowsInSection)` method as follows:

```
override func tableView(tableView: UITableView,
            numberOfRowsInSection section: Int) -> Int
{
        if photos != nil {
            return photos!.count
        }

        return 0
}
```

2. Implement the `tableview(tableView, cellForRowAtIndexPath)` method as follows

```
override func tableView(tableView: UITableView,
            cellForRowAtIndexPath indexPath: NSIndexPath) -> UITableViewCell
{
    let cell:UITableViewCell =
        tableView.dequeueReusableCellWithIdentifier("prototypeCell1",
        forIndexPath: indexPath)

    let somePhoto:Photo! = photos![indexPath.row]

    cell.textLabel?.text = somePhoto.photoCaption

    return cell
}
```

➤ Add code to the `DetailViewController.swift` file to display information on a `Photo` instance.

1. Declare an optional variable called `modelObject` in the `DetailViewController` class.

```
var modelObject:Photo?
```

2. Update the code in the `viewDidLoad` method to resemble the following:

```
override func viewDidLoad() {
    super.viewDidLoad()

    guard let
        modelObject = modelObject,
        photoDescription = modelObject.photoDescription,
        photoCaption = modelObject.photoCaption,
        imageFileName = modelObject.fileName else {
            return
    }

    detailLabel.text = photoDescription
    captionLabel.text = photoCaption
    loadImageFromFileInDocumentsDirectory(imageFileName)
}
```

The preceding snippet extracts the `photoCaption`, `photoDescription`, and `fileName` attributes of the `Photo` entity and updates information on the view.

3. Implement a method called `loadImageFromFileInDocumentsDirectory(imageFileName)`, which is given the name of a file in the documents directory and loads the image into the image view:

```
func loadImageFromFileInDocumentsDirectory(imageFileName:String) {

    let documentsURL =
NSFileManager.defaultManager().URLsForDirectory(.DocumentDirectory,
                            inDomains: .UserDomainMask)[0]

    let fileURL = documentsURL.URLByAppendingPathComponent(imageFileName)

    let image:UIImage? = UIImage(contentsOfFile: fileURL.path!)

    if (image != nil) {
        imageView.image = image
        imageView.contentMode = UIViewContentMode.ScaleAspectFit
    }

}
```

➤ Add code to the `AddPhotoViewController.swift` file to allow the user to add a photo to the public CloudKit database.

1. Import the CloudKit framework at the top of the `AddPhotoViewController.swift` file.

2. Create an action method in the `AddPhotoViewController` class and associate it with the Did End On Exit events of the two text fields.

➤ Right-click the first `UITextField` object to display its context menu, and drag from the circle beside the Did End On Exit item to an empty line in the `AddPhotoViewController.swift` file.

➤ Name the new Action `onDismissKeyboard`.

➤ Right-click the second `UITextField` object to display its context menu, and drag from the circle beside the Did End On Exit item to the icon representing the view controller in the dock.

➤ Release the mouse button over the yellow view controller icon in the dock to present a list of existing action methods in the view controller. Select the `onDismissKeyboard` method.

3. Click the `AddPhotoViewController.swift` file in the project navigator to open it.

Add the following code to the implementation of the `onDismissKeyboard` method:

```
captionField.resignFirstResponder()
descriptionField.resignFirstResponder()
```

4. Add a tap gesture recognizer and use it to dismiss the keyboard when the background area of the view is tapped.

➤ Add the following method declaration to the `AddPhotoViewController.swift` file:

```
func handleBackgroundTap(sender: UITapGestureRecognizer) {
    captionField.resignFirstResponder()
    descriptionField.resignFirstResponder()
}
```

➤ Add the following code to the `viewDidLoad` method after the `super.viewDidLoad()` line:

```
let tapRecognizer = UITapGestureRecognizer(target:self,
    action: Selector("handleBackgroundTap:"))

tapRecognizer.cancelsTouchesInView = false
self.view.addGestureRecognizer(tapRecognizer)
```

5. Set up placeholder text in the text fields when the view is loaded.

Add the following code to the `viewDidLoad` method after the `supe.viewDidLoad()` line:

```
captionField.placeholder = "Photo caption"
descriptionField.placeholder = "Photo description"
```

Your `viewDidLoad` method of `AddPhotoViewController.swift` should now resemble the following:

```
override func viewDidLoad() {
    super.viewDidLoad()

    captionField.placeholder = "Photo caption"
    descriptionField.placeholder = "Photo description"
```

```
let tapRecognizer = UITapGestureRecognizer(target:self ,
    action: Selector("handleBackgroundTap:"))

tapRecognizer.cancelsTouchesInView = false
self.view.addGestureRecognizer(tapRecognizer)
}
```

6. Add code to allow the user to select a picture from the photo library on the device. Selecting pictures from the photo library is covered in Lesson 31.

➤ Replace the implementation of the onSelectPicture method with the following:

```
@IBAction func onSelectPicture(sender: AnyObject) {

    guard let cameraButton = sender as? UIButton else {
        return
    }

    let imagePicker:UIImagePickerController = UIImagePickerController()
    imagePicker.sourceType = UIImagePickerControllerSourceType.PhotoLibrary
    imagePicker.delegate = self

    if UIDevice().userInterfaceIdiom == UIUserInterfaceIdiom.Pad
    {
        imagePicker.modalPresentationStyle =
                    UIModalPresentationStyle.Popover

        self.presentViewController(imagePicker,
                                    animated: true, completion: nil)

        let presentationController:UIPopoverPresentationController =
            imagePicker.popoverPresentationController!

        presentationController.permittedArrowDirections =
                            UIPopoverArrowDirection.Left

        presentationController.sourceView = self.view
        presentationController.sourceRect = cameraButton.frame
    }
    else
    {
        self.presentViewController(imagePicker,
                                    animated: true, completion: nil)
    }
}
```

➤ AddPhotoViewController class from

```
class AddPhotoViewController: UIViewController {
```

to

```
class AddPhotoViewController: UIViewController,
                UIImagePickerControllerDelegate,
                UINavigationControllerDelegate  {
```

➤ Add the following implementation of `UIImagePickerDelegate` methods in the `AddPhotoViewController.swift` file:

```
func imagePickerController(picker: UIImagePickerController,
            didFinishPickingMediaWithInfo info: [String : AnyObject]) {
    let image:UIImage =
        info[UIImagePickerControllerOriginalImage] as! UIImage
    imageView.image = image

    picker.dismissViewControllerAnimated(true, completion: nil)
}

func imagePickerControllerDidCancel(picker: UIImagePickerController)
{
    picker.dismissViewControllerAnimated(true, completion: nil)
}
```

7. Add code to dismiss the `AddPhotoViewController` when the Cancel button is tapped.

Replace the implementation of the `OnCancel` method with the following:

```
@IBAction func onCancel(sender: AnyObject) {
    self.dismissViewControllerAnimated(true, completion: nil)
}
```

8. Add code to save the image to the local file system and update CloudKit when the Save button is tapped.

Replace the implementation of the `OnSaveRecord` method with the following:

```
@IBAction func onSaveRecord(sender: AnyObject) {

    // ensure data has been filled.
    guard let
        photoCaption = captionField.text,
        photoDescription = descriptionField.text,
        image = imageView.image else {

        // user has not filled in all fields
        let alert = UIAlertController(title: "Incomplete information!",
        message: "You must select an image, provide a caption and a
                description.",
        preferredStyle: UIAlertControllerStyle.Alert)

        alert.addAction(UIAlertAction(title: "Ok",
            style: UIAlertActionStyle.Default,
            handler: nil))

        self.presentViewController(alert,
            animated: true,
            completion: nil)

            return
        }

        if photoCaption.characters.count == 0 ||
```

```
                    photoDescription.characters.count == 0 {
                        // user has not filled in all fields
                        let alert = UIAlertController(title: "Incomplete
information!",
                            message: "You must select an image, provide a
caption and a description.",
                            preferredStyle: UIAlertControllerStyle.Alert)

                    alert.addAction(UIAlertAction(title: "Ok",
                        style: UIAlertActionStyle.Default,
                        handler: nil))

                    self.presentViewController(alert,
                        animated: true,
                        completion: nil)

                    return

                }


            // generate a unique record identifier
            let uuid:String = NSUUID().UUIDString
            let photoRecordID:CKRecordID = CKRecordID(recordName: uuid)

            // save the image to a file in the documents directory
            let fileName:String = "\(uuid).jpg"
            let fileURL:NSURL =
            Photo.saveImageToDocumentsDirectory(image, fileName)

            // make a CKAsset from the file.
            let photoAsset:CKAsset = CKAsset(fileURL: fileURL)

            // create a photoRecord
            let photoRecord:CKRecord = CKRecord(recordType: "Photo",
                                        recordID: photoRecordID)

            photoRecord["photoCaption" ] = photoCaption
            photoRecord["photoDescription"] = photoDescription
            photoRecord["dateTaken"] = NSDate()
            photoRecord["filename"] = fileName
            photoRecord["photoAsset"] = photoAsset

            // save the record to the public database with CloudKit
            let publicDatabase:CKDatabase =
                CKContainer.defaultContainer().publicCloudDatabase

            publicDatabase.saveRecord(photoRecord)
            { (newRecord, error) -> Void in

                if error != nil {
                    let alert = UIAlertController(title: "Error!",
                        message: "Error saving to Cloudkit",
                        preferredStyle: UIAlertControllerStyle.Alert)

                    alert.addAction(UIAlertAction(title: "Ok",
```

```
            style: UIAlertActionStyle.Default,
            handler: nil))

    self.presentViewController(alert,
        animated: true,
        completion: nil)

        return
    }
    self.dismissViewControllerAnimated(true,
        completion: nil)
}


}
```

➤ Test your app in the iOS Simulator.

1. Click the Run button in the Xcode toolbar. Alternatively, you can select Project ⇨ Run.

2. When you launch the app for the first time, you will be presented with an empty table view. Use the Add button to add a photo to your CloudKit database. Once you have added a photo, wait for a few seconds for the table view to refresh its contents. You will see a row in the table view for each photo you add to CloudKit.

REFERENCE *To see some of the examples from this lesson, watch the Lesson 25 video online at* www.wrox.com/go/swiftiosvid.

26

Introduction to Core Data

The Core Data framework provides solutions to tasks commonly associated with managing the lifecycle of objects in your application, including object serialization. Prior to Core Data, programmers relied on SQLite to store their application data; Core Data can be viewed as an object-oriented wrapper around a SQLite database. It provides you with a convenient mechanism to create, update, and delete entities in the database without having to write a single line of SQL. In this lesson, you learn to use Core Data to implement simple object persistence in your applications.

BASIC CONCEPTS

Core Data is based on the Model-View-Controller pattern and essentially fits in at the model stage. It forces you to think of your applications data in terms of objects. Core Data introduces quite a few new concepts and terminology. These are discussed briefly in this section. Figure 26-1 provides an overview of the key classes introduced by Core Data.

Managed Object

A managed object is a representation of the object that you want to save to the data store. This is conceptually similar to a record in a relational database table and typically contains fields that correspond to properties in the object you want to save. The lifecycle of managed objects is managed by Core Data; you should not hold strong references in your code to managed objects. Managed objects are subclasses of NSManagedObject and not NSObject.

Managed Object Context

The managed object context is akin to a buffer between your application and the data store. It contains all your managed objects before they are written to the data store and manages their lifecycles. Inside this context you can add, delete, or modify managed objects. When you load data from the underlying data store, managed objects that are created as a result will live within the managed object context. When you need to read, insert, or delete objects, you will call methods on the managed object context. A managed object context is represented by an instance of the NSManagedObjectContext class. Managed object contexts should only be accessed from the thread in which they were created. An application can have multiple managed object contexts all of which can be connected to a single persistent store coordinator, and in effect are talking to the same database.

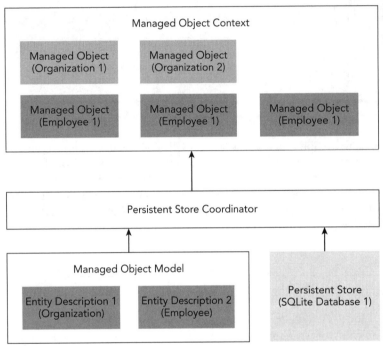

FIGURE 26-1

Persistent Store Coordinator

The persistent store coordinator is an instance of NSPersistentStoreCoordinator and represents the connection to the data store. It contains low-level information, such as the name, location, and type of the data store to be used, as well as handling the task of communicating with the store. Your application will have one instance of the persistent store coordinator for each database that it needs to interact with.

The persistent store coordinator is used by the managed object context, and in most cases, you will not need to deal with it directly. Multiple managed object contexts can share the same instance of the persistent store coordinator, and Core Data handles the synchronization of data across all these contexts.

You may have more than one managed object context sharing the persistent store coordinator if you want to access your managed objects from different threads. In such cases you will have one managed object context per thread.

Entity Description

An entity description is an instance of NSEntityDescription and essentially describes a table within the database. In Core Data terms, database tables are called entities. It is rare for a programmer to create entity descriptions programmatically, but it can be done. The most common method to create entity descriptions is to use the graphical Core Data editor included within XCode.

It is worth nothing that an entity description is similar to the schema for a database table. It does not contain the actual data; it is used internally by Core Data to create tables in the underlying database.

Managed Object Model

The managed object model is an instance of NSManagedObjectModel and is a collection of entity descriptions. When Core Data is used in a project, the project contains a file that ends with the extension .xcdatamodeld. This file is used by XCode to build a graphical editor for the managed object model (see Figure 26-2).

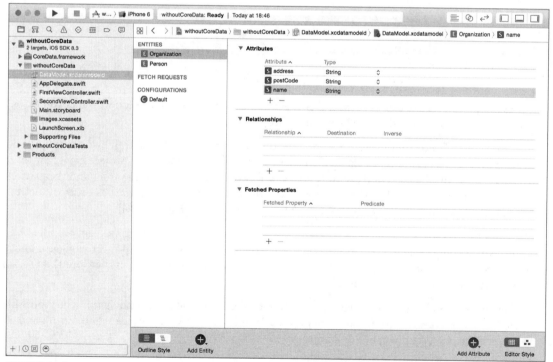

FIGURE 26-2

When your project is compiled into an executable, this file is compiled into a .mom file, which is the managed object model in binary format. For most practical purposes, the .xcdatamodel file can be considered to be the managed object model. However, it is important to keep in mind that this file will be compiled to produce the managed object model.

ADDING CORE DATA TO A PROJECT

When you create a new project based on the Master Detail or Single View Application templates, you have the option to include Core Data in the project in the project options dialog box (see Figure 26-3).

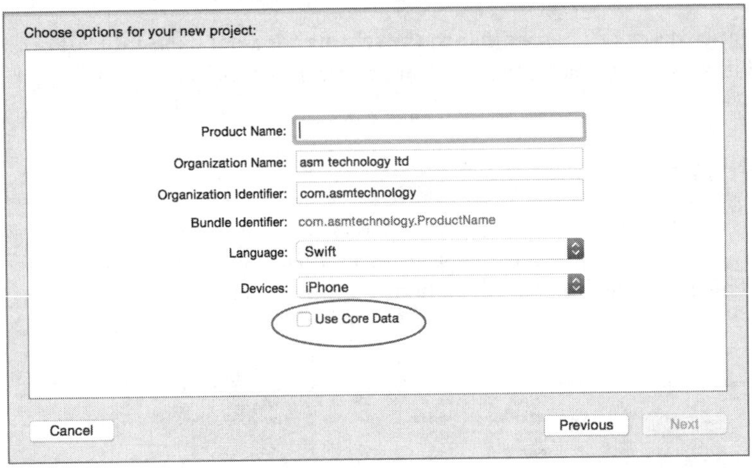

FIGURE 26-3

However, for other application types, this checkbox does not exist. This section walks you through what you need to do to add Core Data into a project manually.

To add Core Data to your project, you first need to add a reference to the framework. You can do this from the Project Settings page in Xcode. Select the project node in the project navigator to display the settings page. On the settings page, select the appropriate build target and then switch to the Build Phases tab. Click the + button under the Link Binary With Libraries category. Select CoreData.framework from the list of available frameworks (see Figure 26-4).

The next step is to create a managed object model for the project. To create an empty model file (into which you will later add entities), right-click the project group in the project navigator and select New File from the context menu. Select the Data Model template from the Core Data section and create the new file (see Figure 26-5).

To open the model in the Xcode editor, simply click the file in the project navigator (the model file has the .xcdatamodeld extension). The new model file is initially empty (see Figure 26-6), and as such is not much use to you in this state.

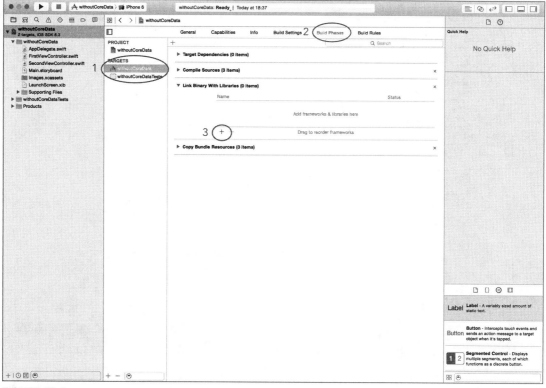

FIGURE 26-4

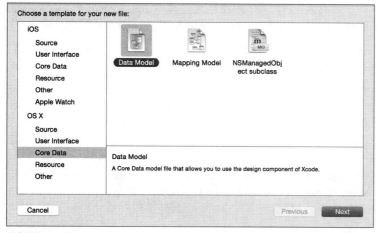

FIGURE 26-5

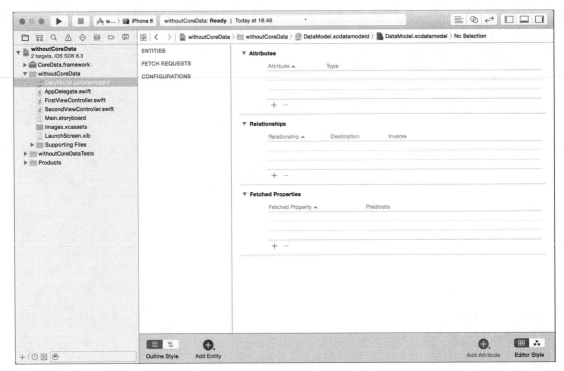

FIGURE 26-6

To persist objects into the underlying data store, you first need to define an entity in the data model for each object that you want to persist. Defining entities is trivial with the Xcode editor: To add a new entity called `ContactData`, select Editor ⇨ Add Entity and name the new entity appropriately. You will see the new entity listed under the Entities section of the Xcode editor (see Figure 26-7).

After you have defined an entity, you need to add attributes to it. Attributes represent the actual data fields in the entities themselves. Assuming the `ContactData` entity represents customer contact information, some of its attributes may be:

➤   Customer Name

➤   Phone Number

➤   Postcode

To add an attribute to the currently selected entity, select Editor ⇨ Add Attribute. This adds a new row to the Attributes section of the Xcode model editor (see Figure 26-8).

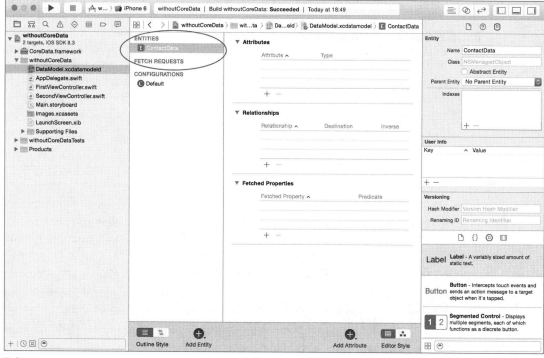

FIGURE 26-7

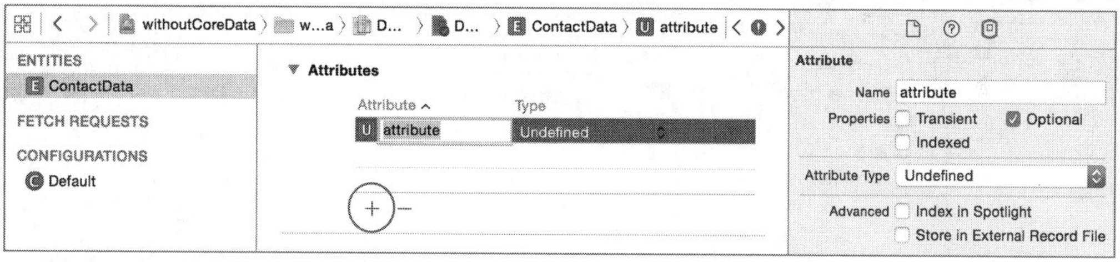

FIGURE 26-8

Type in an appropriate name for the attribute and specify the attribute type. Attribute names must begin with a lowercase letter and cannot contain whitespace. The attribute type is similar to the data type of a variable, and determines what type of data the attribute contains. Core Data provides several data types that can be selected from a drop-down list (see Figure 26-9). The type for each attribute of the ContactData entity can be String.

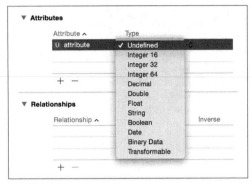

FIGURE 26-9

At this stage, you have created a new data model and added an entity to it. Now you need an actual Swift class that maps to the entity defined in the model. To do this, select Editor ➪ Create NSManagedObject Subclass. This presents a dialog box asking you where to save the `file` for the new class. In this dialog box, ensure the language is set to Swift (see Figure 26-10).

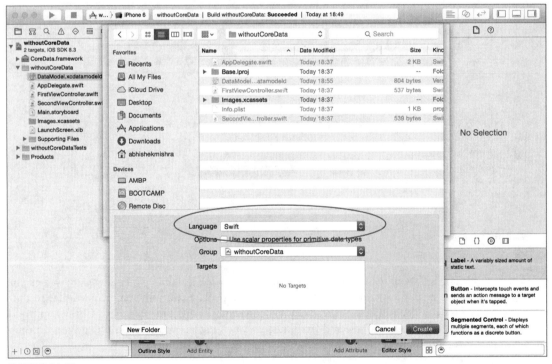

FIGURE 26-10

The name of the class will be the same as the name of the entity. The `ContactData` class that is created for you by Xcode is a subclass of `NSManagedObject` and maps to the entity with the same name. Its interface is listed here:

```
import Foundation
import CoreData

class ContactData: NSManagedObject {

    @NSManaged var customerName: String
    @NSManaged var phoneNumber: String
    @NSManaged var postCode: String

}
```

You need to ensure that the name of the class that corresponds to the entity in the data model is set up correctly. To do this, select the Entity in the `xcdatamodeld` file and switch to the Data Model Inspector by selecting View ⇨ Utilities ⇨ Show Data Model Inspector. Examine the value of the Class property; it should be set to `<your project name>.ContactData`.

It is worth mentioning that if you now decided to make changes to the entity in the `.xcdatamodel` file, the managed object class will not automatically update. You will need to regenerate the managed object class and this process will overwrite the contents of the previous managed object class header and implementation files. If you need to add code to the Core Data–generated class files, it is best to do so in a subclass of the class generated by Core Data.

INSTANTIATING CORE DATA OBJECTS

Before you can read or write model objects to the underlying data store, you will need to instantiate the managed object model, the managed object context, and the persistent store coordinator.

The managed object model is represented by an instance of the `NSManagedObjectModel` class, and you instantiate a single instance for the `.xcdatamodeld` file in your project using the following snippet.

```
let modelURL = NSBundle.mainBundle().URLForResource("withCoreData",
    withExtension: "momd")!

var managedObjectModel: NSManagedObjectModel =
    NSManagedObjectModel(contentsOfURL: modelURL)!
```

Once you have an `NSManagedObjectModel` instance, you can create an instance of the `NSPersistentStoreCoordinator` class, which represents the persistent store coordinator. Recall that the persistent store coordinator handles the low-level connection with underlying data stores. Individual databases are referred to as *persistent stores*.

To create an `NSPersistentStoreCoordinator` instance, use the following snippet:

```
var coordinator: NSPersistentStoreCoordinator? =
NSPersistentStoreCoordinator(managedObjectModel:
self.managedObjectModel)
```

Once you have the store coordinator, you need to give it a data store to manage. You do this by call-ing the `addPersistentStoreWithType(storeType, configuration, URL, options)` method on the store coordinator object. For instance, the following code snippet sets up a SQLite database as the data store:

```
let urls =
NSFileManager.defaultManager().URLsForDirectory(.DocumentDirectory,
inDomains: .UserDomainMask)

var applicationDocumentsDirectory:NSURL = urls[urls.count-1] as! NSURL

let url = applicationDocumentsDirectory.URLByAppendingPathComponent("data.sqlite")

do {
    try coordinator.addPersistentStoreWithType(NSSQLiteStoreType,
        configuration: nil, URL: url, options: nil)
    } catch {
        // Report any error.
    }
```

Finally, with the store coordinator object in place, it is time to instantiate a managed object context. Recall that a managed object context is like a buffer where you place your managed objects before writing to (or reading from) the database. The managed object context is represented by an instance of the `NSManagedObjectContext` class and can be created as follows:

```
var managedObjectContext = NSManagedObjectContext(
    concurrencyType: .MainQueueConcurrencyType)
managedObjectContext.persistentStoreCoordinator = coordinator
```

WRITING MANAGED OBJECTS

Instantiating a managed object is slightly different from the usual process. With managed objects, you allow Core Data to instantiate them within a managed object context. Once the object has been instantiated, you can use it as you would any other object. To instantiate a `ContactData` object, use the following code:

```
let newContact =
NSEntityDescription.insertNewObjectForEntityForName("ContactData",
inManagedObjectContext:managedObjectContext) as! ContactData
```

Now that you have instantiated a `ContactData` object, you can set up its attributes just as you would for any object:

```
newContact.customerName = "John Smith";
newContact.phoneNumber = "+44 78901 78192";
newContact.postcode = "PB2 7YK";
```

To write managed objects to the data store, simply call the `save` method of the managed object context. Doing so saves any new objects to the underlying data store (by using the persistent store coordinator). The `save` method returns a Boolean value indicating success or failure.

```
do {
    try managedObjectContext.save()
} catch {
    // handle error.
}
```

READING MANAGED OBJECTS

Reading objects from a data store with Core Data is quite straightforward. You simply create an appropriate fetch request and ask the managed object context to execute the request. The managed object context will then return an array of objects read from the data store.

A fetch request is an instance of the `NSFetchRequest` class, and is similar to a SELECT statement in SQL. When creating a fetch request, you need to specify the entity that you want to fetch. The entity has to be one that exists in the data model. To create a fetch request that retrieves all `ContactData` entities from the data store, use the following code:

```
let fetchRequest = NSFetchRequest(entityName: "ContactData")
```

To retrieve an array of managed objects from the data store, you need to ask the managed object context to execute the fetch request, as shown in the following snippet:

```
do {
    if let fetchResults = try
    appDelegate.manaedObjectContext!.executeFetchRequest(fetchRequest)
    as? [ContactData] {
        // fetchReults is now an array of ContactData objects.
    }
} catch {
    // handle errors here.
}
```

TRY IT

In this Try It, you build an iPhone application based on the Single View Application template called `CoreDataTest` that can serialize/de-serialize object data to an SQLite database using Core Data.

Lesson Requirements

➤   Launch Xcode.

➤   Create a new project based on the Single View Application template.

➤   Add an entity to the data model.

➤   Create an `NSManagedObject` subclass.

➤   Create a simple user interface with a storyboard.

➤ Initialize Core Data objects.

➤ Save managed objects to the database with Core Data.

➤ Read managed objects from the database with Core Data.

> **REFERENCE** *The code for this Try It is available at* www.wrox.com/go/
> swiftios.

Hints

➤ When creating a new project, you can use your website's domain name as the Company Identifier in the Project Options dialog box.

➤ To show the Object library, select View ➪ Utilities ➪ Show Object Library.

➤ To show the assistant editor, select View ➪ Assistant Editor ➪ Show Assistant Editor.

➤ Ensure the Use Core Data option is selecting when creating the project.

Step-by-Step

➤ Create a Single View Application in Xcode called CoreDataTest.

1. Launch Xcode and create a new application by selecting File ➪ New ➪ Project.

2. Select the Single View Application template from the list of iOS project templates.

3. In the project options screen, use the following values:

   ➤ **Product Name:** CoreDataTest

   ➤ **Organization Name:** your company

   ➤ **Organization Identifier:** com.yourcompany

   ➤ **Language:** Swift

   ➤ **Devices:** iPhone

   ➤ **Use Core Data:** Checked

4. Save the project onto your hard disk.

➤ Edit the data model file.

1. Select the CoreDataTest.xcdatamodeld file in the project navigator to open it in the Xcode editor.

2. Add an Entity to the data model to represent contact data instances.

   Select Editor ➪ Add Entity and name the new entity ContactData.

3. Add attributes to the ContactData entity.

➤ Select Editor ⇨ Add Attribute to create a new attribute. Name it `customer-Name` and set its type to `String`.

➤ Add two more `String` attributes, `phoneNumber` and `postCode`, to the entity.

➤ Create an `NSManagedObject` subclass to represent the `ContactData` entity.

1. Select Editor ⇨ Create NSManagedObject Subclass. You will be aksed to select the entities for which you wish to create `NSManagedObject` subclasses. Ensure the check box beside the ContactData entity is selected.

2. Accept the default file location, but ensure the language is set to Swift. Click Save to create a new class called `ContactData` in your project.

3. Select the Entity in the `CoreDataTest.xcdatamodeld` file and switch to the Data Model Inspector by selecting View ⇨ Utilities ⇨ Show Data Model Inspector.

4. Ensure the value of the Class field is `CoreDataTest.ContactData`.

➤ Create a simple user interface using a storyboard.

1. Open the `Main.storyboard` file in Interface Builder.

2. From the Object library, drag and drop five Label objects, three Text Field objects, one Button object, and one Table View object onto the scene.

3. Arrange these objects to resemble Figure 26-11.

FIGURE 26-11

4. Create three outlets in the view controller class corresponding to the three Text Field objects in the scene. Name the outlets `nameField`, `phoneNumberField`, and `postcode-Field`, respectively.

5. Create an action method called `onAdd` in the view controller class and connect it to the Touch Up Inside event of the Add New Record To Database button.

6. Create an outlet in the view controller class corresponding to the Table View object in the scene. Name the outlet `tableOfContacts`.

7. Select the table view in the scene. Use the Assistant Editor to set its content type to Dynamic Prototypes and the number of prototype cells for the table view to 1.

8. Select the prototype cell within the table view. Use the Assistant Editor to set the table view cell style to Basic and the Identifier to `ContactDataTableViewCellIdentifier`.

➤ Setup constraints in the default scene.

1. Select the New Contact label.

   ➤ Select Editor ⇨ Size To Fit Contents. This will ensure the size of the label is precisely what is needed to show all its contents.

   ➤ Select Editor ⇨ Align ⇨ Horizontal Center in Container to center this label horizontally in the scene.

   ➤ Ensure the label is selected and bring up the Pin Constraints dialog box.

   ➤ Ensure the Constrain to Margins option is unchecked.

   ➤ Pin the distance from the top of the label to the view to 20.

   ➤ Pin the width of the label.

   ➤ Pin the height of the label.

2. Select the Name label and use the Pin Constraints dialog box to set up the following constraints while ensuring the Constrain to Margins option is unchecked.

   ➤ **Left:** 31

   ➤ **Top:** 37

   ➤ **Width:** 46

   ➤ **Height:** 21

3. Select the Phone number label and use the Pin Constraints dialog box to set up the following constraints while ensuring the Constrain to Margins option is unchecked.

   ➤ **Left:** 31

   ➤ **Top:** 18

   ➤ **Width:** 113

   ➤ **Height:** 21

4. Select the Postcode label and use the Pin Constraints dialog box to set up the following constraints while ensuring the Constrain to Margins option is unchecked.

   ➤ **Left:** 31

   ➤ **Top:** 18

➤ **Width:** 79

➤ **Height:** 21

5. Select the Name text field and use the Pin Constraints dialog box to set up the following constraints while ensuring the Constrain to Margins option is unchecked.

➤ **Left:** 114

➤ **Top:** 12

➤ **Right:** 26

➤ **Height:** 30

6. Select the Phone number text field and use the Pin Constraints dialog box to set up the following constraints while ensuring the Constrain to Margins option is unchecked.

➤ **Left:** 47

➤ **Top:** 10

➤ **Right:** 26

➤ **Height:** 30

7. Select the Postcode text field and use the Pin Constraints dialog box to set up the following constraints while ensuring the Constrain to Margins option is unchecked.

➤ **Left:** 81

➤ **Top:** 8

➤ **Right:** 26

➤ **Height:** 30

8. Select the Add New Record To Database button and use the Pin Constraints dialog box to set up the following constraints while ensuring the Constrain to Margins option is unchecked.

➤ **Top:** 13

➤ **Right:** 26

➤ **Width:** 236

➤ **Height:** 37

9. Select the Existing Contacts label.

➤ Select Editor ➪ Size To Fit Contents. This will ensure the size of the label is precisely what is needed to show all its contents.

➤ Select Editor ➪ Align ➪ Horizontal Center in Container to center this label horizontally in the scene.

➤ Ensure the label is selected and bring up the Pin Constraints dialog box.

➤ Ensure the Constrain to Margins option is unchecked.

➤ Pin the distance from the top of the label to the view to 18.

➤ Pin the width of the label.

➤ Pin the height of the label.

10. Select the table view and use the Pin Constraints dialog box to set up the following constraints while ensuring the Constrain to Margins option is unchecked.

➤ **Left:** 31

➤ **Top:** 13

➤ **Right:** 26

➤ **Bottom:** 15

11. Update the frames to match the constraints you have set.

➤ Click on the View controller item in the dock above the storyboard scene. This is the first of the three icons located directly above the selected storyboard scene.

➤ Select Editor ➪ Resolve Auto Layout Issues ➪ Update Frames.

➤ Create a managed object in the data store when the Add New Record To Database button is tapped.

1. Import the `CoreData` header files at the top of the `ViewController.swift` file by adding this line:

```
import CoreData
```

2. Update the implementation of the `onAdd` method to the following:

```
@IBAction func onAdd(sender: AnyObject) {

        nameField.resignFirstResponder()
        phoneNumberField.resignFirstResponder()
        postCodeField.resignFirstResponder()

        let appDelegate = UIApplication.sharedApplication().delegate
            as! AppDelegate

        let newCustomerName:String! = nameField.text
        let newCustomerPhoneNumber:String! = phoneNumberField.text
        let newCustomerPostcode:String! = postCodeField.text

        if newCustomerName.isEmpty &&
           newCustomerPhoneNumber.isEmpty &&
           newCustomerPostcode.isEmpty
        {
            return
        }

        let newItem =
```

```
NSEntityDescription.insertNewObjectForEntityForName(
"ContactData",
inManagedObjectContext: appDelegate.managedObjectContext)
as! ContactData

newItem.customerName = newCustomerName
newItem.phoneNumber = newCustomerPhoneNumber
newItem.postCode = newCustomerPostcode

var error:NSError? = nil
appDelegate.managedObjectContext!.save(&error)

fetchExistingContacts()
tableOfContacts.reloadData()

}
```

➤ Read managed objects from the database and display them in a table view.

1. Ensure the `ViewController` class implements the `UITableViewDataSource` and `UITableViewDelegate` protocols by changing its declaration to the following:

```
class ViewController: UIViewController,
                      UITableViewDataSource,
                      UITableViewDelegate
```

2. Add the following variable declaration to the `ViewController.swift` file:

```
var listOfContacts:Array<ContactData>? = nil
```

3. Create a new method in the `ViewController.swift` file called `fetchExisting ContactData` as follows:

```
func fetchExistingContacts()
    {
    let fetchRequest = NSFetchRequest(entityName: "ContactData")

    let appDelegate = UIApplication.sharedApplication().delegate
                      as! AppDelegate

    do {
        self.listOfContacts = try
        appDelegate.managedObjectContext.executeFetchRequest
        (fetchRequest) as? [ContactData]
        } catch {
          // handle errors here.
        }
    }
```

4. Add the following lines of code to the end of the `viewDidLoad` method. These lines set up the `datasource` and `delegate` properties of the table view object and call the `fetchExistingContactData` method.

```
fetchExistingContacts()
tableOfContacts.dataSource = self
tableOfContacts.delegate = self
```

5. Implement `UITableViewDataSource` and `UITableViewDelegate` methods in the `ViewController.swift` file as follows:

```swift
func tableView(tableView: UITableView,
               numberOfRowsInSection section: Int)
               -> Int
{
    return listOfContacts!.count;
}

func tableView(tableView: UITableView,
    cellForRowAtIndexPath indexPath: NSIndexPath)
    -> UITableViewCell
{
  let cell = tableView.dequeueReusableCellWithIdentifier(
  "ContactDataTableViewCellIdentifier",
  forIndexPath: indexPath)

    var someContactData:ContactData! =
        listOfContacts![indexPath.row]

    cell.textLabel?.text = someContactData.customerName

    return cell
}
```

➤ Test your app in the iOS Simulator.

Click the Run button in the Xcode toolbar. Alternatively, you can select Project ➪ Run.

REFERENCE *To see some of the examples from this lesson, watch the Lesson 26 video online at* `www.wrox.com/go/swiftiosvid`.

27

Consuming RESTful JSON Web Services

A web service is essentially a web application that runs on a web server and provides a list of methods that allow users to access server-side resources. These resources can be web pages, business data, images, or video files. You access the web service as you would any other website using a URL.

Web services themselves can be written using one of several technologies including Node.js, PHP, ASP.NET, and ColdFusion. Creating a web service is outside the scope of this book.

The examples in this lesson use a simple web service called `MathService`. Table 27-1 lists the operations supported by the web service, the web service end point, and a brief description of each.

TABLE 27-1: MathService Methods

METHOD NAME	ENDPOINT URL	SUPPORTED HTTP OPERATIONS	DESCRIPTION
CircleArea	www.asmtechnol-ogy.com/MathService/CircleArea/?radius=X	GET	Input: radius Output: Returns the area of a circle with specified radius.
RectangleArea	www.asmtechnology.com/MathService/RectangleArea/?length=X&breadth=Y	GET	Input: length, breadth Output: Returns the area of a rectangle with specified length and breadth.

continues

TABLE 27-1 *(continued)*

METHOD NAME	ENDPOINT URL	SUPPORTED HTTP OPERATIONS	DESCRIPTION
SquareArea	www.asmtechnol-ogy.com/MathService/SquareArea/?length=X	GET	Input: `length` Output: Returns the area of a square whose sides are of specified length.
TriangleArea	www.asmtechnol-ogy.com/MathService/TriangleArea?base=X&height=Y	GET	Input: `base`, `height` Output: Returns the area of a triangle with specified base length and height.

TYPES OF WEB SERVICES

There are two kinds of web services:

➤ RESTful

➤ SOAP

RESTful Web Services

REST is an acronym for Representational State Transfer. REST is an architecture style, primarily used to build lightweight, scalable web services. Each server-side resource that is exposed by a RESTful web service will have at least one URL. It is quite common for RESTful web services to return responses in either XML or JSON formats with the latter gaining popularity in recent years.

A RESTful service URL resembles a directory-like structure and identifies a resource or collection of resources as objects. A key differentiating point between web services that are RESTful and those that aren't is how resources are accessed.

When a resource is accessed through a RESTful web service, the actual operation that will be performed on the server is determined by the HTTP verb specified when making the request. The response from the server includes a status code that can be inspected to determine success or failure. A list of HTTP status codes can be found at http://www.w3.org/Protocols/rfc2616/rfc2616-sec10.html.

The most common HTTP verbs are GET, POST, and DELETE. The same URL can be called with different HTTP verbs to perform different operations. This is different from non-RESTful web services where one would have a different URL for each operation that is to be performed on the server.

For instance, if you had a database of employees on a server that you wished to expose publicly with a RESTful web service, the URL to identify an employee (with unique identifier of 1790716) would resemble the following:

```
http://www.example.com/Employee/1790716
```

If you were to send an HTTP GET request to this URL, the service would typically return some information about that particular employee. If, on the other hand, you were to send an HTTP DELETE request to the same URL, the service could potentially delete the employee record.

Needless to say, web service designers carefully decide which operations will be supported on a web service.

SOAP Web Services

SOAP is an acronym for Simple Object Access Protocol. It is an XML-based message format, which allows different applications to exchange objects with each other. SOAP web services often contain a machine-readable description of the functions exposed by the web service written in WSDL (Web Services Description Language). SOAP web services are generally used when communicating between enterprise applications. SOAP requests and responses are larger than equivalent RESTful versions and are therefore not suited to processing on mobile devices.

JSON AND NSJSONSERIALIZATION

JSON is an acronym for JavaScript Object Notation and provides constructs that allow you to conveniently serialize objects to UTF-8 text. It is used primarily to communicate between servers and clients as an alternative to XML.

JSON is preferred over XML because JSON data takes fewer bytes to represent the same information. For example, the following snippet shows how a collection of Organization objects would be encoded in JSON and XML. As you can see, the JSON representation is more compact, which translates to fewer bytes being sent over the network.

```
{"organizations":[
    {«name»:"ACME Corportation", "address":"112, Fleming Drive, LE3 4F6, UK"},
    {«name»:"Bright Ideas LLC", "address":"26, Syon Lane, London TW3 3P2"},
    {«name»:"Chromatic Inks Ltd", "address":"178, Lexuar Drive, Langley, SL6 3U0"}
]}


<organizations>
    <organization>
        <name>ACME Corportation</name>
```

```
    <address>112, Fleming Drive, LE3 4F6, UK</address>
        </organization>
        <organization>
            <name>Bright Ideas LLC</name>
    <address>26, Syon Lane, London TW3 3P2</address>
        </organization>
        <organization>
            <name>Chromatic Inks Ltd</name>
    <address>178, Lexuar Drive, Langley, SL6 3U0</address>
        </organization>
    </organizations>
```

NSJSONSerialization is a class that is part of the Foundation framework and can be used to convert JSON objects into Foundation objects and vice versa. NSJSONSerialization requires that the top level object is an array or dictionary and that all objects in the JSON are either strings, numbers, arrays, or dictionaries. Table 27 -2 lists the mapping between Foundation types and JSON types

TABLE 27-2: Mapping Foundation to JSON Types

JSON TYPE	FOUNDATION TYPE
Array	NSArray
Dictionary	NSDictionary
String	NSString
Number	NSNumber

Assuming you have an NSData instance that contains JSON objects, you can convert them to Foundation objects using the JSONObjectWithData class method:

```
class func JSONObjectWithData(_data: NSData, options opt: NSJSONReadingOptions)
        throws -> AnyObject
```

The first parameter to this method is an NSData instance that contains JSON objects, encoded using either UTF-8, or UTF-16. The second parameter is used to specify how Foundation objects are generated from JSON objects, and can be a combination of the following:

➤ **MutableContainers:** Creates NSMutableArray and NSMutableDictionary instead of NSArray and NSDictionary.

➤ **MutableLeaves:** Specifies that leaf nodes that contain string data will convert to NSMutableString instead of NSString.

➤ **AllowFragments:** Specifies that the parser should allow top-level objects that are not arrays or dictionaries.

This method returns a non-optional result and will throw an error if it was unable to parse the JSON input. The following snippet shows how you would use this method:

```
do {
    let JSONObject = try NSJSONSerialization.JSONObjectWithData(data!,
```

```
                         options: .MutableContainers)

    // use JSONObject
}
catch {
    // handle exceptions.
}
```

NSURLSESSION AND APPLICATION TRANSPORT SECURITY

NSURLSession refers to a class from a set of related classes that allow you to download content via HTTP. It was introduced in iOS7 and supersedes the NSURLConnection API. The new NSURLSession API is asynchronous by design and provides several improvements over NSURLConnection including the following:

➤ Support for HTTP2.0 out of the box

➤ Support for per-session cache, cookies, and auth credentials

➤ Support for background downloads

> **NOTE** NSURLConnection *is deprecated on iOS 9 and is not available for WatchOS. If you are developing a WatchOS application and need access to networking APIs then you must use* NSURLSession.

With the NSURLSession API, your app can create multiple sessions, with each session coordinating a group of data transfer tasks. A session is analogous to a tab in a browser window, and a data transfer task to a request to fetch a single resource such as an image. Within each session you could hit the server multiple times for different resources. Each session has its own cache and HTTP security credentials.

Some of the key classes in the NSURLSession API are:

➤ NSURLSession: Represents a session object

➤ NSURLSessionConfiguration: Represents a configuration object used while creating a session object

➤ NSURLSessionDataTask: Represents a task for retrieving the contents of a URL as an NSData object

➤ NSURLSessionDownloadTask: Represents a task for retrieving the contents of a URL as a temporary file on the disk

➤ NSURLSessionUploadTask: A task for uploading an NSData object to a file

➤ NSURLSessionStreamTask: A task that lets you communicate using raw TCP/IP sockets. This is useful if you want to use a protocol other than HTTP/HTTPS such as IRC.

The API also provides several protocols that define delegate methods you can implement in your code for better control over session and task behavior:

➤ `NSSessionDelegate`: Contains delegate methods to handle session level events

➤ `NSURLSessionTaskDelegate`: Contains delegate methods to handle events common to all task types

➤ `NSURLSessionDataDelegate`: Contains delegate methods to handle events specific to data and upload tasks

➤ `NSURLSessionDownloadDelegate`: Contains delegate methods to handle events specific to download tasks

➤ `NSURLSessionStreamDelegate`: Contains delegate methods to handle events specific to stream tasks

Creating an NSURLSession

To create an `NSURLSession` instance, you must first create a session configuration; use the `default-SessionConfiguration()` method of the `NSURLSessionClass`:

```
let configuration = NSURLSessionConfiguration.defaultSessionConfiguration()
```

Once you have a session configuration, you can fine-tune it by editing some of its attributes, including the following:

➤ `allowsCellularAccess`: A value that indicates if the request should proceed over cellular networks

➤ `timeoutIntervalForRequests`: A value that will cause a timeout if no data is transmitted after this interval has elapsed

➤ `HTTPAdditionalHeaders`: Additional headers for outgoing HTTP requests

➤ `HTTPMaximumConnectionsPerHost`: Limits the maximum number of simultaneous connections to a server

> **NOTE** `NSURLSession` *also provides two more class methods to create sessions:*
>
> ➤ `ephemeralSessionConfiguration()` returns a configuration with no persistent store for cookies, caching, or user credentials. This could be ideal to create a private browsing mode like feature in an app.
>
> ➤ `backgroundSessionConfigurationWithIdentifier(identifier:)` returns a configuration that can be used to create a background session. A background session is one that can upload and download data when the app is in the suspended or inactive modes.

The following code snippet shows how to set a custom HTTP request header to support HTTP basic authentication in your code:

```
let configuration = NSURLSessionConfiguration.defaultSessionConfiguration()

let userPasswordString = "username@yourcompany.com:password"

let userPasswordData = userPasswordString.dataUsingEncoding(NSUTF8StringEncoding)

let base64EncodedCredential =
userPasswordData!.base64EncodedStringWithOptions(
NSDataBase64EncodingOptions.Encoding64CharacterLineLength)

let authString = "Basic \(base64EncodedCredential)"
configuration.HTTPAdditionalHeaders = ["Authorization" : authString]
```

To learn more about how HTTP basic authentication works, refer to the section "Basic Authentication Scheme" in the HTTP reference documentation at `http://www.w3.org/Protocols/HTTP/1.0/spec.html#BasicAA`.

Once you have a session configuration, you can create a session using the following:

```
let session: NSURLSession! = NSURLSession(configuration: configuration,
                    delegate: nil, delegateQueue: nil)
```

The delegate is optional, and is an object that implements the NSURLSession protocol. The final parameter, delegateQueue, is a queue for scheduling the delegate calls and completion handlers. If nil, the session creates a serial operation queue. It is important to note that your delegate methods (or completion handler) will be called on this queue. If you intend to update the user interface within these callbacks, then you must make sure that the code that updates the UI is called on the main queue.

One way to do this is by using `NSOperationQueue.mainQueue()` as the final parameter while creating the NSURLSesssion:

```
let session: NSURLSession! = NSURLSession(configuration: configuration,
                    delegate: nil,
                    delegateQueue: NSOperationQueue.mainQueue())
```

Creating a Data Task

If you wanted to call a method on a web service, chances are that you will end up using a data task. To create a data task, you can use any of the following methods of the session object.

```
dataTaskWithRequest(urlRequest)
```

```
dataTaskWithRequest(urlRequest:completionHandler:)
```

There are two versions of this method. Use the first one if you want to supply a delegate object; the second one takes a block that is called when the request completes. The following code snippet shows how you could create a data task with a completion handler:

```
let task : NSURLSessionDataTask! = session.dataTaskWithRequest(request,
                        completionHandler: {(data, response, error) in

});
```

The first parameter to both these methods is an NSURLRequest instance. An NSURLRequest instance allows you to specify not only the URL but also additional information such as the request type (GET/POST). NSURLRequest defaults to creating a GET request, but Apple provides a mutable version called NSMutableURLRequest that allows you to set the content type. In general, it is common practice to use NSMutableURLRequest in your code as you always have the option of changing the request type when needed.

The following code snippet shows how you could create an NSMutableURLRequest from a URL and set the request type to POST:

```
let serviceURL:String =
"http://www.asmtechnology.com/MathService/CircleArea/?radius=\(radius)"

let url:NSURL! = NSURL(string: serviceURL)
let request: NSMutableURLRequest = NSMutableURLRequest(URL: url)
request.HTTPMethod = "POST"
```

> **NOTE** *To find out how to create, download, and upload tasks, refer to the NSURLSession programming guide at:*
>
> ```
> https://developer.apple.com/library/ios/documentation/Foundation/
> Reference/NSURLSession_class/#//apple_ref/occ/instm/NSURLSession/
> dataTaskWithURL:completionHandler
> ```

Once you have created an appropriate task, you need to call its resume() method to begin it:

```
task.resume()
```

Application Transport Security

Application Transport Security (ATS) is a new feature in iOS 9 that helps prevent accidental disclosure of data while making network requests by encouraging your application to make secure connections to web services.

By default, ATS prevents calls to HTTP URLs. In fact, even if you provided an http:// prefix to your URL, The NSURLSession API will end up making an HTTPS call. This is fine if your server supports HTTPS, but if it doesn't, then you will need to configure an exception for one or more URLs in your application's Info.plist file.

To configure ATS, you need to add a new key to your `Info.plist` file called `NSAppTransportSecurity` and set its type to be a `Dictionary`.

To disable ATS completely (not recommended), thereby allowing all http:// URL requests to pass through, add a new Boolean value to this dictionary called `NSAllowsArbitraryLoads` and set its value to `YES` (Figure 27-1).

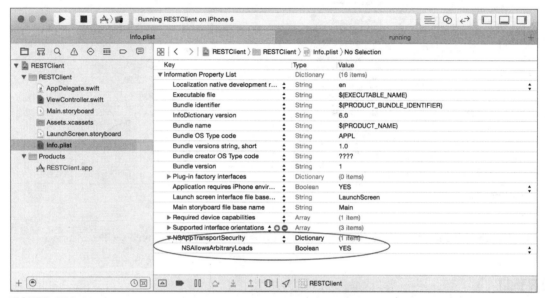

FIGURE: 27-1

If, on the other hand, you want ATS to allow only specific insecure connections, you need to use a different key called `NSExceptionDomains` (which is also a dictionary). Within this dictionary, you can configure exceptions on a domain basis.

For each domain you want to configure, you need to provide a child dictionary within the `NSExceptionDomains` dictionary. This domain-specific configuration dictionary can have any of the following keys:

➤ `NSIncludesSubdomains`

➤ `NSExceptionAllowsInsecureHTTPLoads`

➤ `NSExceptionRequiresForwardSecrecy`

➤ `NSExceptionMinimumTLSVersion`

For instance, if you wanted to allow insecure http requests for all URLs in the `asmtechnology.com` domain, your `Info.plist` file would resemble Figure 27-2.

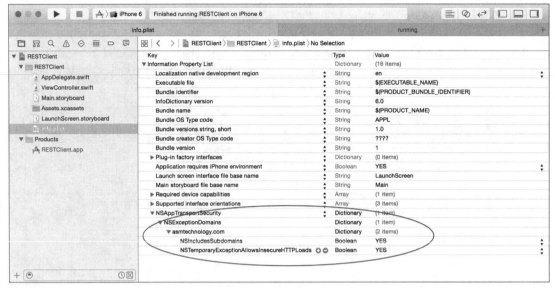

FIGURE 27-2

In the next session you will see how to put all of this together to call a web service.

TRY IT

In this Try It, you create a simple iPhone application based on the Single View Application template called RESTClient, which uses a RESTful web service (described in Table 27-1) to calculate the area of a circle.

Lesson Requirements

➤ Launch Xcode.

➤ Create a new iPhone project based on the Single View Application template.

➤ Add a UIButton to the default scene and an appropriate action method to the view controller class.

➤ Add a UITextField to the default scene and an appropriate outlet to the view controller class.

➤ Add a scrolling UITextView to the default scene and an appropriate outlet to the view controller class.

➤ Dismiss the text field when the Return button is pressed on the keyboard by implementing a UITextFieldDelegate method.

➤ Send a GET request to a RESTful web service when the `UIButton` is pressed.

➤ Parse and display the response in the `UITextView`.

> **REFERENCE** *The code for this Try It is available at* www.wrox.com/go/
> swiftios.

Hints

➤ The math web service implements a web method called `CircleArea` that requires a single parameter called `radius`. The service endpoint is `http://www.asmtechnology.com/MathService/CircleArea`.

➤ When creating a new project, you can use your website's domain name as the Company Identifier in the Project Options dialog box.

➤ To show the Object library, select View ➪ Utilities ➪ Show Object Library.

➤ To show the assistant editor, select View ➪ Assistant Editor ➪ Show Assistant Editor.

Step-by-Step

➤ Create a Single View Application in Xcode called `RESTClient`.

1. Launch Xcode and create a new application by selecting File ➪ New ➪ Project.

2. Select the Single View Application template from the list of iOS project templates.

3. In the project options screen, use the following values:

   ➤ **Product Name:** RESTClient

   ➤ **Organization Name:** your company

   ➤ **Organization Identifier:** com.yourcompany

   ➤ **Language:** Swift

   ➤ **Devices:** iPhone

   ➤ **Use Core Data:** Unchecked

   ➤ **Include UI Tests:** Unchecked

   ➤ **Include Unit Tests:** Unchecked

4. Save the project onto your hard disk.

➤ Add UI elements to the default scene.

1. Open the `Main.storyboard` file in the Interface Editor

2. From the Object library, drag and drop a button, text field, and text view objects onto the scene and place to resemble Figure 27-3.

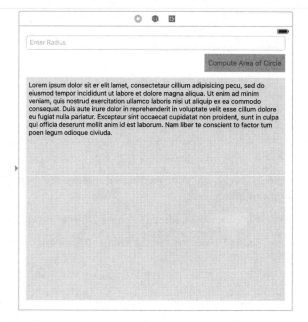

FIGURE 27-3

3. Select the Text field and use the Attribute inspector, to change the value of the Placeholder attribute to Enter Radius.

4. Select the Button and use the Attribute inspector to change its background color to a shade of gray and its caption to "Compute Area of Circle"

5. Select the Text view and use the Attribute inspector to change its background color to a lighter shade of gray than the button.

6. With the Text view still selected, uncheck the Editable attribute (see Figure 27-4). This will ensure that the user cannot change the contents of the text view.

7. Create layout constraints for each of the elements on the storyboard scene using the information in Table 27-3. When creating layout constraints using the pin constraints popup, ensure the Constrain to margins option is unchecked and Update Frames is set to Items of New Constraints.

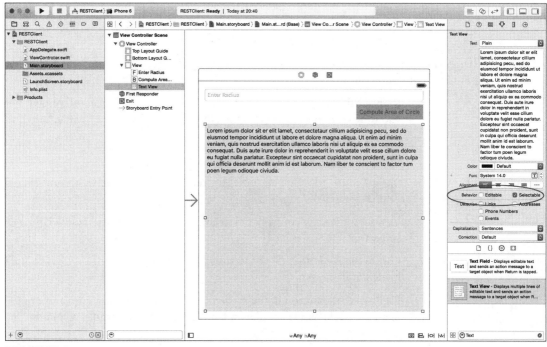

FIGURE 27-4

TABLE 27-3: Layout Constraints

ELEMENT	LEFT	TOP	RIGHT	BOTTOM	WIDTH	HEIGHT
Text Field	16	20	16			30
Button		56	16		176	38
Text View	16	8	16	20		

8. Use the assistant editor to create an outlet for the Text field in the view controller class. Name the outlet `radiusField`.

9. Set up the delegate property for the Text field.

➤ Ensure the Assistant Editor is visible and the `ViewController.swift` file is loaded in it.

➤ Right-click the table view to bring up a context menu. Drag from the item labeled "delegate" in the context menu to the item labeled "View Controller" in the document outline.

10. Create an action method in the `ViewController` class and associate it with the Did End On Exit event of the text field.

➤ Right-click the `UITextField` object on the scene to display its context menu, and drag from the circle beside the Did End On Exit item to an empty line in the `ViewController.swift` file.

➤ Name the new Action `onDismissKeyboard`.

11. Use the assistant editor to create an outlet for the Text view in the view controller class. Name the outlet `serverResponseView`.

12. Create an action in the view controller class and connect it with the Touch Up Inside event of the button.

➤ Ensure the Assistant editor is visible and the `ViewController.swift` file is loaded in it.

➤ Right-click the button in the scene to display its context menu, and drag from the circle beside the Touch Up Inside item to an empty line in the `ViewController.swift` file.

➤ Name the new action `onCalculateArea`.

➤ Ensure the `ViewController` class implements the `UITextFieldDelegate` protocol.

Modify the declaration of the `ViewController` class from:

```
class ViewController: UIViewController
```

to

```
class ViewController: UIViewController, UITextFieldDelegate
```

➤ Modify code in the view controller class.

1. Open the `ViewController.swift` file in the project explorer.

2. Add the following line to the implementation of the `onDismissKeyboard` method:

```
radiusField.resignFirstResponder()
```

➤ Add a tap gesture recognizer and use it to dismiss the keyboard when the background area of the view is tapped.

1. Add the following method to the `ViewController.swift` file:

```
func handleBackgroundTap(sender: UITapGestureRecognizer) {
        radiusField.resignFirstResponder()
}
```

2. Add the following code to the `viewDidLoad` method of the view controller class, after the `super.viewDidLoad()` line:

```
let tapRecognizer = UITapGestureRecognizer(target:self ,
action: Selector("handleBackgroundTap:"))
```

```
tapRecognizer.cancelsTouchesInView = false

self.view.addGestureRecognizer(tapRecognizer)
```

3. Add code to clear the initial contents of the text view when the view is loaded.

   ➤ Add the following line to the end of the `viewDidLoad` method:

   ```
   serverResponseView.text = ""
   ```

   ➤ The `viewDidLoad` method in your `ViewController.swift` file should now resemble the following:

   ```
   override func viewDidLoad() {

       super.viewDidLoad()

       let tapRecognizer = UITapGestureRecognizer(target:self ,
           action: Selector("handleBackgroundTap:"))

       tapRecognizer.cancelsTouchesInView = false

       self.view.addGestureRecognizer(tapRecognizer)

       serverResponseView.text = ""
   }
   ```

4. Replace the implementation of the `onCalculateArea` method with the following:

   ```
   @IBAction func onCalculateArea(sender: AnyObject) {

       let radius:String = radiusField.text!
       if radius.isEmpty
       {
           return;
       }

       let serviceURL:String =
   "http://www.asmtechnology.com/MathService/CircleArea/?radius=\(radius)"
       let url:NSURL! = NSURL(string: serviceURL)
       let request: NSMutableURLRequest = NSMutableURLRequest(URL: url)

       let configuration =
   NSURLSessionConfiguration.defaultSessionConfiguration()
       configuration.timeoutIntervalForRequest = 15.0

       let session: NSURLSession! =
           NSURLSession(configuration: configuration,
                       delegate: nil,
                       delegateQueue: NSOperationQueue.mainQueue())

       let task : NSURLSessionDataTask! =
                       session.dataTaskWithRequest(request,
                       completionHandler: {(data, response, error) in

           if data != nil
   ```

```
        {
            let decodedString = NSString(data: data!,
                           encoding: NSUTF8StringEncoding)
            self.serverResponseView.text = decodedString as! String
        }

    });


    task.resume()
}
```

➤ Configure Application Transport Security to allow an insecure HTTP connection for the asmtechnology.com domain.

1. Expand the `RESTClient` group in the project navigator and click on the `Info.plist` file to open it in the property list editor.

2. Add a new key to the `Info.plist` file called `NSAppTransportSecurity` and set its type as `Dictionary`.

3. Expand the `NSAppTransportSecurity` key and add a new child key called `NSExceptionDomains`, also of type `Dictionary`.

4. Expand the `NSExceptionDomains` key and add a child key called `asmtechnology.com`, also of type `Dictionary`.

5. Expand the `asmtechnology.com` key and add two Boolean keys, both set to YES, called `NSIncludesSubdomains` and `NSExceptionAllowsInsecureHTTPLoads`.

➤ Test your app in the iOS Simulator.

1. Click the Run button in the Xcode toolbar. Alternatively, you can select Project ➪ Run.

2. Ensure your computer has an active Internet connection.

3. Enter a numeric value for the radius field and tap the Compute Area of Circle button.

REFERENCE *To see some of the examples from this lesson, watch the Lesson 27 video online at* www.wrox.com/go/swiftiosvid.

SECTION IV
Beyond the Basics

28

Social Media Integration

Social media integration is not something that most apps can ignore. These days, social media integration in apps is the norm rather than the exception. Fortunately for you, Apple has integrated support for Facebook Twitter, Sina Webo, and Tecent Webo into iOS 9. Posting to social media services has never been easier!

In this lesson, you learn to integrate the Social framework in your iOS apps and allow the user to share a post on Facebook and Twitter from your apps. You can build more complex clients that can access the entire Facebook/Twitter API, but this topic is beyond the scope of this book.

The Social framework is not included in any of the standard iOS project templates that you use when creating a new project. You will need to add a reference to this framework manually. You can do this from the Project Settings page in Xcode. Select the project node in the project navigator to display the settings page. On the settings page, select the build target and switch to the Build Phases tab. Click the plus (+) button under the Link Binary With Libraries category and select `Social.framework` from the list of available frameworks (see Figure 28-1).

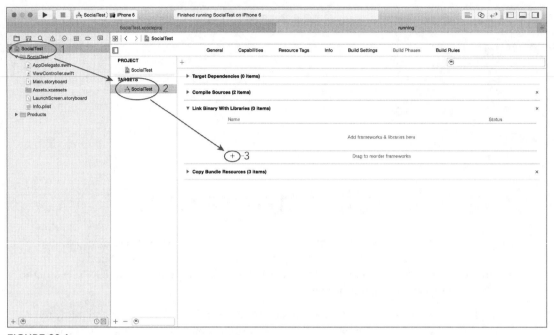

FIGURE 28-1

THE SHARE SHEET

The Social framework provides a share sheet that you should use in your apps if all you want is a simple "share" feature. The share sheet is an instance of the SLComposeViewController class and provides a convenient user interface to allow the user to type a message, attach an image, and add the current location (see Figure 28-2).

The keyboard is displayed automatically when the share sheet appears and disappears automatically when the user presses the Send or Cancel buttons. Creating and displaying the share sheet configured to one of the supported services is a simple matter of instantiating it and presenting it modally:

```
let facebookMessageComposer:SLComposeViewController =
SLComposeViewController(forServiceType: SLServiceTypeFacebook)

self.presentViewController(facebookMessageComposer,
animated: true, completion: nil)
```

When creating an SLComposeViewController instance, you must provide a single argument that indicates what social media service you want to use. This argument can have one of four possible values:

➤   SLServiceTypeTwitter

➤   SLServiceTypeFacebook

➤ `SLServiceTypeSinaWeibo`

➤ `SLServiceTypeTencentWeibo`

FIGURE 28-2

The options displayed in the share sheet will vary depending on the social media service that is configured. Typically, you will want to do this in an action method that is triggered when your user taps on a button in the user interface. Before you show the share sheet for a particular service, you must check to see if the user has created an appropriate account on the system (see Figure 28-3).

For instance, if you detect that the user has not created a Twitter account on the system, you may want to hide the Tweet button from your user interface entirely, or display an alert when the user taps it.

To check the availability of a service, use the `isAvailableForServiceType(serviceType: String!)` class method of the `SLComposeViewController` class as follows:

```
if SLComposeViewController.isAvailableForServiceType(SLServiceTypeFacebook)
{
    // service is available
}
else
{
    // service is not available, perhaps show an alert to the user?
}
```

You can set up the initial text displayed in the tweet sheet prior to displaying it by calling the `setInitialText()` method on the `SLComposeViewController` instance:

```
func setInitialText(text: String!) -> Bool
```

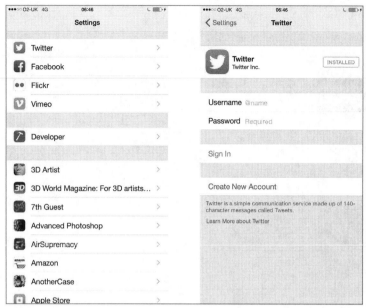

FIGURE 28-3

This method takes one `String` argument that contains the text you want to set and returns a Boolean value that contains the result of the operation. Common reasons why the operation may not be successful are:

➤ The length of the message is longer than the maximum character limit set by the service.

➤ You are trying to set the text in the share sheet after it has been displayed.

➤ The social media service does not allow you to pre-populate content in a share sheet because of legal reasons.

You can attach an image to the share sheet by calling the `addImage()` method on the `SLComposeViewController` instance:

```
func addImage(image: UIImage!) -> Bool
```

This method has one argument that is a `UIImage` object and returns a Boolean result. The image is automatically resized and uploaded to the appropriate social media service by the framework. You must examine the return value to determine if the operation was successful.

To add a URL to the share sheet, use the `addURL()` method:

```
func addURL(url: NSURL!) -> Bool
```

As with the `setInitialText()` and `addImage()` methods, the `addURL()` method returns a Boolean value indicating success or failure. It is important to note that images and URLs take up part of the character limit imposed by the social media service.

You can provide an optional block completion handler that will be executed when the operation has completed. Assuming `messageComposer` is an instance of an `SLComposeViewController` configured for Twitter, you can do this as follows:

```
messageComposer.completionHandler = (result:SLComposeViewControllerResult) in
            // place your code here
}
```

Within the block, you can examine the value of the `result` parameter to get more information on the result of the operation. The value of the `result` parameter depends on which button was pressed by the user, and can be either of the following:

➤   `Cancelled`

➤   `Done`

You will need to dismiss the tweet sheet by calling the `dismissModalViewControllerAnimated()` method of the presenting view controller. If you do not provide a block completion handler, the tweet sheet is dismissed automatically regardless of the result of the operation.

TRY IT

In this Try It, you create a simple iPhone application based on the Single View Application template called `SocialTest` that displays Facebook and Twitter share sheets with pre-populated contents.

Lesson Requirements

➤   Launch Xcode.

➤   Create a new iPhone project based on the Single View Application template.

➤   Add two `UIButton` instances to the default scene and appropriate action methods to the view controller class.

➤   Add the Social framework to the build target.

➤   Add code to display pre-populated share sheets.

> **REFERENCE** *The code for this Try It is available at* www.wrox.com/go/ swiftios.

Hints

➤   To use a share sheet you must add a reference to the Social framework.

➤   When creating a new project, you can use your website's domain name as the Company Identifier in the Project Options dialog box.

➤ To show the Object library, select View ➪ Utilities ➪ Show Object Library.

➤ To show the assistant editor, select View ➪ Assistant Editor ➪ Show Assistant Editor.

Step-by-Step

➤ Create a Single View Application in Xcode called `ShareTest`.

1. Launch Xcode and create a new application by selecting File ➪ New ➪ Project.

2. Select the Single View Application template from the list of iOS project templates.

3. In the project options screen, use the following values:

   ➤ **Product Name:** ShareTest

   ➤ **Organization Name:** your company

   ➤ **Organization Identifier:** com.yourcompany

   ➤ **Language:** Swift

   ➤ **Devices:** iPhone

   ➤ **Use Core Data:** Unchecked

   ➤ **Include UI Tests:** Unchecked

   ➤ **Include Unit Tests:** Unchecked

4. Save the project onto your hard disk.

➤ Add image resources to your project.

1. Ensure the project navigator is visible. To show it, select View ➪ Navigators ➪ Show Project Navigator.

2. Open the `Assets.xcassets` file by clicking on it in the project navigator.

3. Navigate to the `Images` folder in this chapter's resources from the website.

4. Create a new Image set by selecting Editor ➪ New Image Set, and name this new image set `Petal`.

5. Drag the `Petal_1x.jpg`, `Petal_2x.jpg`, and `Petal_3x.jpg` images from this chapter's resources into the appropriate placeholders in the image set.

➤ Add UI elements to the default scene.

1. Open the `Main.storyboard` file in the Interface Editor.

2. From the Object library, drag and drop two buttons onto the scene and place to resemble Figure 28-4.

3. Select the first button and use the Attribute inspector to change its caption to Share on Facebook and the background color to a shade of gray.

4. Select the second button and use the Attribute inspector to change its caption to Share on Twitter and the background color to a shade of gray.

FIGURE 28-4

5. Create layout constraints for each of elements on the storyboard scene using the information in Table 28-1. When creating layout constraints using the constraints editor popover, ensure the Constrain to margins option is unchecked and Update Frames is set to Items of New Constraints.

TABLE 28-1: Layout Constraints

ELEMENT	LEFT	TOP	RIGHT	HEIGHT
Facebook button	20	20	20	40
Twitter button	20	20	20	40

6. Create an action in the view controller class and connect it with the Touch Up Inside event of the Share on Facebook button.

➤ Ensure the Assistant editor is visible and the `ViewController.swift` file is loaded in it.

➤ Right-click the Share on Facebook button in the scene to display its context menu, and drag from the circle beside the Touch Up Inside item to an empty line in the `ViewController.swift` file.

➤ Name the new action `onFacebookShare`.

7. Create an action in the view controller class and connect it with the Touch Up Inside event of the Share on Twitter button.

➤ Ensure the Assistant editor is visible and the `ViewController.swift` file is loaded in it.

➤ Right-click the Share on Twitter button in the scene to display its context menu, and drag from the circle beside the Touch Up Inside item to an empty line in the `ViewController.swift` file.

➤ Name the new action `onTwitterShare`.

➤ Import the Social framework into the project. The Social framework is not included in any of the standard iOS project templates that you use when creating a new project. You will need to add a reference to this framework manually. You can do so from the Project Settings page in Xcode.

Ensure the following import statements are located at the top of the `ViewController` class:

```
import UIKit
import Social
```

➤ Add code to post a tweet.

1. Open the `ViewController.swift` file in the project explorer.

2. Update the empty implementation of the `onTwitterShare` method to resemble the following:

```
@IBAction func onTwitterShare(sender: AnyObject) {

    if
SLComposeViewController.isAvailableForServiceType(SLServiceTypeTwitter)
    {
        let twitterMessageComposer:SLComposeViewController =
    SLComposeViewController(forServiceType: SLServiceTypeTwitter)

        twitterMessageComposer.setInitialText("Test Twitter Post")

    twitterMessageComposer.addURL(NSURL(string: "http://www.asmtechnology.com"))

        twitterMessageComposer.addImage(UIImage(named: "Petal"))

        self.presentViewController(twitterMessageComposer,
        animated: true, completion: nil)
    }
    else
    {
        let twitterNotConfiguredAlert =
        UIAlertController(title: "Twitter Not Configured",
        message: "Please setup a twitter account.",
        preferredStyle: UIAlertControllerStyle.Alert)

        twitterNotConfiguredAlert.addAction(UIAlertAction(title: "OK",
        style: UIAlertActionStyle.Default, handler: nil))
```

```
    self.presentViewController(twitterNotConfiguredAlert,
    animated: true, completion: nil)
    }
}
```

➤ Add code to post to the Facebook timeline.

1. Open the `ViewController.swift` file in the project explorer.

2. Update the empty implementation of the `onFacebookShare` method to resemble:

```
@IBAction func onFacebookShare(sender: AnyObject) {

if
SLComposeViewController.isAvailableForServiceType(SLServiceTypeFacebook)
{
    let facebookMessageComposer:SLComposeViewController =
    SLComposeViewController(forServiceType: SLServiceTypeFacebook)

    facebookMessageComposer.addURL(NSURL(string:
                                    "http://www.asmtechnology.com"))

    facebookMessageComposer.addImage(UIImage(named: "Petal"))

    self.presentViewController(facebookMessageComposer,
    animated: true, completion: nil)

}
else
{
    let facebookNotConfiguredAlert =
    UIAlertController(title: "Facebook Not Configured",
    message: "Please setup a facebook account.",
    preferredStyle: UIAlertControllerStyle.Alert)

    facebookNotConfiguredAlert.addAction(UIAlertAction(title: "OK",
    style: UIAlertActionStyle.Default, handler: nil))

    self.presentViewController(facebookNotConfiguredAlert,
    animated: true, completion: nil)
}
    }
```

➤ Test your app in the iOS Simulator.

1. Click the Run button in the Xcode toolbar. Alternatively, you can select Project ➪ Run.

2. Ensure your computer has an active Internet connection.

3. Enter a numeric value for the radius field and tap the Compute Area of Circle button.

> **REFERENCE** *To see some of the examples from this lesson, watch the Lesson 28 video online at* www.wrox.com/go/swiftiosvid.

29

Where Am I? Introducing Core Location

Core Location is a framework that allows applications to retrieve the location and heading of the device they are running on. To do this, Core Location can use a combination of a compass for heading, and either GPS, cellular radio, or WiFi technologies for location. Cellular radio and WiFi-based location is less accurate than GPS.

Applications cannot specify which method will be used, but they can specify a desired level of accuracy. Depending on the desired level of accuracy, Core Location tries to use the GPS hardware, cellular radio, or WiFi in that order.

This framework is not included in any of the standard iOS application templates. To use this framework in your code, you will need to add it manually to your project. You can do this from the Project Settings page in Xcode. Select the project node in the project navigator to display the settings page. On the settings page, switch to the Build Phases tab and click the + button under the Link Binary With Libraries category. Select CoreLocation.framework from the list of available frameworks (see Figure 29-1).

Core Location defines a manager class called `CLLocationManager` that you can use to interact with the framework. It allows you to specify the desired frequency and accuracy of location information. To receive location updates in an application, you need to create an instance of the `CLLocationManager` class and provide a delegate object to receive location updates and errors. This delegate object must implement the `CLLocationManagerDelegate` protocol.

The delegate object is often a view controller class but could also be any other class in your application. Using location hardware can have a significant drain on the device's batteries, and hence applications need to turn on and turn off receiving location updates.

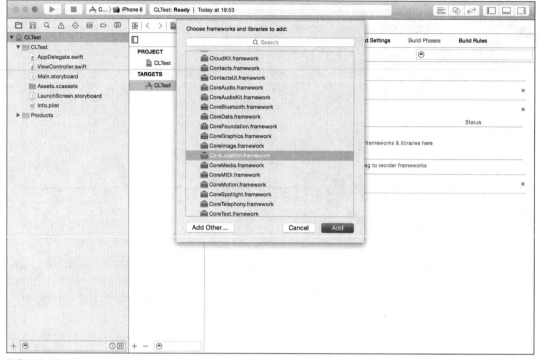

FIGURE 29-1

PERMISSIONS

From iOS 8 onward, Apple requires that applications ask the user for permission before attempting to access location information. There are two types of permissions available:

➤ **Always Authorization:** For apps that need to access location information while in both the foreground and background modes

➤ **When In Use Authorization:** For apps that need only access location information in the foreground mode

You need to ask for either type of permission, but not both. The process of asking for permission has two parts. The first part involves adding a key to the `Info.plist` file that contains some text that will be presented to the user while asking for permission. This text should describe the reason for application requiring access to location data.

Depending on the type of permission you wish to ask for, you need to add either of the following keys to the `Info.plist` file (see Figure 29-2).

➤ `NSLocationAlwaysUsageDescription`

➤ `NSLocationWhenInUseUsageDescription`

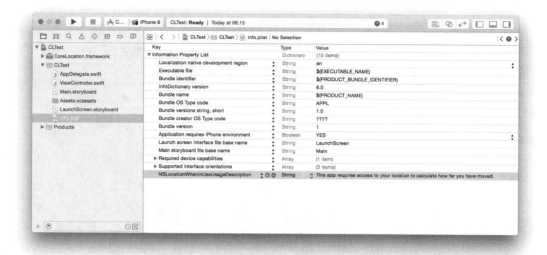

FIGURE 29-2

The second part requires that you make a call to either the requestWhenInUseAuthorization() or requestAlwaysAuthorization() class methods of CLLocationManager and find out the user's decision in a delegate method:

```
func locationManager(manager: CLLocationManager,
    didChangeAuthorizationStatus status: CLAuthorizationStatus)
```

The user's decision is returned in the second parameter of this delegate method and can be one of the following:

➤ Denied

➤ AuthorizedAlways

➤ AuthorizedWhenInUse

The following code assumes that you wish to request When-in-use authorization, and demonstrates the basic setup required to receive location updates:

```
let locationManager = CLLocationManager()
locationManager.delegate = self
locationManager.desiredAccuracy = kCLLocationAccuracyBestForNavigation
locationManager.requestWhenInUseAuthorization()

...
...
...

func locationManager(manager: CLLocationManager,
    didChangeAuthorizationStatus status: CLAuthorizationStatus)
{
```

```
        var shouldAllow = false

        switch status {
            case CLAuthorizationStatus.AuthorizedWhenInUse:
                shouldAllow = true
            case CLAuthorizationStatus.AuthorizedAlways:
                shouldAllow = true
            default:
                shouldAllow = false
        }

        if shouldAllow == true {
            manager.startUpdatingLocation()
        }

    }
```

If your application just cannot function without location services, add the
UIRequiredDeviceCapabilities key to the Info.plist file. This key is a dictionary and can contain a list of strings each of which describe a single capability required by your application. The App
Store examines the information in this key when users try to download your app and will prevent
users from downloading your application to devices that don't contain the listed features.

The values to include for location service hardware are:

➤   location-services: Your application requires location services in general.

➤   gps: Your application requires the accuracy offered only by GPS hardware.

ACCURACY

An application can set up the desiredAccuracy property of the CLLocationManager instance to
specify a desired accuracy. Core Location will try its best to achieve the desired accuracy. The more
accurate a reading required, the more battery power is needed.

Applications should, in general, try to use the least accuracy possible to satisfy their requirements.
The property can have the following values, listed in decreasing order of accuracy:

➤   kCLLocationAccuracyBestForNavigation

➤   kCLLocationAccuracyBest

➤   kCLLocationAccuracyNearestTenMeters

➤   kCLLocationAccuracyHundredMeters

➤   kCLLocationAccuracyKilometer

➤   kCLLocationAccuracyThreeKilometers

An application can also set up the distanceFilter property of the CLLocationManager instance
to specify the minimum distance in meters a device must move before an update is provided to the
application.

The default value of this property is kCLDistanceFilterNone, which specifies the application wants
to know of all movements.

RECEIVING LOCATION UPDATES

To start receiving location updates, you must call the `startUpdatingLocation()` method on the `CLLocationManager` instance.

```
locationManager.startUpdatingLocation()
```

When your application does not want to receive location updates, it must call the `stopUpdating Location` method of the `CLLocationManager` instance:

```
locationManager.stopUpdatingLocation()
```

The `CLLocationManagerDelegate` protocol defines two methods that are used by an application to handle a location update:

```
func locationManager(manager: CLLocationManager,
    didUpdateLocations locations: [AnyObject])

func locationManager(manager: CLLocationManager,
    didFailWithError error: NSError)
```

A typical implementation of the `locationManager(manager: CLLocationManager, didUpdate-Locations locations: [AnyObject])` would resemble the following:

```
func locationManager(manager: CLLocationManager,
    didUpdateLocations locations: [AnyObject])
{
    let locationArray = locations as NSArray
    for newLocation in locationArray
    {
        // lat/lon values should only be considered if
        // horizontalAccuracy is not negative.
        if newLocation.horizontalAccuracy >= 0
        {
            let currentLatitude:CLLocationDegrees =
                newLocation.coordinate.latitude;

            let currentLongitude:CLLocationDegrees =
                newLocation.coordinate.longitude;

            // do something with currentLatitude and currentLongitude.
        }

        // altitude values should only be considered if
        // verticalAccuracy is not negative.
        if (newLocation.verticalAccuracy >= 0)
        {
            let currentAltitude:CLLocationDegrees = newLocation.altitude;

            // do something with currentAltitude
        }

    }

}
```

The `locationManager(manager: CLLocationManager, didUpdateLocations locations: [AnyObject])` method's arguments are the `CLLocationManager` instance, and an array of location updates in chronological order. Each element in this array is an instance of `CLLocation`.

A `CLLocation` object encapsulates a location. It contains a `coordinate` property that is a structure containing a `latitude` and `longitude` member, each expressed as `CLLocationDegrees` values. `CLLocationDegrees` is an alias for a floating-point (decimal) value.

The location object also has the `horizonalAccuracy` property that signifies the radius of a circle centered at the coordinate property. The device can be anywhere within this circle. A larger `horizontalAccuracy` implies a larger circle, and thus a less accurate measurement. If the `horizontalAccuracy` property is negative, the reading should be discarded as being inaccurate.

The `CLLocation` object also provides altitude information using two properties: `altitude` and `verticalAccuracy`. A positive `altitude` value is a height above sea level, and a negative altitude is below sea level. A positive `verticalAccuracy` implies that the altitude measurement is off that amount; a negative value implies an invalid altitude measurement.

> **NOTE** *Although the location updates are served to your delegate in chronological order, the* `horizontalAccuracy` *and* `verticalAccuracy` *values may vary across the updates. In general, if you wait for more updates, the accuracy of the readings will increase. When using the* `startUpdatingLocation()` *method, you need to provide custom logic in your application to pick the reading with the best accuracy and this can be a tradeoff between taking an earlier but somewhat inaccurate location, or waiting until you get a sufficiently accurate reading.*

Starting with iOS9, Core Location has a new method called `requestLocation()`, which can be used to get a single location reading. When you call `requestLocation()`, behind the scenes Core Location will collect a number of readings and provide you one that it feels is reasonably accurate.

`requestLocation()` is mutually exclusive with `startUpdatingLocation()` with the latter taking precedence. Thus, if you call `startUpdatingLocation()` while a previous call to `requestLocation()` hasn't completed, the call to `requestLocation()` will automatically be cancelled.

You can measure the distance between two locations using the `distanceFromLocation()` method of the `CLLocation` class. The distance in meters is expressed as a `CLLocationDistance` value, which is also an alias for a floating-point value:

```
Let distanceTravelled = oldLocation.distanceFromLocation(newLocation)
```

To compute the distance of a location update from a fixed point, you can instantiate a `CLLocation` object that represents the fixed point and use the `distanceFromLocation()` method as normal. For example, if you want to find out the distance of a location update from the center of London (lat = 51.5001524, lon = –0.1262362), you can use code similar to the following:

```
let londonLocation = CLLocation(latitude: 51.5001524, longitude: -0.1262362)

let distanceTravelled = londonLocation.distanceFromLocation(newLocation as!
        CLLocation)
```

HANDLING ERRORS AND CHECKING HARDWARE AVAILABILITY

If Core Location is unable to get a location fix, your delegate's `locationManager(manager:
CLLocationManager, didFailWithError error: NSError)` method will be called. The error
argument is of type `NSError`. Its `code` property can be examined to determine the reason for failure:

➤ `kCLErrorDenied`: The user has denied access to location data.

➤ `kCLErrorLocationUnknown`: Core Location has tried, but could not get a location fix.

➤ `kCLErrorNetwork`: There is no means for Core Location to get a location fix.

If the user has denied access to Core Location, then the `CLLocationManager` will not try to get a
location fix again, and in such a case, it is best to call the `stopUpdatingLocation()` method to the
instance.

Some location services require the presence of specific hardware on the device. In general, you must
check whether the desired service is available before attempting to use it. Table 29-1 lists some of the
methods provided by the `CLLocationManager` class to test service availability.

TABLE 29-1: CLLocationManager Service Availability Methods

METHOD	DESCRIPTION
`func locationServicesEnabled() -> Bool`	Returns True if location services are enabled on the device. The user can disable location services from device settings.
`func isMonitoringAvailableForClass (regionClass: AnyClass) -> Bool`	Returns True if region monitoring is supported on the current device for the specific type of region.
`isRangingAvailable() -> Bool`	Returns True if ranging is supported on the current device.
`func headingAvailable() -> Bool`	Returns True if the location manager is able to generate heading-related events.
`func significantLocationChange MonitoringAvailable() -> Bool`	Returns True if significant location change monitoring is available on the current device.
`func authorizationStatus() -> CLAuthorizationStatus`	Returns a value indicating whether an application is authorized to use location services.

> **NOTE** *The iOS Simulator can simulate either a device at a fixed location or
> a device that is moving along one of three preset routes. These features can be
> accessed from the Debug ⇨ Location menu of the iOS Simulator.*

GEOCODING AND REVERSE GEOCODING

Geocoding involves converting between a latitude/longitude coordinate pair and an address. Core Location provides the CLGeocoder class that provides methods to perform both forward and reverse geocoding. Forward-geocoding involves converting from an address to a latitude/longitude value. Reverse-geocoding involves converting a latitude/longitude value into an address. The result of a geocoding request is represented by a CLPlacemark object. A forward-geocoding request returns an array of CLPlacemark objects because multiple results may be returned.

You should try to use one geocoding request per action and avoid making the same geocoding request multiple times. To perform a forward-geocoding request from an address string, you can call the geocodeAddressString(addressString: String, completionHandler: CLGeocodeCompletionHandler) method on a geocoder instance. This message requires you to specify a String object that contains an address string and a block handler that is called when the geocoding operation is complete. The following code snippet converts an address string into a latitude/longitude coordinate pair:

```
let localGeocoder = CLGeocoder()
let addressString = "170 Bilton Road, Perivale, UB6 7HL, United Kingdom"

localGeocoder.geocodeAddressString(addressString) { (placemarks:[CLPlacemark]?,
                                    error:NSError?) -> Void in

    if placemarks != nil
    {
        let firstPlacemark = placemarks!.first
        let latValue = firstPlacemark!.location.coordinate.latitude;
        let lonValue = firstPlacemark!.location.coordinate.longitude;
    }
}
```

You can send the geocoder a reverse-geocoding request by calling the reverseGeocodeLocation (location: CLLocation, completionHandler: CLGeocodeCompletionHandler) method, as shown in the following snippet:

```
let localGeocoder = CLGeocoder()
let londonLocation = CLLocation(latitude: 51.5001524, longitude: -0.1262362)

localGeocoder.reverseGeocodeLocation(londonLocation) {
            (placemarks:[CLPlacemark]?,
             error:NSError?) -> Void in

    if placemarks != nil {

        let firstPlacemark = placemarks!.first

        let countryCode = firstPlacemark!.ISOcountryCode
        let countryName = firstPlacemark!.country
        let adminArea = firstPlacemark!.administrativeArea
        let city = firstPlacemark!.locality
        let postCode = firstPlacemark!.postalCode
        let streetAddress1 = firstPlacemark!.thoroughfare
    }
};
```

The message requires you to provide a CLLocation object that represents a latitude/longitude coordinate pair and block handler that is called with the results of the reverse-geocoding operation. The CLLocation instance in this example is created with a fixed set of coordinates (lat=51.5001524, lon=−0.1262362) but could have just as well been obtained from a location update.

The actual geocoding operation is performed asynchronously. The results are supplied as an array of CLPlacemark objects, but in this case, the array will contain just one element. If an error occurred, the array is nil and the error variable contains more information on the error.

A CLPlacemark object contains several properties that encapsulate information on an address associated with a specific coordinate. Some of the properties are:

- ➤ location: A CLLocation object that provides the coordinate pair associated with the placemark

- ➤ ISOcountryCode: An NSString object that contains the abbreviated country code

- ➤ country: An NSString object that contains the name of country

- ➤ postalCode: An NSString object that contains the postal code

- ➤ administrativeArea: An NSString object that contains the state/province

- ➤ locality: An NSString object that contains the city

- ➤ thoroughfare: An NSString object that contains the street address

- ➤ subThoroughfare: An NSString object that contains additional street address information

If the coordinates lie over an inland water body, or an ocean, this information can be accessed through the inlandWater and ocean properties, respectively, both of which are String objects.

OBTAINING COMPASS HEADINGS

You can determine if a compass is available on a device by calling the headingAvailable() method of the location manager. If a compass is available on the device, you can use the location manager to receive heading updates. Heading updates work much like location updates. Once you have set up the CLLocationManager instance, you can call the startUpdatingHeading() and stopUpdating-Heading() methods to begin receiving heading updates.

The CLLocationManagerDelegate protocol defines two methods that are related to heading updates:

```
func locationManager(manager: CLLocationManager,
    didUpdateHeading newHeading: CLHeading)

func locationManagerShouldDisplayHeadingCalibration(manager: CLLocationManager)
    -> Bool
```

Heading data is supplied as a CLHeading object to the locationManager(manager: CLLocationManager, didUpdateHeading newHeading: CLHeading) delegate method. The CLHeading class encapsulates the magnetic heading, the true heading, and an accuracy measure in its magneticHeading, trueHeading, and headingAccuracy properties, respectively.

The earth's geographic North Pole is different from the magnetic north pole. The geographic North Pole is fixed at the North Pole, whereas the magnetic north pole is a few hundred miles away. Make sure you know the difference between geographic north and magnetic north when you build any application that uses the compass feature.

The geographic North Pole heading is contained in the `trueHeading` member of the `CLHeading` instance. Data in this member is available only if you enable both heading updates and location updates.

The `locationManagerShouldDisplayHeadingCalibration(manager: CLLocationManager)` is called on the delegate object when the location manager wants to display a calibration prompt to the user. If you find this prompt annoying, you can implement this method to return `NO`. If you were to do so, the compass would try to calibrate itself automatically but the results of the calibration process might not be accurate.

> **NOTE** *The iOS Simulator cannot simulate compass headings. You need to test applications that require this feature on an actual device.*

TRY IT

In this Try It, you create a simple iPhone application based on the Single View Application template called `CLTest` that displays the current location and the distance traveled since the last location reading was obtained.

Lesson Requirements

➤   Launch Xcode.

➤   Create a new iPhone project based on the Single View Application template.

➤   Add a few `UILabel` elements that will display the location readings. Create outlets for these in the view controller class.

➤   Add a `UIButton` that will be used to stop/start receiving location updates. Create an appropriate outlet and action.

➤   Initialize Core Location when the button is pressed. Stop receiving location updates when the button is pressed a second time.

➤   Implement `CLLocationManagerDelegate` methods.

> **REFERENCE** *The code for this Try It is available at* www.wrox.com/go/swiftios.

Hints

➤ You must add the NSLocationWhenInUseUsageDescription key to the Info.plist file in the project. The value of this key should be a string that describes what your application will do with the user's location data.

➤ Before calling startUpdatingLocation() on the CLLocationManager instance, you must check if the user has allowed your app to access location data.

➤ When creating a new project, you can use your website's domain name as the Company Identifier in the Project Options dialog box.

➤ You will need to add a reference to the Core Location framework to the project.

➤ To show the Object library, select View ⇨ Utilities ⇨ Show Object Library.

➤ To show the assistant editor, select View ⇨ Assistant Editor ⇨ Show Assistant Editor.

Step-by-Step

➤ Create a Single View Application in Xcode called CLTest.

1. Launch Xcode and create a new application by selecting File ⇨ New ⇨ Project.

2. Select the Single View Application template from the list of iOS project templates.

3. In the project options screen use the following values:

   ➤ **Product Name:** CLTest

   ➤ **Organization Name:** your company

   ➤ **Organization Identifier:** com.yourcompany

   ➤ **Language:** Swift

   ➤ **Devices:** iPhone

   ➤ **Use Core Data:** Unchecked

   ➤ **Include UI Tests:** Unchecked

   ➤ **Include Unit Tests:** Unchecked

4. Save the project onto your hard disk.

➤ Add a reference to the Core Location framework.

1. In Xcode, make sure the project navigator is visible. To show it, select View ⇨ Navigators ⇨ Show Project Navigator.

2. Click the root (project) node of the project navigator to display project settings.

3. Select the Build Phases tab.

4. Expand the Link Binary With Libraries group in this tab.

5. Click the + button at the bottom of this group and select `CoreLocation.framework` from the list of available frameworks.

6. Click the Add button.

➤ Add UI elements to the default scene.

1. Open the `Main.storyboard` file in the Interface Editor.

2. From the Object library, drag and drop six labels onto the scene and place to resemble Figure 29-3.

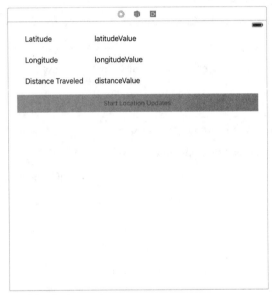

FIGURE 29-3

3. Double-click each label in turn and change its text to Latitude, Longitude, Distance Traveled, latitudeValue, longitudeValue, and distanceValue respectively.

4. Create layout constraints for each of the elements on the storyboard scene using the information in Table 29-2. When creating layout constraints using the pin constraints dialog box, ensure the Constrain to margins option is unchecked and Update Frames is set to Items of New Constraints.

TABLE 29-2: Layout Constraints

ELEMENT	LEFT	TOP	WIDTH	HEIGHT
Latitude label	39	8	63	21
Longitude label	39	26	77	21

ELEMENT	LEFT	TOP	WIDTH	HEIGHT
Distance Travelled label	39	26	141	21
latitudeValue label	99	8	99	21
longitudeValue label	85	26	114	21
distanceValue label	21	26	107	21

5. Using the assistant editor, create outlets for the `latitudeValue`, `longitudeValue`, and `distanceValue` labels. Call these outlets `latitudeValue`, `longitudeValue`, and `distanceValue`, respectively.

➤ Add a `UIButton` instance to start/stop receiving location updates.

1. Ensure the Object library is visible. You can show it by selecting View ➪ Utilities ➪ Show Object Library.

2. Use the Object library to add a `UIButton` instance and place it below the labels.

3. Double-click the button and set its title to Start Location Updates.

4. Select the button and display the pin constraints dialog box. Ensure the Constrain to margins options is unchecked and Update Frames is set to Items of New Constraints. Create the following layout constraints:

    ➤ Left: 20

    ➤ Top: 20

    ➤ Right: 20

    ➤ Height: 40

5. Using the assistant editor, create an outlet called `toggleButton` in the `ViewController` class and connect it to the button.

6. Using the assistant editor, create an action method in the view controller class and connect it to the Touch Up Inside event of the button. Call the new method `onButtonPressed`.

➤ Add code to receive location updates to the View controller class.

1. Open the `ViewController.swift` file in the project explorer.

2. Import the Core Location framework into the view controller.

3. Ensure the following import statements are located at the top of the `ViewController` class:

    ```
    import UIKit
    import CoreLocation
    ```

4. Add the following variable declarations to the view controller class:

    ```
    var locationManager:CLLocationManager? = nil
    ```

```
var lastLocation:CLLocation? = nil
var isReceivingLocationUpdates:Bool = false
```

5. Ensure the View controller class implements the `CLLocationManager` delegate protocol by ensuring the class is declared as:

```
class ViewController: UIViewController, CLLocationManagerDelegate
```

6. Update the stub implementation of the `viewDidLoad` method to resemble the following:

```
override func viewDidLoad() {

    super.viewDidLoad()

    locationManager = CLLocationManager()
    locationManager!.delegate = self
    locationManager!.desiredAccuracy = kCLLocationAccuracyBestForNavigation

    lastLocation = CLLocation(latitude: 51.5001524, longitude: -0.1262362)

    toggleButton.titleLabel!.text = "Start location updates"
}
```

7. Update the empty implementation of the `onButtonPressed` method to resemble the following:

```
@IBAction func onButtonPressed(sender: AnyObject) {

    if isReceivingLocationUpdates == false
    {
        if CLLocationManager.authorizationStatus() !=
           CLAuthorizationStatus.AuthorizedWhenInUse
        {
            locationManager!.requestWhenInUseAuthorization()
        }
        else
        {
            isReceivingLocationUpdates = true
            toggleButton.titleLabel!.text = "Stop location updates"
            locationManager!.startUpdatingLocation()
        }
    }
    else
    {
        isReceivingLocationUpdates = false
        toggleButton.titleLabel!.text = "Start location updates"
        locationManager!.stopUpdatingLocation()
    }

}
```

8. Implement the `locationManager`(`manager: CLLocationManager, didChange AuthorizationStatus status: CLAuthorizationStatus`) delegate method in the view controller class:

```
func locationManager(manager: CLLocationManager,
    didChangeAuthorizationStatus status: CLAuthorizationStatus)
{
    var shouldAllow = false

    switch status {
        case CLAuthorizationStatus.AuthorizedWhenInUse:
            shouldAllow = true
        case CLAuthorizationStatus.AuthorizedAlways:
            shouldAllow = true
        default:
            shouldAllow = false
    }

    if shouldAllow == true {
        isReceivingLocationUpdates = true
        toggleButton.titleLabel!.text = "Stop location updates"
        manager.startUpdatingLocation()
    }
}
```

9. Implement the `locationManager(manager: CLLocationManager, didUpdateLocations locations: [CLLocation])` delegate method in the view controller class:

```
func locationManager(manager: CLLocationManager,
    didUpdateLocations locations: [CLLocation])
{
    let locationArray = locations as NSArray
    for newLocation in locationArray
    {
        // lat/lon values should only be considered if
        // horizontalAccuracy is not negative.
        if newLocation.horizontalAccuracy >= 0
        {
            let currentLatitude:CLLocationDegrees =
                newLocation.coordinate.latitude;

            let currentLongitude:CLLocationDegrees =
                newLocation.coordinate.longitude;

            let distanceTravelled =
                newLocation.distanceFromLocation(lastLocation!)

            latitudeValue.text = "\(currentLatitude)"
            longitudeValue.text = "\(currentLongitude)"
            distanceValue.text = "\(distanceTravelled)"

            lastLocation = newLocation as? CLLocation
        }
    }
}
```

➤ Test your app in the iOS Simulator.

1. Click the Run button in the Xcode toolbar. Alternatively you can select Project ➪ Run.

2. Click the Start Location Updates button.

3. Use the iOS Simulator's ability to simulate a device on the move by selecting Debug ➪ Location ➪ City Bicycle Ride.

REFERENCE *To see some of the examples from this lesson, watch the Lesson 29 video online at* `www.wrox.com/go/swiftiosvid`.

30

Introduction to Map Kit

In the previous lesson, you learned how to locate a device using Core Location. In this lesson, you learn how to integrate a map within your application.

The Map Kit framework provides the `MKMapView` class for adding maps into your views. Map Kit also provides additional classes for annotating the map. The Map Kit framework uses Apple's map service internally.

The Map Kit framework is often used in conjunction with the Core Location framework, neither of which are included in any of the standard iOS application templates. To use these frameworks in your code, you need to add them manually to your project. You can do this from the Project Settings page in Xcode. Select the Project node in the project navigator to display the settings page. On the settings page, switch to the Build Phases tab and click the + button under the Link Binary With Libraries category. Select the Map Kit framework from the list of available frameworks (see Figure 30-1). Repeat this step for the Core Location framework.

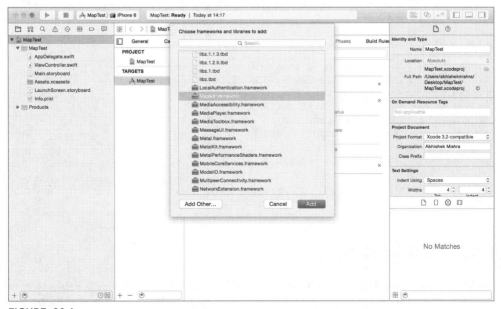

FIGURE: 30-1

You can add a Map Kit view to an existing view controller or storyboard using the Object library. Simply drag an instance of a Map Kit view and create an outlet for it in the view controller class.

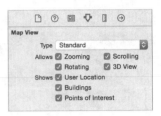

The map view handles zooming and scrolling automatically. You can use the Attribute inspector to choose from Map, Satellite, and Hybrid modes (see Figure 30-2). You can also set up the map to use Core Location to display the user's location by checking the Shows User Location property.

FIGURE: 30-2

You can also set up these properties programmatically by using the `mapType` property of the `MKMapView` instance to specify the map mode. The `mapType` property can take one of five values:

➤ `Standard`

➤ `Satellite`

➤ `Hybrid`

➤ `SatelliteFlyover`

➤ `HybridFlyover`

To enable/disable zooming and scrolling, use the `zoomEnabled` and `scrollEnabled` properties, respectively. To have the map display the user's location, set the `showsUserLocation` property to `true`.

You can set up the initial coordinate and zoom factor of the map by defining a map region and using the `setRegion(region: MKCoordinateRegion, animated: Bool)` method of the `MKMapView` instance.

A region is represented by the `MKCoordinateRegion` structure and has members called `center` and `span`. The `center` member is a `CLLocationCoordinate2D` structure and has the members `latitude` and `longitude`. The `span` member is an `MKCoordinateSpan` structure and has the member's `latitudeDelta` and `longitudeDelta`, which specify a rectangular region around the center in degrees of latitude and longitude.

To create a region and apply it, you use code similar to the following:

```
// setup the map's location and zoom factor
var mapRegion:MKCoordinateRegion = MKCoordinateRegion();
mapRegion.center.latitude = 51.5001524;
mapRegion.center.longitude = -0.1262362;
mapRegion.span.latitudeDelta = 0.2;
mapRegion.span.longitudeDelta = 0.2;

mapView.setRegion(mapRegion, animated: true)
```

The preceding code snippet assumes that `mapView` is an outlet connected to the Map View object created with Interface Builder.

ADDING ANNOTATIONS

The `MKMapView` class enables you to add custom annotations to a map. Because a map can potentially display several annotations at the same time, the designers of Map Kit decided to use separate objects to represent the data contained in an annotation and the view used to display it. The idea was that view objects could be reused with different data objects.

The data portion of an annotation is encapsulated by an instance of a class that implements the MKAnnotation protocol and contains information about the coordinates on the map and a description that is displayed in a callout.

The MKAnnotation protocol defines the coordinate, title, and subtitle properties. The coordinate property is a CLLocationCoordinate2D structure, and the title and subtitle properties are NSString objects. To conform to this protocol, your class must contain these properties. An example of such a class, PlacemarkClass.swift, is shown here:

```swift
import Foundation
import MapKit

class PlacemarkClass: NSObject, MKAnnotation {

    var coordinate:CLLocationCoordinate2D
    var title:String?
    var subtitle:String?

    init(coordinate: CLLocationCoordinate2D, title: String, subtitle: String) {
        self.coordinate = coordinate
        self.title = title
        self.subtitle = subtitle
    }

}
```

Note that the class has an initializer method that enables you to specify an initial coordinate, title, and subtitle. To instantiate a PlacemarkClass object and add it as an annotation to the mapView object, you can use the addAnnotation:animated: method, as demonstrated by the following code:

```swift
// drop a pin on parliament square
let parliamentLocation:CLLocationCoordinate2D =
 CLLocationCoordinate2DMake(51.5001524, -0.1262362)

let parliamentAnnotation = PlacemarkClass(coordinate: parliamentLocation,
 title: "Parliament Square",
subtitle: "Big Ben is here!")

mapView.addAnnotation(parliamentAnnotation)
```

The view portion of an annotation is represented by a subclass of the MKAnnotationView class. Apple provides a subclass called MKPinAnnotationView that you can use for standard pin/callout annotations. The MKMapView instance requests this view from a delegate object when it is required. The delegate object must implement the MKMapViewDelegate protocol, which defines the mapView(mapView: MKMapView, viewForAnnotation annotation: MKAnnotation) -> MKAnnotationView? method.

Typically, the delegate object will be your view controller class. You can set up the delegate by using either the Interface Builder (see Figure 30-3) or setting the delegate property of the MKMapView instance.

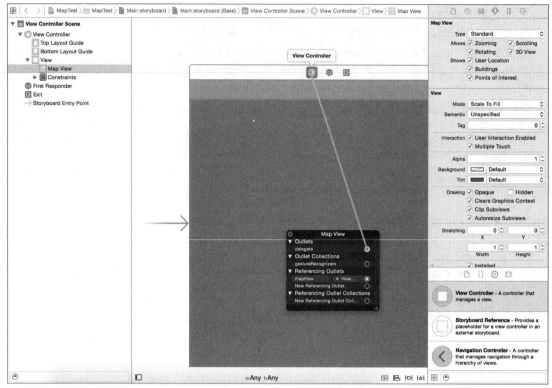

FIGURE 30-3

A typical implementation of this `delegate` method follows:

```
func mapView(mapView: MKMapView,
viewForAnnotation annotation: MKAnnotation) -> MKAnnotationView?
{
    let newAnnotation:MKPinAnnotationView =
    MKPinAnnotationView(annotation: annotation,
                    reuseIdentifier: "annotation1")

    newAnnotation.pinTintColor = UIColor.yellowColor()
    newAnnotation.animatesDrop = true
    newAnnotation.canShowCallout = true
    newAnnotation.setSelected(true, animated: true)

    return newAnnotation
}
```

The annotation object for which a view is required is specified in the `annotation` parameter. Once you have allocated an `MKPinAnnotationView` instance, you can set up its pin color using the `pintTintColor` property. If you want the pin to display a callout when tapped, set the `canShowCallout` property to YES. If you want the pin drop animation, set `animatesDrop` to YES. The resulting pin and callout box is shown in Figure 30-4.

FIGURE 30-4

ACCESSORY VIEWS

An annotation callout can have up to three accessory views (see Figure 30-5):

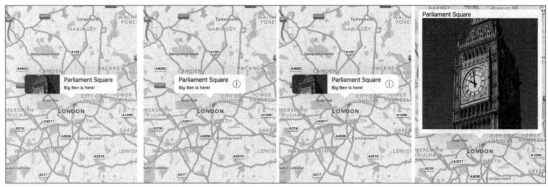

FIGURE 30-5

➤ `leftCalloutAccessoryView`: This view is displayed to the left of the popup content. It displays alongside the title and subtitle.

➤ `rightCalloutAccessoryView`: This view is displayed to the right of the popup content. It displays alongside the title and subtitle.

➤ `detailedCalloutAccessoryView`: Added in iOS9, this property can be used to present a custom `UIView` subclass in place of the subtitle of the annotation view. For instance, to use an image of Big Ben in the callout box attached to an annotation, you can use the following snippet:

```
let newAnnotation:MKPinAnnotationView =
   MKPinAnnotationView(annotation: annotation,
   reuseIdentifier: "annotation1")

newAnnotation.pinTintColor = UIColor.yellowColor()
newAnnotation.animatesDrop = true
newAnnotation.canShowCallout = true

let bigBenImageSmall = UIImage(named: "BigBen")
newAnnotation.detailCalloutAccessoryView =
UIImageView(image: bigBenImageSmall)

newAnnotation.setSelected(true, animated: true)
```

TRY IT

In this Try It, you create a simple iPhone application based on the Single View Application template called `MapTest` that displays the current location and the location of Big Ben on a map. The user can use a segmented control to change the map style to standard, satellite, or hybrid.

> **NOTE** *Although this book does not have a lesson dedicated specifically to the segmented control, it is often used with maps. You can follow the steps outlined in this Try It to use a segmented control with a map. However, if you would like more information on the segmented control, refer to the* UISegmentedControl *class reference, available at:*
>
> http://developer.apple.com/library/ios/#documentation/uikit/reference/UISegmentedControl_Class/Reference/UISegmentedControl.html

Lesson Requirements

➤ Launch Xcode.

➤ Create a new iPhone project based on the Single View Application template.

➤ Add a map kit view to the default scene and create an outlet for it in the view controller class.

➤ Add a segmented control and add an action for it in the view controller class.

➤ Add a reference to the Map Kit and Core Location frameworks.

➤ Create a subclass of NSObject that implements the MKAnnotation protocol to use as the annotation data class.

➤ Initialize the map view in the view controller's viewDidLoad method.

➤ Implement the MKMapViewDelegate protocol in your view controller class.

➤ Change the map style when the active segment in the segmented control is changed.

> **REFERENCE** *The code for this Try It is available at* www.wrox.com/go/swiftios.

Hints

➤ When creating a new project, you can use your website's domain name as the Company Identifier in the Project Options dialog box.

➤ You will need to add a reference to both the Map Kit and the Core Location frameworks to the project.

➤ To show the Object library, select View ➪ Utilities ➪ Show Object Library.

➤ To show the assistant editor, select View ➪ Assistant Editor ➪ Show Assistant Editor.

Step-by-Step

➤ Create a Single View Application in Xcode called `MapTest`.

1. Launch Xcode and create a new application by selecting File ⇨ New ⇨ Project.

2. Select the Single View Application template from the list of iOS project templates.

3. In the project options screen, use the following values:

   ➤ **Product Name:** MapTest

   ➤ **Organization Name:** your company

   ➤ **Organization Identifier:** com.yourcompany

   ➤ **Language:** Swift

   ➤ **Devices:** iPhone

   ➤ **Use Core Data:** Unchecked

   ➤ **Include UI Tests:** Unchecked

   ➤ **Include Unit Tests:** Unchecked

4. Save the project onto your hard disk.

➤ Add a reference to the Core Location framework.

1. In Xcode, make sure the project navigator is visible. To show it, select View ⇨ Navigators ⇨ Show Project Navigator.

2. Click the root (project) node of the project navigator to display project settings.

3. Select the Build Phases tab.

4. Expand the Link Binary With Libraries group in this tab.

5. Click the + button at the bottom of this group and select `CoreLocation.framework` from the list of available frameworks.

6. Click the Add button.

➤ Add a reference to the Map Kit framework.

1. In Xcode, make sure the project navigator is visible. To show it, select View ⇨ Navigators ⇨ Show Project Navigator.

2. Click the root (project) node of the project navigator to display project settings.

3. Select the Build Phases tab.

4. Expand the Link Binary With Libraries group in this tab.

5. Click the + button at the bottom of this group and select `MapKit.framework` from the list of available frameworks.

6. Click the Add button.

➤ Add a segmented control to the scene.

1. Ensure the Object library is visible. You can show it by selecting View ⇨ Utilities ⇨ Show Object Library.

2. Use the Object library to add a Segmented Control instance.

3. Use the Attribute inspector to set the number of segments to 3.

4. Use the Attribute inspector to name the three segments Map, Satellite, and Hybrid, respectively (see Figure 30-6).

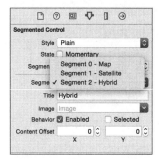

FIGURE 30-6

5. Select the segment control and display the pin constraints popup window. Ensure the Constrain to margins options is unchecked and Update Frames is set to Items of New Constraints. Create the following layout constraints:

   ➤ **Left:** 20

   ➤ **Top:** 20

   ➤ **Width:** 275

   ➤ **Height:** 28

6. Using the assistant editor, create an outlet in the view controller class called `mapMode-SegmentControl` and connect it to the segmented control in the default scene.

7. Using the assistant editor, create an action in the view controller class and connect it to the Value Changed event of the `UISegmentedControl`. Call the new method `onSegmentChanged`.

➤ Ensure the top of the `ViewController.Swift` file contains the following import statements:

```
import UIKit
import MapKit
```

➤ Add a Map Kit view to the default scene.

1. Ensure the Object library is visible. You can show it by selecting View ⇨ Utilities ⇨ Show Object Library.

2. Use the Object library to add a Map Kit view to the default scene of the storyboard.

3. Using the Assistant editor, create an outlet called `mapView` and connect it to the map view instance in the default scene.

4. With the Map Kit view selected, sqitch to the Attribute inspector and ensure the "Shows User Location" attribute is unchecked.

5. Select the Map Kit view and display the pin constraints dialog box. Ensure the Constrain to margins option is unchecked and Update Frames is set to Items of New Constraints. Create the following layout constraints:

   ➤ **Left:** 0

   ➤ **Top:** 20

   ➤ **Right:** 0

   ➤ **Bottom:** 0

➤ Create a new Swift class to represent annotation data.

1. Create a new Swift class by selecting File ➪ New ➪ File.

2. Select the Swift File template and click Next.

3. Name the new class `PlacemarkClass`.

4. Edit the class to resemble the following:

```
import Foundation
import MapKit

class PlacemarkClass: NSObject, MKAnnotation {

    var coordinate:CLLocationCoordinate2D
    var title:String?
    var subtitle:String?

    init(coordinate: CLLocationCoordinate2D,
        title: String, subtitle: String) {
        self.coordinate = coordinate
        self.title = title
        self.subtitle = subtitle
    }

}
```

➤ Declare the `ViewController.Swift` class to conform to the `MKMapViewDelegate` protocol by modifying its declaration as follows:

```
class ViewController: UIViewController, MKMapViewDelegate
```

➤ Update the `viewDidLoad` method of the `ViewController` class to resemble the following:

```
override func viewDidLoad() {

    super.viewDidLoad()

    // setup the map's location and zoom factor
```

```
        var mapRegion:MKCoordinateRegion = MKCoordinateRegion();
        mapRegion.center.latitude = 51.5001524;
        mapRegion.center.longitude = -0.1262362;
        mapRegion.span.latitudeDelta = 0.2;
        mapRegion.span.longitudeDelta = 0.2;
        mapView.setRegion(mapRegion, animated: true)

        // drop a pin on parliament square
        let parliamentLocation:CLLocationCoordinate2D =
    CLLocationCoordinate2DMake(51.5001524, -0.1262362)
        let parliamentAnnotation = PlacemarkClass(coordinate:
    parliamentLocation, title: "Parliament Square", subtitle: "Big Ben is here!")
        mapView.addAnnotation(parliamentAnnotation)
    }
```

➤ Implement the `MKMapViewDelegate` method `mapView(mapView: MKMapView, viewFor Annotation annotation: MKAnnotation) -> MKAnnotationView?` in your view controller class as follows:

```
    func mapView(mapView: MKMapView, viewForAnnotation annotation:
    MKAnnotation) -> MKAnnotationView?
    {
        let newAnnotation:MKPinAnnotationView =
    MKPinAnnotationView(annotation: annotation, reuseIdentifier: "annotation1")

        newAnnotation.pinTintColor = UIColor.yellowColor()
        newAnnotation.animatesDrop = true
        newAnnotation.canShowCallout = true
        newAnnotation.setSelected(true, animated: true)

        return newAnnotation
    }
```

➤ Add the following code to the `onSegmentChanged(sender: AnyObject)` method of the view controller class:

```
    if mapModeSegmentControl.selectedSegmentIndex == 0
    {
        mapView.mapType = MKMapType.Standard;
    }
    else if mapModeSegmentControl.selectedSegmentIndex == 1
    {
        mapView.mapType = MKMapType.Satellite;
    }
    else if mapModeSegmentControl.selectedSegmentIndex == 2
    {
        mapView.mapType = MKMapType.Hybrid;
    }
```

➤ Test your app in the iOS Simulator.

   1. Click the Run button in the Xcode toolbar. Alternatively you can use the Project ⇨ Run menu item.

   2. Switch between the different segments on the segment control to change map types.

> **REFERENCE** *To see some of the examples from this lesson, watch the Lesson 30 video online at* www.wrox.com/go/swiftiosvid.

31

Using the Camera and Photo Library

All iOS 9 devices have at least one camera. When a user takes a picture with the camera, the image is stored in the device's photo library. This lesson shows you how to allow the user to pick an image from the photo library or take a new picture with the camera and use it in your application.

The UIKit framework contains a class called `UIImagePickerController` designed specifically to allow you to access the camera and photo library from your applications. This class presents its own user interface (see Figure 31-1) that allows a user to browse through the photo library or control the camera. All you have to do is present this view controller in your application and provide a delegate method whose methods are called when the user has finished selecting an image.

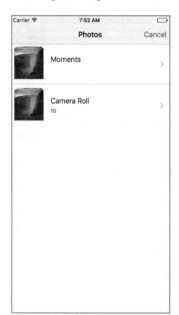
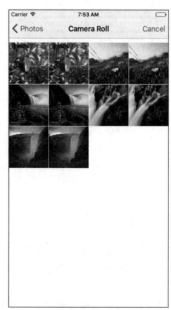

FIGURE 31-1

The image picker controller can also be used to record videos and access these recorded videos within your application.

SELECTING THE IMAGE SOURCE

The `UIImagePickerController` class can be used to access the contents of either the photo library, saved photos album, or the camera. You can specify the source by providing a value for the `sourceType` property. This value can be one of the following:

- ➤ `UIImagePickerControllerSourceType.PhotoLibrary`

- ➤ `UIImagePickerControllerSourceType.Camera`

- ➤ `UIImagePickerControllerSourceType.SavedPhotosAlbum`

To check if a particular source type is available, use the `isSourceTypeAvailable(sourceType: UIImagePickerControllerSourceType) -> Bool` class method of the `UIImagePickerController` class as follows:

```
let hasCamera:Bool = UIImagePickerController.isSourceTypeAvailable(
UIImagePickerControllerSourceType.Camera)
```

When the `sourceType` is set to use the camera, you can specify which camera is to be used if your device has multiple cameras. By default, the image picker uses the rear camera. To find out if front and rear cameras are available, use the `isCameraDeviceAvailable(cameraDevice: UIImagePickerControllerCameraDevice) -> Bool` class method, as shown in the following code snippet:

```
let hasFrontCamera:Bool =
UIImagePickerController.isCameraDeviceAvailable(
UIImagePickerControllerCameraDevice.Front);

let hasRearCamera:Bool =
UIImagePickerController.isCameraDeviceAvailable(
UIImagePickerControllerCameraDevice.Rear);
```

Once you have determined that the camera you want to use is available, you can specify it using the `cameraDevice` property of the image picker instance. For instance, to use the front camera, use the following code:

```
imagePicker.cameraDevice = UIImagePickerControllerCameraDevice.Front;
```

PRESENTING THE IMAGE PICKER

To display the image picker as a modal sheet, use the `presentViewController(viewControllerTo Present: UIViewController, animated flag: Bool, completion: (() -> Void)?)` method on your active view controller object:

```
self.presentViewController(imagePicker, animated: true, completion: nil)
```

On an iPad, you can also display an image picker in a popover controller. The following code snippet shows how this can be done programmatically from a method in your view controller class:

```
if UIDevice().userInterfaceIdiom == UIUserInterfaceIdiom.Pad
{
    imagePicker.modalPresentationStyle = UIModalPresentationStyle.Popover
    self.presentViewController(imagePicker, animated: true, completion: nil)

    // Get the popover presentation controller and configure it.
    let presentationController:UIPopoverPresentationController =
        imagePicker.popoverPresentationController!

    presentationController.permittedArrowDirections =
    UIPopoverArrowDirection.Left

    presentationController.sourceView = self.view
    presentationController.sourceRect = popoverPresetingButton.frame
}
```

The preceding code assumes that you have `imagePicker` as an instance of `UIImagePickerController` and `popoverPresentingButton` as an outlet in your view controller class.

`UIImagePickerController` requires a delegate object that implements both the `UIImagePickerControllerDelegate` and `UINavigationControllerDelegate` protocols. The former defines two methods that are called when the user has selected an image or selected the Cancel button in the image picker:

```
func imagePickerController(picker: UIImagePickerController,
didFinishPickingMediaWithInfo info: [String : AnyObject])

func imagePickerControllerDidCancel(picker: UIImagePickerController)
```

The `imagePickerControllerDidCancel(picker: UIImagePickerController)` delegate method has one parameter that contains a reference to the image picker controller. A typical implementation of this delegate method dismisses the image picker controller if it was presented modally:

```
picker.dismissViewControllerAnimated(true, completion: nil)
```

The `imagePickerController(picker: UIImagePickerController, didFinishPicking MediaWithInfo info: [String : AnyObject])` delegate method has two parameters, the first of which is a reference to the image picker. The second parameter is an `NSDictionary` object that contains a `UIImage` object corresponding to the selected image.

To access this image in this delegate method, you can use code similar to the following to retrieve the value in the dictionary that corresponds to the `UIImagePickerControllerOriginalImage` key:

```
let image:UIImage = info[UIImagePickerControllerOriginalImage] as! UIImage
```

Often, you may want to save this `UIImage` instance to a file. To do that, you must first obtain an `NSData` instance that contains the pixels in the `UIImage` instance in a specific file format. Once you have this `NSData` instance, you can write it to a file by sending it the `writeToFile:atomically:` message.

To obtain an NSData instance that contains the image as a PNG file, use the UIImagePNGRepresentation function as follows:

```
let imageData:NSData = UIImagePNGRepresentation(image)!
```

To obtain an NSData instance that contains the image in JPEG format, use the UIImageJPEGRepresentation function as follows:

```
let imageData:NSData = UIImageJPEGRepresentation(image, 1.0)!
```

The first parameter to this function is the UIImage instance; the second is a number between 0.0 and 1.0 that indicates the desired JPEG quality, with 0.0 being representing the lowest quality and 1.0 the highest quality.

The following implementation of the imagePickerController(picker: UIImagePickerController, didFinishPickingMediaWithInfo info: [String : AnyObject]) delegate method shows how to save the selected image to a PNG file in the Documents directory:

```
func imagePickerController(picker: UIImagePickerController,
    didFinishPickingMediaWithInfo info: [String : AnyObject])
{
    let image:UIImage = info[UIImagePickerControllerOriginalImage] as!
        UIImage

    let imageData:NSData = UIImagePNGRepresentation(image)!

    let documentsDirectory =
        NSSearchPathForDirectoriesInDomains(.DocumentDirectory,
                                            .UserDomainMask,
                                            true)[0]

    let outFile:String = documentsDirectory + "savedImage.png"

    imageData.writeToFile(outFile, atomically: true)

    picker.dismissViewControllerAnimated(true, completion: nil)
}
```

If you provide a delegate for the image picker, then you are responsible for dismissing the picker. To do so, add the following line of code:

```
picker.dismissViewControllerAnimated(true, completion: nil)
```

to the end of both delegate methods:

➤ imagePickerControllerDidCancel(picker: UIImagePickerController)

➤ imagePickerController(picker: UIImagePickerController, didFinishPicking
MediaWithInfo info: [String : AnyObject])

TRY IT

In this Try It, you build an iPhone application based on the Single View Application template called `ImagePicker` that allows the user to select an image from the photo library, or take a picture using the camera and display the image in an image view.

Lesson Requirements

➤ Launch Xcode.

➤ Create a new iPhone project based on the Single View Application template.

➤ Add a `UIImageView` instance to the scene and an appropriate outlet in the view controller file.

➤ Add two `UIButton` instances to the scene and connect them to appropriate action methods in the view controller class.

➤ Allow the user to select an image from the photo library and display the selected image in the image view.

➤ Allow the user to take a picture using the camera and display the image in the image view.

➤ Hide the camera button if the device does not have a camera.

> **REFERENCE** *The code for this Try It is available at* www.wrox.com/go/swiftios.

Hints

➤ When creating a new project, you can use your website's domain name as the Company Identifier in the Project Options dialog box.

➤ To show the Object library, select View ➪ Utilities ➪ Show Object Library.

➤ To show the assistant editor, select View ➪ Assistant Editor ➪ Show Assistant Editor.

Step-by-Step

➤ Create a Single View Application in Xcode called `ImagePicker`.

   1. Launch Xcode and create a new application by selecting File ➪ New ➪ Project.

   2. Select the Single View Application template from the list of iOS project templates.

3. In the project options screen use the following values:

    ➤   **Product Name:** ImagePicker

    ➤   **Organization Name:** your company

    ➤   **Organization Identifier:** com.yourcompany

    ➤   **Language:** Swift

    ➤   **Devices:** iPhone

    ➤   **Use Core Data:** Unchecked

    ➤   **Include UI Tests:** Unchecked

    ➤   **Include Unit Tests:** Unchecked

4. Save the project onto your hard disk.

➤   Add a `UIImageView` instance to the default scene and connect it to an outlet in the view controller class.

1. Open the storyboard file and use the Object library to drag and drop an image view onto the scene.

2. Select the image view and display the pin constraints dialog box. Ensure the Constrain to margins options is *unchecked* and Update Frames is set to Items of New Constraints. Create the following layout constraints:

    ➤   **Left:** 0

    ➤   **Right:** 0

    ➤   **Top:** 20

    ➤   **Bottom:** 0

3. Use the assistant editor to create an outlet in the view controller class and connect it to the image view. Name the outlet `imageView`.

4. Select the image view and use the attribute editor to set the view mode of the image view to Aspect Fit.

➤   Add two `UIButton` instances to the scene and connect their Touch Up Inside events to appropriate action methods in the view controller class.

1. Drag and drop two `UIButton` instances onto the default scene and position them one below the other (see Figure 31-2).

2. Set the title of the first button to `Camera`. Set its background color to a shade of gray.

3. Set the title of the second button to `Photo Library`. Set its background color to a shade of gray.

4. Name the action method corresponding to the first button `onCamera`.

5. Name the action method corresponding to the second button `onPhotoLibrary`.

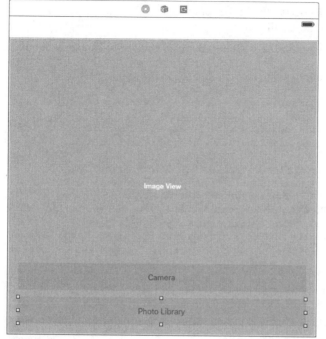

FIGURE 31-2

6. Create an outlet called `cameraButton` in the view controller class and connect it to the button titled Camera in the scene.

7. Create layout constraints for the buttons on the storyboard scene using the information in Table 31-1. When creating layout constraints using the pin constraints dialog box, ensure the Constrain to margins option is unchecked and Update Frames is set to Items of New Constraints.

TABLE 31-1: Layout Constraints

ELEMENT	LEFT	BOTTOM	RIGHT	HEIGHT
Camera button	20	13	20	51
Photo Library	20	20	20	51

➤ Ensure the view controller class conforms to the `UINavigationControllerDelegate` and `UIImagePickerControllerDelegate` protocols. Modify the declaration of the `ViewController` class to resemble the following.

```
class ViewController: UIViewController,
        UIImagePickerControllerDelegate,
        UINavigationControllerDelegate
```

➤ Add the following code to the implementation of the `onCamera()` method in the `ViewController.swift` file:

```
let imagePicker:UIImagePickerController = UIImagePickerController()
imagePicker.sourceType = UIImagePickerControllerSourceType.Camera
imagePicker.delegate = self

if UIDevice().userInterfaceIdiom == UIUserInterfaceIdiom.Pad
{
    imagePicker.modalPresentationStyle = UIModalPresentationStyle.Popover
    self.presentViewController(imagePicker, animated: true, completion: nil)

    let presentationController:UIPopoverPresentationController =
        imagePicker.popoverPresentationController!
    presentationController.permittedArrowDirections =
        UIPopoverArrowDirection.Left
    presentationController.sourceView = self.view
    presentationController.sourceRect = cameraButton.frame
}
else
{
    self.presentViewController(imagePicker, animated: true, completion: nil)
}
```

➤ Add the following code to the implementation of the `onPhotoLibrary()` method in the `ViewController.swift` file:

```
let imagePicker:UIImagePickerController = UIImagePickerController()
imagePicker.sourceType = UIImagePickerControllerSourceType.PhotoLibrary
imagePicker.delegate = self

if UIDevice().userInterfaceIdiom == UIUserInterfaceIdiom.Pad
{
    imagePicker.modalPresentationStyle = UIModalPresentationStyle.Popover
    self.presentViewController(imagePicker, animated: true, completion: nil)

    let presentationController:UIPopoverPresentationController =
        imagePicker.popoverPresentationController!
    presentationController.permittedArrowDirections =
        UIPopoverArrowDirection.Left
    presentationController.sourceView = self.view
    presentationController.sourceRect = cameraButton.frame
}
else
{
    self.presentViewController(imagePicker,
                                animated: true,
                                completion: nil)
}
```

➤ Implement UIImagePickerControllerDelegate methods in your view controller class.

1. Add the following code in your ViewController.swift file to implement the image PickerControllerDidCancel(picker: UIImagePickerController) delegate method:

```
func imagePickerControllerDidCancel(picker: UIImagePickerController)
{
    picker.dismissViewControllerAnimated(true, completion: nil)
}
```

2. Add the following code in your ViewController.swift file to implement the imagePickerController(picker: UIImagePickerController, didFinish PickingMediaWithInfo info: [String : AnyObject]) delegate method:

```
func imagePickerController(picker: UIImagePickerController,
    didFinishPickingMediaWithInfo info: [String : AnyObject])
{
  let image:UIImage = info[UIImagePickerControllerOriginalImage] as!
      UIImage

   imageView.image = image

   picker.dismissViewControllerAnimated(true, completion: nil)
}
```

➤ Hide the camera button if the device does not have a camera. Add the following code to the end of the viewDidLoad method of your view controller class:

```
override func viewDidLoad() {
    super.viewDidLoad()

    let hasCamera = UIImagePickerController.isSourceTypeAvailable(
                    UIImagePickerControllerSourceType.Camera)
    if hasCamera == false
    {
        cameraButton.hidden = true;
    }
}
```

➤ Test your application on an iPhone or iPod touch.

1. Connect your device to your Mac and select it from the Scheme/Target selector in the Xcode toolbar.

2. Click the Run button in the Xcode toolbar. Alternatively you can select Project ⇨ Run.

3. Tap the Photo Library button and select a photo from the contents of your device's photo library. Alternately, tap the Camera button to take a picture. After selecting the image, your device screen will resemble Figure 31-3.

FIGURE 31-3

REFERENCE *To see some of the examples from this lesson, watch the Lesson 31 video online at* www.wrox.com/go/swiftiosvid.

32

Introduction to User Interface Testing

User Interface Testing (UI Testing) is a new feature in Xcode 7 that allows you to write code that can launch an instance of your application, interact with UI elements of the application programmatically, and validate the state and properties of these elements.

A related feature, called *UI recording*, has been introduced in Xcode 7. When UI recording is enabled, you can launch the app and interact with it as you normally would. XCode records your interaction with the app and builds a user interface test that can perform the same sequence of interactions for you.

UI Testing is built upon XCTest, which is Xcode's testing framework. XCTest is used by both user interface tests as well as traditional unit tests. Unit tests are covered in Lesson 34.

ADDING SUPPORT FOR UI TESTING TO YOUR PROJECT

Adding support for UI testing involves making a few changes to an Xcode project. For starters a new build target must be added that will be used to run the user interface tests. A suitable unit testing framework will also need to be linked with the project.

If you are creating a new project in Xcode, adding support for unit tests is a simple matter of ensuring the Include UI Tests check box is selected in the project options dialog box (see Figure 32-1).

When you do this, you will notice a few changes:

➤ A new group has been added to the project explorer. This group will be used to contain your unit test files.

➤ A new build target is added to the project settings. This new build target is called the *test target*.

➤ The test target is preconfigured to test the host application.

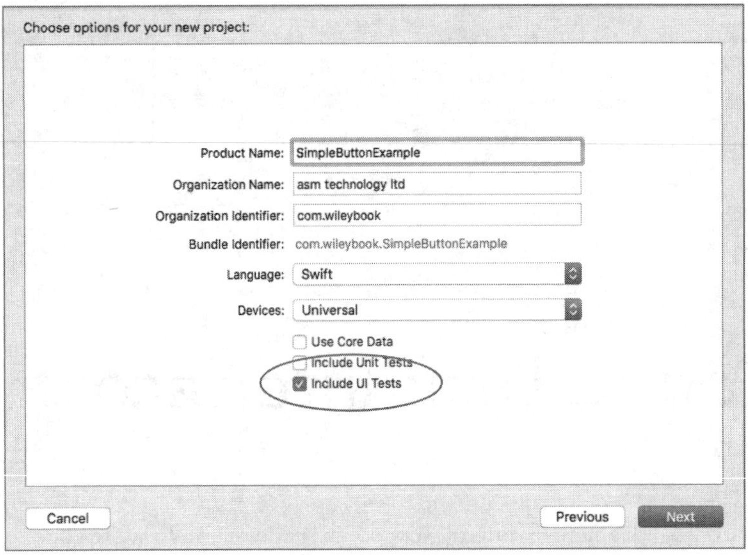

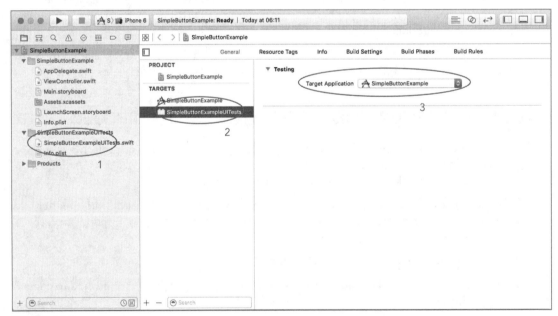

FIGURE 32-1

All of these points are visible in Figure 32-2.

FIGURE 32-2

Adding support for UI tests to an existing project is slightly more tricky. First you need to add a new build target to your Xcode project by selecting File ➪ New ➪ Target.

In the target template dialog box, select iOS UI Testing Bundle under the Test category (see Figure 32-3).

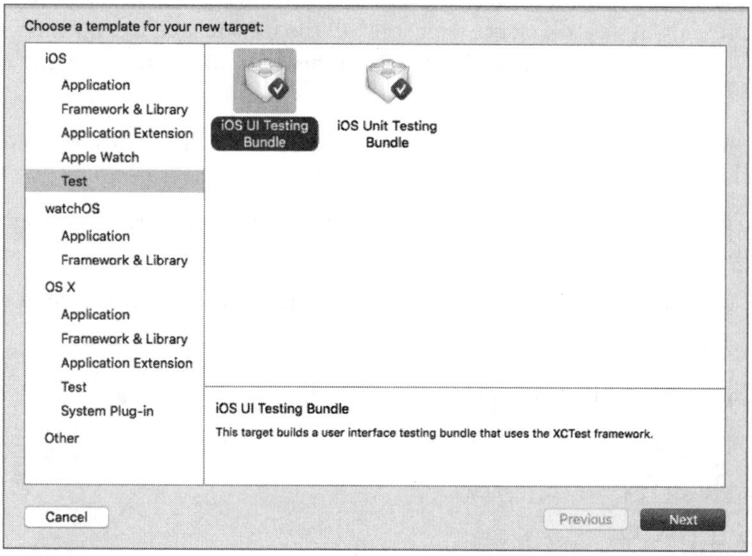

FIGURE 32-3

You will then be presented with the target options dialog box, which is similar in many respects to the project options dialog box you encounter when creating a new project. Accept the default values in this dialog box and click Finish (see Figure 32-4).

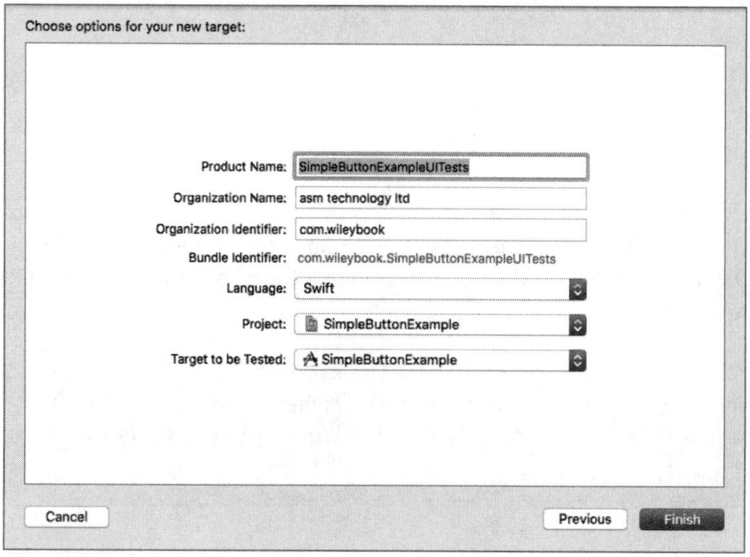

FIGURE 32-4

ANATOMY OF A TEST CASE

Previously in this lesson, you learned that UI tests are stored under their own group in the project explorer. The unit being tested is always a .swift class file, and all the tests related to that class are grouped in a single test class. A test class is just a Swift class that inherits from XCTestCase and can contain three types of methods:

➤   **Setup method:** This method appears as setUp() and is called before each test method is executed in the test class.

➤   **Teardown method:** This method appears as tearDown() and is called after each test method is executed in the test class.

➤   **Test methods:** These methods all begin with the word test. Each method encapsulates a single test.

The following code snippet shows what a typical UI test class looks like:

```
import XCTest

class SwiftTableViewSampleUITests: XCTestCase {

    override func setUp() {
        super.setUp()

        continueAfterFailure = false
        XCUIApplication().launch()
    }

    override func tearDown() {
        super.tearDown()
    }

    func testExample() {

    }

}
```

To execute all unit tests (in all test classes) in a project, use the Product ⇨ Test menu item. Doing so will launch the app on the iOS Simulator or iOS device and execute all methods that begin with the word test in each test case sequentially.

> **NOTE** *If your project has both unit tests and user interface tests, then the user interface tests will be executed only after all the unit tests finish regardless of any unit test failures.*

The result of the testing phase is visible in the Test Navigator, which can be accessed by selecting View ⇨ Navigators ⇨ Show Test Navigator (see Figure 32-5).

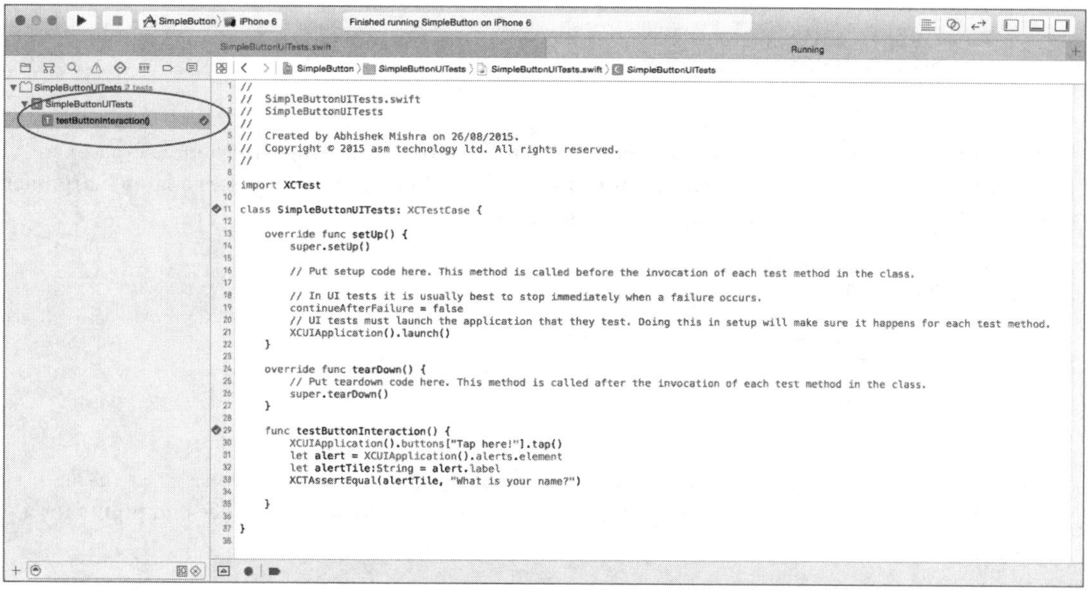

FIGURE 32-5

You will see a green tick box next to each test that has passed, and a red one next to each test that has failed. Keep in mind that test code must be able to compile for the tests to begin executing. If your project has compilation errors, you will need to fix these before the tests can run.

You can add additional test classes to your project by using the Add button (+) and the New UI Test Class command in the Test Navigator (see Figure 32-6).

FIGURE 32-6

NEW CLASSES FOR UI TESTING

UI testing is part of the XCTest framework, which is Xcode's standard testing framework. UI testing introduces four new classes, and two new protocols, which are discussed in this section.

XCUIApplication

An XCUIApplication instance is used to launch an instance of your application for testing. Typically, you instantiate an XCUIApplication instance in your test class's setup() method and call the launch method:

```
override func setUp() {
    super.setUp()
XCUIApplication().launch()
}
```

You can also set specific arguments of environment variables by setting the `launchArguments` and `launchEnvironment` properties. For example, the following snippet passes a launch argument `USE_DEBUG_SERVER` to the `UIApplication` instance:

```
override func setUp() {
    super.setUp()

    let application = XCUIApplication()
    application.launchArguments = ["USE_DEBUG_SERVER"]
    application.launch()
}
```

The application can look out for this argument in `application(application, didFinish LaunchingWithOptions)` and take appropriate action (such as load web service end points for a staging server):

```
func application(application: UIApplication,
    didFinishLaunchingWithOptions launchOptions:
[NSObject: AnyObject]?)
    -> Bool {

    let launchArguments = Process.arguments

    for var index = 1; index < launchArguments.count; index++ {
        let argument = launchArguments[index] as String
        if argument.compare("USE_DEBUG_SERVER") ==
            NSComparisonResult.OrderedSame{
            // do something here to load endpoints for a debug server.
        }
    }

    return true
}
```

The preceding snippet retrieves any launch arguments as an array of strings by calling `Process.arguments`. The first element in this array is always the full path to the application, which is why it examines elements from index 1 onward.

To terminate an app, you could call the `terminate()` method on and `XCUIApplication` instance. This is not strictly necessary as `XCTest` will terminate the application instance automatically every time a test finishes executing.

XCUIDevice

An instance of this class represents the device on which the test is running. There is always only one instance of this device that can be accessed as follows:

```
let device = XCUIDevice.sharedDevice()
```

At the time of this writing, XCUIDevice has only one property called orientation that returns the orientation of the device. Setting this property changes the orientation of the device.

The following setup method passes a launch argument and changes the device to landscape orientation before running a UI test.

```
override func setUp() {
    super.setUp()

    let application = XCUIApplication()
    application.launchArguments = ["USE_DEBUG_SERVER"]
    application.launch()

    let device = XCUIDevice.sharedDevice()
    device.orientation = UIDeviceOrientation.LandscapeLeft
}
```

XCUIElementQuery

An instance of this class can be used to locate a UI element in the application's user interface. This class, along with XCUIElement is the primary class used for UI testing.

In most cases you will not instantiate an XCUIElementQuery explicitly; instead you will use one of the properties defined by the XCUIElementTypeQueryProvider protocol on the XCUIApplication instance to obtain an XCUIElementQuery instance.

XCUIApplication implements the XCUIElementTypeQueryProvider protocol; the protocol is discussed later in this lesson.

XCUIElementQuery defines several instance methods, as shown in Table 32-1. Some of these methods return an XCUIElement, while others return another XCUIElementQuery instance. In the latter case, the returned XCUIElementQuery instance is usually used to obtain a smaller subset of elements.

TABLE 32-1: XCUIElementQuery Methods

PROPERTY/METHOD NAME	DESCRIPTION
var count: UInt { get }	Resolves the query and returns the number of elements matched by the query
func elementBoundByIndex(index: UInt) -> XCUIElement	Resolves the query and returns an element at the specified index
func elementMatchingType(elementType: XCUIElementType, identifier: String?) -> XCUIElement	Resolves the query and returns an element that matches a specific type and accessibility identifier
func childrenMatchingType(type: XCUIElementType) -> XCUIElementQuery	Returns a query that can be used to extract children of a specific type

Figure 32-7 shows the storyboard of an application that has a single view controller with three buttons on it.

FIGURE 32-7

The following code snippet will return the number of buttons in the view controller that is currently visible on the screen (which in this case will be 3). The code snippet uses `application.buttons` to create a query that returns all the visible buttons on the device's screen. This query will be explained when we discuss XCUIElementQueryProvided later in this lesson.

```
let application = XCUIApplication()
let query = application.buttons

print (query.count)
```

XCUIElement

An `XCUIElement` instance encapsulates the information required to locate a user interface element in your application. It is almost always obtained by calling one of the methods on an `XCUIElementQuery` instance.

The information within an `XCUIElement` is only evaluated when a method is called on the `XCUIElement`. At the time of evaluation, if the `XCUIElement` does not resolve into an actual element an error will be raised.

It is important to keep in mind that the `XCUIElement` instance does not let you access the underlying user element directly. For instance, if you had an `XCUIElement` that represents a text field instance on a view, you cannot dereference the `XCUIElement` to arrive at the underlying `UITextField` object and then attempt to manipulate the underlying object.

However, an `XCUIElement` does allow you to interact with the underlying element programmatically as an end user would while using your app. To achieve this, `XCUIElement` provides a number of properties and methods that you could call on a concrete instance, some of which are listed in Table 32-2.

TABLE 32-2: XCUIElement Methods

PROPERTY/METHOD NAME	DESCRIPTION
`var exists: Bool { get }`	Returns true if the `XCUIElement` resolves into an actual UI element in the app
`func tap()`	Sends a tap event to the underlying UI element
`func doubleTap()`	Sends a double tap event to the underlying UI element
`func pressForDuration(duration: NSTimeInterval)`	Sends a long press gesture event to the underlying UI element
`pressForDuration(duration: NSTimeInterval, thenDragToElement otherElement: XCUIElement)`	Sends a press and hold gesture to the underlying UI element that then drags to another element
`func swipeUp()`	Sends a swipe up gesture to the underlying UI element
`func swipeDown()`	Sends a swipe down gesture to the underlying UI element
`func swipeLeft()`	Sends a swipe left gesture to the underlying UI element
`func swipeRight()`	Sends a swipe left gesture to the underlying UI element

`XCUIElement` also conforms to the `XCUIElementAttributes` and `XCUIElementTypeQueryProvider` protocols, both of which are defined later in the lesson.

Take a moment to look at Figure 32-7 again. In the previous section you learned that the following snippet will result in an `XCUIElementQuery` that resolves to three objects:

```
let application = XCUIApplication()
let query = application.buttons

print (query.count)
```

That being the case, you could attempt to get an `XCUIElement` instance that represents the green button using the `elementBoundByIndex` method:

```
let greenButton = query.elementBoundByIndex(1)
```

To verify you have indeed gotten the green button, simply inspect the value of the `label` property on the `XCUIElement` instance (`greenButton`):

```
print (greenButton.label)
```

In case you were wondering, the `label` property is defined in the `XCUIElementAttributes` protocol, which is implemented by `XCUIElement`. As mentioned earlier, this protocol will be discussed later in this lesson.

This type of code is sensitive to the layout of the user interface. A far better approach is to set up an accessibility identifier for the buttons in the storyboard and use the accessibility identifier to retrieve the green button regardless of how the storyboard scene was laid out.

To set up an accessibility identifier for your user interface elements, select the user interface element in the storyboard and use the Identity Inspector (see Figure 32-8)

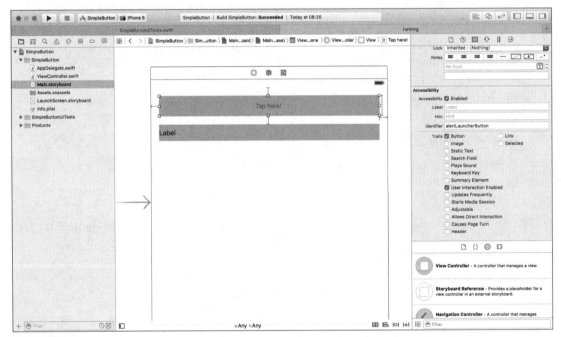

FIGURE 32-8

Once an element has an accessibility identifier set up, you could use the following snippet to return an `XCUIElement` instance that will resolve to the green button regardless of how the user interface is laid out.

```
let application = XCUIApplication()
let query = application.buttons
let greenButton = query.elementMatchingType(.Button, identifier: "greenButton")
```

The last line of the preceding snippet retrieves an `XCUIElement` of a specific type with a specific identifier. Alternately, you could have written the last line as:

```
let greenButton = query["greenButton"]
```

This alternate statement uses the subscript operator ([ ]) to retrieve an element by accessibility identifier.

XCUIElementAttributes

The `XCUIElementAttributes` protocol defines several properties that return commonly used attributes and is implemented by `XCUIElement` as one would expect. Table 32-3 lists some of the commonly used properties defined in `XCUIElementAttributes`.

TABLE 32-3: XCUIElementAttribute Properties

PROPERTY NAME	DESCRIPTION
`var identifier: String { get }`	Returns the accessibility identifier of the element
`var frame: CGRect { get }`	Returns the frame property of the element
`var title: String { get }`	Returns the accessibility title of the element
`var label: String { get }`	Returns the caption of the element (if applicable)
`var elementType: XCUIElementType`	Returns an enumeration value that represents the type of the element
`var enabled: Bool { get }`	Returns true if the element is enabled for user interaction
`func swipeDown()`	Sends a swipe down gesture to the underlying UI element
`func swipeLeft()`	Sends a swipe left gesture to the underlying UI element
`func swipeRight()`	Sends a swipe right gesture to the underlying UI element

The `elementType` property is an enumerated value that represents the type of element. `XCUIElementType` is a very large enumeration and some of its members do not apply to iOS applications. Some of the more commonly used values are listed here:

➤ `XCUIElementType.Alert`

➤ `XCUIElementType.Button`

➤ `XCUIElementType.NavigationBar`

➤ `XCUIElementType.TabBar`

➤ `XCUIElementType.ToolBar`

➤ `XCUIElementType.ActivityIndicator`

➤ `XCUIElementType.SegmentedControl`

➤ `XCUIElementType.Picker`

➤ `XCUIElementType.Image`

➤ `XCUIElementType.StaticText`

➤ `XCUIElementType.TextField`

➤ `XCUIElementType.DatePicker`

➤ `XCUIElementType.TextView`

➤ `XCUIElementType.WebView`

XCUIElementTypeQueryProvider

`XCTest` also defines a new protocol `XCUIElementTypeQueryProvider`. This protocol defines several properties that return preconfigured `XCUIElementQuery` instances. Both `XCUIApplication` and `XCUIElement` implement this protocol.

Some of the properties defined in this protocol are listed in Table 32-4. Typically, you will use one of these methods on the `XCUIApplication` instance to return an initial `XCUIElementQuery`, and you will then use the methods defined in `XCUIElementQuery` to filter down to a specific element.

TABLE 32-4: XCUIElementTypeQueryProvider Methods

PROPERTY/METHOD NAME	DESCRIPTION
`var windows: XCUIElementQuery { get }`	Returns a query that provides access to all windows that are currently visible in app. iOS applications have just a single window.
`var alerts: XCUIElementQuery { get }`	Returns a query that provides access to all alerts that are currently visible in app. Usually there is only one alert visible in an app at a time.
`var buttons: XCUIElementQuery { get }`	Returns a query that provides access to all buttons that are currently visible in app.
`var navigationBars: XCUIElementQuery { get }`	Returns a query that provides access to all navigation bars that are currently visible in app.
`tables: XCUIElementQuery { get }`	Returns a query that provides access to all table views that are currently visible in app.
`var collectionViews: XCUIElementQuery { get }`	Returns a query that provides access to all collection views that are currently visible in app.

PROPERTY/METHOD NAME	DESCRIPTION
`var staticTexts: XCUIElementQuery { get }`	Returns a query that provides access to all labels that are currently visible in app.
`var textFields: XCUIElementQuery { get }`	Returns a query that provides access to all text fields that are currently visible in app.
`textViews: XCUIElementQuery { get }`	Returns a query that provides access to all text views that are currently visible in app.
`var maps: XCUIElementQuery { get }`	Returns a query that provides access to all map views that are currently visible in app.
`var otherElements: XCUIElementQuery { get }`	Returns a query that provides access to all view controllers that are currently visible in app.

TEST ASSERTIONS

An assertion represents a failure of a unit test. Typically your UI test case will use one of the properties defined by the `XCUIElementTypeQueryProvider` protocol on the `XCUIApplication` instance to obtain an `XCUIElementQuery` instance. It will then resolve the `XCUIElementQuery` into an `XCUIElement` and inspect some of the attributes of the underlying UI element.

If the value of the underlying attribute being tested does not match the expected value, the test will fail by firing an assertion. XCTest provides several macros to help you create assertions. Table 32-5 lists some of the more commonly used assertions.

TABLE 32-5: XCTest Assertion Macros

MACRO	DESCRIPTION
`XCTAssert(expression, String)`	Generates a failure if the expression evaluates to false. An optional string message may be provided to indicate failure.
`XCTAssertEqual(expression1, expression2, String)`	Generates a failure when `expression1` is not equal to `expression2`. This test is for primitive data types.
`XCTAssertNil (expression, String)`	Generates a failure when the expression is not nil.
`XCTAssertNotNil(expression, String)`	Generates a failure when the expression is nil.
`XCTAssertTrue (expression)`	Generates a failure when the expression evaluates to false. Identical to `XCTAssert()`.
`XCTAssertFalse (expression)`	Generates a failure when the expression evaluates to true.

The following code snippet lists a UI test case that will try to locate a button with a specific accessibility identifier and assert if the button was not found:

```
func testGreenButtonExists() {
    let application = XCUIApplication()
    let query = application.buttons
    let greenButton = query.elementMatchingType(.Button, identifier: "greenButton")
    XCTAssert(greenButton.exists)
}
```

It is worth noting that `XCTAssert` was used instead of `XCTAssertNotNil`. This is because `green-Button` is an `XCUIElement` instance.

Recall that `XCUIElement` is not the actual user element on the screen; it just represents the information needed by the testing framework to attempt to locate a user interface element. Only when you try to access the underlying element (by calling `exists()` on the `XCUIElement`) will the testing framework try to resolve the `XCUIElement` into an actual user interface element.

The following snippet builds on the previous test and asserts if the label on the button does not match a specific value.

```
func testGreenButtonHasCorrectLabel(){
    let application = XCUIApplication()
    let query = application.buttons
    let greenButton = query.elementMatchingType(.Button,
        identifier: "greenButton")
    let buttonLabel = greenButton.label
    XCTAssertEqual(buttonLabel, "Green",
    "expected button label to be Green, but
     found \(buttonLabel) instead.")
    }
```

UI RECORDING

One of the coolest new features added to Xcode 7 is UI recording. With UI recording, you can launch an instance of your application and interact with it as normal. While you interact with your app, Xcode will record your taps, gestures, selections, and key strokes into a UI test script.

UI recording is tightly coupled with UI testing. To begin UI recording, simply place the text cursor within a UI test case and tap the red record button at the bottom of the Xcode editor (see Figure 32-9).

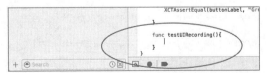

FIGURE 32-9

To stop recording simply tap the stop button, which replaces the record button during a recording session. UI recording provides a good starting point to build your UI tests; you can then fine-tune the code generated by UI recording and add appropriate `XCTAssert` statements.

WAITING FOR ELEMENTS IN A UI TEST

Sometimes it is necessary to wait for an asynchronous operation to complete and verify the data displayed on the screen when this asynchronous operation has completed. For instance, imagine a button that attempts to retrieve the current time from a web service and displays the result in a label on the screen.

You could easily simulate a tap on the button using a simple statement such as this:

```
XCUIApplication().buttons["serviceLauncherButton"].tap()
```

However, you could not immediately go and inspect the text of the label and expect it to have changed because tapping the button has sent out a web service request to an external resource and could take a few seconds to come back with the response.

You need to be able to wait for a few seconds for the text in the label to change. Fortunately, XCTest has just the thing in the form of test expectations.

A test expectation is an instance of XCTestExpectation and represents an expected result. For example, to set up an expectation that indicates a UILabel with the caption "11 December, 2015" exists, you could use the following snippet:

```
let label = XCUIApplication().staticTexts["Hello Alex"]
let predicate = NSPredicate(format: "exists == 1", argumentArray: nil)
self.expectationForPredicate(predicate, evaluatedWithObject: label, handler: nil
```

The preceding snippet starts out by retrieving an XCUIElement instance for a label with text Hello Alex.

```
let label = XCUIApplication().staticTexts["Hello Alex"]
```

The label does not yet exist, but that is not a problem as an XCUIElement just represents the information needed to locate an element and not an actual element. An attempt to locate the actual element is only made when you call a method such as exists() on the XCUIElement instance.

Once an XCUIElement instance has been obtained, an expectation is set up using the expectation ForPredicate () method of the XCTestCase class. (Recall that all UI test classes inherit from XCTestCase)

```
let predicate = NSPredicate(format: "exists == 1", argumentArray: nil)
self.expectationForPredicate(predicate, evaluatedWithObject: label, handler: nil
```

The expectation is expressed as a predicate that is evaluated on an object. The object in this case is the label, and the predicate is set up to call the exists() method and ensure the result is 1.

The net result is that the expectation represents a situation where a label with the caption Hello Alex exists.

Once an expectation has been set up, you need to call the waitForExpectationsWithTimeout() method on an XCTestCase instance:

```
self.waitForExpectationsWithTimeout(5, handler: nil)
```

The `waitForExpectationsWithTimeout()` method waits a specified amount of time (in seconds) and then evaluates all expectations that have been set up in the test method. If any of the expectations are not fulfilled, the test will fail.

If multiple expectations have been set up, they are evaluated in the order in which they are created. Use of `XCTestExpectation` is demonstrated in this lesson's Try It.

TRY IT

In this Try It, you build an iPhone application based on the Single View Application template called `SimpleButton` that presents a simple user interface to the user with a button and a label.

When the button is tapped, the user is prompted to type in her name. The name is displayed in the text field when the alert is dismissed. You will then write a few UI test cases to augment the application and verify that things are working as expected.

Lesson Requirements

➤ Launch Xcode.

➤ Create a new iPhone project based on the Single View Application template with UI testing support.

➤ Add a `UIButton` instance to the scene and connect it to the appropriate action method in the view controller class.

➤ Add a `UILabel` instance to the scene and connect it to an outlet in the view controller.

➤ Add code to display an alert when the button is tapped.

➤ Write UI test cases to verify the behavior of the application.

> **REFERENCE** *The code for this Try It is available at* www.wrox.com/go/swiftios.

Hints

➤ When creating a new project, you can use your website's domain name as the Company Identifier in the Project Options dialog box.

➤ To include support for UI tests in your project, ensure the Include UI Tests check box is enabled in the project options dialog box.

➤ To show the Test navigator, select View ➪ Navigators ➪ Show Test Navigator.

➤ To show the Object library, select View ➪ Utilities ➪ Show Object Library.

➤ To show the assistant editor, select View ➪ Assistant Editor ➪ Show Assistant Editor.

Step-by-Step

➤ Create a Single View Application in Xcode called SimpleButton.

1. Launch Xcode and create a new application by selecting File ➪ New ➪ Project menu item.

2. Select the Single View Application template from the list of iOS project templates.

3. In the project options screen use the following values:

> ➤ **Product Name:** SimpleButton
>
> ➤ **Organization Name:** your company
>
> ➤ **Organization Identifier:** com.yourcompany
>
> ➤ **Language:** Swift
>
> ➤ **Devices:** iPhone
>
> ➤ **Use Core Data:** Unchecked
>
> ➤ **Include Unit Tests:** Unchecked
>
> ➤ **Include UI Tests:** Checked

4. Save the project onto your hard disk.

➤ Add user interface elements to your storyboard's scene.

1. Use the Object library to add a UIButton and a UILabel instance to the default scene. Name and position them to resemble Figure 32-10.

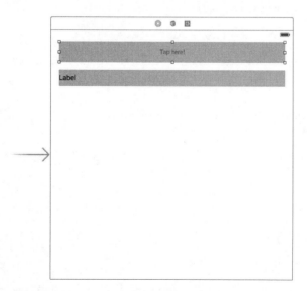

FIGURE 32-10

2. Create layout constraints for each of elements on the storyboard scene using the information in Table 32-6. When creating layout constraints using the pin constraints dialog box, ensure the Constrain to margins option is unchecked and the Update Frames combo box is set to None.

TABLE 32-6: Layout Constraints

ELEMENT	LEFT	TOP	RIGHT	HEIGHT
Button	20	20	20	50
Label	20	20	20	40

3. Select the view controller object and update frames by selecting Editor ➪ Resolve Auto Layout Issues ➪ Update Frames.

4. Use the assistant editor to create outlets for the label in the view controller class. Name the outlet greetingLabel.

5. Use the assistant editor to create an action method in the view controller class called onButtonTapped and connect it to the button on the scene.

6. Using the Identity Inspector to set the accessibility identifier of the button to alert-LauncherButton and the accessibility identifier of the label to alertResultLabel.

➤ Present an alert when the button is tapped.

1. Replace the implementation of the onButtonTapped method with the following:

```
@IBAction func onButtonTapped(sender: AnyObject) {

    var inputTextField: UITextField?

    let alert = UIAlertController(title: "What is your name?",
message: nil,
preferredStyle: UIAlertControllerStyle.Alert)

    let alertAction = UIAlertAction(title: "Ok",
style: UIAlertActionStyle.Default,
handler: { action -> Void in
        guard let textField = inputTextField else {
            return
        }

        self.greetingLabel.text = "Hello \(textField.text!)"

})

    alert.addAction(alertAction)

    alert.addTextFieldWithConfigurationHandler { (textField) -> Void in
        inputTextField = textField;
        inputTextField!.text = ""
```

```
        }

        self.presentViewController(alert, animated: true, completion: nil)
    }
```

2. Replace the implementation of the `viewDidLoad` method with the following:

```
override func viewDidLoad() {
        super.viewDidLoad()
        greetingLabel.text = ""
}
```

➤ Test your app in the iOS Simulator.

1. Click the Run button in the Xcode toolbar. Alternatively, you can use the Project ➪ Run menu item.

2. Tap the button, type in your name when asked, and observe the text in the label changes.

➤ Create a UI test that will tap the button, type in some text in the alert view, and verify that the text on the label updates correctly.

1. Locate the `SimpleButtonUITests.swift` file in the Project Explorer and open it.

2. Delete the `textExample()` method at the bottom of the file.

3. Add a new method, `testWhenButtonTapped_AlertAppears`, to the UI test class:

```
func testWhenButtonTapped_AlertAppears () {
    XCUIApplication().buttons["alertLauncherButton"].tap()
    let alert = XCUIApplication().alerts.element
     XCTAssertNotNil(alert.exists)
    }
```

This test aims to verify that an alert view is displayed when the button is tapped.

4. Add another method called `testWhenButtonTapped_AlertAppearsWithCorrectTitle` to the UI test class:

```
func testWhenButtonTapped_AlertAppearsWithCorrectTitle () {
    XCUIApplication().buttons["alertLauncherButton"].tap()
    let alert = XCUIApplication().alerts.element
    let alertTile:String = alert.label
    XCTAssertEqual(alertTile, "What is your name?")
}
```

This test aims to verify that the alert view that is displayed when the button is tapped has the correct title.

5. Add another method called `testWhenAlertDismissed_LabelUpdatesCorrectly` to the unit test class:

```
func testWhenAlertDismissed_LabelUpdatesCorrectly () {

    XCUIApplication().buttons["alertLauncherButton"].tap()
    let alert = XCUIApplication().alerts.element
```

```
        alert.textFields.elementBoundByIndex(0).typeText("Alex")
        alert.buttons.elementBoundByIndex(0).tap()

        let label = XCUIApplication().staticTexts["Hello Alex"]
        let predicate = NSPredicate(format: "exists == 1",
                        argumentArray: nil)

        self.expectationForPredicate(predicate,
                        evaluatedWithObject: label,
                        handler: nil)

        self.waitForExpectationsWithTimeout(5, handler: nil)
    }
```

This test enters the name Alex in the alert view and dismisses the alert view by tapping OK on the alert view. It then verifies that the text on the label has been updated to Hello Alex.

6. Run the unit tests using the Product ⇨ Test menu item once again and observe that the product compiles and all tests pass.

REFERENCE *To see some of the examples from this lesson, watch the Lesson 32 video online at* www.wrox.com/go/swiftiosvid.

33

Introduction to Test Driven Development

Test Driven Development (TDD) is an approach to software development that aims to reduce the number of bugs in the final product. A developer who practices TDD techniques not only writes actual code to carry out the app's functionality but also test code that ensures his applications code does what it is supposed to do.

This test code is called a unit test, and it is common for an application to have several hundred unit tests with each test testing a very small piece of the code base. The code that forms these unit tests is not part of the code base that will ship to the end users of the application. Typically these units tests are executed every time a developer attempts to create a build and if any unit tests were to fail then a build would not be created. TDD makes it very cost effective to catch *regression bugs* (bugs that were fixed at an earlier point in time but have been reintroduced due to subsequent development work).

It is not necessary for the same developer to write both the class as well as the test case. In fact, it is quite common for a senior developer to specify the behavior of a class for a junior developer by creating a bunch of unit tests. Given these tests, the junior developer can implement the class and knows his work is done when all the unit tests pass.

One of the key principles of TDD is that the tests are written first and development focuses on writing the minimum amount of code needed to make all tests pass. Once all tests pass, the feature in question is deemed to be complete. This process is iterative, with each iteration creating new tests and code to make these tests pass.

A company that practices TDD will discover that over time not only will the number of defects decrease, but also defects are found earlier in the development process.

TDD requires an upfront investment in the time required to write the test code in addition to the production code, and the time required to maintain test code as the application is developed further, but it could be argued that teams that do not practice TDD techniques could end up spending a significant amount of time fixing bugs.

ADDING SUPPORT FOR UNIT TESTING TO YOUR PROJECT

Adding support for TDD involves making a few changes to an Xcode project. For starters, a new build target must be added that will be used to run the unit tests. A suitable unit testing framework will also need to be linked with the project.

If you are creating a new project in Xcode, adding support for unit tests is a simple matter of ensuring the Include Unit Tests check box is checked in the project options dialog box (see Figure 33-1).

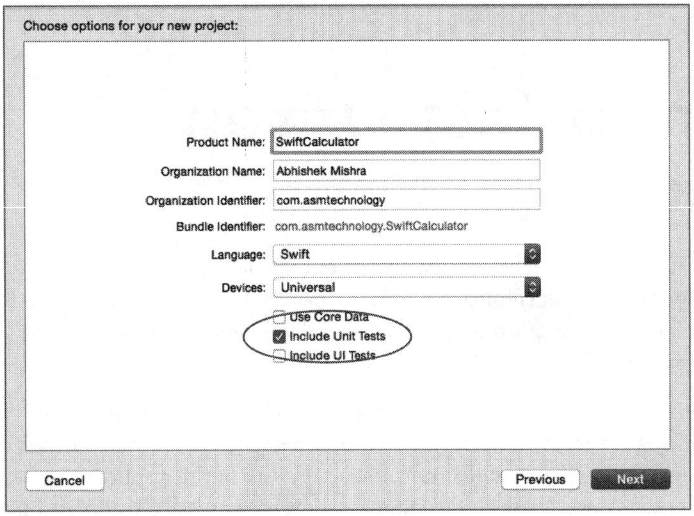

FIGURE: 33-1

When you do this, you will notice a few changes:

➤ A new group has been added to the project explorer. This group will be used to contain your unit test files.

➤ A new build target is added to the project settings. This new build target is called the test target.

➤ The test target is pre-configured to test the host application.

All of these points are visible in Figure 33-2.

Adding support for unit tests to an existing project is slightly more tricky. First you need to add a new build target to your Xcode project by selecting File ➪ New ➪ Target.

In the target template dialog box, select iOS Unit Testing Bundle under the Test category (see Figure 33-3).

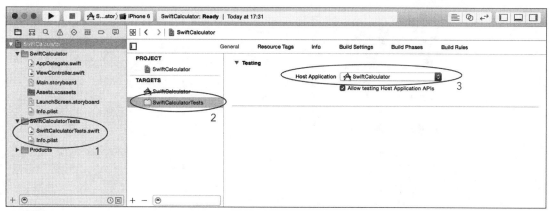

FIGURE: 33-2

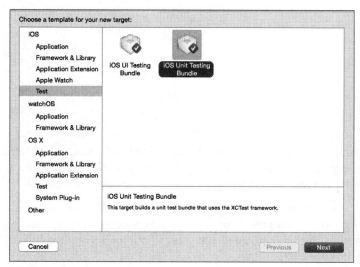

FIGURE: 33-3

You will then be presented with the target options dialog box, which is similar in many respects to the project options dialog box you encounter when creating a new project. Accept the default values in this dialog box and click Finish (see Figure 33-4).

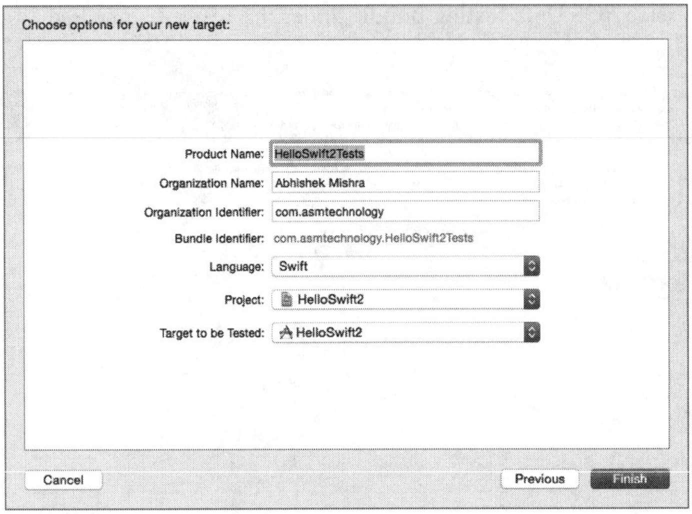

FIGURE: 33-4

TDD TECHNIQUES

This section examines some of the common techniques practiced by developers who work in a TDD environment.

Test First

This practice encourages developers to write the tests before the code that will be tested. The tests define the acceptance criteria of the project. If you have a comprehensive suite of tests, the code is considered ready as soon as all tests pass and no further changes to the code base are required.

In practice, a developer writes a single test, and then runs it to check if it fails. The developer then proceeds to write the code to make this one test pass. This is an iterative process and over time a comprehensive set of tests is created by the developer, which serves as both the acceptance criteria as well as living documentation for the code base.

Red-Green-Refactor

This practice builds upon the previous principle. When a test is written for code that does not yet exist, it is quite possible the test may not even compile, and if it does it will definitely fail. This stage of development that involves writing a failing test that encapsulates the desired behavior of a system is called the Red stage. The color red has to do with popular IDE's like Xcode and Visual Studio using red as the color to indicate failed tests in a summary view.

If the first stage toward implementing TDD is getting a failing test, then the next one is obviously writing the code to make the test pass. This second stage is called the Green stage. Reaching this second stage may mean creating a new class or method, or changing some existing code. At this stage, you should not focus on writing the most optimum code to fix the test; something that is good enough will do fine.

The final stage involves optionally refactoring the code that was written in the second stage while ensuring that you do not break any existing tests.

Don't Write Code You Do Not Yet Need

This practice requires the developer to not write any code that is not needed at the moment. It is tempting to add features to a class anticipating future uses of the class, but a good TDD practitioner must resist this temptation. There may be a user story in the future that could use this code that you want to write now; it is best to write it when you are addressing the specific user story, complete with its own set of tests.

ANATOMY OF A TEST CASE

Previously in this lesson, you learned that unit tests are stored under their own group in the project explorer. The unit being tested is always a `.swift` class file, and all the tests related to that class are grouped in a single test class. A test class is just a Swift class that inherits from `XCTestCase` and can contain five types of methods:

➤ **Setup method:** This method is called `setUp()` and is called before each test method is executed in the test class.

➤ **Teardown method:** This method is called `tearDown()` and is called after each test method is executed in the test class.

➤ **Test methods:** These methods all begin with the word "test." Each method encapsulates a single test.

➤ **Performance testing methods:** These methods all begin with `testPerformance`. Performance testing is outside the scope of this book.

➤ **Other Swift methods:** A test class is a Swift class and can contain any other methods just like any other Swift class. These methods are usually written to support other test methods.

The following code snippet shows what a typical test class looks like:

```swift
import XCTest
@testable import SwiftCalculator

class SwiftCalculatorTests: XCTestCase {

    override func setUp() {
        super.setUp()
        // Put setup code here. This method is called
        // before the invocation of each test method in the class.
    }

    override func tearDown() {
        // Put teardown code here. This method is called
```

```
        // after the invocation of each test method in the class.
        super.tearDown()
    }

    func testExample() {
        // This is an example of a functional test case.
        // Use XCTAssert and related functions to verify your
        // tests produce the correct results.
    }

}
```

To execute all unit tests (in all test classes) in a project, select Product ⇨ Test. Doing so will launch the app on the iOS Simulator or iOS device and execute all methods that begin with the word "test" in each test case sequentially.

It is important to note that only setUp(), teardown(), and methods that begin with test (or test-Performance) will be executed automatically as part of the testing cycle.

The result of the testing phase is visible in the Test Navigator, which can be accessed by selecting View ⇨ Navigators ⇨ Show Test Navigator (see Figure 33-5).

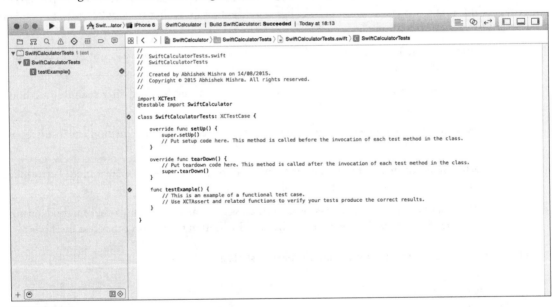

FIGURE 33-5

You will see a green tick box next to each test that has passed and a red one next to each test that has failed. Keep in mind that test code is also code and must be able to compile for the tests to be executed. If your project has compilation errors, you will need to fix these before the tests can run.

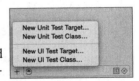

FIGURE 33-6

You can add additional test classes to your project by using the Add button (+) and the new test class command in the Test Navigator (see Figure 33-6).

TEST ASSERTIONS

Assertions are the bread and butter of unit tests. An assertion represents a failure of a unit test. Typically, your unit test will call a method on an object and this method will change some values in your application. The unit test will call the method with known inputs and expect a specific output. If the output from the method being tested does not match the expected value, the test will fail by firing an assertion. The standard unit testing framework in XCode is called XCTest and it provides several macros to help you create assertions. Table 33-1 lists some of the more commonly used macros.

TABLE 33-1: XCTEST ASSERTION MACROS

MACRO	DESCRIPTION
XCTAssert(expression, String)	Generates a failure if the expression evaluates to false. An optional string message may be provided to indicate failure.
XCTAssertEqualObjects(expression1, expression2, String)	Generates a failure when expression1 is not equal to expression2 (or one object is nil and the other is not).
XCTAssertNotEqualObjects(expression1, expression2, String)	Generates a failure when expression1 is equal to expression2.
XCTAssertEqual(expression1, expression2, String)	Generates a failure when expression1 is not equal to expression2. This test is for primitive data types.
XCTAssertNotEqual(expression1, expression2, String)	Generates a failure when expression1 is equal to expression2. This test is for primitive data types.
XCTAssertNil(expression, String)	Generates a failure when the expression is not nil.
XCTAssertNotNil(expression, String)	Generates a failure when the expression is nil.
XCTAssertTrue(expression)	Generates a failure when the expression evaluates to false. Identical to XCTAssert().
XCTAssertFalse(expression)	Generates a failure when the expression evaluates to true.

The following code snippet lists a unit test that will fail using the `XCTAssertEqual` macro:

```
func testNumbersAreEqual() {
        let number1 = 10
        let number2 = 20
        XCTAssertEqual(number1, number2, "number1 and number2 should be equal")
}
```

Figure 33-7 shows the Test Navigator with the failed unit test.

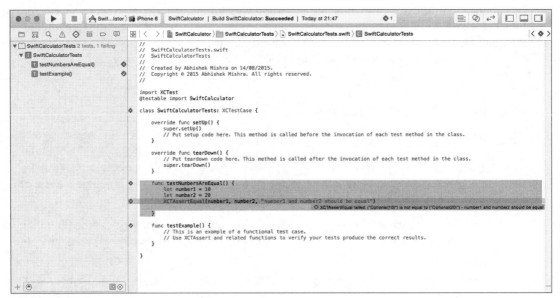

FIGURE 33-7

This test fails because the test expects `number1` and `number2` to have the same value. Fixing it is a simple matter of setting number 2 to 10:

```
func testNumbersAreEqual() {
        let number1 = 10
        let number2 = 10
        XCTAssertEqual(number1, number2, "number1 and number2 should be equal")
}
```

This particular test method does not test any production code. It is only presented to serve as an example of how assertions work. In a real-world scenario, the items being compared will be member variables in classes from your production code base.

A more practical example of TDD techniques is presented in this lesson's Try It, where you build a simple calculator app using TDD techniques.

TRY IT

In this Try It, you build an iPhone application based on the Single View Application template called `SwiftCalculator` that allows the user to perform simple arithmetic operations on a pair of numbers and display the result. You will approach this application with a TDD mindset, writing unit tests and incrementally adding functionality.

Lesson Requirements

➤ Launch Xcode.

➤ Create a new iPhone project based on the Single View Application template with unit test support.

➤ Add two `UILabel` and two `UITextField` instances to the scene with appropriate outlets in the view controller file.

➤ Add four `UIButton` instances to the scene and connect them to appropriate action methods in the view controller class.

➤ Create a class `ArithmeticCalculator` that performs arithmetic operations on two numbers.

➤ Write unit tests for the `ArithmeticCalculator` class.

➤ Connect the `ArithmeticCalculator` class to the action methods of the `UIButton` instances.

➤ Display results in an alert.

> **REFERENCE** *The code for this Try It is available at* www.wrox.com/go/swiftios.

Hints

➤ When creating a new project, you can use your website's domain name as the Company Identifier in the Project Options dialog box.

➤ To include support for unit tests in your project, ensure the Include Unit Tests check box is enabled in the project options dialog box.

➤ To show the Test navigator, select View ➪ Navigators ➪ Show Test Navigator.

➤ To show the Object library, select View ➪ Utilities ➪ Show Object Library.

➤ To show the assistant editor, select View ➪ Assistant Editor ➪ Show Assistant Editor.

Step-by-Step

➤ Create a Single View Application in Xcode called `SwiftCalculator`.

1. Launch Xcode and create a new application by selecting File ➪ New ➪ Project.

2. Select the Single View Application template from the list of iOS project templates.

3. In the project options screen use the following values:

   ➤ **Product Name:** SwiftCalculator

   ➤ **Organization Name:** your company

   ➤ **Organization Identifier:** com.yourcompany

   ➤ **Language:** Swift

   ➤ **Devices:** iPhone

   ➤ **Use Core Data:** Unchecked

   ➤ **Include Unit Tests:** Checked

   ➤ **Include UI Tests:** Unchecked

4. Save the project onto your hard disk.

➤ Add user interface elements to your storyboard's scene.

1. Use the Object library to add two `UILabel` instances, two `UITextField` instances, and four `UIButton` instances to the default scene. Name and position them to resemble Figure 33-8.

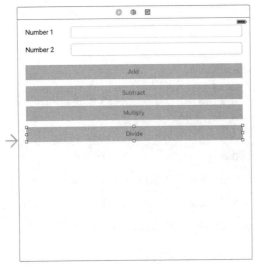

FIGURE 33-8

2. Create layout constraints for each of the elements on the storyboard scene using the information in Table 33-2. When creating layout constraints using the pin constraints

dialog box, ensure the Constrain to margins option is unchecked and the Update Frames combo box is set to None.

TABLE 33-2: Layout Constraints

ELEMENT	LEFT	TOP	RIGHT	WIDTH	HEIGHT
Number 1 (Label)	20	20		92	21
Number 1 (Text field)	28	20	20		30
Number 2 (Label)	20	20		92	21
Number 2 (Text field)	28	14	20		30
Add (Button)	20	22	20		37
Subtract (Button)	20	15	20		37
Multiply (Button)	20	15	20		37
Divide (Button)	20	15	20		37

3. Select the view controller object and update frames by selecting Editor ➪ Resolve Auto Layout Issues ➪ Update Frames.

4. Use the assistant editor to create outlets for each of the text fields in the view controller class. Name the outlets `numberField1` and `numberField2`.

5. Use the assistant editor to create action methods in the view controller class. Name the action methods `onAdd`, `onSubtract`, `onDivide`, and `onMultiply` and connect these methods to the buttons on the scene.

➤ Create Unit Tests and develop the `ArithmeticCalculator` class from the unit tests.

1. Add a new test class to the `SwiftCalculatorTests` group called `ArithmeticCalculatorTests` by selecting File ➪ New ➪ File. Use the Unit Test Case template under the iOS ➪ Source category.

2. Delete the contents of the `ArithmeticCalculatorTests.swift` file and replace it with the following:

```
import XCTest

class ArithmeticCalculatorTests: XCTestCase {

    override func setUp() {
        super.setUp()

    }

    override func tearDown() {

        super.tearDown()
    }
```

```swift
func testInitializerDoesNotReturnNilInstance() {
    XCTAssertNotNil(ArithmeticCalculator())
}
}
```

The preceding code snippet adds a new test method called `testInitializerDoes-NotReturnNilInstance`. This test will fail if an `ArithmeticCalculator` instance could not be instantiated.

3. Run the unit tests by selecting Product ⇨ Test and observe that the product fails to compile. The specific error you will get in this case is "Use of undeclared identifier `'ArithmeticCalculator'`" in the test case class (see Figure 33-9).

FIGURE 33-9

This failure to compile can be thought of as an indication that you need to write some code to rectify the situation and can be used as the starting point for implementing TDD methods in this project.

4. In order to make this first test pass, create a new class called `ArithmeticCalculator` by selecting File ⇨ New ⇨ File. Use the Swift File template under the iOS ⇨ Source category. In the file location dialog box, ensure that the new class will be available to both the `SwiftCalculator` and `SwiftCalculatorTests` targets by ensuring that the corresponding checkboxes beside these items are checked (see Figure 33-10).

5. Replace the contents of `ArithmeticCalculator.swift` with the following empty class definition:

```swift
import Foundation

class ArithmeticCalculator: NSObject {

}
```

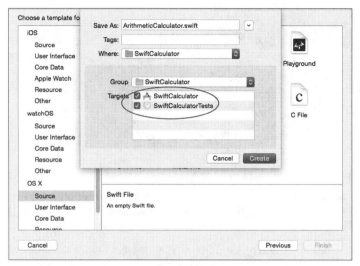

FIGURE 33-10

6. Run the unit tests by selecting Product ⇨ Test once again and observe that the product compiles and all tests pass.

7. The `ArithmeticCalculator` class will end up containing the following methods, each of which accepts two Doubles as input and returns a Double as output:

➤ `addNumbers()`

➤ `subtractNumbrs()`

➤ `divideNumbers()`

➤ `multiplyNumbers()`

The `divideNumbers()` method returns an optional that will be `nil` if the denominator is zero. With this design in mind, you need to work out some of the test cases that could be used to test the behavior of these methods. In order to keep this Try It focused, you will develop unit tests for the following test cases (see Table 33-3). These test cases are by no means exhaustive but should give you a starting point to create some of your own test cases.

TABLE 33-3: Test Cases

METHOD	N1	N2	EXPECTED RESULT
`addNumbers`	10	20	30
`addNumbers`	10	0	10
`subtractNumbers`	20	10	10
`multiplyNumbers`	20	10	200

continues

TABLE 33-3 *(continued)*

METHOD	N1	N2	EXPECTED RESULT
multiplyNumbers	–20	–10	20
divideNumbers	20	10	2
divideNumbers	–20	–10	2
divideNumbers	20	0	nil

8. Add the following unit tests to the `ArithmeticControllerTests.swift` file:

```swift
func testAddNumbers_PositiveN1_PositiveN2_ReturnsValidResult() {
    let calculator:ArithmeticCalculator = ArithmeticCalculator()
    let n1:Double = 10
    let n2:Double = 20
    let result:Double = calculator.addNumbers(firstNumber: n1,
                        secondNumber: n2)
    XCTAssertEqual(result, n1 + n2)
}


func testAddNumbers_PositiveN1_ZeroN2_ReturnsNumber1() {
    let calculator:ArithmeticCalculator = ArithmeticCalculator()
    let n1:Double = 10
    let n2:Double = 0
    let result:Double = calculator.addNumbers(firstNumber: n1
                        secondNumber: n2)
    XCTAssertEqual(result, n1)
}

func testSubtractNumbers_PositiveN1_SmallerPositiveN2_ReturnsValidResult()
{
    let calculator:ArithmeticCalculator = ArithmeticCalculator()
    let n1:Double = 20
    let n2:Double = 10
    let result:Double = calculator.subtractNumbers(firstNumber: n1,
                        secondNumber: n2)
     XCTAssertEqual(result, n1 - n2)
}

func testMultiplyNumbers_PositiveN1_PositiveN2_ReturnsValidResult() {
    let calculator:ArithmeticCalculator = ArithmeticCalculator()
    let n1:Double = 20
    let n2:Double = 10
    let result:Double = calculator.multiplyNumbers(firstNumber: n1,
                        secondNumber: n2)
    XCTAssertEqual(result, n1 * n2)
}

func
testMultiplyNumbers_NegativeeN1_NegativeN2_ReturnsValidPositiveResult() {
    let calculator:ArithmeticCalculator = ArithmeticCalculator()
    let n1:Double = 20
```

```
        let n2:Double = 10
        let result:Double = calculator.multiplyNumbers(firstNumber: n1,
                         secondNumber: n2)
        XCTAssert(result >= 0)
    }


    func testDivideNumbers_PositiveN1_PositiveN2_ReturnsValidResult() {
        let calculator:ArithmeticCalculator = ArithmeticCalculator()
        let n1:Double = 20
        let n2:Double = 10
        let result:Double? = calculator.divideNumbers(numerator: n1,
                         denominator: n2)
        XCTAssertEqual(result!, n1 / n2)
    }

    func testDivideNumbers_NegativeN1_NegativeN2_ReturnsValidPositiveResult() {
        let calculator:ArithmeticCalculator = ArithmeticCalculator()
        let n1:Double = -20
        let n2:Double = -10
        let result:Double? = calculator.divideNumbers(numerator: n1,
                         denominator: n2)
        XCTAssert(result! >= 0)
    }

    func testDivideNumbers_PositiveN1_ZeroN2_ReturnsNil() {
        let calculator:ArithmeticCalculator = ArithmeticCalculator()
        let n1:Double = 20
        let n2:Double = 0
        let result:Double? = calculator.divideNumbers(numerator: n1,
                         denominator: n2)
        XCTAssertNil(result)
    }
```

9. Run the unit tests by selecting Product ➪ Test once again and observe that, once again, the product does not compile. This is because you have not implemented the add Numbers, subtractNumbers, divideNumbers, and multiplyNumbers methods.

10. In order to ensure these new unit tests also pass, update the code in the ArithmeticCalculator.swift file to resemble the following:

```
import Foundation

class ArithmeticCalculator: NSObject {

    func addNumbers(firstNumber number1:Double,
        secondNumber number2:Double) -> Double{

        return number1 + number2
    }

    func subtractNumbers(firstNumber number1:Double,
        secondNumber number2:Double) -> Double{
```

```
        return number1 - number2
    }

    func divideNumbers(numerator number1:Double,
        denominator number2:Double) -> Double? {

        if number2 == 0 {
            return nil
        }

        return number1 / number2
    }

    func multiplyNumbers(firstNumber number1:Double,
        secondNumber number2:Double) -> Double{

        return number1 * number2
    }
}
```

11. Run the unit tests by selecting Product ⇨ Test once again and observe that the product compiles and all tests pass.

➤ Integrate the `ArithmeticCalculator` class into the `ViewController` class.

1. Implement the `onAdd` action method in the `ViewController.swift` file as follows:

```
@IBAction func onAdd(sender: AnyObject) {

    numberField1.resignFirstResponder()
    numberField2.resignFirstResponder()

    let number1:String? = numberField1.text
    let number2:String? = numberField2.text

    if let n1 = number1, n2 = number2 {

        if n1.isEmpty || n2.isEmpty {
            return
        }

        let firstNumber:Double? =
NSNumberFormatter().numberFromString(n1)?.doubleValue

        let secondNumber:Double? =
NSNumberFormatter().numberFromString(n2)?.doubleValue

        if let fN = firstNumber, sN = secondNumber {

            let calculator:ArithmeticCalculator = ArithmeticCalculator()
            let result:Double = calculator.addNumbers(firstNumber: fN,
                        secondNumber: sN)

            let alert = UIAlertController(title: "",
                    message: "\(fN) + \(sN) = \(result)",
                    preferredStyle: UIAlertControllerStyle.Alert)

            alert.addAction(UIAlertAction(title: "Ok",
```

```
            style: UIAlertActionStyle.Default,
        handler: nil))

            self.presentViewController(alert, animated: true,
        completion: nil)
            }
        }
    }
```

2. Implement the `onSubtract` action method in the `ViewController.swift` file as follows:

```
@IBAction func onSubtract(sender: AnyObject) {

    numberField1.resignFirstResponder()
    numberField2.resignFirstResponder()

    let number1:String? = numberField1.text
    let number2:String? = numberField2.text

    if let n1 = number1, n2 = number2 {

        if n1.isEmpty || n2.isEmpty {
            return
        }

        let firstNumber:Double? =
NSNumberFormatter().numberFromString(n1)?.doubleValue

        let secondNumber:Double? =
NSNumberFormatter().numberFromString(n2)?.doubleValue

        if let fN = firstNumber, sN = secondNumber {

            let calculator:ArithmeticCalculator = ArithmeticCalculator()
            let result:Double = calculator.subtractNumbers(firstNumber: fN,
        secondNumber: sN)

            let alert = UIAlertController(title: "",
                message: "\(fN) - \(sN) = \(result)",
                preferredStyle: UIAlertControllerStyle.Alert)

            alert.addAction(UIAlertAction(title: "Ok",
        style: UIAlertActionStyle.Default, handler: nil))

            self.presentViewController(alert, animated: true,
        completion: nil)
        }
    }

}
```

3. Implement the `onDivide` action method in the `ViewController.swift` file as follows:

```
@IBAction func onDivide(sender: AnyObject) {

    numberField1.resignFirstResponder()
```

```
        numberField2.resignFirstResponder()

    let number1:String? = numberField1.text
    let number2:String? = numberField2.text

    if let n1 = number1, n2 = number2 {

        if n1.isEmpty || n2.isEmpty {
            return
        }

        let firstNumber:Double? =
NSNumberFormatter().numberFromString(n1)?.doubleValue

        let secondNumber:Double? =
NSNumberFormatter().numberFromString(n2)?.doubleValue

        if let fN = firstNumber, sN = secondNumber {

            let calculator:ArithmeticCalculator = ArithmeticCalculator()
            let result:Double! = calculator.divideNumbers(numerator: fN,
                            denominator: sN)

            if result == nil {

                let alert = UIAlertController(title: "Error",
                    message: "Division by Zero",
                    preferredStyle: UIAlertControllerStyle.Alert)

                alert.addAction(UIAlertAction(title: "Ok",
    style: UIAlertActionStyle.Default, handler: nil))

                self.presentViewController(alert, animated: true,
    completion: nil)
            }
            else
            {
                let alert = UIAlertController(title: "",
                    message: "\(fN) / \(sN) = \(result!)",
                    preferredStyle: UIAlertControllerStyle.Alert)

                alert.addAction(UIAlertAction(title: "Ok",
    style: UIAlertActionStyle.Default, handler: nil))

                self.presentViewController(alert, animated: true,
        completion: nil)
            }
        }
    }
}
```

4. Implement the `onMultiply` action method in the `ViewController.swift` file as
    follows:

```
@IBAction func onMultiply(sender: AnyObject) {

    numberField1.resignFirstResponder()
```

```
                numberField2.resignFirstResponder()

            let number1:String? = numberField1.text
            let number2:String? = numberField2.text

            if let n1 = number1, n2 = number2 {

                if n1.isEmpty || n2.isEmpty {
                    return
                }

                let firstNumber:Double? =
        NSNumberFormatter().numberFromString(n1)?.doubleValue

                let secondNumber:Double? =
        NSNumberFormatter().numberFromString(n2)?.doubleValue

                if let fN = firstNumber, sN = secondNumber {

                    let calculator:ArithmeticCalculator = ArithmeticCalculator()
                    let result:Double = calculator.multiplyNumbers(firstNumber: fN,
                secondNumber: sN)

                    let alert = UIAlertController(title: "",
                        message: "\(fN) * \(sN) = \(result)",
                        preferredStyle: UIAlertControllerStyle.Alert)

                    alert.addAction(UIAlertAction(title: "Ok",
                                style: UIAlertActionStyle.Default,
                                handler: nil))

                self.presentViewController(alert, animated: true, completion: nil)
                }
            }

        }
```

➤ Test your app in the iOS Simulator. Click the Run button in the Xcode toolbar. Alternatively, you can select Project ⇨ Run.

REFERENCE *To see some of the examples from this lesson, watch the Lesson 33 video online at* www.wrox.com/go/swiftiosvid.

SECTION V
Reference

- ▶ **APPENDIX A:** Testing Your App on a Device

- ▶ **APPENDIX B:** Beta Testing with TestFlight

- ▶ **APPENDIX C:** App Store Distribution

Testing Your App on a Device

The iOS Simulator is a handy tool for testing your application as you are developing it. However, it is no substitute for testing on an actual device. Certain features, such as the accelerometer and camera, cannot be tested on the simulator at all.

Testing your application on your device is slightly different from giving it to a small number of users for beta testing. When it is your own device, you can physically connect it to your Mac and use Xcode to test/debug your app while it executes on the device. Distributing your app to a few users for beta testing is achieved through TestFlight, a process covered in detail in Appendix B.

Before you can test your app on a device, you need to prepare the device for testing and configure a few options in Xcode. The process itself can seem quite complicated at first. This appendix goes through the various steps required to test your apps on a device with Xcode.

OBTAINING AND REGISTERING UDIDS

Each iOS device has a unique 40-digit identifier, commonly referred to as the device UDID. Before you can test your app on a device with Xcode, you will need to register the UDID of that device with the iOS Provisioning Portal. You can obtain this UDID through the Xcode Device Manager.

To obtain the UDID for a device, simply connect it to your Mac and access the Devices Manager by selecting Window ➪ Devices. Click the device in the list on the left-hand side and note the value of the Identifier field (see Figure A-1).

FIGURE A-1

To register a device for development, simply click the Use for Development button in the Devices Manager window. You will be asked to provide the Apple ID and password you used to register as an iOS developer. If the device has already been set up for development, then the Use for Development button will not be visible.

You can also register UDIDs manually. To do this, you must log in to your iOS developer account at `https://developer.apple.com/ios`. Click the Member Center link on the top-right corner of the page to navigate to the member center. Within the member center, click the Certificates, Identifiers & Profiles link (see Figure A-2).

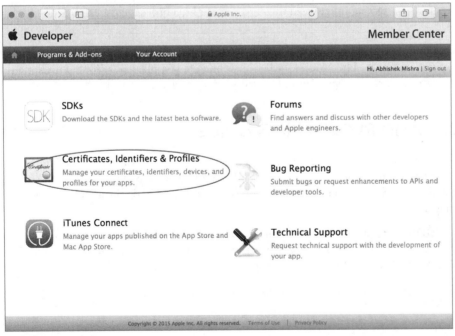

FIGURE A-2

Next, click the Devices link in the iOS Apps category on the left-hand side of the page (see Figure A-3).

FIGURE A-3

The Devices screen shows you a list of devices registered to your account. You can register up to 100 devices of each type a year (note that deleting a device does not count toward this limit). There are five device types:

➤ iPhone

➤ iPad

➤ iPod Touch

➤ Apple Watch

➤ Apple TV

To add a device to your account, click the Add button located above the list of devices and fill in the UDID of the device along with a name with which you would like to refer to the device (see Figure A-4). Click Continue to add the UDID to the device list. This list can be reset once a year, when you renew your paid membership.

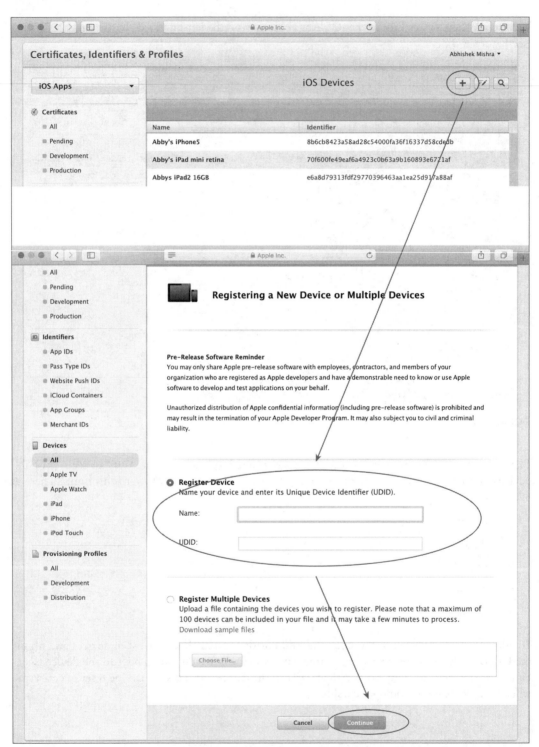

FIGURE A-4

CREATING AN APP ID (BUNDLE IDENTIFIER)

The next step involves creating and registering a unique identifier for your app; this is known as the App ID (or Bundle ID). In addition to uniquely identifying your application, an App ID allows your application to receive remote notifications, communicate with external accessories, or share keychain data with other applications in a suite, and use iCloud services.

An App ID consists of an organization identifier and an application identifier (see Figure A-5). When you create a new project in Xcode, you are asked to provide an organization identifier, and the App ID is generated for you by appending the name of the project to the organization identifier. To distribute the application through the App Store, the identifier used to create the Xcode project must be registered with your iOS developer account. You can always change the Bundle Identifier for an existing application by editing the Bundle Identifier key in the project's `info.plist` file.

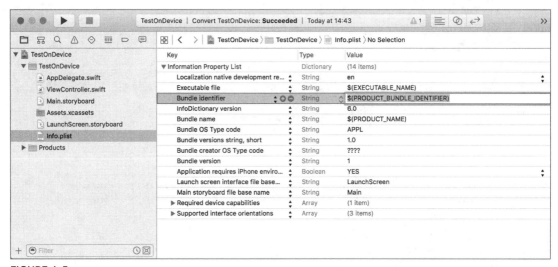

FIGURE A-5

To create an appropriate App ID, log in to your iOS developer account at `https://developer` `.apple.com/ios`. Click the Member Center link in the top-right corner of the page to navigate to the member center. Within the member center, click the Certificates, Identifiers & Profiles link, and then in the Identifiers section under the iOS Apps category click on the link to App IDs.

To create a new App ID, click the New App ID button on the top-right side (see Figure A-6).

Provide a descriptive name for the new App ID in the Name field and select Team ID in the App ID prefix drop-down. Select the Explicit App ID radio button under the App ID suffix section and provide a unique identifier in the Bundle ID field that ends in the name of the Xcode project you are going to create (or have created).

Typically, you create this identifier by combining the reverse-domain name of your website and the name of your Xcode project. For example, if your company identifier is com.acmecorp and your Xcode project is called `cloudkitphotos`, then the bundle identifier specified should resemble `com` `.acmecorp.cloudkitphotos`. Your browser window should resemble Figure A-7.

FIGURE A-6

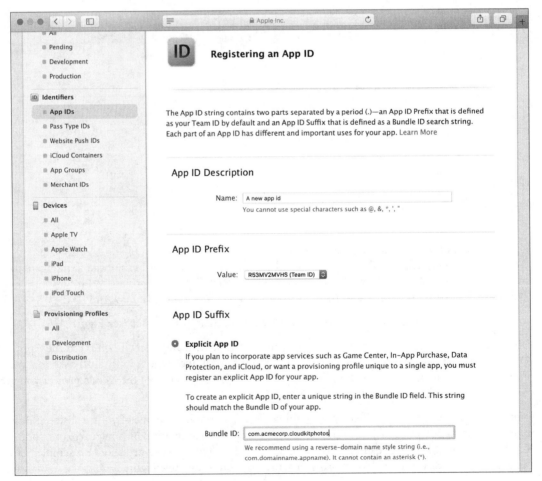

FIGURE A-7

If you do not mind your apps sharing data between them, you can use an asterisk instead of the application name, thus creating a string of the form `com.domainname.*`.

Such an App ID is called a *wildcard* App ID and can be used repeatedly across multiple applications. If you want to create a wildcard App ID, simply select the relevant radio button on the page (see Figure A-8).

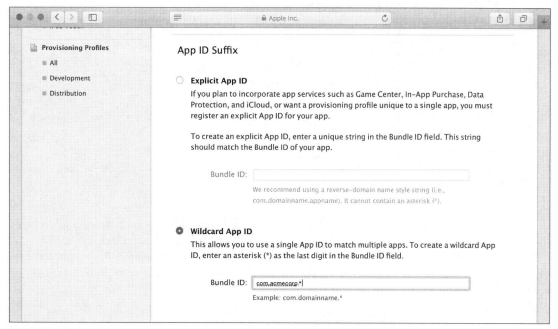

FIGURE A-8

The downside of wildcard App IDs is that certain features such as Remote Push Notifications and iCloud support are not available.

Click the Continue button to proceed. You will be presented with a summary of the App ID information. Click on Submit to finish creating the App ID.

CREATING A DEVELOPMENT CERTIFICATE

The next step is to create and install a development certificate. Creating a development certificate involves creating an appropriate certificate request and submitting this request to the iOS Provisioning Portal. Once the certificate is ready, you will be able to download and install it on your Mac.

To create a certificate request, launch the Keychain Access utility from the `Applications` folder on your Mac. When the Keychain Access utility is running, choose Keychain Access ➪ Certificate Assistant ➪ Request a Certificate from a Certificate Authority.

In the Certificate Assistant dialog box (see Figure A-9), specify the e-mail address and account name used to access the iOS Developer Program, and ensure the Saved to Disk radio button is selected. Click the Continue button to save the certificate request as a file on your Mac.

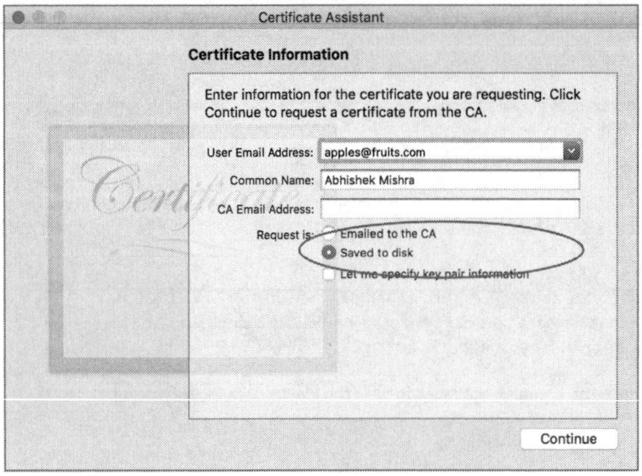

FIGURE A-9

To create a development certificate from your certificate request file, log in to your iOS developer account at `https://developer.apple.com/ios`. Click the Member Center link on the top-right corner of the page to navigate to the member center. Within the member center, click the Certificates, Identifiers & Profiles link, and then under the iOS Apps category, look under the Certificates category and click on All.

To create a new development certificate, click the Add button (+) on the top-right side (see Figure A-10).

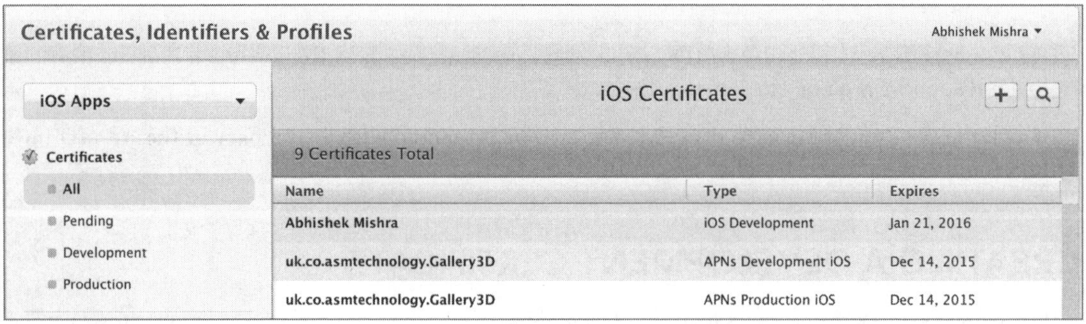

FIGURE A-10

You will now be asked to choose the type of certificate you want to create. Select iOS App Development from the list of options (see Figure A-11), scroll down to the bottom of the page, and click Continue.

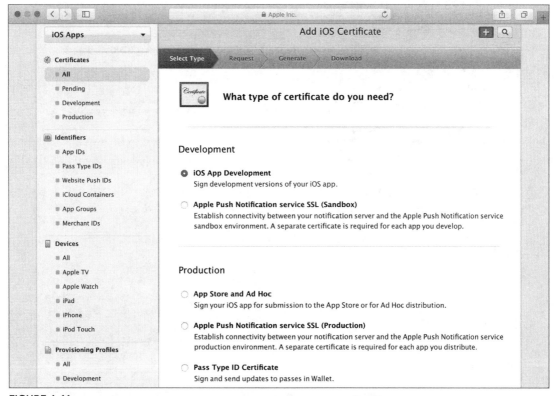

FIGURE A-11

The next screen contains some general information on what a certificate request file is and how to create one (see Figure A-12). Because you have already created one, scroll to the bottom of the page and click Continue.

In the next screen, use the Choose File button to select the certificate request file that you saved on your Mac and then click the Generate button to create the development certificate (see Figure A-13).

If you are not part of a team, and are solely responsible for handling your iOS Developer account, your certificate is issued automatically and available to download in a few minutes. You may need to refresh your browser window. If you are part of a team, your team manager will need to first approve the certificate request. When your certificate is ready to download, you will see its status listed as Issued, and a Download link will be available.

Download the certificate and save it to your Mac; by default, the certificate should be saved to your `Downloads` folder.

If you haven't done so already, download the Worldwide Developer Relations Certificate from the Apple PKI authority page (see Figure A-14). This page is located at `https://www.apple.com/certificateauthority/`.

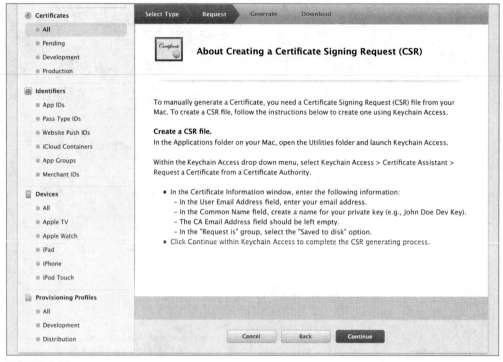

FIGURE A-12

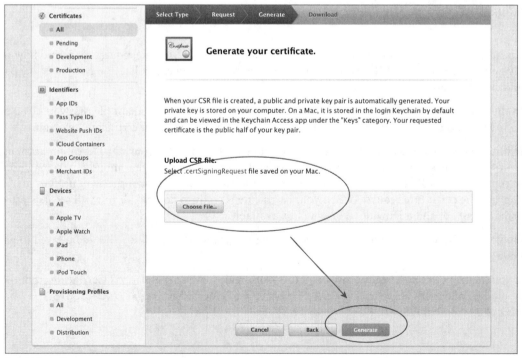

FIGURE A-13

This certificate is also available to download at the bottom of the Create Certificate page, where you select the type of certificate to generate (Figure A-15).

FIGURE A-14

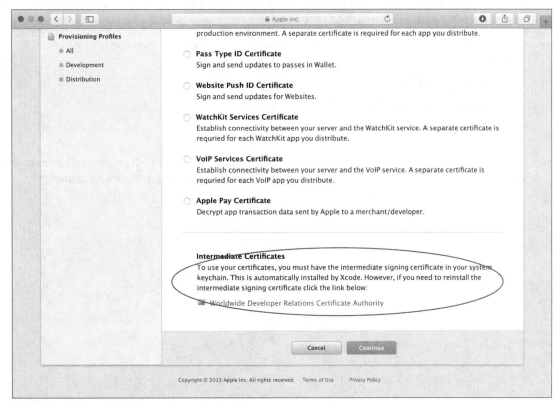

FIGURE A-15

CREATING A PROVISIONING PROFILE

After having registered your device UDID, App ID, and creating a development certificate, you will need to create a development provisioning profile. A provisioning profile groups an App ID, a certificate, and device UDIDs into a single entity. The certificate in question would be the development certificate you just generated in the previous section, and the device-specific information would be a list of UDIDs on which you want to debug your application.

To create a development provisioning profile, log in to your iOS developer account at `https://developer.apple.com/ios`. Click the Member Center link on the top-right corner of the page to navigate to the member center. Within the member center, click the Certificates, Identifiers & Profiles link, and then under the iOS Apps category, find Provisioning Profiles and click All.

Click the New Profile button on the top-right side (see Figure A-16).

FIGURE A-16

You will be asked to choose between a development or a distribution provisioning profile. A distribution provisioning profile is used to submit applications to iTunes Connect. For the moment, select the iOS App Development option and click Continue (see Figure A-17).

As mentioned earlier in this section, a development provisioning profile connects three pieces of information:

➤   A single App ID

➤   One or more public keys

➤   A list of test device IDs

The next step requires you to select an App ID that will be associated with this provisioning profile. Select an App ID from the list of available identifiers (see Figure A-18) and click Continue.

Select one or more development certificates that will be included in the profile. You must make sure to sign the app in Xcode using one of the certificates you select here. Select a suitable certificate and click Continue (see Figure A-19).

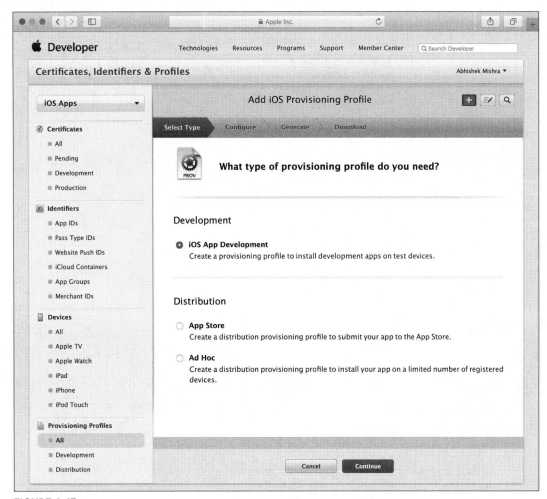

FIGURE A-17

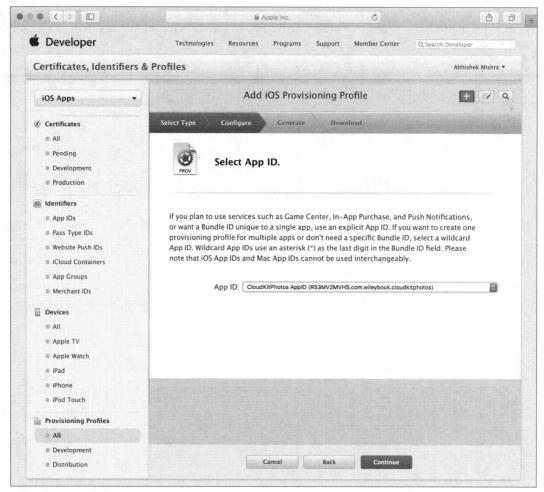

FIGURE A-18

Next, you must select one or more devices that will be included in this provisioning profile. The corresponding identifiers for these devices must be registered with your development account. Your app will only be testable on these devices (see Figure A-20).

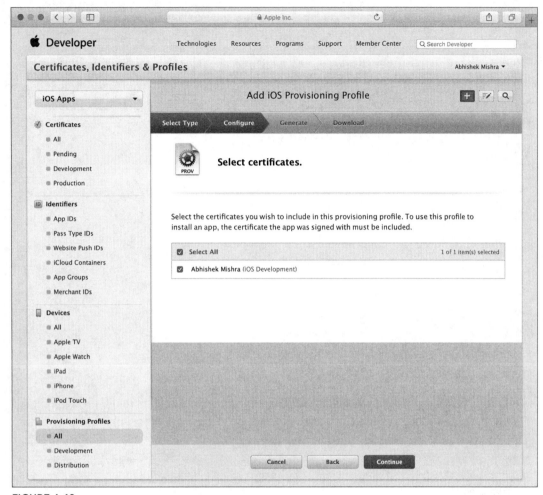

FIGURE A-19

The final step involves providing a suitable name for the profile and clicking the Generate button. When the profile is created, you will be provided an option to download it onto your computer. (see Figure A-21).

FIGURE A-20

If you were to now click the All link under the Provisioning section of the left-hand side menu, you should see an entry for the new profile in the list of available profiles. You can also download a provisioning profile from this list.

Once the profile has been downloaded, simply locate it in the Downloads folder on your Mac and double-click it to install it in Xcode.

FIGURE A-21

CONFIGURING YOUR PROJECT

The final step in the process involves setting up your Xcode project and preparing an appropriate build. Before you begin, make sure you have installed both your development certificate and development provisioning profile.

Open the project that you want to test on a device. If the project's App ID is different from what has been registered with the iOS Provisioning Portal, edit the value of the Bundle identifier key in the project's `info.plist` file to match.

Save the `info.plist` file if you have edited it, and then connect one of the provisioned iOS devices to your Mac and ensure that the Scheme/Target selector in the Xcode toolbar is set to build for an iOS device (see Figure A-22).

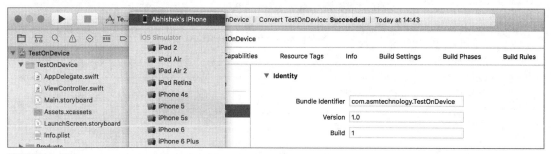

FIGURE A-22

Access the project's properties by selecting the root project node in the project navigator. Select the build target and then switch to the Build Settings tab.

Scroll down to the Code Signing section and locate the node labeled Provisioning Profile. You may need to expand this node to see the values for individual build configurations (such as debug, release). Select the provisioning profile you created earlier from the list of profiles for the debug configuration (see Figure A-23).

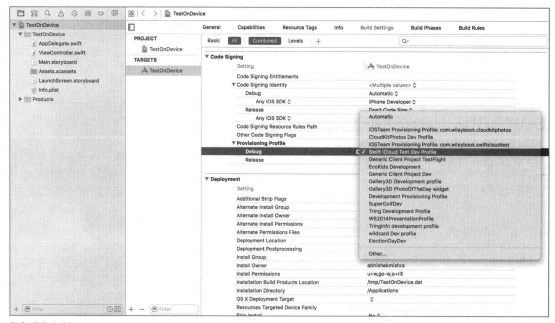

FIGURE A-23

Now look for a node called Code Signing Identity. Expand this node to reveal a node called Debug, and then expand the Debug node to reveal a node called Any iOS SDK. Ensure the value of this node is set to be the development certificate you created and installed earlier (see Figure A-24).

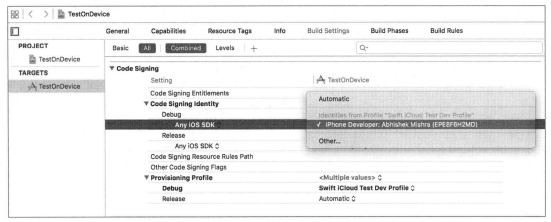

FIGURE A-24

Your Xcode project is now ready to be tested on an iOS device. Simply click the Run button on the Xcode toolbar to begin.

Beta Testing with TestFlight

As an iOS application developer, there will be times when you need to try out your app on multiple test devices before submitting it to Apple for the App Store approval process.

If the number of test devices are few and you are the only person doing all the testing, then you can always set up the devices for development and use Xcode to debug applications on the devices.

However, in most cases, you will have a team of beta testers and product owners, each with their own devices. Connecting each team member's device to your Mac one by one and deploying debug builds with Xcode is simply not feasible anymore. Add to this the fact that you will need to repeat the entire deployment process every time a bug is fixed and your app needs retesting.

TestFlight is a service provided by Apple that acts as a central build deployment solution where you upload the new build, and all interested parties are sent notifications to download the new build onto their devices. TestFlight is available to apps that target iOS8 or later.

PREPARING A DISTRIBUTION BUILD FOR TESTFLIGHT

To distribute your app to testers, you will first need to prepare a suitable build and upload it to iTunes Connect using Xcode. In order to prepare the build, you will need the following:

➤ An App ID that is registered with your iOS developer account

➤ A distribution certificate installed on your Mac

➤ A distribution provisioning profile installed on your Mac

➤ An iTunes Connect record for the application

➤ An appropriately configured Xcode project

Creating an App ID

An App ID is a unique identifier that is used internally by Apple to identify your app in the App store. The process of creating an App ID (also known as a Bundle ID) is covered in Appendix A.

Creating a Distribution Certificate

Creating a distribution certificate is similar to creating a development certificate and involves creating an appropriate certificate request and submitting this request to the iOS Provisioning Portal. Once the certificate is ready, you will be able to download and install it on your Mac.

To create a certificate request, launch the Keychain Access utility from the `Applications` folder on your Mac. When the Keychain Access utility is running, choose Keychain Access ⇨ Certificate Assistant ⇨ Request a Certificate from a Certificate Authority.

In the Certificate Assistant dialog box (see Figure B-1), specify the e-mail address and account name used to access the iOS Developer Program, and ensure the Saved to Disk radio button is selected. Click the Continue button to save the certificate request as a file on your Mac.

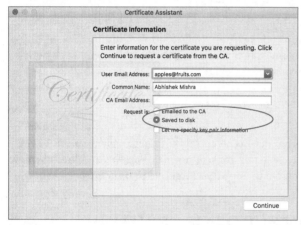

FIGURE B-1

To create a distribution certificate from your certificate request file, log in to your iOS developer account at `https://developer.apple.com/ios`, navigate to the Certificates link under the Member Center ⇨ Certificates, Identifiers & Profiles ⇨ iOS Apps category, and click the New Certificate button on the top-right side (see Figure B-2).

You will now be asked to choose the type of certificate you want to create. Select App Store and Ad Hoc from the list of options in the Production category (see Figure B-3).

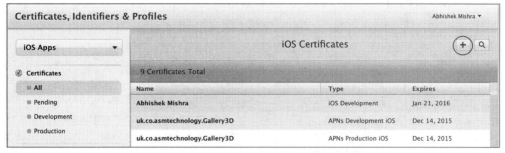

FIGURE B-2

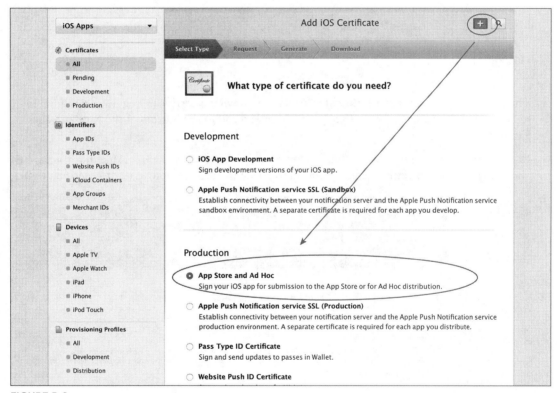

FIGURE B-3

Scroll down to the bottom of the page and use the link provided to download the Intermediate Certificate (see Figure B-4) and click Continue. The intermediate certificate is used to validate your distribution certificate and must be present in your Mac's keychain in addition to the distribution certificate.

FIGURE B-4

The next screen contains some general information on what a certificate request file is and how to create one. Because you have already created one, scroll to the bottom of the page and click Continue.

In the next screen, use the Choose File button to select the certificate request file that you saved on your Mac and then click the Generate button to create the distribution certificate (see Figure B-5).

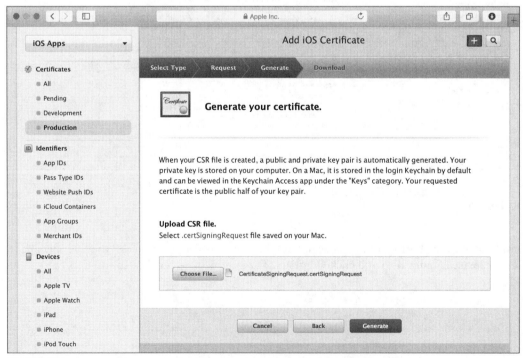

FIGURE B-5

If you are not part of a team, and are solely responsible for handling your iOS Developer account, your certificate is issued automatically and available to download in a few minutes. You may need to refresh your browser window. If you are part of a team, your team manager will need to first approve the certificate request. When your certificate is ready to download, you will see its status listed as Issued, and a Download link will be available.

Download the certificate and save it to your Mac. By default, the certificate should be saved to your `Downloads` folder.

Creating a Distribution Provisioning Profile

To create a distribution provisioning profile, log in to your iOS developer account at `https://developer.apple.com/ios`, navigate to the Provisioning Profiles link under the Member Center ⇨ Certificates, Identifiers & Profiles ⇨ iOS Apps category, and click the New Profile button on the top-right side (see Figure B-6).

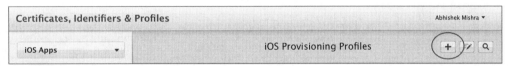

FIGURE B-6

You will now be asked to choose the type of profile you want to create. Select App Store from the list of options under the Distribution category (see Figure B-7) and click Continue.

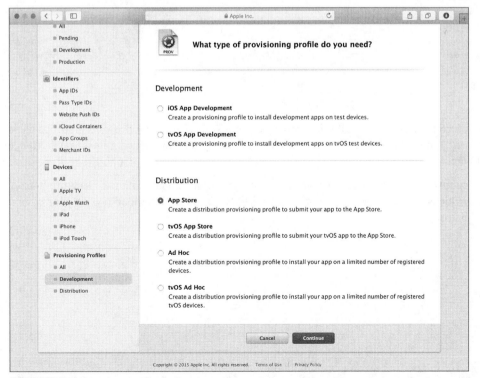

FIGURE B-7

The next step requires you to select an App ID that will be associated with this provisioning profile. Select an App ID from the list of available identifiers (see Figure B-8) and click Continue.

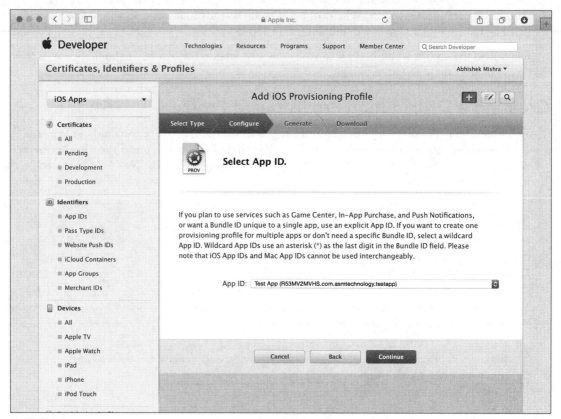

FIGURE B-8

On the next screen, select the distribution certificate that you created in a previous step and click Continue (see Figure B-9). You must make sure to sign the app in Xcode using the same certificate you select here.

The final step involves providing a suitable name for the profile and clicking the Generate button. When the profile is created, you will be provided with an option to download it onto your computer (see Figure B-10).

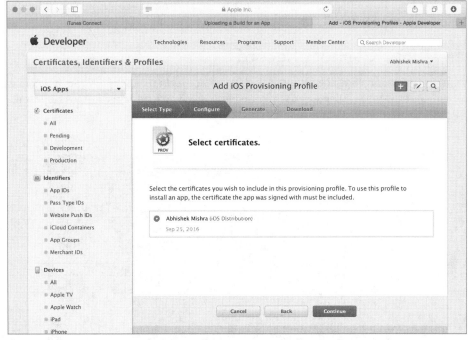

FIGURE B-9

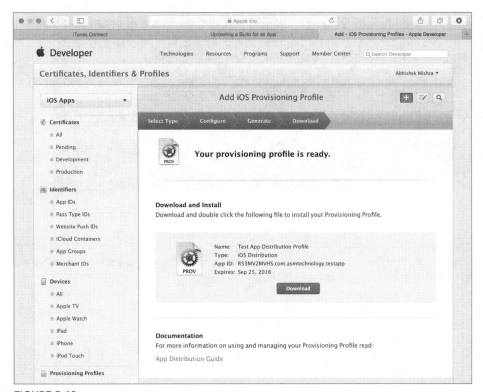

FIGURE B-10

Once the profile has been downloaded, simply locate it in the Downloads folder on your Mac and double-click it to install it in Xcode.

Creating an iTunes Connect Record

To create an iTunes Connect record, log in to the iTunes Connect portal at `https://itunesconnect.apple.com/` with your iOS developer account credentials. Once you have logged in to the portal, click the My Apps link (see Figure B-11).

FIGURE B-11

On this screen, you will see all your iOS and MacOS applications. You can either add a new application or manage one of the existing ones. To create a new application profile, click the Add New App button in the top-left corner of the window (see Figure B-12).

FIGURE B-12

When you select the New App option, a popup window appears. You'll need to enter some basic information on your new app, including the name, Bundle ID, and version number (see Figure B-13).

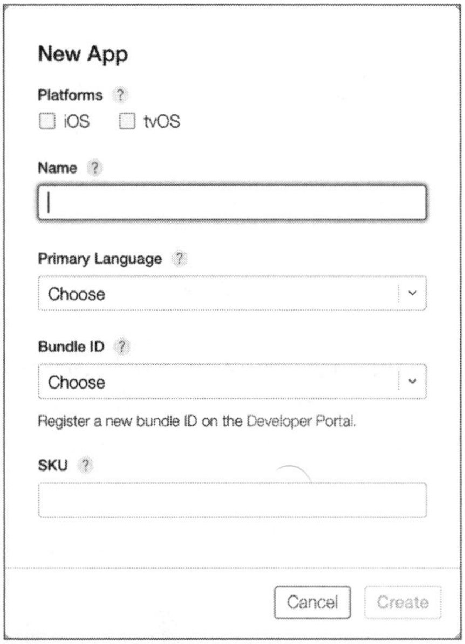

FIGURE B-13

The Bundle ID (also known as an App ID) must be registered with your iOS developer account. If you haven't created an App ID, you will need to do so now, before you can proceed with the next steps. Once you have filled in the fields in the popup window, click Create to go to the Application Information screen (see Figure B-14).

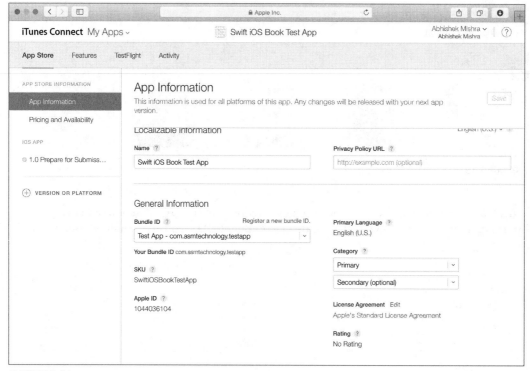

FIGURE B-14

At the top of the page is a tabbed menu bar (see Figure B-15) with four tabs: App Store, Features, TestFlight, and Activity.

FIGURE B-15

The App Store tab is selected by default, and the new application's status is displayed on the left side of the screen. A new application profile starts out in the Prepare For Submission state. You then fill in all the relevant information to complete the application profile and click on the Save button to save this information (see Figure B-16).

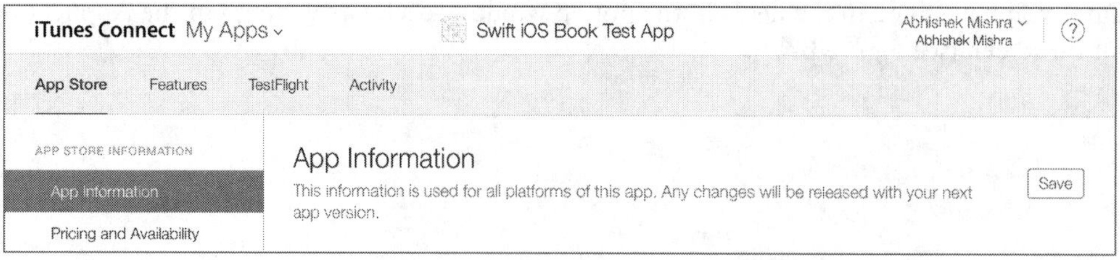

FIGURE B-16

Creating an iTunes Connect record for an application requires that you fill in several screens of information, select pricing and distribution information, configure app rating, and upload screenshots. If your aim is to just distribute the app to beta testers (and not release to the app store just yet), you can get away with filling in very little information at this stage.

If your testers are all internal testers, then you do not need to add any metadata beyond creating a barebones application record, which you have just done by following the steps in this section so far.

If your test team involves external testers, then you only need to supply a small subset of information to begin testing with TestFlight. You will, however, need to create a complete application record before you can submit the app to the App Store. Submitting applications to the App Store is covered in Appendix C.

The subset of information you need to provide in order to begin using TestFlight with external testers is located on the App Store tab.

The screen accessed via the App Store tab has a menu on the left side that provides the following options:

➤ App Information

➤ Pricing and Availability

➤ Versions

App Information

On this screen, you need to specify basic information on the app, including an application name, a SKU code, and an application Bundle ID. The Bundle ID you specify on this screen must match the one have used in your Xcode project's `info.plist` file.

The SKU code is not used by Apple, but is used to identify the application on the monthly financial report provided by Apple.

Toward the bottom-right corner of the screen, you will find options to select a Primary and Secondary Category under which your app will be listed in the App Store (see Figure B-17).

Pricing and Availability

You do not need to fill out this section for beta testing with TestFlight.

Versions

This section enables you to provide screenshots and videos, and to configure application metadata for each version of your app. A node in the left-hand side menu represents each version (see Figure B-18).

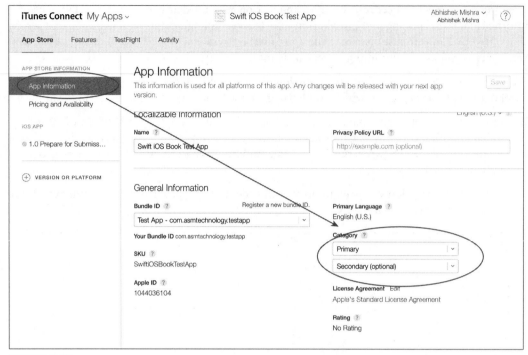

FIGURE B-17

FIGURE B-18

The options in this screen are grouped into several subsections:

➤ Version Information

➤ Apple Watch

➤ Build

➤ General App Information

➤ Game Center

➤ App Review Information

➤ Version Release

Version Information

The Version Information section is shown in Figure B-19. Here you need to specify the following information:

➤ **Screenshots:** You do not need to provide screenshots for beta testing with TestFlight.

➤ **Description:** This is the description, as you want it to appear on the App Store. It can be no more than 4,000 characters.

➤ **Keywords:** One or more keywords that describe the app you are adding. When users search the App Store, the terms they enter are matched with these keywords.

➤ **Support URL:** A URL that links to the application's support site.

➤ **Marketing URL:** An optional URL that links to the application's website.

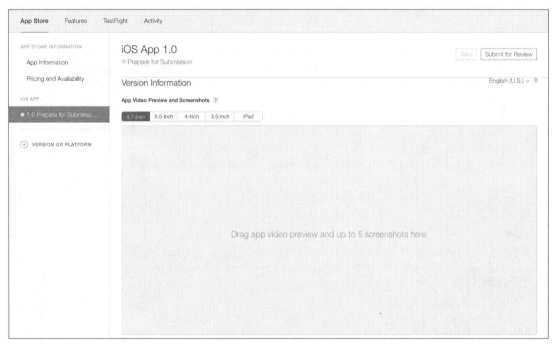

FIGURE B-19

Apple Watch

The Apple Watch section contains options that allow you to upload screenshots and an icon for your Apple Watch app (see Figure B-20). Creating Apple Watch apps is beyond the scope of this book. If you are interested, you should read the Apple Watch Programming Guide at `https://developer.apple.com/library/prerelease/ios/documentation/General/Conceptual/WatchKitProgrammingGuide/`.

FIGURE B-20

Build

The Build section contains the application binary that has been uploaded for the current application version. If no binary has been uploaded, this section is empty (see Figure B-21). The process of uploading an application binary to iTunes Connect with Xcode is covered later in this appendix.

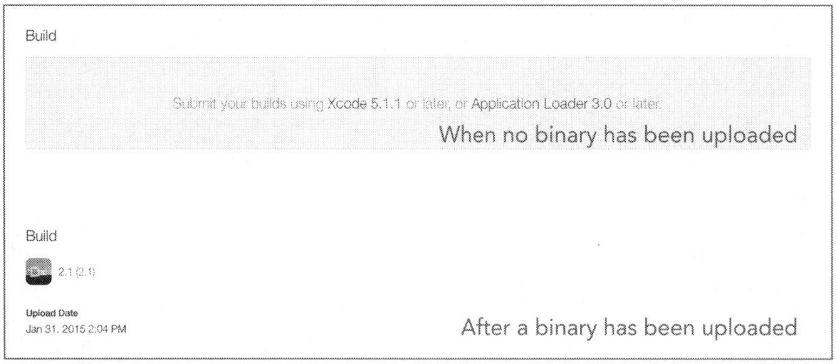

FIGURE B-21

General App Information

The general app information section resembles Figure B-22. Here you need to specify the following information:

➤ **App Icon:** The icon that will be used on the App store. This icon must be 1024 x 1024 in the JPEG or PNG format and must not have rounded corners.

➤ **Version:** This must match the value set in the Xcode project.

➤ **Copyright:** The name of the person or entity that owns the copyright to the app.

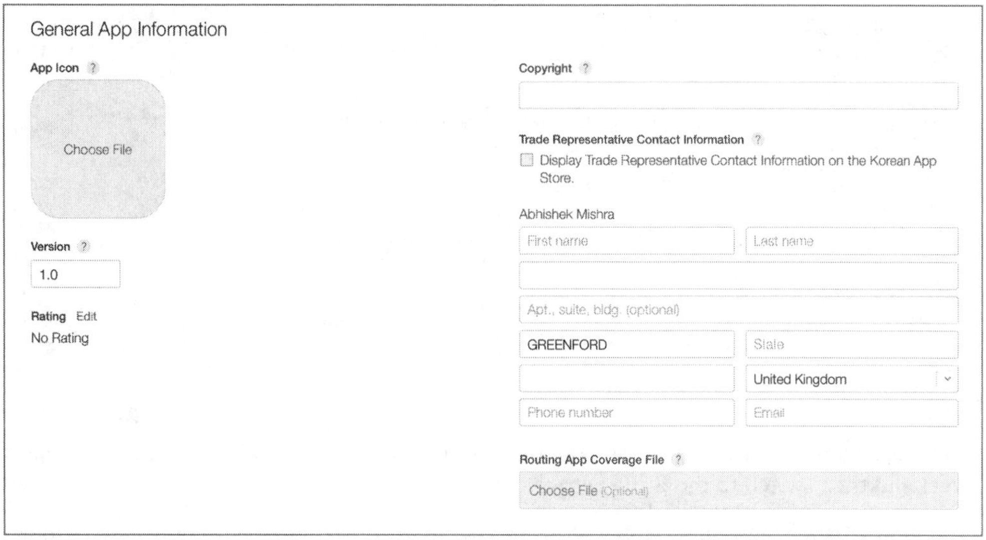

FIGURE B-22

Game Center

The Game Center section is disabled by default and should be enabled for applications that support Game Center. When enabled, you will have options to configure leader boards, achievements, and multiplayer compatibility. A detailed discussion of Game Center is beyond the scope of this book. If you are interested, you should read the Game Center Programming Guide at `https://developer`
`.apple.com/library/ios/documentation/NetworkingInternet/Conceptual/GameKit_Guide/`
`Introduction/Introduction.html`.

App Review

The App Review section allows you to provide special testing instructions to Apple engineers when they review your app, as well as contact information for a person in your company who will be contacted if there are problems with your app.

Configuring Your Xcode Project

The next step in the process involves setting up your Xcode project and submitting a build to iTunes Connect. Before you begin, make sure you have installed both your distribution certificate and distribution provisioning profile.

Open the project that you want to submit in Xcode. If the project's App ID is different from what has been registered with the iOS Provisioning Portal, edit the value of the Bundle identifier key in the project's `info.plist` file to match.

Save the `info.plist` file. Disconnect any connected devices, and ensure that the Scheme/Target selector in the Xcode toolbar is set to build for a generic iOS device (see Figure B-23).

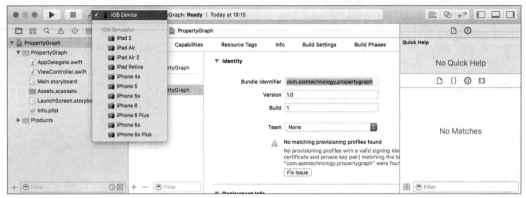

FIGURE B-23

Access the project's properties by selecting the root project node in the project navigator. Select the build target and then switch to the Build Settings tab.

Scroll down to the Code Signing section and locate the node labeled Provisioning Profile. You may need to expand this node to see the values for individual build configurations (such as Debug, Release). Select the provisioning profile you created earlier from the list of profiles for the release configuration (see Figure B-24).

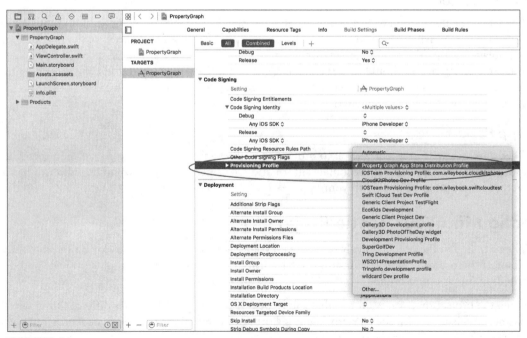

FIGURE B-24

Now look for a node called Code Signing Identity. Expand this node to reveal a node called Release, and then expand the Release node to reveal a node called Any iOS SDK. Ensure the value of this node is set to be the distribution certificate you created and installed earlier (see Figure B-25).

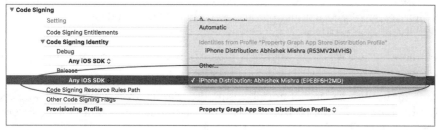

FIGURE B-25

Select the Edit Scheme menu from the Scheme/Target multi-selector in the Xcode toolbar (see Figure B-26).

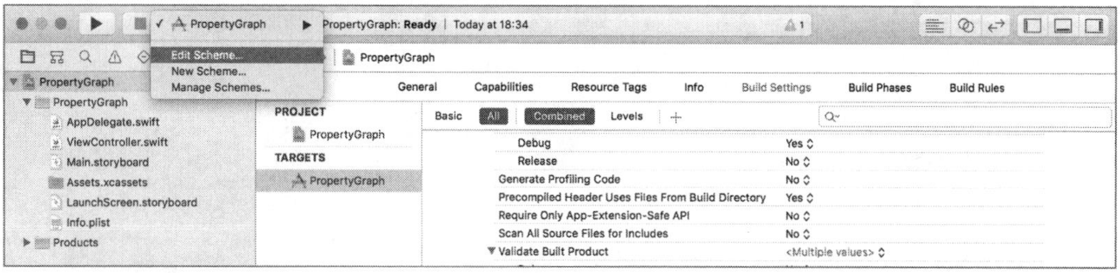

FIGURE B-26

In the Edit Scheme dialog box, select Archive from the left menu to bring up archive-specific options. Ensure the Reveal Archive in Organizer option is checked and the Build Configuration is set to Release (see Figure B-27). Click OK to dismiss this dialog.

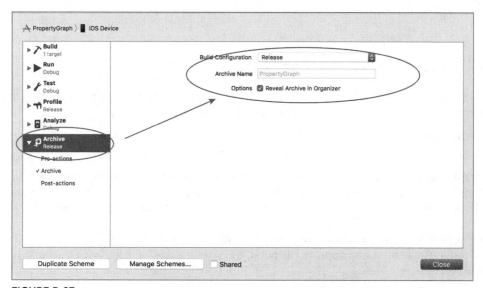

FIGURE B-27

Uploading a Build to iTunes Connect

If you have followed all the steps so far, you are ready to prepare an archive that can be distributed to your clients/beta testers. To prepare an archive, simply select Product ➪ Archive in Xcode. This builds your project for App Store distribution. During the build process, Xcode may ask you to allow access to your distribution certificate.

If it does, click the Allow button. When the archive is successfully built, the Organizer opens automatically, revealing the archive.

To submit the archive to the iTunes Connect portal, ensure the relevant archive is selected, and click the Upload to App Store button. The Organizer will ask you for your iTunes Connect login credentials, and upload the archive to iTunes Connect (see Figure B-28).

FIGURE B-28

INTERNAL AND EXTERNAL TESTERS

With TestFlight you can distribute prerelease builds of your app to your beta test team. TestFlight requires that members in your beta test team be part of one of two groups:

> **Internal testers:** These are individuals who are part of your iTunes Connect team with the Admin, Legal, or Technical role. You can invite up to 25 internal testers per app.

> **External testers:** These are individuals who are not part of your iTunes Connect team. They do not need to be in your organization. In fact, you can invite any user with an e-mail address to be an external tester. The maximum number of external testers per app is 1,000.

Another key difference between internal and external testers is that in order to distribute a build to an external tester, Apple must first approve the build. This is not a requirement when the build is being distributed to internal testers.

Registering Internal Testers

Before you can invite internal testers to test your app, you must make sure they have been added to your iTunes Connect team with the Admin, Legal, or Technical role.

To add a user to your iTunes Connect team, log in to the iTunes Connect portal at `https://itunesconnect.apple.com/` with your iOS developer account credentials. Once you have logged in to the portal, click the Users and Roles link (see Figure B-29).

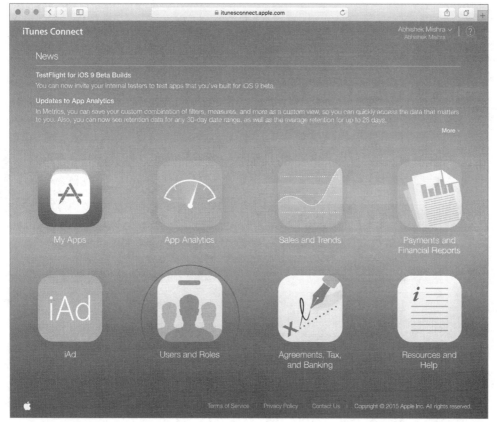

FIGURE B-29

On this screen, you will see all your team members listed along with their roles. Click on the (+) link on the page to add a new user (see Figure B-30).

You are presented with a screen where you need to type the name and e-mail address of the new user (see Figure B-31). An invitation to join your team will be sent to this e-mail address. Fill in the fields and click Next.

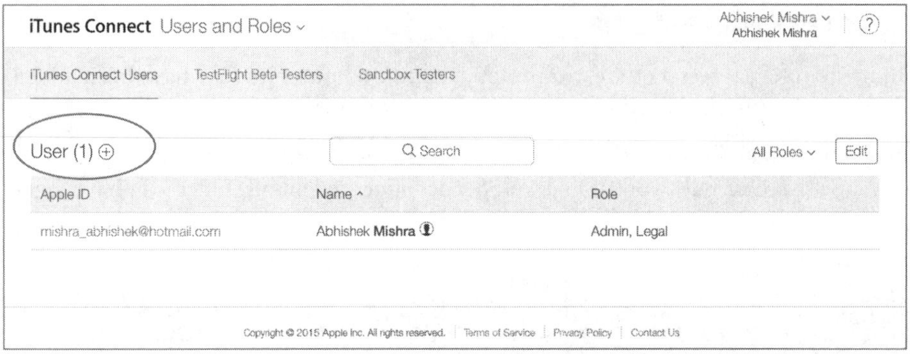

FIGURE B-30

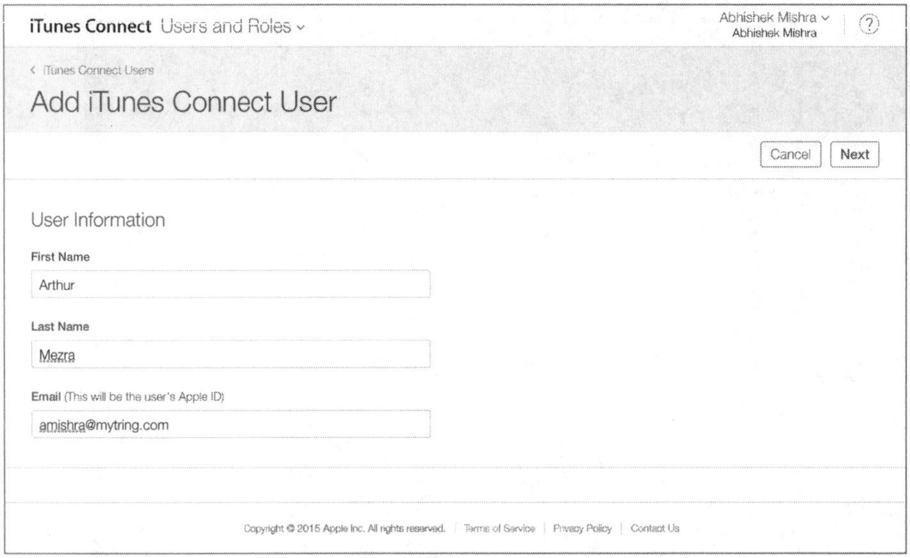

FIGURE B-31

On the screen that follows, you will need to assign a role to the new user. You can choose from Admin, Technical, Finance, Sales, or Marketing (see Figure B-32). Select the role for the new team member and click Next.

The next screen lets you to set up e-mail notifications that will be sent to the new user account (see Figure B-33). You can decide whether the new user account should receive notifications pertaining to:

➤ App Status

➤ Legal Agreements

➤ Financial (Sales) Reports

➤ Payments

Once you have set up the options on this screen, click Save to add the new user to your team.

FIGURE B-32

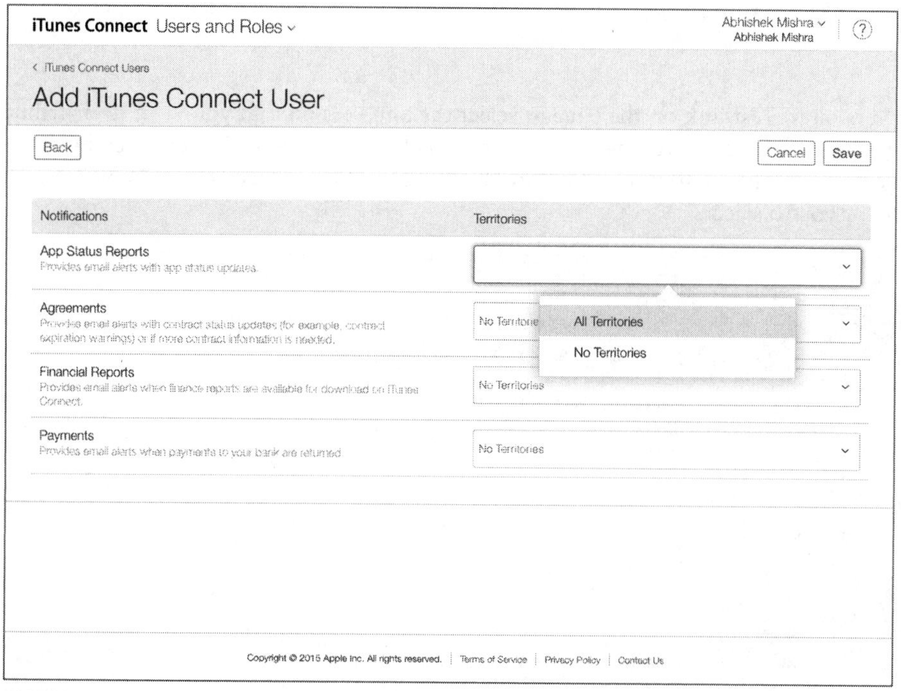

FIGURE B-33

Once a user has been added to your iTunes Connect team, adding that user as a beta tester for an app is fairly straightforward. A user in your team can beta test up to 10 of your apps simultaneously.

Access your application record on iTunes Connect and navigate to the TestFlight tab (see Figure B-34).

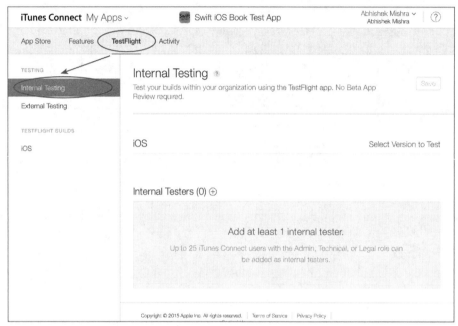

FIGURE B-34

Use the Select Version to Test link on the page to select the app version that you want to distribute via TestFlight (see Figure B-35). If you have only just uploaded a build with Xcode, keep in mind that you may need to wait up to 30 minutes before the build has been processed by Apple's servers and is available for you to select.

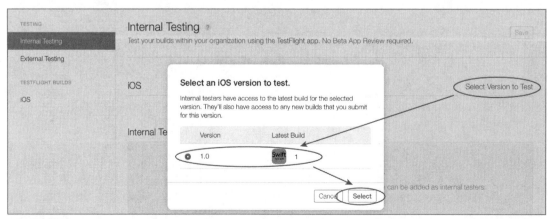

FIGURE B-35

Use the Add button (+) to add up to 25 internal testers. When you click the Add button, you will be presented with a list of iTunes Connect team members see (see Figure B-36). If a team member's e-mail address is not present in the list, then it is likely that he has not confirmed his membership in your team. When you add an individual to your team, a message with a confirmation link is sent out to the new member's e-mail address.

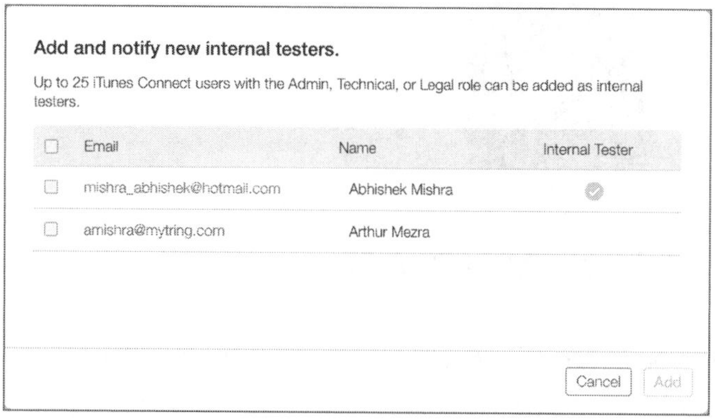

☐	Email	Name	Internal Tester
☐	mishra_abhishek@hotmail.com	Abhishek Mishra	✓
☐	amishra@mytring.com	Arthur Mezra	

Add and notify new internal testers.

Up to 25 iTunes Connect users with the Admin, Technical, or Legal role can be added as internal testers.

Cancel   Add

FIGURE B-36

When you invite one or more team members to beta test your build, the Start Testing button at the top-right corner of the page will be enabled (see Figure B-37). Click this button to start the beta test process.

App Store   Features   **TestFlight**   Activity

TESTING

Internal Testing

Internal Testing ⍰
Test your builds within your organization using the TestFlight app. No Beta App Review required.

Start Testing

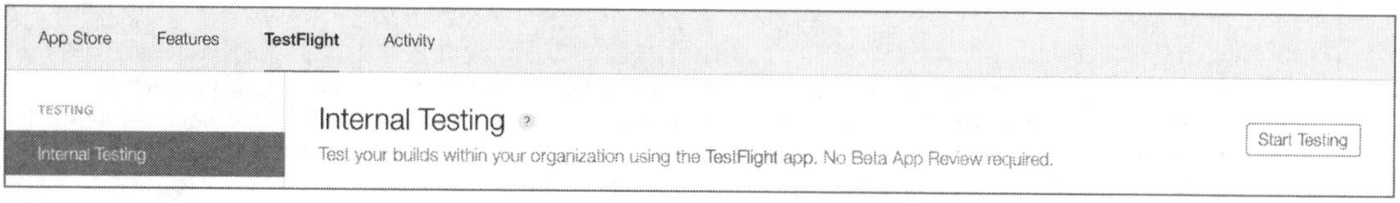

FIGURE B-37

Once you start the beta test process, each tester will receive an e-mail with instructions on how to download and install the beta version of your app on his or her test device (Figure B-38). For the beta test process to work correctly, the tester should access this e-mail message on the test device, as the email contains links that will install an app on his or her device).

Registering External Testers

To register external testers, access your application record on iTunes Connect and navigate to the TestFlight tab. Within the TestFlight tab, navigate to the External Testing section (see Figure B-39).

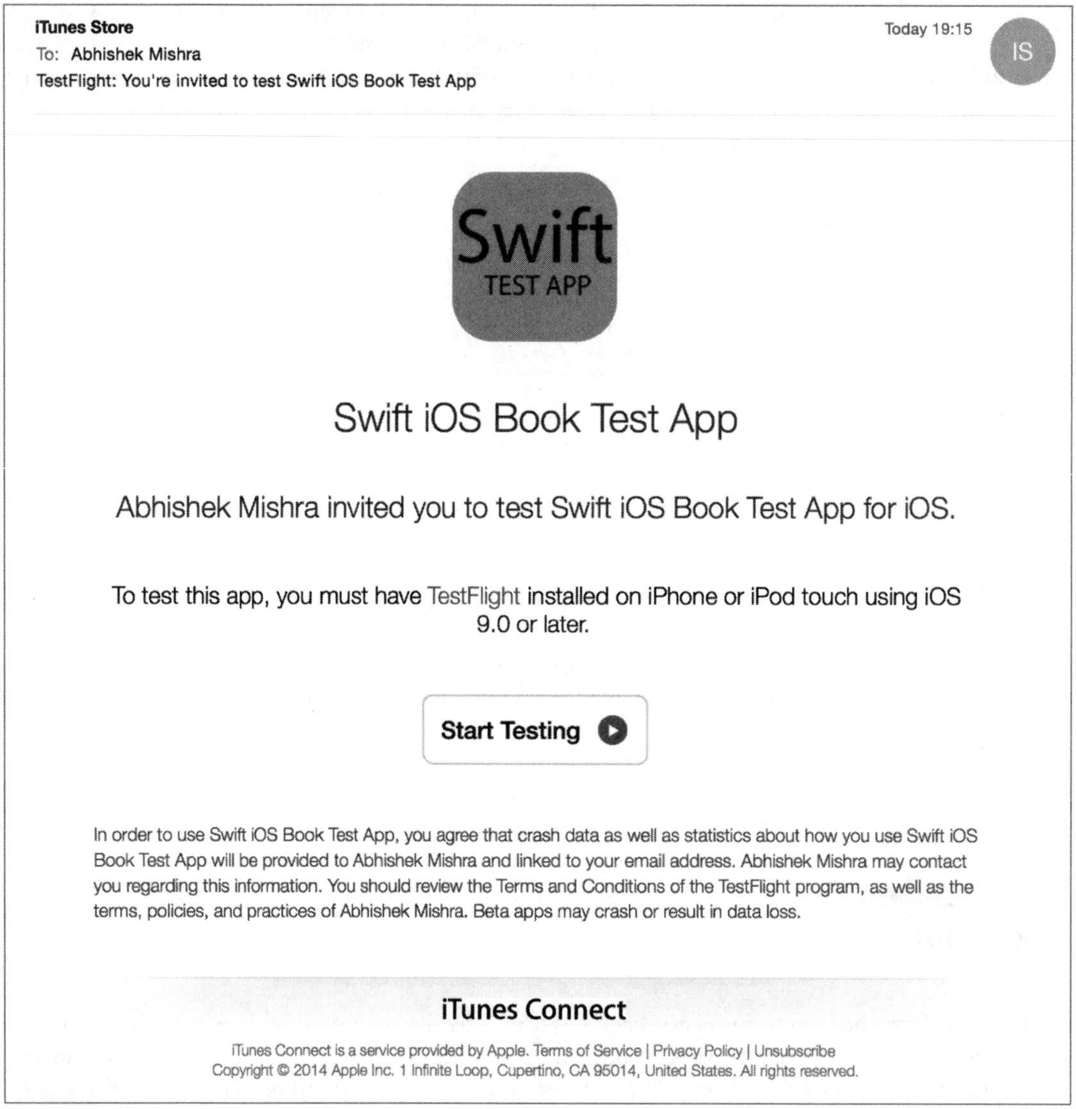

---

iTunes Store   Today 19:15
To: Abhishek Mishra
TestFlight: You're invited to test Swift iOS Book Test App

Swift iOS Book Test App

Abhishek Mishra invited you to test Swift iOS Book Test App for iOS.

To test this app, you must have TestFlight installed on iPhone or iPod touch using iOS 9.0 or later.

Start Testing

In order to use Swift iOS Book Test App, you agree that crash data as well as statistics about how you use Swift iOS Book Test App will be provided to Abhishek Mishra and linked to your email address. Abhishek Mishra may contact you regarding this information. You should review the Terms and Conditions of the TestFlight program, as well as the terms, policies, and practices of Abhishek Mishra. Beta apps may crash or result in data loss.

iTunes Connect

iTunes Connect is a service provided by Apple. Terms of Service | Privacy Policy | Unsubscribe
Copyright © 2014 Apple Inc. 1 Infinite Loop, Cupertino, CA 95014, United States. All rights reserved.

FIGURE B-38

The process of registering external testers is very similar to that of registering internal testers. You need to click the Select Version to Test link on the page to select the app version that you want to distribute via TestFlight. After you select the version, you may be prompted to fill in some application meta data if you have not done so when you created the application record (see Figure B-40).

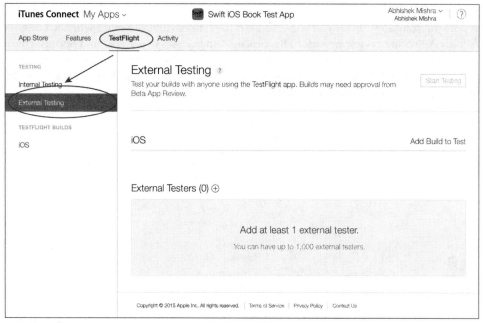

FIGURE B-39

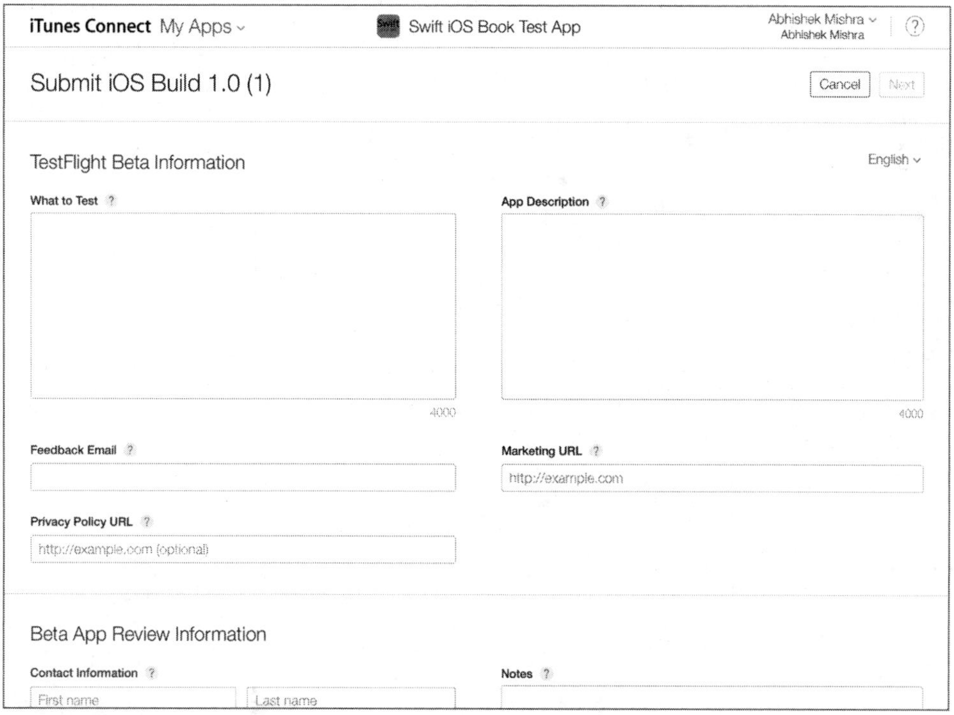

Submit iOS Build 1.0 (1)

[Cancel] [Next]

TestFlight Beta Information

English ﹀

What to Test ?

4000

App Description ?

4000

Feedback Email ?

Marketing URL ?

http://example.com

Privacy Policy URL ?

http://example.com (optional)

Beta App Review Information

Contact Information ?

First name | Last name

Notes ?

FIGURE B-40

External testers need not be members of your iTunes Connect team. You can invite up to 1,000 external testers for your app. When you click the Start Testing button, the build will need to go through Apple's App Store review process. This process can take up to a week, and once the build has passed the review process, your testers will get an e-mail notifying them that a build is ready to download. Your testers will need to access this e-mail message on their test device and follow the instructions contained in the message to begin testing.

App Store Distribution

In most cases, after your app is ready and tested, you will want to list it in the App Store. Regardless of your pricing strategy (free or paid) every application that is submitted to Apple for distribution via the App Store is subject to an approval process. The approval process usually takes about a week. Updated versions of an existing application also need to go through an approval process.

To distribute your application via the App Store, you will need a standard, paid, iOS developer account. If you have an enterprise iOS developer account, you cannot distribute your applications through the App Store. Submitting an application to Apple for inclusion in the App Store is a two-stage process. First, you need to create an *application profile* on the iTunes Connect portal, and then you need to upload your application binary to iTunes Connect using Xcode.

CREATING AN APPLICATION PROFILE

To start the App Store submission process, log in to the iTunes Connect portal at `https://itunesconnect.apple.com/` with your iOS developer account credentials. Once you have logged in to the portal, click the My Apps link (see Figure C-1).

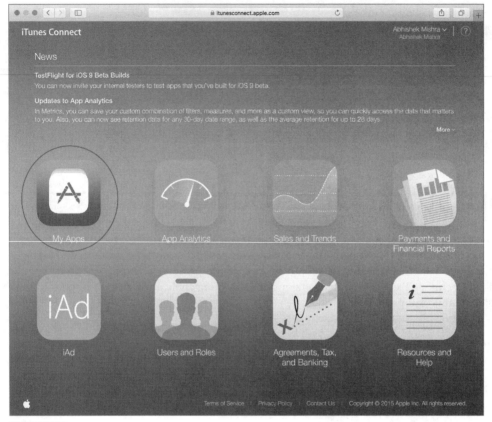

FIGURE C-1

On this screen you will see all your iOS and Mac OS applications. You can either add a new application or manage one of the existing ones. To create a new application profile, click the Add New App button in the top-left corner of the window (see Figure C-2).

FIGURE C-2

Selecting the New App option will display a popup window where you need to enter some basic information on your new app, including the Name, Bundle ID, and version number (see Figure C-3).

New App

Platforms ?
☐ iOS   ☐ tvOS

Name ?
[   ]

Primary Language ?
[Choose   ∨]

Bundle ID ?
[Choose   ∨]
Register a new bundle ID on the Developer Portal.

SKU ?
[   ]

[Cancel] [Create]

FIGURE C-3

The Bundle ID (also known as an App ID) must be registered with your iOS developer account. If you haven't created an App ID, you will need to do so now, before you can proceed with the next steps. Creating an App ID has been discussed in Appendix A. To get started, log in to your iOS developer account at `https://developer.apple.com/ios` and navigate to the Identifiers section of the website.

Once you have filled in the fields in the popup window, click Create to go to the Application Information screen (see Figure C-4).

At the top of the page is a tabbed menu bar (see Figure C-5) with four tabs labeled App Store, Features, TestFlight, and Activity.

The App Store tab is selected by default, and the new application's status is displayed in the left-hand side of the screen. A new application profile starts out in the Prepare For Submission state. You then fill in all the relevant information to complete the application profile and click the Save button to save this information (see Figure C-6).

Once you have saved the application profile, you will need to upload a build from Xcode. The process of uploading a build is covered later in this appendix. First let's examine each of the tabs on the application profile screen.

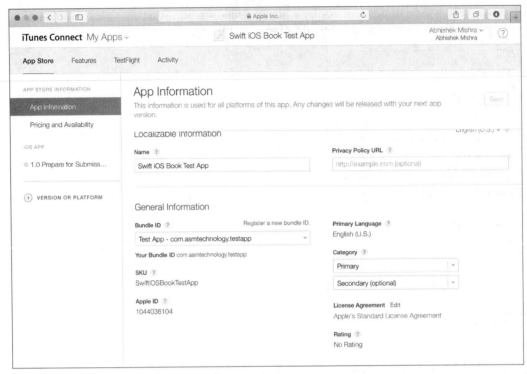

FIGURE C-4

FIGURE C-5

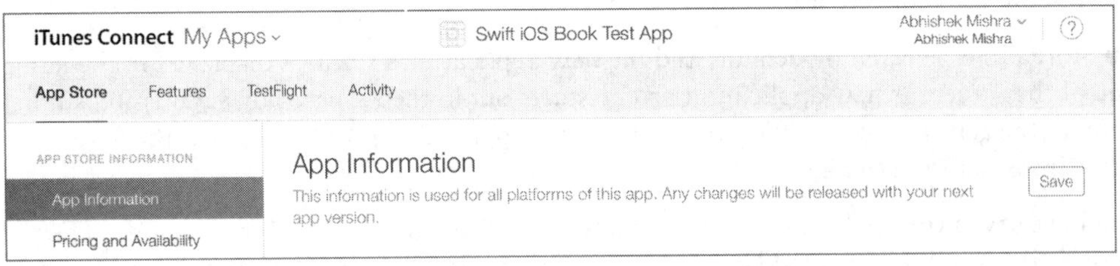

FIGURE C-6

App Store Tab

This screen has a menu on the left-hand side that provides the following options:

➤ App Information

➤ Pricing and Availability

➤ Versions

App Information

On this screen you need to specify basic information on the app, including an application name, a SKU code, and an application Bundle ID. The Bundle ID you specify on this screen must match the one have used in your Xcode project's `info.plist` file.

The SKU code is not used by Apple, but is used to identify the application on the monthly financial report provided by Apple.

Toward the bottom-right corner of the screen, you will find options to select a Primary and Secondary Category under which your app will be listed in the App Store (see Figure C-7).

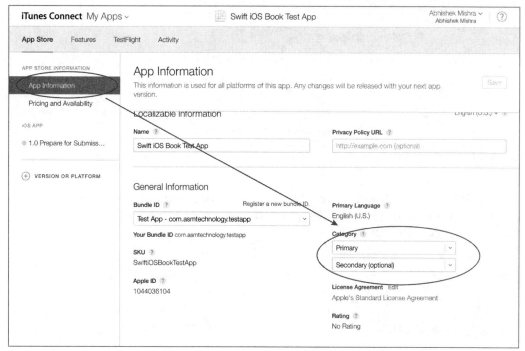

FIGURE C-7

Pricing and Availability

This screen contains options that let you specify the price of the app as well as the territories where your app will be available for purchase (see Figure C-8).

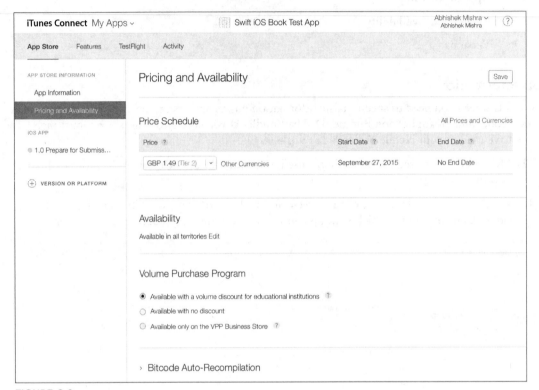

FIGURE C-8

If you would like to provide a discount to business buyers, or educational institutions when they buy multiple copies of your app, you can select one of the options under the Volume Purchase Program section of the page (see Figure C-9).

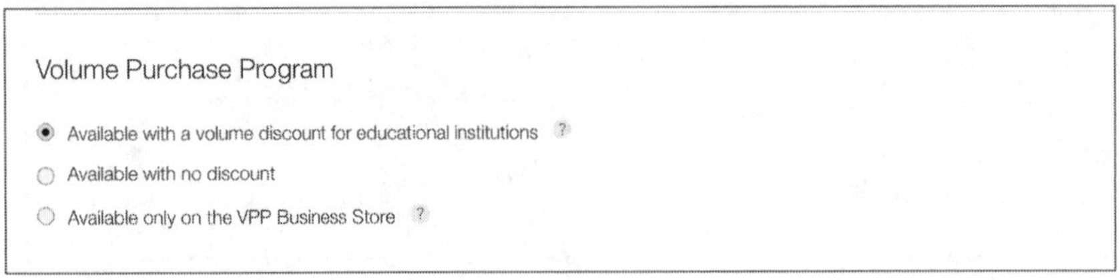

FIGURE C-9

Click the Save button to save the changes you have made to this page before moving on to the next section.

Versions

This section allows you to provide screenshots and videos, and to configure application metadata for each version of your app. A node in the menu on the left-hand side represents each version (see Figure C-10).

FIGURE C-10

The options in this screen are grouped into several subsections:

➤ Version Information

➤ Apple Watch

➤ Build

➤ General App Information

➤ Game Center

➤ App Review Information

➤ Version Release

Version Information

The version information section resembles Figure C-11. Here you need to specify the following information:

➤ **Screenshots:** You can provide up to five screenshots and a video preview for different devices. If you are submitting a universal application, you will need to provide both iPhone and iPad screenshots.

➤ **Description:** This is the description, as you want it to appear on the App Store. It can be no more than 4,000 characters.

➤ **Keywords:** One or more keywords that describe the app you are adding. When users search the App Store, the terms they enter are matched with these keywords.

➤ **Support URL:** A URL that links to the application's support site.

➤ **Marketing URL:** An optional URL that links to the application's website.

FIGURE C-11

Apple Watch

The Apple Watch section contains options that allow you to upload screenshots and an icon for your Apple Watch app (see Figure C-12). Creating Apple Watch apps is a topic beyond the scope of this book; if you are interested, you should read the Apple Watch Programming Guide located at `https://developer.apple.com/library/prerelease/ios/documentation/General/Conceptual/WatchKitProgrammingGuide/`.

FIGURE C-12

Build

The Build section will contain the application binary that has been uploaded for the current application version. If no binary has been uploaded, this section will be empty (see Figure C-13). The process of uploading an application binary to iTunes Connect with Xcode is covered later in this appendix.

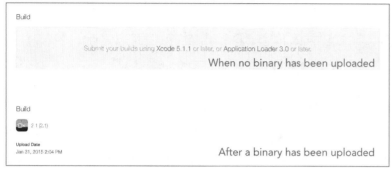

FIGURE C-13

General App Information

The general app information section resembles Figure C-14. Here you need to specify the following information:

➤ **App Icon:** The icon that will be used on the App store. This icon must be 1024 x 1024 in the JPEG or PNG format and must not have rounded corners.

➤ **Version:** This must match the value set in the Xcode project.

➤ **Copyright:** The name of the person or entity that owns the copyright to the app.

FIGURE C-14

Tapping on the Edit button next to the Rating link will bring up a popup window that consists of a series of questions, the answers to which determine a rating category for your application (see Figure C-15). The rating determines the parental controls that will apply to your application. As you change the answers to these questions, the age limit will change.

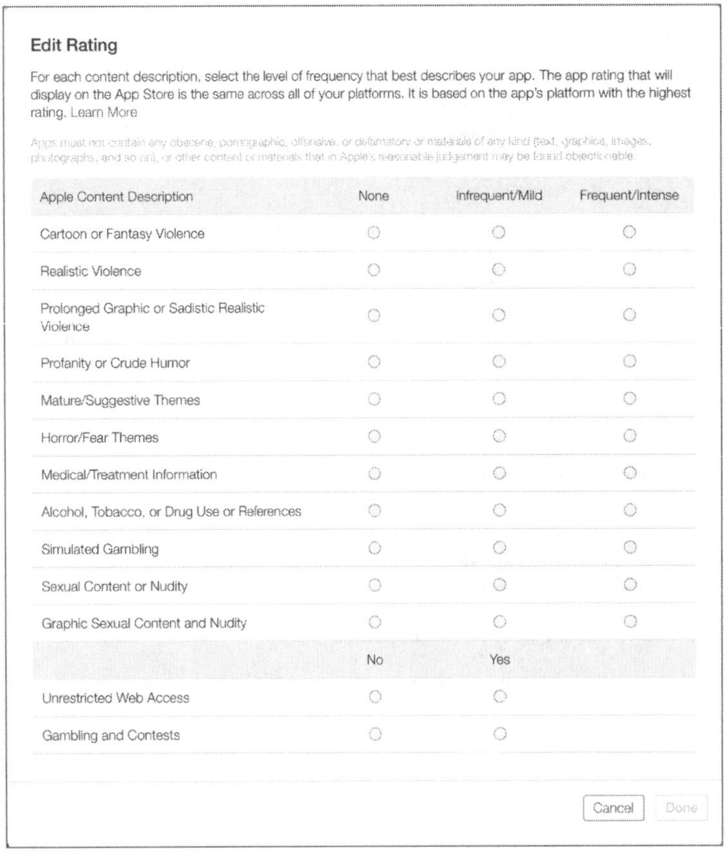

Edit Rating

For each content description, select the level of frequency that best describes your app. The app rating that will display on the App Store is the same across all of your platforms. It is based on the app's platform with the highest rating. Learn More

Apps must not contain any obscene, pornographic, offensive, or defamatory or materials of any kind (text, graphics, images, photographs, and so on), or other content or materials that in Apple's reasonable judgement may be found objectionable.

Apple Content Description	None	Infrequent/Mild	Frequent/Intense
Cartoon or Fantasy Violence	○	○	○
Realistic Violence	○	○	○
Prolonged Graphic or Sadistic Realistic Violence	○	○	○
Profanity or Crude Humor	○	○	○
Mature/Suggestive Themes	○	○	○
Horror/Fear Themes	○	○	○
Medical/Treatment Information	○	○	○
Alcohol, Tobacco, or Drug Use or References	○	○	○
Simulated Gambling	○	○	○
Sexual Content or Nudity	○	○	○
Graphic Sexual Content and Nudity	○	○	○
	No	Yes	
Unrestricted Web Access	○	○	
Gambling and Contests	○	○	

Cancel   Done

FIGURE C-15

Game Center

The Game Center section is disabled by default, and should be enabled for applications that support Game Center. When enabled, you will have options to configure leader boards, achievements, and multiplayer compatibility. Game Center is a topic beyond the scope of this book, but if you are interested, you should read the Game Center Programming Guide located at `https://developer` `.apple.com/library/ios/documentation/NetworkingInternet/Conceptual/GameKit_Guide/` `Introduction/Introduction.html`.

App Review

The App Review section allows you to provide special testing instructions to Apple engineers when they review your app, as well as contact information for a person in your company who will be contacted if there are problems with your app.

Features Tab

The features tab provides options to configure In-App purchases and Game Center for an app. In-App Purchases and Game Center are not covered in this book. If your app does not utilize either of these technologies, you can ignore the contents of this tab.

TestFlight Tab

This tab provides options to distribute prerelease builds of your app to internal and external testers using TestFlight. This is covered in Appendix B.

Activity Tab

This tab provides options to examine beta test activity. This is covered in Appendix B.

PREPARING AND UPLOADING THE APPLICATION BINARY

Once you have created and saved the application profile, the next step involves using Xcode to upload the binary to iTunes Connect. Before you can do this, you may need to do certain housekeeping tasks; these are especially relevant when you are submitting your first application.

Creating a Distribution Certificate

The process of creating a distribution certificate is very similar to that of creating a development certificate. Creating a development certificate is covered in Appendix A.

To create a distribution certificate, create a Certificate Signing Request (.csr file) using the Keychain Access utility on your Mac, and save this file onto your computer. You can use the same .csr file that you used to create a development certificate.

Log in to your iOS developer account at https://developer.apple.com/ios and navigate to the Certificates section of the developer portal. Click the New Certificate button on the top-right side of the screen and choose App Store and Ad Hoc under the Production category (see Figure C-16).

Scroll down to the bottom of the page and download the Worldwide Developer Relations Intermediate Certificate using the link provided if you haven't done so already. To proceed with creating the distribution certificate, click Continue.

On the next screen, upload the certificate request file that you saved on your Mac and then click the Generate button to create the distribution certificate.

If you are not part of a team, and are solely responsible for handling your iOS Developer account, your certificate is issued automatically and available to download in a few minutes. You may need to refresh your browser window. If you are part of a team, your team manager will need to first approve the certificate request. When your certificate is ready to download, you will see its status listed as Issued, and a Download link will be available.

Download the certificate and save it to your Mac. By default, the certificate should be saved to your Downloads folder.

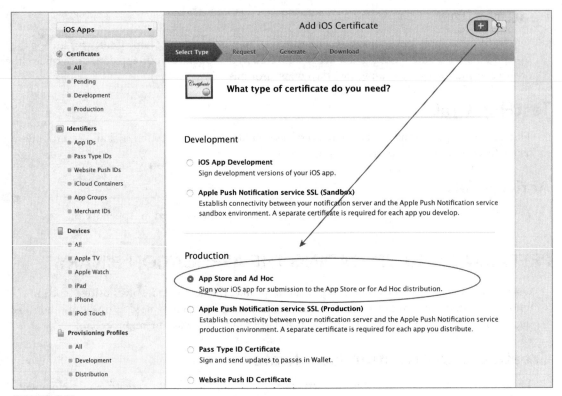

FIGURE C-16

Creating a Distribution Provisioning Profile

The process of creating a distribution provisioning profile is similar to that of creating a development provisioning profile. Creating a development provisioning profile has been covered in Appendix A.

Before you create a distribution provisioning profile, you must ensure that you have created a distribution certificate and have registered an App ID with your developer account.

The main differences between a distribution provisioning profile and a development provisioning profile are that a distribution profile does not have a list of devices included in it and requires a distribution certificate.

To create a distribution provisioning profile, log in to your iOS developer account at https://developer.apple.com/ios. Navigate to the Provisioning Profiles section and click the New Profile button on the top-right side of the screen.

When you are asked to choose the profile type, choose App Store from the list of available options and click Continue (see Figure C-17).

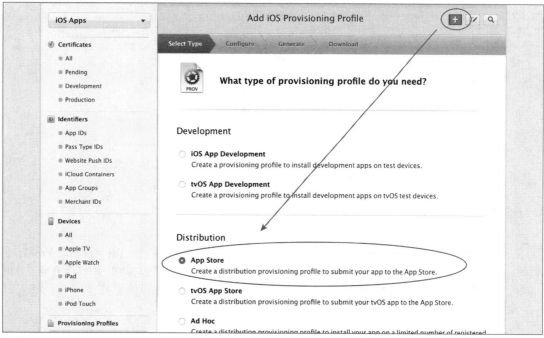

FIGURE C-17

In the next screen, select the App ID that corresponds to the app that you want to submit to iTunes Connect and click Continue. Finally, select the distribution certificate and generate the provisioning profile. Download the provisioning profile and double-click the downloaded file to install the distribution profile in Xcode.

Configuring the Xcode Project

The next step in the process involves setting up your Xcode project and submitting a build to iTunes Connect. Before you begin, make sure you have installed both your distribution certificate and distribution provisioning profile.

Open the project that you want to submit in Xcode. If the project's App ID is different from what has been registered with the iOS Provisioning Portal, edit the value of the Bundle identifier key in the project's info.plist file to match.

Save the info.plist file, disconnect any connected devices, and ensure that the Scheme/Target selector in the Xcode toolbar is set to build for a generic iOS Device (see Figure C-18).

Access the project's properties by selecting the root project node in the project navigator. Select the build target and then switch to the Build Settings tab.

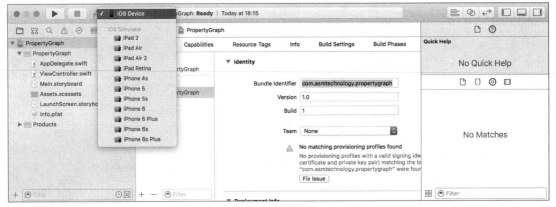

FIGURE C-18

Scroll down to the Code Signing section and locate the node that's labeled Provisioning Profile. You may need to expand this node to see the values for individual build configurations (such as Debug or Release). Select the provisioning profile you created earlier from the list of profiles for the release configuration (see Figure C-19).

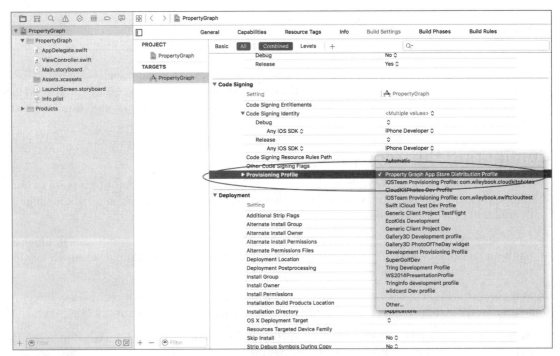

FIGURE C-19

Now look for a node called Code Signing Identity. Expand this node to reveal a node called Release, and then expand the Release node to reveal a node called Any iOS SDK. Ensure the value of this node is set to be the distribution certificate you created and installed earlier (see Figure C-20).

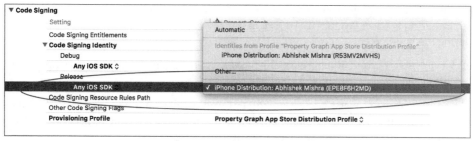

FIGURE C-20

Select the Edit Scheme menu from the Scheme/Target multi-selector in the Xcode toolbar (see Figure C-21).

FIGURE C-21

In the Edit Scheme dialog box, select Archive from the left menu to bring up archive-specific options. Ensure the Reveal Archive in Organizer option is selected and Build Configuration is set to Release (see Figure C-22). Click OK to dismiss this dialog box.

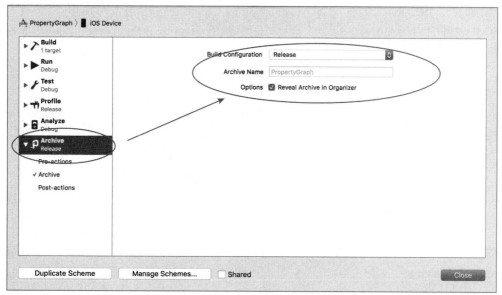

FIGURE C-22

At this point you are ready to prepare an archive that can be distributed to your clients/beta-testers. To prepare an archive, simply select Product ➪ Archive in Xcode. This builds your project for App Store distribution. During the build process, Xcode may ask you to allow access to your distribution certificate.

If it does, click the Allow button. When the archive is successfully built, the Organizer opens automatically, revealing the archive.

To submit the archive to the iTunes Connect portal, ensure the relevant archive is selected, and click the Upload to App Store button. The Organizer will ask you for your iTunes Connect login credentials, and upload the archive to iTunes Connect (see Figure C-23).

FIGURE C-23

SUBMITTING THE APP FOR REVIEW

Once the application binary has been uploaded to iTunes Connect, you will need to log in to iTunes Connect once again, and click the Submit for Review button in your application record page to submit the app for review (see Figure C-24).

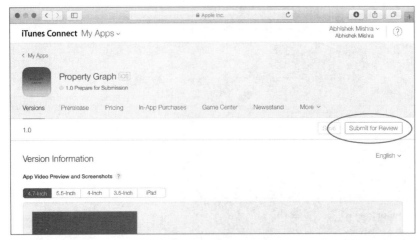

FIGURE C-24

INDEX